Adolescence and Beyond

Adolescence and Beyond

Family Processes and Development

EDITED BY PATRICIA K. KERIG

MARC S. SCHULZ

AND

STUART T. HAUSER

OXFORD
UNIVERSITY PRESS

Oxford University Press, Inc., publishes works that further
Oxford University's objective of excellence
in research, scholarship, and education.

Oxford   New York
Auckland   Cape Town   Dar es Salaam   Hong Kong   Karachi
Kuala Lumpur   Madrid   Melbourne   Mexico City   Nairobi
New Delhi   Shanghai   Taipei   Toronto

With offices in
Argentina   Austria   Brazil   Chile   Czech Republic   France   Greece
Guatemala   Hungary   Italy   Japan   Poland   Portugal   Singapore
South Korea   Switzerland   Thailand   Turkey   Ukraine   Vietnam

Copyright © 2012 by Oxford University Press.

Published by Oxford University Press, Inc.
198 Madison Avenue, New York, New York 10016
www.oup.com

Oxford is a registered trademark of Oxford University Press

Library of Congress Cataloging-in-Publication Data

Adolescence and beyond : family processes and development / edited by Patricia K. Kerig,
Marc S. Schulz, Stuart T. Hauser.
p. cm.
ISBN 978-0-19-973654-6 (hardback : acid-free paper) 1. Adolescence.
2. Adolescent psychology. 3. Teenagers—Family relationships. 4. Teenagers—Sexual behavior.
I. Kerig, Patricia. II. Schulz, Marc S. III. Hauser, Stuart T.
BF724.A253 2011
155.5'18924—dc23
2011027086

9 8 7 6 5 4 3 2 1

Printed in the United States of America
on acid-free paper

To Bob, beyond all
—PK

To my family, especially Joan, Jacob, and Sam, for their love,
support, and inspiration
—MS

To Stuart, for all the wisdom he has graced us with
—PK and MS

ACKNOWLEDGMENTS

The editors gratefully acknowledge the generosity and kindness of Barbara Hauser, without whom this volume would not have been possible. We also want to extend our appreciation to the reviewers of the manuscript in its earlier stages, who made valuable comments that enriched the final product greatly. In addition, we offer heartfelt thanks to Sarah Harrington of Oxford University Press, who has been unflaggingly encouraging, patient, and a pleasure to work with, as well as Jodi Narde, who has wrested order out of chaos with good humor and aplomb. Lastly, our thanks and admiration go to the wonderful contributors to this volume who have taught us so much as we traveled this journey together.

CONTENTS

Contributors **xiii**

Introduction to the Volume: The Transition from Adolescence
to Adulthood: What Lies Beneath and What Lies Beyond **3**
Patricia K. Kerig and Marc S. Schulz

SECTION ONE

Introduction to Section I: Self-Development and
Regulatory Processes **13**
Marc S. Schulz and Patricia K. Kerig

1. Regulating Emotion in Adolescence:
A Cognitive-Mediational Conceptualization **19**
Marc S. Schulz and Richard S. Lazarus

2. Risk and Protective Factors for Suicidality during the Transition to
Adulthood: Parenting, Self-Regulatory Processes, and Successful
Resolution of Stage-Salient Tasks **43**
Daria K. Boeninger and Rand D. Conger

3. The Status of Identity: Developments in Identity Status Research **64**
Jane Kroger

SECTION TWO

Introduction to Section II: Friendship and Intimate Relationships **85**
Patricia K. Kerig and Marc S. Schulz

4. The Quality of Friendships during Adolescence: Patterns across
Context, Culture, and Age **91**
Niobe Way and Lisa R. Silverman

5. The Intergenerational Transmission of Adolescent
Romantic Relationships **113**
Shmuel Shulman, Miri Scharf, and Lital Shachar-Shapira

6. Autonomy with Connection: Influences of Parental
   Psychological Control on Mutuality in Emerging Adults'
   Close Relationships 134
   Patricia K. Kerig, Julie A. Swanson, and Rose Marie Ward

SECTION THREE

   Introduction to Section III: Shifts in Family Roles
   and Relationships 155
   Marc S. Schulz and Patricia K. Kerig

7. Sociocultural Perspectives on Adolescent Autonomy 161
   Kathleen Boykin McElhaney and Joseph P. Allen

8. "Mama, I'm a Person, Too!": Individuation and Young
   African-American Mothers' Parenting Competence 177
   *Laura D. Pittman, Lauren S. Wakschlag,
   P. Lindsay Chase-Lansdale, and Jeanne Brooks–Gunn*

9. Young Fathers and the Transition to Parenthood:
   An Interpersonal Analysis of Paternal Outcomes 200
   Paul Florsheim and David R. Moore

SECTION FOUR

   Introduction to Section IV: Life Events and Coping
   with Challenges 225
   Patricia K. Kerig and Marc S. Schulz

10. Exceptional Outcomes: Using Narratives and Family
    Observations to Understand Resilience 231
    Stuart T. Hauser, Joseph P. Allen, and Marc S. Schulz

11. Sexual-Minority Development in the Family Context 249
    Lisa M. Diamond, Molly R. Butterworth, and Kendrick Allen

12. Resilience and Vulnerability of Mexican Origin Youth and
    Their Families: A Test of a Culturally Informed Model of
    Family Economic Stress 268
    *Rand D. Conger, Hairong Song, Gary D. Stockdale,
    Emilio Ferrer, Keith F. Widaman, and Ana M. Cauce*

13. Psychiatric Hospitalization: The Utility of Using Archival
    Records to Understand the Lives of Adolescent Patients 287
    Karin M. Best and Stuart T. Hauser

    Conclusion: Looking Beyond Adolescence: Translating Basic
    Research into Clinical Practice 304
    Marc S. Schulz and Patricia K. Kerig

Index 315

CONTRIBUTORS

Joseph P. Allen, Ph.D.
Department of Psychology
University of Virginia
Charlottesville, Virginia

Kendrick Allen, BA
Department of Psychology
University of Utah
Salt Lake City, Utah

Karin M. Best, Ph.D.
Judge Baker Children's Center
University of California, Los Angeles

Daria K. Boeninger, Ph.D.
Prevention Research Center
Arizona State University
Tempe, Arizona

Kathleen Boykin McElhaney, Ph.D.
Clinical Psychologist
FamilyFirst Psychological Services
Vienna, Virginia

Jeanne Brooks-Gunn, Ph.D.
Teachers College
Columbia University
New York, New York

Molly R. Butterworth, MA
Department of Psychology
University of Utah
Salt Lake City, Utah

Ana M. Cauce, Ph.D.
College of Arts and Sciences
University of Washington
Seattle, Washington

P. Lindsay Chase-Lansdale, Ph.D.
School of Education and Social Policy
Northwestern University
Evanston, Illinois

Rand D. Conger, Ph.D.
Human and Community Development
University of California, Davis
Davis, California

Lisa M. Diamond, Ph.D.
Department of Psychology
University of Utah
Salt Lake City, Utah

Emilio Ferrer, Ph.D.
Department of Psychology
University of California, Davis
Davis, California

Paul Florsheim, Ph.D.
School of Public Health
University of Wisconsin-Milwaukee
Milwaukee, Wisconsin

Stuart T. Hauser, Ph.D.
Department of Psychiatry
Harvard Medical School
Boston, Massachusetts

Patricia K. Kerig, Ph.D.
Department of Psychology
University of Utah
Salt Lake City, Utah

Jane Kroger, Ph.D.
Department of Psychology
University of Tromsø
Tromsø, Norway

Richard S. Lazarus, Ph.D.
Department of Psychology
University of California, Berkeley
Berkeley, California

David R. Moore, Ph.D.
Department of Psychology
University of Puget Sound
Tacoma, Washington

Laura D. Pittman, Ph.D.
Department of Psychology
Northern Illinois University
DeKalb, Illinois

Miri Scharf, Ph.D.
Department of Counseling and
   Human Development
University of Haifa
Haifa, Israel

Marc S. Schulz, Ph.D.
Department of Psychology
Bryn Mawr College
Bryn Mawr, Pennsylvania

Lital Shachar-Shapira, Ph.D.
Department of Psychology
Bar Ilan University
Ramat-Gan, Israel

Shmuel Shulman, Ph.D.
Department of Psychology
Bar Ilan University
Ramat-Gan, Israel

Lisa R. Silverman, Ph.D.
Department of Applied Psychology
New York University
New York, New York

Hairong Song, Ph.D.
Department of Psychology
University of Oklahoma
Norman, Oklahoma

Gary D. Stockdale, Ph.D.
Department of Human and
   Community Development
University of California, Davis
Davis, California

Julie A. Swanson, Ph.D.
The Counseling Center
Sam Houston State University
Huntsville, Texas

Lauren S. Wakschlag, Ph.D.
Feinberg School of Medicine
Northwestern University
Chicago, Illinois

Rose Marie Ward, Ph.D.
Department of Kinesiology and
   Health
Miami University
Oxford, Ohio

Niobe Way, Ed.D
Department of Applied Psychology
New York University
New York, New York

Keith F. Widaman, Ph.D.
Department of Psychology
University of California, Davis
Davis, California

Adolescence and Beyond

The Transition from Adolescence to Adulthood

What Lies Beneath and What Lies Beyond

PATRICIA K. KERIG AND MARC S. SCHULZ

The interplay between adolescents' social contexts and their development and well-being is of compelling interest to clinical child psychologists, family scientists, developmental researchers, child mental health practitioners, as well as countless parents working to make sense of their teenage children. An issue that has attracted considerable contemporary interest within academic fields is the nature of adolescents' transition to emerging adulthood (Arnett & Tanner, 2006). As theorists, investigators, and clinicians interested in the links between family process and individual development, we especially want this dialogue to focus on how experiences in one's family of origin influence this key passage in youths' life course. Increased autonomy from one's family and the establishment of more mature peer and romantic relationships are important markers of the transition through adolescence, but the context and nature of this autonomy continue to merit close study. Important social and cultural influences ensure that there is variation in the degree to which these hallmarks of adolescent maturation are valued. As theorists, investigators, and clinicians interested in the influence and importance of family relationships, we want to ensure that research on the transition to emerging adulthood focuses on both the influence of one's family of origin and adolescents' emerging relationships with peers and romantic partners that become the basis of their families in adulthood. To this end, as its name implies, the purpose of this volume is to explore our current understanding regarding how development in the family context during a youth's adolescent years sets the stage for the adulthood that lies just beyond.

This interdisciplinary volume—which includes contributors from the fields of child development, clinical psychology, social psychology, and adolescent psychiatry—was inspired initially by conversations among participants in the long-standing NIMH Family Research Consortium. Building on these conversations, we set out to bring together some of the leading researchers and thinkers in the field to offer their insights about cutting-edge conceptual and empirical issues in the study of family process and development during adolescence, including self-development, emotion regulation, romantic relationships, beginning new families, resilience in contexts of risk, and sociocultural and ethnic influences on development. Our goal has been to cover these topics and introduce the reader to a wide range of methodological approaches, from questionnaires to direct family observation to interview and narrative analyses. The study of adolescents and their families presents many challenges, and it is clear that no single method can adequately address the important questions in the field. A particular strength of this volume is its presentation of state-of-the-art quantitative methods along with intensive qualitative approaches that provide a more wholistic or organismic understanding of adolescent development.

This interplay between quantitative and qualitative approaches was a hallmark of the career of Stuart Hauser, who provided the initial vision for conceptualizing this volume. Stuart passed away before the volume was complete, but his long tradition of integrating methods and bridging theoretical gulfs provided a clear roadmap for the volume. Integrating a final kind of diversity was also a critical driving force. Social, economic, and cultural factors shape the family and larger contexts in which adolescents grow. The researchers contributing to this volume present studies of adolescents that vary in important ways in these dimensions.

The task we set for our contributors was to be forward-looking and cutting-edge rather than looking backward and merely providing a review of past research. Rather than a textbook, in which each of the authors is asked to produce an overview of previous research on a specific topic, we asked leading investigators to present their own recent research as an exemplar of where the field is heading regarding key topics in adolescent development. In this way, we strove for chapters that were lively, engaging, and promised to lead the way for the next generation of adolescence researchers.

DEVELOPMENTAL PSYCHOPATHOLOGY AS AN OVERARCHING FRAMEWORK

The contributors to this volume ground their work in a wide variety of theoretical perspectives, including classical psychoanalysis (Shulman et al., Chapter 5), ego psychology (Hauser et al., Chapter 10; Kroger, Chapter 3), family systems (Conger et al., Chapter 12), interpersonal (Florsheim & Moore, Chapter 9) and dynamic systems (Diamond et al., Chapter 11), cognitive (Boeninger & Conger, Chapter 2; Schulz & Lazarus, Chapter 1), and attachment theory (Kerig et al., Chapter 6), as well as approaches that integrate theories within a developmental framework (e.g., Pittman et al., Chapter 8; Way & Silverman, Chapter 4). However, despite the vast range of theoretical perspectives represented in these chapters, an overarching framework that unites them is the developmental psychopathology perspective.

As Achenbach (1990) has argued, developmental psychopathology is not a unitary theory but rather a conceptual umbrella under which a number of different ways of understanding development—biological, cognitive, behavior, psychodynamic, systemic, sociological—are organized and integrated while their individual richness and complexity are still retained. In regard to the work presented in this volume, the developmental psychopathology perspective enriches our understanding of the adolescent–adult transition in a number of ways. The idea that there is a continuum between normative and pathological development suggests that an understanding of positive adaptation and resilience in adolescence is as important to us as is an understanding of development in contexts of risk and adversity (Sroufe, 1997). To this end, this volume includes chapters investigating both positive and negative outcomes in adolescence.

Perspectives from developmental psychopathology (Cicchetti, 2006; Cicchetti & Toth, 2009; Kerig, Ludlow, & Wenar, 2012) inform and shape this volume in important ways. One important tenet from developmental psychopathology posits that development can be most meaningfully understood through attention to the stage-salient issues that rise to the fore in each period. Although some stage-salient issues are not *exclusively* associated with any one time of life—for example, adolescent struggles related to individuation and autonomy have been referred to as the "second toddlerhood" (Blos, 1967; Kroger, 1998; see Pittman and colleagues, Chapter 8)—these represent developmental tasks that interact with the most pressing demands the social context places on the youth at that time in life. In this way, certain tasks have a uniquely central importance at a particular stage, and they provide a window for assessing the individual's success and failure at navigating future challenges. Adolescence, it is said, is unique among developmental periods in that there are distinct transitions both into and out of the stage (Kerig et al., 2012). For example, the onset of adolescence traditionally has been marked by the striking biological changes associated with puberty, with all their powerful socioemotional ramifications. At the end of adolescence, in turn, the developmental tasks of early adulthood loom and challenge the youth to come to terms with such weighty issues as the formation of committed romantic attachments and the development of a sense of purpose and meaning in life. This volume includes attention to stage-salient themes that arise in all three phases of the adolescent period: the transition into adolescence (e.g., identity, self-regulation, and the mastery of challenging emotions), mid-adolescence (e.g., friendships, dating, and competence in the extrafamilial realm), and emergent adulthood (e.g., intimate relationships, the renegotiation of family roles, and the transition to parenthood).

DEFINING THE BOUNDARIES AND MARKERS OF ADOLESCENCE AND ITS TRANSITIONS

The chronological boundaries of adolescence typically are defined by a combination of biological, social, and psychological markers that themselves are dynamic

Table 1. Stage-Salient Issues of the Adolescent Transition

Across the Transition	Emerging Adulthood (Ages 18–25)	Late Adolescence (Ages 17–18)	Mid-Adolescence (Ages 14–16)	Emerging/Early Adolescence (Ages 10–13)
• Achievement[1]	• Achieving new forms of independence from parents while maintaining meaningful connections with them[12]	• Academic or occupational achievement[8]	• Balancing autonomy and accountability[10]	• Adjusting to pubertal changes[10]
• Autonomy, separation, emancipation[1,2,4,9]	• Committed romantic attachments[3,8,9]	• Consolidating an identity[10]	• Independence from family[2,3,5,6]	• Dealing with gender-related expectations[10]
• Identity[1,2,4] versus role confusion[7]	• Deepening and enduring intimate relationships[4,12]	• Experiencing a new level of intimacy[10]	• Friendships deepening[3,4,8,10]	• Empathy, understanding of others' needs[11]
• Intimacy[1,2]	• Identity explorations concerning love, work, worldviews[4,9]	• Leaving home[10]	• Metacognition[5]	• Identity[1,2,3,5]
• Metacognition, higher level cognitive skills[4]	• Independent decision-making ability, accepting responsibility for yourself[9]	• Renegotiation of role relationships with family of origin[6]	• Moral decision-making[10]	• Individuation[3]
• Peer relations increasingly central and deep[4,11]		• Romantic relationships[3,5,8]	• Sexuality and sexual orientation[1,3,10]	• Learning to use new cognitive capacities[10]
• Responsibility[9]				• Mastery[2,3]
• Self-regulation[8]				
• Sexuality[1,4]				
• Transformations in parent–child relationships[2,3,4]				
• Vocation and mastery[2,3,4]				

- Purpose and meaning in life[3]
- Transition to parenthood[6]
- Work, long-term adult occupation, financial independence[2,3,4,8,9]

- Need for intimacy[11]
- Peer relations[1,2,3,11]; finding a place in a peer group[10]
- Self-regulation[8]

[1]Holmbeck, Friedman, Abad, and Jandasek (2006).
[2]Task Force on Adolescent Assault Victim Needs (1996).
[3]Kerig and Wenar (2006); Kerig, Ludlow, and Wenar (2012).
[4]Holmbeck, Greenley, and Franks (2003).
[5]Forehand and Wierson (1993).
[6]McGoldrick and Gerson (1988).
[7]Erikson (1950).
[8]Roisman, Masten, Coatsworth, and Tellegen (2004).
[9]Arnett (2007).
[10]Miccuci (2009).
[11]Sullivan (1953).
[12]Hauser, Allen, and Schulz (this volume).

across history. The onset of adolescence has commonly been marked by the unique biological changes associated with puberty, but the onset of puberty, particularly for girls, is increasingly occurring at ages that we traditionally consider to be preadolescent. The end of adolescence, in turn, is marked by developmental tasks and social markers of early adulthood including the formation of lasting intimate attachments, pursuing a means of self-support, and the development of a sense of purpose and meaning in life. As historical, cultural, and socioeconomic forces continue to shape the social demands that spur development across the entire span of adolescence they also blur the exact boundaries of the adolescence period.

In soliciting contributions to the present volume, we sought research that spanned the entire spectrum of the adolescent transition, from the entry into the early adolescent stage (e.g., Conger et al., Chapter 12), through mid-adolescence (e.g., Way & Silverman, Chapter 4), to late adolescence (e.g., Shulman et al., Chapter 5) and emerging adulthood (e.g., Kerig et al., Chapter 6). In addition, we sought longitudinal studies that investigated processes that connect functioning across different stages (e.g., Best & Hauser, Chapter 13; Boeninger & Conger, Chapter 2; Hauser et al., Chapter 10; Kroger, Chapter 3; Pittman et al., Chapter 8). In all of the chapters, authors make explicit reference to the underlying developmental processes that are targeted by their research and the conceptualization of the key stage-salient tasks that informed their choices of measures and methods. The concept of stage-salient tasks is an enormously rich idea that is essential to informing developmentally sensitive theory and research, but it is also a concept that is still in its own adolescence, with all the fluidity and ambivalence characteristic of the stage. To whit, Table 1 displays an overview and integration of a wide range of theoretical conceptualizations of the stages of adolescence and their corresponding tasks for mastery. Despite the harmony of themes that can be derived from the various developmental theorists summarized in the table, there are also some evident discordances. For example, developmentalists do not always agree regarding the specific ages that demarcate the subphases in the adolescence transition. In particular, the delineation of a separate stage of emerging adulthood has been rife with controversy (Arnett, 2007; Hendry & Kloep, 2007). Particularly noteworthy in this regard, some investigators view the resolution of certain tasks as a key feature of earlier phases of development whereas others believe these are still works in progress at the latest stage of adolescence. For example, Micucci (2009) assigns to the late adolescent the task of "consolidating an identity" whereas for Arnett (2007) the emerging adult is only exploring such questions.

The extent to which the concept of adolescence itself is a modern creation is hotly debated, and certainly there are important historical, cultural, and ethnic differences in how the transition between childhood and adulthood has been conceptualized (Demos & Demos, 1969; Gielen, 2004). As McElhany and Allen (Chapter 7) remind us, the *meanings* of constructs, such as parental restraint and adolescent autonomy-seeking, change according to the functions they serve in a specific sociocultural environment. In seeming defiance of our developmental theories, youth often involve themselves in adult-oriented activities for which they may, in fact, be socially and emotionally unprepared. For example, in most cultural contexts in the United States, not until emerging adulthood is it considered desirable for youth to begin making the transition to parenthood, but the onset of puberty makes pregnancy a biological possibility and, indeed, increasing numbers of U.S. teenagers are becoming parents (Hamilton, Martin, & Ventura, 2007). Such newly formed families may take nontraditional forms, including three-generation grandparent-headed families (e.g., Pittman et al., Chapter 8) and teen fathers with only loose affiliations with their offspring (e.g., Florsheim & Moore, Chapter 9), but these are family forms that are common, accepted, and to some degree considered normative in subcultures outside of the middle-class mainstream, and that provide the contexts in which increasing numbers of U.S. children are being raised. On the other hand, particularly among more affluent families, the phenomenon of an extended adolescence, in which the assumption of full adult responsibilities is delayed, appears to be increasingly common. For example, although Micucci (2009) associates leaving home with the late adolescent phase, this for many youth is only a metaphoric leave-taking given that reduced career prospects in the current economy are causing many young people to return to the family home after finishing college (Kaplan, 2009).

DIVERSE METHODOLOGIES

Proponents of a developmental psychopathology approach have argued that the methods used to study the adolescent transition must be as complex and multifaceted as the problem itself. Given the complexity of adolescent development, the task of understanding this process requires the integration of a variety of perspectives and methodologies (e.g., Cicchetti & Hinshaw, 2003). In particular, developmental psychopathology has emphasized the advantages of integrating knowledge that is gained from traditional "variable-centered" research with findings from "person-centered" research that may include repeated measurement of individuals across time, the study of narratives, and individual case studies. In keeping with this perspective, the contributions to this volume were selected to represent a wide range of research methodologies. These include the use of sophisticated multivariate approaches such as path analysis and structural equation modeling (e.g., Boeninger & Conger, Chapter 2; Conger et al., Chapter 12; Kerig et al., Chapter 6), person-centered methods and intensive qualitative analyses of narratives (e.g., Hauser et al., Chapter 10; Shulman & colleagues, Chapter 5), careful observational coding of adolescent family interactions (e.g., Pittman et al., Chapter 8), archival research (e.g., Best & Hauser, Chapter 13), and meta-analysis (e.g., Kroger, Chapter 3). Moreover, many of the authors present state-of-the-art integrations among person-centered and variable-centered approaches (e.g., Hauser et al., Chapter 10; Florsheim & Moore, Chapter 9; Way & Silverman, Chapter 4) and speak to the ways in which those methods can complement and inform one another, a direction that is critical for the field in the future Also included in this book are conceptually based critiques of our current methodologies that challenge us to develop new strategies for capturing complicated phenomena, such as the reciprocal and dynamic relationships in family systems as they emerge over time (e.g., Diamond et al., Chapter 11) or the elusive processes of emotion regulation (e.g., Schulz & Lazarus, Chapter 1). Of particular value for the reader of the present volume is the care that the contributors take to provide clear explications of the rationale and procedures involved in their methodologies, including their study designs and choices of measures and analytic techniques, as well providing discussions of the strategic choices, benefits, and limitations of various research strategies. The introductions to each section and the concluding chapter in this volume further highlight the ways in which these different approaches can inform and complement each other.

DIVERSITY IN ETHNICITY, FAMILY FORMS, LIFE PATHWAYS, AND FUNCTIONING

In soliciting contributions to this volume, we also were committed to seeking diversity in its many guises. To this end, international (Kroger, Chapter 3; Shulman et al., Chapter 5) and cross-cultural work are represented (McElhaney & Allen, Chapter 7), as are the experiences of diverse American samples including inner-city youth (Way & Silverman, Chapter 4), African American three-generational families (Pittman et al., Chapter 8), teenage fathers (Florsheim & Moore, Chapter 9), Mexican-origin families (Conger et al., Chapter 12), and sexual minority youth (Diamond et al., Chapter 11). In addition, and also in keeping with a developmental psychopathology perspective, the chapters in this volume intentionally incorporate research that focuses on the entire continuum of adaptation, including the normative and the pathological. A core principle underlying developmental psychopathology is the idea that we can better understand psychopathology by investigating normative development, and that our understanding of typical development is improved by studying deviations from the normal (Sroufe, 1990). Such an assertion demands that a serious look at adolescence include a focus on normative transitions and changes as well as a focus on disrupted development and nontypical pathways. An important contribution of developmental psychopathology researchers, including Stuart Hauser (e.g., Hauser, Allen, & Golden, 2006), has been a focus on resilience in the face of adversity. The chapters in this volume include a number of studies devoted to youth whose pathways deviate from the norm by virtue of precocious engagement in adult roles (e.g., Florsheim & Moore, Chapter 9; Pittman et al., Chapter 8), or who face extraordinary challenges through exposure to highly risky (e.g., Conger et al., Chapter 12; Way & Silverman, Chapter 4), nonnormative (e.g., Best & Hauser, Chapter 13; Hauser et al., Chapter 10), or unsupportive (e.g., Diamond et al., Chapter 11) environments.

ORGANIZATION AND CONTENT OF THE VOLUME

The volume is organized into four main sections that reflect key developmental tasks and challenges in the transition between adolescence and adulthood. The first section of the volume, Self-Development and Regulatory Processes, includes chapters focusing on emotion regulation (Schulz & Lazarus, Chapter 1), self-regulatory capacity (Boeninger & Conger, Chapter 2), and the development of identity (Kroger, Chapter 3). The second section, Friendship and Intimate Relationships, includes chapters on the development of friendships during adolescence (Way & Silverman, Chapter 4), and two chapters exploring different elements of family influence on adolescent romantic relationships (Shulman et al., Chapter 5 and Kerig et al., Chapter 6). The third section, Shifts in Family Roles and Relationships, concerns ways in which adolescent development is affected by relationships with parents (McElhaney & Allen, Chapter 7), or by becoming a parent (Florsheim & Moore, Chapter 9), or, in the case of young mothers, by both of the above (Pittman et al., Chapter 8). The fourth section, Life Events and Challenging Contexts, includes work that speaks to how youth navigate the challenges of the stage-salient issues of the period in the context of life challenges, including racial and economic stress (Conger et al., Chapter 12), psychiatric hospitalization (Hauser et al., Chapter 10), and coming out in a heterosexist environment (Diamond et al., Chapter 11). Each of these chapters illustrates potential sources of risk and protective factors that promise to shed new light on development during the adolescent-emerging adult transition, whether in the direction of healthy or pathological development.

References

Achenbach, T. M. (1990). Conceptualization of developmental psychopathology. In M. Lewis & S. M. Miller (Eds.), *Handbook of developmental psychopathology* (pp. 3–14). New York: Plenum.

Arnett, J. J. (2007). Emerging adulthood: What is it, and what is it good for? *Child Development Perspectives, 1*, 68–73.

Arnett, J. J. & Tanner, J. L. (2006). *Emerging adults in America: Coming of age in the 21st century*. Washington, DC: American Psychological Association.

Blos, P. (1967). The second individuation process of adolescence. *Psychoanalytic Study of the Child, 22*, 162–186.

Cicchetti, D. (2006). Development and psychopathology. In D. Cicchetti & D. J. Cohen (Eds.), *Developmental psychopathology. Vol I: Theory and method* (2nd ed., pp. 1–23). New York: Wiley.

Cicchetti, D., & Hinshaw, S. P. (2003). Conceptual, methodological, and statistical issues in developmental psychopathology: A special issue in honor of Paul E. Meehl. *Development and Psychopathology, 15*, 497–499.

Cicchetti, D., & Toth, S. L. (2009). The past achievements and future promises of developmental psychopathology: The coming of age of a discipline. *Journal of Child Psychology and Psychiatry, 50*, 16–25.

Demos, J., & Demos, V. (1969). Adolescence in historical perspective. *Journal of Marriage and the Family, 31,* 632–638.

Erikson, E. H. (1950). *Childhood and society.* New York: Norton.

Forehand, R., & Wierson, M. (1993). The role of developmental factors in planning behavioral interventions for children: Disruptive behavior as an example. *Behavior Therapy, 24,* 117–141.

Gielen, U. P. (2004). The cross-cultural study of human development: An opinionated historical introduction. In U. P. Gielen & J. Roopnarine (Eds.), *Childhood and adolescence: Cross-cultural perspectives and applications* (pp. 3–44). Westport, CT: Prager.

Hamilton, B. E., Martin, J. A., & Ventura, S. J. (2007). Births: Preliminary data for 2006. *National Vital Statistics Reports, 56,* DHHS Publication No. (PHS) 2008–1120.

Hauser, S. T., Allen, J. P., & Golden, E. (2006). *Out of the woods: Tales of resilient teens.* Cambridge, MA: Harvard University Press.

Hendry, L. B., & Kleop, M. (2007). Conceptualizing emerging adulthood: Inspecting the emperor's new clothes? *Child Development Perspectives, 1,* 64–79.

Holmbeck, G. N., Friedman, D., Abad, M., & Jandasek, B. (2006). Development and psychopathology in adolescence. In D. A. Wolfe & E. J. Mash (Eds.), *Behavioral and emotional disorders in adolescents* (pp. 21–55). New York: Guilford.

Holmbeck, G. N., Greenley, R. N., & Franks, E. A. (2003). Developmental issues and considerations in research and practice. In A. E. Kazdin & J. R. Weisz (Eds.), *Evidence-based psychotherapies for children and adolescents* (pp. 21–41). New York: Guilford.

Kaplan, G. (2009). *Boomerang kids: Labor market dynamics and moving back home.* Unpublished paper, Research Department, Federal Reserve Bank of Minneapolis.

Kerig, P. K., Ludlow, A., & Wenar, C. (2012). *Developmental psychopathology: From infancy through adolescence* (6th ed.). New York: McGraw-Hill.

Kerig, P. K, & Wenar, C. (2006). *Developmental psychopathology: From infancy through adolescence* (5th ed.). New York: McGraw-Hill.

Kroger, J. (1998). Adolescence as a second separation-individuation process: Critical review of an object relations approach. In E. Skoe & A. von der Lippe (Eds.), *Personality development in adolescence: A cross national life-span perspective* (pp. 141–192). London: Routledge.

McGoldrick, M., & Gerson, R. (1988). Genograms and the family life cycle. In B. Carter & M. McGoldrick (Eds.), *The changing family life cycle: A framework for family therapy.* (pp. 164–189). New York: Gardner.

Micucci, J. A. (2009). *The adolescent in family therapy: Harnessing the power of relationships.* New York: Guilford.

Roisman, G. I., Masten, A. S., Coatsworth, J. D., & Tellegan, A. (2004). Salient and emerging developmental tasks in the transition to adulthood. *Child Development, 75*(1), 123–133.

Sroufe, L. A. (1990). Considering normal and abnormal together: The essence of developmental psychopathology. *Development and Psychopathology, 2,* 335–348.

Sroufe, L. A. (1997). Psychopathology as an outcome of development. *Development and Psychopathology, 9,* 251–268.

Sullivan, H. S. (1953). *The interpersonal theory of psychiatry.* New York: Norton.

Task Force on Adolescent Assault Victim Needs. (1996). Adolescent assault victim needs: A review of issues and a model protocol. *Pediatrics, 98,* 991–1001.

Introduction to Section I

Self-Development and Regulatory Processes

MARC S. SCHULZ AND PATRICIA K. KERIG

The chapters in this section of the volume explore two defining features of adolescence—the development of self-identity and the role of regulatory skills that shape the experience of emotion and behavior in challenging circumstances. Adolescence is marked by changes in many domains, but a defining hallmark of adolescence, at least since the influential writings of Erik Erikson, is the attempt to develop a more well-defined and stable sense of identity. Along with the physical changes that puberty ushers in, changes in preferred clothes, hair styles, and personal grooming are common and easily observed markers of the transition into adolescence in many cultures. These outward displays are linked to a deeper and more complex set of changes that involves adolescents' efforts at figuring out who they are and who they want to be. These efforts include representations of how they want to be perceived by others. For many adults, these fledgling efforts to develop an identity and personal style comprise some of the most discomforting memories of adolescence.

Popular conceptualizations of adolescence also tend to highlight emotional and behavioral volatility as an important marker of this time of life (Larson & Sheeber, 2008). Although it has become clear that volatility is not a necessary rite of passage for adolescents (Offer, Kaiz, Ostrov, & Albert, 2002), the development of a range of emotional and behavioral regulatory skills is indeed a key feature of adolescence. Foremost among these skills are emotion regulatory and coping strategies invoked in stressful circumstances. These regulatory processes as well as an exploration of the self are part of a larger set of psychological processes increasingly referred to as *self-regulation*. Self-regulation is typically understood to include both efforts that shape the development of one's self or identity and efforts to alter and coordinate other inner states or psychological processes in the service of one's goals in life or in particular situations (Baumeister & Vohs, 2010). The focus of such regulatory efforts may include thoughts, emotions, impulses, attentional processes, or behaviors. Successful regulatory efforts are a key to success in life—a recent review suggests that "nearly every major personal or social problem affecting large numbers of modern citizens involves come kind of failure of self regulation" (Vohs & Baumeister, 2004, p. 3). Emotion regulatory failures, for example, may underlie the development of anxiety or mood disorders (Moses & Barlow, 2006).

Modern research on emotion regulation originated in two research traditions that are well represented in this volume—developmental research and family research. Developmentalists focused on the emergence of emotions and affective regulatory processes in childhood, such as the ability to mask disappointment in the service of social conventions (e.g., Saarni & Crowley, 1990). Other developmentally oriented researchers explored mutual regulation of affect in early parent–child interactions (e.g., Weinberg & Tronick, 1996). Similar explorations of regulatory processes in dyadic interactions were initiated by investigators interested in understanding adult intimate partnerships (e.g., Levenson & Gottman, 1985). From these early influential explorations, interest in emotion regulation has exploded across many areas of psychology and related fields. In Chapter 1, Schulz and Lazarus take on the challenging task of defining and identifying a construct (emotion regulation) that has become quite popular. They anchor their chapter in an influential cognitive-mediational theory of emotion that emerged from the stress and coping literature (Lazarus & Folkman, 1984). By carefully embedding emotion regulatory processes in the context of an existing, influential theory of emotion, they identify important ways in which research on emotion regulation can build on an established empirical literature. Consistent with most modern conceptualizations of emotions, their theory emphasizes the systemic and dynamic nature of emotion. Subjective experience and personal meaning also play a central role in this conceptualization of emotion. An important contribution of their chapter is the identification of methodological challenges posed by this and other modern conceptualizations of emotion. Accounting for the multiple components of the emotion system and its changing nature over time requires innovative methodologies, such as intensive observations of interactions or repeated daily assessments using electronic diaries. Assessing fluctuating subjective experience and personal meaning in a reliable and valid way is particularly challenging.

Schulz and Lazarus also consider important developmental forces that influence emotion regulation in adolescence. Despite longstanding interest in the emotional volatility of adolescence, research on the factors that shape emotion regulation in adolescence has lagged behind early childhood explorations. Boeninger and Conger, in Chapter 2, extend this focus on regulatory processes in adolescence by using a self-regulatory perspective to examine a major public health risk for adolescence—suicidality. They identify key self-regulatory processes across behavioral, cognitive-affective, and motivational domains that may put adolescents at risk for suicidality or other maladaptive responses when challenged by difficult life circumstances. The very same self-regulatory processes are likely to shape success in educational, occupational, and romantic pursuits in late adolescence. As Boeninger and Conger elaborate, these pursuits are central developmental tasks of the stage that is increasingly being referred to as "emerging adulthood" (Arnett, 2001). These pursuits represent strivings for independence and the attainment of adult social roles as marked by achievements in the realm of work, advanced schooling, and the establishment of a stable intimate relationship. Failure to attain these goals during emergent adulthood is likely to put individuals at greater risk for self-harm, as their study demonstrates.

Conger's influential studies in rural Iowa have long been recognized for their careful attention to the influence of family processes, especially parenting, in shaping adolescent and early adult development. In their contribution to this volume, Boeninger and Conger continue to build on this important tradition by exploring the ways in which parenting might contribute to the development of self-regulatory skills and ultimately suicidal behaviors. They put their conceptual model to an empirical test using multiple measures collected across time. Their findings indicate that parenting in early adolescence is linked to self-development in later adolescence, which is, in turn, linked to functioning in multiple areas and suicidality in emerging adulthood. Their study follows adolescents over a 6-year period from age 15 through to age 20 and establishes that a self-regulatory framework has great utility in understanding adaptive functioning and the risk for suicidality across the transition from adolescence into young adulthood.

The final chapter in this section, Chapter 3, addresses another central issue in self-regulatory research, that of identity development. As Kroger notes in this chapter, Erikson's psychosocial stage theory has had a major influence on how adolescence itself is conceived and what are typically identified as the primary developmental challenges for adolescents. The notion of identity and identity seeking that emerged from Erikson's work has been studied extensively by researchers interested in ego identity models and change. Identity is described elegantly in this volume by Kroger in her paraphrasing of Erikson as "that sense of sameness and continuity that enables one to move with a sense of well being, purpose and direction in life, and to recognize and be recognized by significant others" (Erikson, 1968). Kroger provides an overview of Marcia's (1966) influential approach to studying the process of identity formation during adolescence and young adulthood. In addition to providing an historical review, Kroger highlights the new directions that researchers of identity status are exploring, including notable examples from Kroger's own productive and influential research on identity in Norway. Her review also identifies important questions that remain unanswered in research on the role of identity exploration.

Kroger's chapter demonstrates the power of meta-analytic tools to address critical questions in a maturing literature. Objective reviews of existing studies are critical for any scientific field, but they are notoriously difficult to do. Kroger employs meta-analysis to systematically integrate findings from multiple studies to refine our understanding of the links between identity status and other markers of adaptive functioning, such as personality characteristics and relationship functioning, and also to address important questions about the developmental timing and patterning of identity status changes and exploration.

References

Arnett, J. J. (2001). Conceptions of the transition to adulthood: Perspectives from adolescence through midlife. *Journal of Adult Development, 8*, 133–143.

Baumeister, R. F., & Vohs, K. D. (Eds.) (2010). *Handbook of self-regulation: Research, theory, and applications*, 2nd ed. New York: Guilford.

Erikson, E. H. (1968). *Identity, youth and crisis.* New York: W. W. Norton.

Larson, R., & Sheeber, L. (2008). The daily emotional experience of adolescents. In N. Allen & L. Sheeber (Eds.), *Adolescent emotional development and the emergence of depressive disorders* (pp. 11–32). New York: Cambridge University Press.

Lazarus, R. S., & Folkman, S. (1984). *Stress, appraisal, and coping.* New York: Springer.

Levenson, R. W., & Gottman, J. M. (1985). Physiological and affective predictors of change in relationship satisfaction. *Journal of Personality and Social Psychology, 49*, 85–94.

Marcia, J. E. (1966). Development and validation of ego identity status. *Journal of Personality and Social Psychology, 3,* 551–558.

Moses, E. B., & Barlow, D. H. (2006). A new unified treatment approach for emotional disorders based on emotion science. *Current Directions in Psychological Science, 15*(3), 146–150.

Offer, D., Kaiz, M., Ostrov, E., & Albert, D. B. (2002). Continuity in family constellation. *Adolescent and Family Health, 31,* 3–8.

Saarni, C., & Crowley, M. (1990). The development of emotion regulation: Effects on emotional state and expression. In E. A. Blechman (Ed.), *Emotions and the family: For better or worse.* Hillsdale, NJ: Erlbaum.

Vohs, K. D., & Baumeister, R. F. (2004). Understanding self-regulation: An introduction. In R. F. Baumeister & K. D. Vohs (Eds.), *Handbook of self-regulation: Research, theory and applications* (pp. 1–9). New York: Guilford Press.

Weinberg, M. K., & Tronick, E. Z. (1996). Maternal depression and infant maladjustment: A failure of mutual regulation. In J. Noshpitz (Ed.), *The handbook of child and adolescent psychiatry* (pp. 242–257). New York: Wiley and Sons.

1

Regulating Emotion
in Adolescence

A Cognitive-Mediational Conceptualization

MARC S. SCHULZ AND RICHARD S. LAZARUS

Adolescents experience many emotions throughout the day (Larson & Richards, 1994), and each of these experiences presents an opportunity for regulating emotions. Consider the swirl of emotions that fill part of an ordinary day in the life of a typical adolescent:

> Johnny, a shy 15-year-old boy accidentally dropped a book on his foot during English class in second period. He was embarrassed and concerned that if he revealed his embarrassment to his classmates they would make fun of him. He struggled to pay attention to his teacher and to get through the class without embarrassing himself further. At lunch in the cafeteria, a girl that Johnny had a crush on sat at the next table. She told him that she liked his shirt. He felt pleased about the compliment but also a little nervous about the sudden attention. As some of his male friends gently teased him, he attempted to respond to her in the "coolest" way he could. At home in the evening, his parents started arguing after dinner about a problem with the family car. Johnny always felt uncomfortable when they argued but tried hard to hide his distress.

Circumstances or pressing personal goals often compel adolescents to attempt to alter their emotions in some way. How adolescents regulate emotions—that is, manage their feelings, behaviors, and physiological arousal during emotional encounters—has a great impact on their ability to succeed at school, to maintain positive peer relationships, and to negotiate the challenges of changing relationships with their parents during adolescence (Silk, Steinberg, & Morris, 2003; Schulz, Waldinger, Hauser, & Allen, 2005). Interest in the regulation of emotion has grown dramatically over the past few decades. Cole, Martin, and Dennis (2004) argue that "there is no question the concept dominates the clinical research literature" (p. 1327). A search of the PsycInfo database confirms the explosive growth in interest in emotion regulation. Variants of the words "emotion regula-tion" appeared in only seven publications in the 1970s and 169 publications in the 1980s. Since that time there has been at least a 10-fold increase each decade with over 18,000 publications appearing from 2000 to 2009 that included a refer-ence to emotion regulation. The increased attention to emotion regulation has been accompanied by a range of definitions and ways of operationalizing the con-struct (Cole et al., 2004). A critical task for researchers studying emotion regula-tion is the development of a clearer theoretical framework within which to conceptualize the core components of emotion and emotion regulation and to conduct meaningful research.

In this chapter, we describe how a cognitive-mediational theory of emotion that emerged from the stress and coping literature (e.g., Lazarus & Folkman, 1984) can be used as a framework for understanding the processes involved in emotion regulation. This framework has traditionally been employed largely to examine adult experience (for a notable exception, see Compas, Jaser, & Benson, 2008), and, as Gross and Thompson (2007) observe, there is surprisingly little integra-tion across the developmental and adult literatures on emotion regulation. We use this conceptual framework to identify aspects of emotion regulation that might change or develop during adolescence and to highlight important areas for fur-ther research by developmental and family investigators interested in emotion regulation.

CONCEPTUALIZING EMOTION

Over two decades ago, Campos, Campos, and Barrett (1989) observed that emo-tion was in the process of being reconceptualized from a narrow focus on internal feeling states and behavioral expression to a larger systemic view that incorpo-rated affectively relevant cognitions and emphasized the way in which emotions captured transactions of personal meaning between an individual and the envi-ronment. Central to this reconceptualization was the recognition that well-developed and well-researched theories of stress and coping (e.g., Lazarus & Folkman, 1984) applied to a much broader spectrum of emotional experience than stress. Beginning in the 1980s, Lazarus (e.g., Lazarus, 1991, 1993, 1996; Smith & Lazarus, 2001) and others (e.g., Fridja, Kuipers, & ter-Schure, 1989; Ortony, Clore, & Collins, 1988; Scherer, 1984, 2009; Smith & Ellsworth, 1985, Smith & Kirby, 2009) elaborated comprehensive models of emotion that empha-sized the mediating role of cognitive appraisal processes in the experience of emo-tion. In Lazarus's model (e.g., Lazarus, 1991), emotion is conceptualized as a multidimensional system consisting of appraisals of the personal relevance of a situation, response tendencies that include the subjective experience of a feeling, expressive phenomena, including voice tone and facial displays, and physiological and behavioral reactions. Central to this formulation is the notion that emotions flow from an individual's appraisal of the implications of what is happening in the environment for his or her well-being. Appraisal is a subjective process; not every adolescent would appraise the same situations in the same way that Johnny did during his eventful day described at the beginning of this chapter. Appraisals are shaped both by the context of the encounter and attributes of the individual, especially the individual's personal goals and beliefs about the self and the world. In this way, appraisals and the emotions that flow from them capture relational meaning—the transaction between an individual and his or her environment at a particular time. Campos and colleagues (1989, p. 395) highlighted this relational meaning by arguing that an emotion is "the way the event, the person, and the person's appreciation of significance are interrelated."

In Lazarus's model two categories of appraisal processes work in tandem to shape the quality and intensity of emotional experience. *Primary appraisal* determines whether what is happening in a particular situation is relevant to one's beliefs and goals. Only when an individual assesses that he or she has a personal stake in an encounter, such as preservation of self-image or protection of a highly valued goal or object, does an emotion occur. Emotion, in essence, acts as a signal to the individual and others that something of importance is currently at stake for the individual.

Secondary appraisal, involves an evaluation of how our actions might influence the situation. In the context of stressful encounters, these actions have been referred to as coping. Because an individual's actions can influence the situation in emotional encounters that are not stressful, it is important to enlarge the conceptualization of when coping is engaged and what is incorporated in the construct. Coping in stressful situations might be directed at reducing the sting of the harm or preventing further harm, as in Johnny's attempts not to reveal his embarrassment to his classmates. In a situation that elicits positive emotions, such as when Johnny experiences pride after scoring a basket in gym class, coping efforts may be directed at enhancing the benefit experienced. The fundamental question underlying secondary appraisal is, "What, if anything, can I do in this encounter, and how will what I do and what is going to happen affect my well-being?" (Lazarus, 1991, p. 134).

Core Relational Themes

Both primary and secondary appraisal have several subcomponents that help determine the overall meaning of a specific encounter for an individual and shape the specific emotion that is experienced. The partial meanings of each appraisal subcomponent come together in an integrated whole called a *core relational theme* that captures the individual's overall construal of the situation at a particular moment. Each emotion has a unique pattern of appraisals captured by a core relational theme. Although all cognitive-meditational theories emphasize the role of appraisals in shaping emotions there is no universal agreement on which appraisal dimensions are most important and on the specific contents of the core relational theme for each emotion. This is, in fact, an active focus of research (e.g., Tong et al., 2007). In Lazarus's model, anger implies a demeaning offense, pride an enhancement of our self-identity by taking credit for a valued object or achievement, sadness an irrevocable loss, and happiness a step toward the realization of a goal (Lazarus, 1991). Core relational themes, in effect, provide a shorthand summary of the personal meaning an individual is experiencing during an emotional encounter. They function, however, as more than just a convenient linguistic summary; they facilitate the rapid synthesis of appraisal components that is necessary for virtually instantaneous emotional responses.

Appraisal Subcomponents

Primary appraisal includes three potential subcomponents: goal relevance, goal congruence, and type of ego- or self-involvement. *Goal relevance* refers to an assessment of the extent to which an encounter is relevant to our goals in life. Without an assessment of goal relevance, the encounter will not be emotional. *Goal congruence* refers to whether the encounter fosters or thwarts a person's goals. Congruence of goals leads to positive emotions such as joy and pride, whereas goal incongruence leads to negative emotions such as anger and sadness. Finally, *type of ego- or self-involvement* has to do with the type of goal or aspect of our identity that is at stake in an encounter. These include self or social esteem, moral values, life goals, important assumptions about life, ideals about oneself, and the well-being of others. For example, in anger, it is one's self-esteem or social standing that is at stake; in shame, it is an appraised failure to live up to one's ideals.

The three components of secondary appraisal are blame or credit, coping potential, and future expectations. *Blame or credit* refers to judgments about who or what is responsible or accountable for a perceived harm or benefit in an encounter. Blame or credit can be directed at oneself or externally. *Coping potential* refers to an individual's appraisal of whether and how the individual can manage the demands of or strive toward realization of personal goals in a particular encounter. *Future expectations* refer to appraisals about how the encounter and the stakes raised by the encounter might change in the future.

Using anger as an example, we illustrate these primary and secondary appraisal components. For anger to be experienced there must be a perception that a personal goal is at stake (goal relevance) and is frustrated or threatened (goal incongruence). For Johnny, anger might be initiated when his classmates are joking around with him during lunch while he is trying to impress the girl he likes. Johnny's goal of impressing the girl might be threatened by the classmates' actions. For anger to occur, Johnny must be concerned in the encounter with preserving or enhancing his self-esteem or social standing (type of ego- or self-involvement). In this case, Johnny may worry that the teasing makes him look silly. To experience anger, Johnny must perceive the classmates' actions as demeaning in some way. All negative emotions involve the frustration of a goal in some way. What distinguishes anger from these other emotions is a perceived assault on one's self-esteem or social standing. Finally, a key secondary appraisal component, blame, must also be present. For Johnny to experience anger he must perceive the classmates as intentionally making fun of him, or, at the very least, as being inconsiderate.

Additional secondary appraisal components facilitate anger but are not necessary for its experience. If Johnny believes that he could mount an effective attack of some sort on his classmates (coping potential) and that such an attack is likely to have positive consequences for the future (future expectancy), anger is even more likely. On the other hand, if Johnny is concerned about later retaliation or negative social consequences as a result of attacking his classmates, anger is less likely. For example, if Johnny thinks his classmates are likely to retaliate effectively and perhaps make more fun of him, he may experience fright or anxiety in the encounter either in addition to or instead of anger.

This example from Johnny's day illustrates how an emotion is influenced by appraisals of the possibilities for coping and the consequences of such actions. This link between appraisal and coping makes emotion-regulatory processes an inherent part of the dynamics that underlie the generation of an emotion and not just a reaction to an emotion.

Appraisal is a cognitive process, but it does not imply that wisdom, deliberateness, or consciousness is necessarily involved (Arnold, 1960; Scherer, 2009). Appraisal can be relatively irrational, automatic, and unconscious. In fact, most of our appraisals are hasty and unreflective, but we may continue to evaluate the situation as we process more information and make more subtle judgments. Emotional experiences can be initiated and ended in a very short time, even in fractions of seconds (Ekman, 1984). Neuroscientific evidence is accumulating that shows that basic appraisal processes can indeed operate at this speed (Ochsner & Gross, 2008; Scherer, 2009).

Response Tendencies

The activation of a core relational theme initiates response tendencies that compel an individual to experience a set of coordinated responses across the three main channels of emotional response—subjective experience, expression/action, and physiology. The response tendencies and the rest of the processes involved in the generation of a single emotion are depicted schematically in Figure 1.1. We present this figure with a note of caution, as a schematic figure inherently oversimplifies a complex process. In the case of emotion, researchers are increasingly emphasizing the limitations of linear, information-processing analogues (e.g., Lewis, 2001; Scherer, 2009). Elements of the emotion system depicted in Figure 1.1 may not unfold in a neat linear sequence; rather, there are likely to be complex feedback loops among elements and some of the elemental processes may occur simultaneously.

The response tendencies help coordinate immediate action across multiple channels and are widely viewed as having been shaped by evolutionary forces (Ekman, 1984). They organize an individual and those who care about the

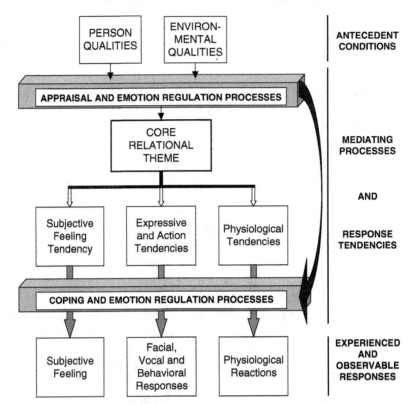

Figure 1.1. Snapshot of a Single Emotion.

individual to orient and respond quickly in situations in which there are personal stakes. When the core relational theme underlying anger is experienced, for example, the individual will *tend* to experience the subjective feeling of anger, express signs of anger through facial, vocal, and gestural channels (e.g., pursing lips together, furrowing brow, staccato speech), and experience changes in the autonomic nervous system that lead to an acceleration in heart rate and an increase in peripheral skin temperature (Levenson, Ekman, & Friesen, 1990).

For many emotions, there is also an impulse to act in a particular way, which has been referred to as an action tendency (Fridja et al., 1989). For example, when angry, we are likely to experience an impulse to attack, when frightened an impulse to flee, and when shamed an impulse to hide. Individuals can attempt to override these action tendencies to accommodate personal or social imperatives they experience in the encounter. The management of these action tendencies and all of the response tendencies is a critical aspect of emotion regulation.

Response tendencies do not unfold in isolation. The three channels of emotional response are part of the same system and can influence one another. For example, the realization that one's heart rate has increased may intensify an individual's subjective experience of a feeling, or, at the very least, make it more likely that an individual attends to the subjective feeling.

EMOTION REGULATION WITHIN
A COGNITIVE-MEDIATIONAL THEORY

Within the cognitive-mediational theory elaborated above, emotion regulation can be viewed as the modulation of any of the subcomponents of the emotion system, including appraisals, feelings, expressive behaviors, and physiological reactions. There are three important questions that must be addressed by any model of emotion regarding emotion regulation. Where in the sequence of processes that constitute the emotion system does emotion regulation take place? How does emotion regulation occur? What goals shape efforts at emotion regulation?

When Does Emotion Regulation Occur?

Advances in neuroscience are beginning to identify the dynamics of a number of aspects of emotion processes, including the timing of regulatory efforts (e.g., Ochsner & Gross, 2008). Clearly elaborated theories are critical to efforts to understand and integrate these neuroscientific findings. As depicted in Figure 1.1, the theory elaborated here suggests that once the response tendencies are initiated by the appraisal of a core relational theme, new information (or feedback) is presented to the individual that may shape or initiate further efforts at emotion regulation. These emotion regulation efforts can be conceptualized as mediating the links between the response tendencies that individuals experience and the emotional responses that might be evident to onlookers and to the individual involved. Much of previous research on emotion regulation has been conceived of as focusing on regulation of responses at this point in the emotion process, but we believe that it is best to conceptualize emotion regulation processes as an inherent part of the emotion generation process. Because secondary appraisal processes involve consideration of actions we might take to influence an encounter and our response to the encounter, emotion regulation processes are engaged at the moment an individual appraises a personal stake in an encounter. These secondary appraisals shape both the actual emotion experienced by the individual and the individual's attempts at regulating emotion. This view is consistent with perspectives in developmental and neurobiological research that highlight the difficulty of separating emotion activation and response from emotion-regulatory processes (Campos, Frankel, & Camras, 2004; Cole & Deater-Deckard, 2009; Goldsmith, Pollak, & Davidson, 2008).

How Does Emotion Regulation Occur?

Emotion regulation is goal directed and governed by processes within the brain that appraise and manipulate information (Ochsner & Gross, 2008; Scherer, 2009). Although it is centrally governed, the targets of emotion regulation extend beyond areas in the brain in which information is appraised. We concur with Campos, Mumme, Kermoian, and Campos (1994) that there are three basic types of mechanisms involved in emotion regulation: input regulation, reappraisal, and output regulation (see also Gross, 2001). Input regulation refers to the alteration of input before it reaches sensory receptors. Through strategies such as niche-picking (Scarr & McCartney, 1983) or selective deployment of attention, individuals can attempt to avoid situations that threaten or frustrate their goals and to engage in encounters that foster attainment of goals and lead to positive emotions. Reappraisal involves attempts to alter the meaning of an encounter, such as re-interpreting a friend's motives during a dispute. Finally, the three channels of emotional response—experiential, expressive, and physiological—can be modified directly through output regulation.

Emotion-regulatory efforts can be planful, deliberate, and rational, but, in many circumstances, they may operate largely out of consciousness in the manner of defenses as described by psychodynamic theorists and investigators (Waldinger & Schulz, 2010). In the context of stress, coping has been defined as cognitive and behavioral efforts to manage specific external or internal demands that are appraised as taxing or exceeding the resources of the person (Lazarus & Folkman, 1984). The reference to internal demands in this definition acknowledges the importance of managing emotional reactions in challenging circumstances. One difficulty, though, with this stress-based conceptualization of coping is its limited focus on "taxing demands" as the stimulus for a regulatory response. As we noted earlier, secondary appraisal in a goal-congruent emotional transaction can include considerations of actions that might extend the benefit that may be experienced. These actions can include efforts to accentuate a positive feeling that might have arisen. Building on a extension of the coping concept elaborated previously by Lazarus (1996), we suggest that coping be thought of more broadly as cognitive and behavioral efforts initiated by the appraisal of personal stakes in an encounter that are aimed at (1) altering the circumstances leading to goal incongruence, (2) sustaining or enhancing the circumstances underlying goal congruence, and/or (3) regulating emotional reactions.

The first two foci of coping in this revised definition comprise what has been described as problem-focused coping (Lazarus & Folkman, 1984). The function of *problem-focused coping* is to change the actual circumstances of the encounter that led to the emotion. Because an emotion encounter represents a transaction between the individual and a particular environment, problem-focused coping efforts can be directed at changing aspects of the environment or something about the individual. For example, if Johnny is worried about an upcoming algebra examination he might elect to spend more time studying so that his increased knowledge in math makes the examination less difficult.

Coping efforts that are intended to transform emotional reactions in some way rather than the situation leading to the emotion have been referred to as *emotion-focused coping*. In the sections that follow, we highlight the specific strategies that are typically used in emotion-focused coping and the circumstances under which emotion-focused coping efforts are particularly important.

Strategies employed in emotion-focused coping. Emotion-focused coping efforts are frequently directed at altering the way the situation that led to an emotion is attended to or interpreted. In addition to seeking to avoid further exposure to a distressing situation, a common strategy involves changing, or reappraising, the meaning of an encounter. This cognitive strategy might be directed at any of the six subcomponents of the original appraisal processes. For example, efforts might be made to change the interpretation of the intent of someone who has just threatened our self-esteem or to reconsider the importance of a belief that was at stake in an encounter. Reappraisal may also be directed at altering evaluations of how particular actions, including emotion-regulatory attempts, might influence the situation. These types of reinterpretation have been labeled reappraisal to capture their similarity to the original appraisal process. In fact, reappraisal is distinguishable from the original appraisal only by its timing in the emotion process. Research has confirmed that this type of cognitive strategy can alter emotional experience and expression in adults (Gross, 1998; Ochsner & Gross, 2008) and in adolescents (Hart, 1991). Emotion-focused coping strategies may also be directed at trying to restrain or alter the response tendencies in each of the three output channels of emotion. Concern about the personal or social consequences of expressing an emotion may motivate an individual to change or mask his or her expression (Gross, 2001). Individuals may also attempt to change the physiological reaction they begin to experience. For example, when frightened we might attempt to slow our heart rate by deliberating taking deep breaths.

Circumstances influencing emotion-focused coping efforts. There are four types of situations in which emotion-focused coping is particularly likely. The first is a situation in which a transaction is perceived as incongruent with our goals and the situation is not amenable to any kind of change. An example of such a situation for an adolescent might be the experience of a defeat in an athletic event that was highly valued or, more seriously, the death of a loved one. Powerful feelings are likely to be engendered by the both types of loss, but there is nothing than can be done to change the situation—it is irreversible. In such circumstances, emotion-focused coping is the only means available to the adolescent to cope with the distress he or she experiences.

Emotion-focused coping is also likely when the full enactment of response tendencies interferes with or threatens important goals the individual has in the encounter. For example, if strong anxiety—both a subjective feeling of anxiousness and physiological signs such as sweaty palms—is experienced during an examination and interferes with an individual's ability to think straight, the individual may attempt to reduce his or her level of anxiety. Another example would be a situation in which the expression of emotion might upset a friend or family member with whom an adolescent is interacting. Under such circumstances, an adolescent may attempt to squelch or, at least, dampen the external signs of the emotion by altering his or her facial expressions, voice, and body language to suggest either another emotion or no emotional experience at all. The individual might also work to avoid enacting an action tendency such as an impulse to become aggressive when angry.

Emotion-focused coping efforts can also be engendered by an unwanted message implied by an emotional experience. Because individuals learn through experience that each of the response tendencies of emotion is an efficient signal of what is at stake in an encounter, the implications of the response tendencies may themselves be experienced as threatening. An adolescent who experiences an unanticipated feeling of anger and an impulse to attack during an interaction with a romantic partner may be uncomfortable at the thought that this partner intentionally did something to harm him or her. The adolescent may respond to this situation by attempting to alter the emotional experience in some way.

Finally, in goal-congruent transactions the individual may seek to enhance the experience of a good feeling. For example, an adolescent may attempt to retain for a longer period or strengthen the intensity of the feeling of joy experienced when a romantic relationship is initiated and mutual attraction is confirmed.

What Are the Goals of Emotion Regulation?

Emotion-regulatory efforts, like all coping efforts, are guided by situational factors and by an individual's personal goals and commitments. As stated earlier, there are two major functions of coping—to alter the actual situation and to regulate the emotion response. Coping efforts in a particular encounter may serve one or both of these functions. Emotion-focused and problem-focused coping are interdependent, and each can be pursued with a variety of overlapping actions. Regulating distress, for example, can help to facilitate problem-focused coping. Consider Johnny's predicament before the algebra examination that worries him. Johnny may attempt to study harder to reduce the threat posed by the examination. If he finds himself so anxious that he is unable to concentrate when he opens up his math book to study, he must work to manage his anxiety first in order to learn.

The functional distinction between emotion-focused and problem-focused coping efforts has often been transformed into an action-based distinction in which certain coping strategies are assumed to serve one function exclusively. In part, this transformation has unfortunately been encouraged by the use of questionnaires that divide coping strategies into emotion-focused and problem-focused categories without considering the meanings or intentions underlying coping choices in particular encounters. People who endorse similar coping actions may differ in their underlying motives for pursuing a particular coping strategy. For example, efforts to squelch the expression of anger in an encounter with a close friend may be motivated by an adolescent's concern about hurting a friend's feelings or by an interest in getting some material benefit from the friend, such as a ride home from school or money for a soda. What is critical to consider is that coping efforts are always guided by the personal goals and commitments of the individual and the specific attributes of the environmental context in a particular encounter. Regardless of whether the coping is directed at changing the situation or the emotional response, the goal is always to reduce thwarting or enhance the realization of an individual's goals and commitments.

Role of Personal Goals, Beliefs, and Self-Identity in Emotion Regulation

Personal goals and commitments define what is important to the person. Goals and commitments, in concert with beliefs about the self and the surrounding world, determine the stakes that individuals experience in their daily lives, shape the meaning of these experiences, and guide coping efforts. Although it would be desirable to be able to identify the most significant goals around which *all* adolescents regulate their emotions, this is, in reality, not possible. There are important normative developmental trends in beliefs and commitments that we will touch on below, but there is sufficient individual variability in these beliefs and commitments that it is difficult to talk about universal goals of emotion regulation.

We believe there is, however, an understudied set of beliefs that has important implications for emotion regulation. The concepts of display rules (Cole & Tamang, 1998; Ekman, 1972; Saarni, 1979) and feeling rules (Hochschild, 1983) capture the conventions that particular cultures or societies embrace about emotional experience and expression. These "rules" are internalized through socialization processes in the family, school, peer culture, and larger society. Hochschild's term, "feeling rules," is an extension of Ekman's emphasis on how culture influences the display or expression of emotions in social situations. Feeling rules apply not only to the expression of emotion but also dictate how we are supposed to experience emotion in particular situations. For example, a parent may remind a teenage son of the rule that he is supposed to be happy when seeing a relative he has not seen for a while. Display rules, although not always explicit, are often backed by powerful social sanctions when violated. Looks of disapproval are often given to those who violate such expectations. These rules shape how our own behavior and that of others is evaluated. During adolescence, peer acceptance is likely to be influenced by the degree to which individuals conform or do not conform to adolescent and societal conventions about how emotions should be expressed and experienced.

Considering Multiple Emotional Encounters and Social Interaction

The representation in Figure 1.1 of a single emotional encounter and the emotion-regulatory processes that it fosters is in many ways overly simplistic. Only rarely does an emotional encounter lead to the experience of a single emotion. Moreover, an emotional experience typically influences the way subsequent encounters are perceived. Individuals continually appraise the changing nature of their transactions with the environment and incorporate the feedback that they receive from their emotions. Johnny, when confronted by the classmates who are teasing him, may vacillate between anger and fright as the environment around him, his construal of the situation, and his awareness of his emotional experiences evolve during the encounter. The experience of an emotion effectively creates the setting for new person–environment transactions (Campos et al., 1994).

Emotions can also lead to the experience of other emotions. We may feel guilty about experiencing too much pride in front of someone who has not enjoyed success. Guilt or shame may flow from anger if we view its expression as unjustified or inappropriate.

Another complication is the recognition that more than one goal may be involved in each encounter and attempting to resolve conflicts between goals may itself be emotion producing. An individual might experience conflict internally between two goals that are strongly valued. Individuals may also experience conflict between their own goals and the goals of another person who they value. Most emotions are experienced in an interpersonal context in which more than one individual's personal goals are likely to be at stake. In a family interaction, for example, multiple emotions unfold at once in different individuals. What makes such a situation so complex is that the unfolding emotions influence each other. For example, when Johnny's parents argue with each other, one parent's emotional expression and behavioral responses strongly influence the way the other parent appraises the encounter and the stakes involved. In the same family encounter, Johnny experiences unease and a string of other cognitions and feelings that are initiated by the ups and downs of his parents' arguments. Johnny's response to his parents' exchange changes the nature of the environment that will be appraised in the next series of emotional experiences by each member of the family.

The implication of this complexity for emotion and family researchers is that studying emotions, particularly in the context of interactions, challenges the relatively simple models we are able to articulate and understand. Each emotion involves an interacting chain of complex processes. Moreover, emotions occur rapidly and are fleeting. Methodologies used in family research must capture this complexity. Using models derived from family systems approaches is one strategy for beginning to account for this complexity (see Boeninger & Conger, this volume and Snyder, Simpson, & Hughes, 2008 for systems-based approaches to research on emotion regulation processes in a family context).

DEVELOPMENTAL CONSIDERATIONS

There have been numerous reviews of factors that shape the development of emotion processes, including emotion regulation, in infancy and early childhood (e.g., Cole, Michel, & Teti, 1994; Thompson & Goodwin, 2007). Less attention has been given to how emotion and emotion regulation processes specifically may change through adolescence, and when attention has been given the focus has often been on the influence of pubertal and other biological changes (e.g., DeRose & Brooks-Gunn, 2008; Nolen-Hoeksema & Girgus, 1994; Steinberg, 2005). Adolescence, however, is also marked by important changes in cognitive capacities, social contexts and challenges, and personal goals, beliefs, and self-identity. Changes in each of these domains have important implications for emotional experience and regulation.

For younger children, the role of parents in helping a child regulate emotional states is critical (Thompson & Meyer, 2007). With increasing cognitive sophistication, the establishment of more intimate and mature peer relationships, and less inclination to depend on parents for their regulatory role, adolescents have the means and the motivation to develop new ways to regulate emotions. Because of shifts in their commitments and beliefs about the self and the world, the contexts that are likely to produce emotions, and the meaning they make of their emotional encounters, adolescents' goals in regulating their emotions are also likely to change. We will briefly touch on the implications of changes in the three domains we have identified.

Cognitive Development

Cognitive development influences the way in which emotional encounters are appraised and the way in which emotions are experienced (Larson & Sheeber, 2008). The increased capacity for abstract thinking, critical reasoning, and perspective taking allows the adolescent to observe more of his or her own emotion processes and those of others (Cowan, 1982; Steinberg, 2005). Larson and Richards (1994) have suggested that these enhanced skills lead adolescents to look beneath the surface of things to see more subtle threats to their well-being. Adolescents become troubled by issues and implications of daily life that younger children do not even consider. Hauser and Safyer (1994) reported that teenagers who have higher levels of ego development, a measure that incorporates constructs such as a capacity for perspective taking and complex reasoning, express more anxiety. They interpreted this finding as evidence that these more cognitively sophisticated individuals have a greater awareness of complexities and uncertainties in themselves and in the world, and that this awareness might underlie the increased anxiety. Adolescents' increased skill in abstract reasoning also contributes to what Erikson (1950) and others have described as the identity crisis of adolescence during which individuals sort through their values and commitments and work to define a new identity for themselves.

Whereas cognitive development might contribute to greater anxiety, conflict, and soul searching for adolescents, it also provides them with the opportunity to take fuller advantage of more complicated types of emotion-focused coping strategies, especially cognitive reappraisal (Aldwin, Yancura, & Boeninger, 2010; Schulz et al., 2005). As we have outlined earlier, cognitive reappraisal can be directed at any of the six subcomponents of primary and secondary appraisal. A more developed ability to engage in abstract thinking and perspective taking increases the opportunities to reappraise an emotional encounter in a different way. For example, an adolescent has a growing capacity to step back and thoughtfully reconsider the importance of his or her own goals and commitments during an emotional encounter. Adolescents are also more able than younger children to reexamine another person's intentions during an emotional encounter. For example, while being teased by his friends in the cafeteria, Johnny might, upon further reflection, consider the possibility that his friend did not intend to hurt his feelings. The friend might instead have intended to engage in some good-spirited fun. This reconsideration of the classmate's intentions is likely to change Johnny's emotional experience.

Changing Social Contexts and Challenges

In addition to the thinking capacities of adolescents becoming more complex, there is evidence that their daily lives become more complicated. Larson and Richards (1994) reported that adolescents experience more conflicting goals and feelings than younger children and that these conflicts reflect an increase in the complexity of their lives. There are a large number of significant transitions (e.g., school changes, preparing for work, college, and leaving home after high school) in the relatively short period of time that is commonly thought of as adolescence. In addition to more varied challenges at school, adolescents are exploring new roles, social groups, and social situations as they move away from the safety of their family. Adolescents may struggle with uncertainty about the rules for appropriate behavior, including emotional experience and expression, in these new situations.

Not surprisingly, findings from several studies indicate that the situations that trigger emotions differ for adolescents as compared to younger children (Haviland, Davidson, Ruetsch, Gebelt, & Lancelot, 1994; Larson & Sheeber, 2008). For younger children, the family appears to be the source of most of their strong feelings, whereas for adolescents, friends and romantic partners, in addition to families, are important stimulators of emotion. Adolescents are especially vulnerable to emotions related to their self-esteem and social standing. Experience sampling methods have shown that adolescents are more likely to report feeling self-conscious, embarrassed, awkward, lonely, and ignored than younger children (Larson & Richards, 1994).

Despite the changing social context of adolescence, there are important underlying continuities in the experience of emotion. Although it is true that a 15 year old is not amused or upset by the same situations as a 5 year old (Davidson & Ekman, 1994), the underlying core relational themes that elicit each emotion remain stable. The infant responds to his or her hands being restrained but not to privileges being reduced or other situations that typically provoke anger in an adolescent (Campos et al., 1989). However, the underlying theme of blocking attainment of an important goal is present across both developmental epochs.

Changing Goals, Beliefs, and Self-Identity

Adolescence is a time in which individuals are actively working on defining their selves, exploring different values and beliefs, and developing a stronger allegiance to particular goals. Individuals at all ages struggle to weave their views of themselves and the world in which they live into a self-consistent system of motives, beliefs, and stories about themselves. This system of beliefs gives meaning to our lives and helps us deal with the conditions of life that are encountered. During adolescence, individuals are working especially hard to prioritize the values, beliefs, and commitments that are central to their identity and those that are peripheral. This developing identity includes beliefs about the self, the self in relation to the larger world, and the nature of this larger world. As we have emphasized, it is this system of values, beliefs, and commitments that helps to determine what is at stake for an individual in his or her encounters in the world and what goals guide coping efforts in emotional encounters. One implication of the shifting values, beliefs, and views of self during adolescence is the likelihood that confusion about or conflict between goals in particular encounters may be more likely.

In addition to this intraindividual variability, there is also significant variation between adolescents in their central goals and beliefs. We must, therefore, be cautious in identifying goals and beliefs that we assume are normatively linked to developmental factors. Clearly, contexts of development, including family, ethnic and cultural background, and socioeconomic factors, influence the development of these goals and beliefs (Mesquita & Albert, 2007).

Many psychologists, including Erikson (1950), have, however, noted common goals that individuals are working to attain during adolescence. Such normative trends allow researchers to examine developmentally salient situations that are likely to engender emotions and in which the stakes are likely to be similar for many adolescents at a similar point in development. For example, several family-based research efforts have examined links between emotional experience and autonomy strivings of adolescents in the context of the family (e.g., Allen, Hauser, Eickholt, Bell, & O'Connor, 1994; Kobak & Ferenz Gillies, 1995). Other researchers have identified overarching goals that may guide individuals' behavior in particular family contexts across childhood and adolescence. For example, building on concepts from the literature on attachment, Davies and Cummings (2006) have theorized that children's desire to preserve a sense of emotional security shapes their responses to parental conflict across developmental periods. Consistent with this theory, when Johnny's parents argue, Johnny might appraise the situation as one that threatens his emotional security because it raises the possibility that his parents may not always be together and there for him. Davies and Cummings believe that his coping response to this threat would be guided by the goal of restoring a sense of emotional security. He might attempt to reappraise the situation as less threatening to his emotional security or he might engage in actions that distract his parents and reduce their conflict.

RESEARCH IMPLICATIONS

We now turn our attention to the implications of the cognitive-mediational model we have outlined for research on adolescent emotional experience and regulation, especially in a family context. Our discussion will necessarily be selective. An important current focus of attention is on explicating the link between aspects of emotion regulation and brain functioning (e.g., Lewis & Mcleod, 2004; Woltering & Lewis, 2009). These efforts have benefited in important ways from appraisal-based emotion frameworks (e.g., Ochsner & Gross, 2008; Scherer, 2009), but we focus, in this section, on the implications of three specific features of the cognitive-mediational model we have elaborated. First, the model's emphasis on the importance of personal meaning points to the need for research that assesses individuals' goals, intentions, and appraisals in emotional encounters. In particular, greater attention to the goals that guide individuals' attempts to regulate their emotions is needed (Fischer, Manstead, Evers, Timmers, & Valk, 2004). Second, because emotion regulation is part of a larger emotion system that has many interdependent components, research on emotion-regulatory processes is likely to be most productive if multiple components of the emotion system are considered simultaneously. Finally, we have emphasized the dynamic unfolding of emotion over time. This process perspective on emotion implies that emotional encounters should be studied as they unfold and that methods that are more microanalytic in nature are critical to understanding these processes.

Capturing Personal Meaning and Intentions When Examining Emotion Regulation

Standard coping questionnaires assess the strategies that individuals employ in emotional encounters (e.g., Folkman & Lazarus, 1988), but they do not typically query about the goals underlying these strategies. Researchers have investigated the intentions motivating coping in emotional contexts by asking individuals how they would respond in *hypothetical* situations (Timmers, Fischer, & Manstead, 1998). More research needs to be directed at identifying the motives that guide emotion-regulatory efforts in *real life* encounters and how these motives may shift as adolescents and young adults develop over time.

Research on adolescents' feeling and display rules can help inform this effort. Investigations of adolescents' perceptions of their family's, peers', and society's expectations or rules regarding appropriate emotional experience and expression in daily life are likely to contribute important information about how emotional expression and behavior are socialized. Studies that trace shifts in feeling and display rules over time would increase our understanding of the developmental processes associated with this important aspect of emotion. It would also be useful to link the feeling and display rules that adolescents perceive to be operative in particular contexts, such as their peers or their families, with their behavior in these contexts.

Related research has been conducted (e.g., Saarni, 1979), but has not generally targeted adolescents. The concept of meta-emotion has been used to refer to an organized set of thoughts and feelings about emotions and the way in which emotions should be expressed and regulated (Gottman, Katz, & Hooven, 1997).

Researchers have presented evidence linking parents' meta-emotion philosophies, parents' behavior toward their children, and children's emotion-regulatory abilities (Gottman et al., 1997; Katz & Hunter, 2007; Yap, Allen, Leve, & Katz, 2008). Stein, Schulz, and Waldinger (2006, 2011) developed a measure, *Beliefs about Emotional Expression* (BEE), that assesses individuals' beliefs about the appropriate ways to express negative emotions in close relationships. Analyses of the responses of over 500 adults identified two dimensions of beliefs. The first dimension captured the belief that expressing negative emotions in close relationships is natural and appropriate (e.g., "Expressing feelings is a natural part of being in a relationship."). The second dimension captured a belief that emotion expression could threaten a close relationship and therefore should be carefully modulated (e.g., "Relationships could be threatened if we let our partners know everything we feel all the time."). Expected links were found between these BEE dimensions and measures of actual emotional expressiveness. This type of research approach needs to be extended to capture adolescents' own views about the role of emotional expression in different types of close relationships (e.g., peer, romantic, family).

Because of the importance of assessing individuals' subjective experience and their intentions during emotional encounters, self-report and interview techniques are critical research tools (Schulz & Waldinger, 2010). However, because some of the processing involved in appraisal may occur outside of full awareness and because we may be motivated to put a good face, or least a socially desirable one, on our emotional experience, self-report data must be interpreted with caution. Concerns about the quality of self-report data are important, but they should motivate us to improve our methods of collecting self-report data to boost reliability and validity, not to abandon their use.

Because it is difficult to study emotions as they are unfolding, researchers often ask individuals to report retrospectively on their thoughts, feelings, and actions. Cued video-recall approaches have been developed to facilitate more accurate recall of specific emotional experiences (e.g., Waldinger & Schulz, 2006; Welsh & Dickson, 2005). Videotapes of an interaction are replayed for participants to cue their memory and induce a psychological state that is similar to the one that was experienced in the original encounter (Gottman & Levenson, 1985). Powers, Welsh, and Wright (1994) have used this video-recall procedure in their research on adolescent-parent interactions to assess repeatedly individuals' feeling states, perceptions of other family members' intentions or purposes, and appraisals of the significance of the interactions. Such an approach could be used to inquire more specifically about appraisal components and the specific regulatory or expressive intentions that adolescents or parents have in emotion-producing family interactions. Data obtained from this type of video-recall procedure can be linked temporally with other aspects of emotion, such as physiology and behaviors from the original interaction (see Schulz & Waldinger, 2010 for an example of this approach with marital interactions).

There have been important efforts by family researchers to incorporate intentions and goals into research on how adolescents cope during emotional encounters.

Researchers building on a tradition of examining attachment behavior in infants and toddlers have focused on adolescents' behavior in family interactions that engage developmentally salient relationship challenges (e.g., Allen et al., 1994; Kobak & Ferenz Gillies, 1995). For example, when an adolescent and a parent are asked to resolve a difference of opinion they have over a moral dilemma, researchers have observed how the adolescent manages conflicting demands for establishing autonomy from parents while still maintaining connection (Allen et al., 1994). These types of circumstances provide a valuable opportunity to examine emotion regulation processes, but we cannot assume that the intentions—or the developmentally salient challenges—are the same for all adolescents engaged in the family tasks. That is, it is still important to assess directly adolescents' intentions and goals during these encounters, especially those that shape their efforts to manage their emotions. Some adolescents may be strongly motivated to demonstrate their persuasive skills and moral reasoning whereas others may be motivated primarily by a desire to avoid an argument with a parent. Without knowing their intentions, it is difficult to assess accurately the nature and effectiveness of their attempts at regulating their emotions.

Need for Multichannel Approaches for Studying Emotion Reactions

Our model emphasizes the multiple components that comprise the emotion system. Examining more than one component simultaneously allows investigators to capture more of the true complexity of emotion processes. For example, combining measures of emotional experience, observations of emotional expression, and psychophysiological assessments during family discussions provides several vantage points from which to understand emotion-regulatory processes. A lack of coherence between observed expression or physiological reactivity and participant-reported experience may help pinpoint the use of emotion-regulatory processes such as expressive suppression (Gross, 1998; Lazarus, 1995).

Need for Methodologies That Capture Dynamic Processes of Emotion

Given the dynamic nature of emotion, research needs to employ methodologies that are capable of capturing processes that unfold over brief periods of time. Observational research on family interaction employing microanalytic coding techniques makes it possible to examine sequences of behavior that may provide clues about important components of emotion regulation. Observing the same person or persons repeatedly over time allows researchers to examine the sequence of important variables and whether these variables covary over the course of an interaction. For example, by intensively observing a series of family interactions, Schulz and colleagues (2005) found covariation across time of hostile exchanges between parents and an adolescents' hostility toward parents. This covariation is consistent with the assumption that interparental conflict is emotionally disequillibrating for adolescents (Davies & Cummings, 2006). Moreover, Schulz and colleagues were able to demonstrate that the degree of covariation was related to individual differences in adolescent emotion-regulatory abilities.

Increasingly, repeated daily questionnaires or momentary assessment approaches have been used to capture thoughts, feelings, and behaviors related to everyday experiences of emotion (e.g., Schulz, Cowan, Cowan, & Brennan, 2004; Silk et al., 2003). These approaches have similar advantages to repeated observations of family interactions and can be extended to incorporate assessments of important appraisal components or goals that are activated during emotional encounters (e.g., Tong et al., 2007). With these data and the use of appropriate multilevel modeling approaches (e.g., Schulz et al., 2004), researchers can examine changes over time in emotion-relevant constructs within particular individuals or families and then see whether particular groupings of individuals or families change in similar ways.

CONCLUSION

In this chapter, we have argued that the conceptualization and study of emotion regulation processes in adolescents would benefit from greater attention to existing cognitive-mediational perspectives on emotion. In these perspectives, emotion is conceptualized as a multidimensional system initiated by an individual's appraisal of his or her personal stakes in a particular situation. Each emotion is believed to be stimulated by a particular set of underlying appraisals referred to as a core relational theme. The appraisal process is subjective and is shaped by the individual's personal goals and beliefs and by the particular situation. The appraisal process involves, in part, consideration of the actions, including emotion-regulatory efforts, that could be taken to influence the outcome of an emotional encounter. For this reason, we have argued that emotion regulation, like other forms of coping, is best conceived of as a mediator of emotion rather than a reaction to emotion.

Emotion-regulatory efforts are guided by individuals' general beliefs and personal goals in an encounter. All aspects of the emotion system can be targeted by emotion-regulatory processes including emotion-provoking environmental contexts, an individual's personal beliefs and goals, appraisal processes, and the response tendencies generated by emotions in the experiential, expressive, and physiological domains.

When considering developmental factors that might shape adolescents' attempts to regulate their emotions, we emphasized changes in cognitive capacities, in social contexts, and in personal goals, beliefs, and self-identity. Our conceptualization of emotion regulation and emotion in general has important implications for research on emotion processes in adolescence. First, we argued for the importance of assessing the beliefs and goals that guide individuals' attempts to regulate emotions. One critical task for researchers is to identify potential developmental patterns in adolescents' beliefs about the appropriate way to experience and express emotions in important contexts, such as family and peer settings. We also believe that more attention must be given to the motives that guide emotion expression and regulation for adolescents in actual emotion encounters. Effective self-report strategies will be critical to efforts to research emotion-regulatory motives.

Second, we noted the importance of incorporating assessment of multiple components of the emotion experience. Multichannel assessment is particularly useful for understanding emotion-regulatory processes, which often involve an uncoupling of the usual coherence in activity across multiple emotional channels. Finally, investigators need to continue to use and develop research strategies that capture the dynamic and fleeting nature of emotion processes. Microanalytic observational research and momentary assessment approaches are two promising strategies for studying emotion-regulatory processes.

Adolescents, such as Johnny, are actively developing styles of regulating their emotions that are likely to be prominent aspects of their personality and relationships for many years to come (Whitton et al., 2008). Research on emotion-regulatory processes during this critical developmental period can help address important questions in the field of emotion. This research can be informed by the rich body of existing conceptual and empirical data on emotion and stress that has been largely focused on adults. Developmentally oriented family researchers are particularly well positioned to integrate work from the adult literature into investigations of adolescent emotion processes.

References

Aldwin, C. M., Yancura, L. A., & Boeninger, D. K. (2010). Coping across the lifespan. In R. E. Lerner, A. M. Freund, & M. E. Lamb (Eds.), *Handbook of Lifespan Development*: Vol. 2 (pp. 298–340). New York: Wiley.

Allen, J. P., Hauser, S. T., Eickholt, C., Bell, K. L., & O'Connor, T. G. (1994). Autonomy and relatedness in family interactions as predictors of expressions of negative adolescent affect. *Journal of Research on Adolescence, 4,* 535–552.

Arnold, M. B. (1960). *Emotion and personality.* New York: Columbia University Press.

Campos, J. J., Campos, R. G., & Barrett, K., (1989). Emergent themes in the study of emotional development and emotion regulation. *Developmental Psychology, 25,* 394–402.

Campos, J. J., Frankel, C. B., & Camras, L. (2004). On the nature of emotion regulation. *Child Development, 75,* 377–394.

Campos, J. J., Mumme, D. L., Kermoian, R., & Campos, R. G. (1994). A functionalist perspective on the nature of emotion. In N. A. Fox (Ed.), *The development of emotion regulation: Biological and behavioral considerations* (Vol. 59, pp. 284–303). Chicago: University of Chicago Press.

Cole, P. M., & Deater-Deckard, K. (2009). Emotion regulation, risk, and psychopathology. *Journal of Child Psychology and Psychiatry, 50,* 1327–1330.

Cole, P. M., Martin, S. E., & Dennis, T. A. (2004). Emotion regulation as a scientific construct: Methodological challenges and directions for child development research. *Child Development, 75*(2), 317–333.

Cole, P. M., Michel, M. K., & Teti, L. O. D. (1994). The development of emotion regulation and dysregulation: A clinical perspective. In N. A. Fox (Ed.), *The development of emotion regulation: Biological and behavioral considerations* (Vol. 59, pp. 73–100). Chicago: University of Chicago Press.

Cole, P. M., & Tamang, B. L. (1998). Nepali children's ideas about emotional displays in hypothetical challenges. *Developmental Psychology, 34,* 640–646.

Compas, B. E., Jaser, S. S., & Benson, M. (2008). Coping and emotion regulation: Implications for understanding depression during adolescence. In S. Nolen-Hoeksema & L. Hilt (Eds.), *Handbook of adolescent depression* (pp. 419–440). New York: Oxford University Press.

Cowan, P. A. (1982). The relationship between emotional and cognitive development. In D. Cicchetti & P. Hesse (Eds.), *Emotional development* (Vol. 16, pp. 49–81). San Francisco: Jossey-Bass.

Davidson, R. J., & Ekman, P. (1994). Afterword to question 11: What develops in emotional development? In P. Ekman & R. J. Davidson (Eds.), *The nature of emotion: Fundamental questions* (pp. 373–375). New York: Oxford University Press.

Davies, P. T., & Cummings, E. M. (2006). Interparental discord, family process, and developmental psychopathology. In D. Cicchetti & D. J. Cohen (Eds.), *Developmental psychopathology: Vol. 3: Risk, disorder, and adaptation* (2nd ed., pp. 86–128). New York: Wiley & Sons.

DeRose, L. M., & Brooks-Gunn, J. (2008). Pubertal development during early adolescence. In N. B. Allen & L. Sheeber (Eds.), *Adolescent emotional development and the emergence of depressive disorders* (pp. 56–73). New York: Cambridge University Press.

Ekman, P. (1972). Universals and cultural differences in facial expressions of emotion. In J. Cole (Ed.), *Nebraska symposium on motivation* (pp. 207–283). Lincoln: University of Nebraska Press.

Ekman, P. (1984). Expression and the nature of emotion. In K. Scherer & P. Ekman (Eds.), *Approaches to emotion* (pp. 319–344). Hillsdale, NJ: Erlbaum.

Erikson, E. H. (1950). *Childhood and society.* New York: Norton.

Fischer, A. H., Manstead, A. S. R., Evers, C., Timmers, M., & Valk, G. (2004). Motives and norms underlying emotion regulation. In R. Feldman & P. Philippot (Eds.), *The regulation of emotion* (pp. 187–210). Mahwah, NJ: Lawrence Erlbaum Associates.

Folkman, S., & Lazarus, R. S. (1988). *Manual for the ways of coping questionnaire.* Palo Alto, CA: Consulting Psychologists Press.

Fridja, N. H., Kuipers, P., & ter-Schure, E. (1989). Relations among emotion, appraisal, and emotional action readiness. *Journal of Personality and Social Psychology, 57,* 212–228.

Goldsmith, H. H., Pollak, S. D., & Davidson, R. J. (2008). Developmental neuroscience perspectives on emotion regulation. *Child Development Perspectives, 2,* 132–140.

Gottman, J. M., Katz, L. F., & Hooven, C. (1997). *Meta-emotion: How families communicate emotionally.* Mahwah, NJ: Erlbaum.

Gottman, J., & Levenson, R. (1985). A valid procedure for obtaining self-report of affect in marital interaction. *Journal of Consulting and Clinical Psychology, 53,* 151–160.

Gross, J. J. (1998). Antecedent- and response-focused emotion regulation: Divergent consequences for experience, expression, and physiology. *Journal of Personality and Social Psychology, 74,* 224–237.

Gross, J. J. (2001). Emotion regulation in adulthood: Timing is everything. *Current Directions in Psychological Science, 10*(6), 214–219.

Gross, J. J., & Thompson, R. A. (2007). Emotion regulation: Conceptual foundations. In J. J. Gross (Ed.), *Handbook of emotion regulation* (pp. 3–24). New York, NY: Guilford Press.

Hart, K. E. (1991). Coping with anger-provoking situations: Adolescent coping in relation to anger-reactivity. *Journal of Adolescent Research, 6,* 357–370.

Hauser, S. T., & Safyer, A. W. (1994). Ego development and adolescent emotions. *Journal of Research on Adolescence, 4,* 487–502.

Haviland, J. M., Davidson, R. B., Ruetch, C., Gebelt, J. L., & Lancelot, C. (1994). The place of emotion in identity. *Journal of Research on Adolescence, 4,* 503–518.

Hochschild, A. R. (1983). *The managed heart: Commercialization of human feeling.* Berkeley: University of California Press.

Katz, L. F., & Hunter, E. C. (2007). Maternal meta-emotion philosophy and adolescent depressive symptomatology. *Social Development, 16,* 343–360.

Kobak, R., & Ferenz Gillies, R. (1995). Emotion regulation and depressive symptoms during adolescence: A functionalist perspective. *Development and Psychopathology, 7,* 183–192.

Larson, R., & Richards, M. H. (1994). *Divergent realities: The emotional lives of mothers, fathers, and adolescents.* New York: Basic Books.

Larson, R., & Sheeber, L. (2008). The daily emotional experience of adolescents. In N. Allen & L. Sheeber (Eds.), *Adolescent emotional development and the emergence of depressive disorders* (pp. 11–32). New York: Cambridge University Press.

Lazarus, R. S. (1991). *Emotion and adaptation.* New York: Oxford.

Lazarus, R. S. (1993). From psychological stress to the emotions: A history of changing outlooks. *Annual Review of Psychology, 44,* 1–21.

Lazarus, R. S. (1995). Vexing research problems inherent in cognitive-mediational theories of emotion—and some solutions. *Psychological Inquiry, 6,* 183–196.

Lazarus, R. S. (1996). The role of coping in the emotions and how coping changes over the life course. In C. Magai & S. H. McFadden (Eds.), *Handbook of emotion, adult development, and aging* (pp. 289–306). San Diego, CA: Academic Press.

Lazarus, R. S., & Folkman, S. (1984). *Stress, appraisal, and coping.* New York: Springer.

Levenson, R. W., Ekman, P., & Friesen, W. V. (1990). Voluntary facial action generates emotion-specific autonomic nervous system activity. *Psychophysiology, 27,* 363–384.

Lewis, M. D. (2001). Personal pathways in the development of appraisal: A complex systems/stage theory perspective. In K. R. Scherer, A. Schorr, & T. Johnstone (Eds.), *Appraisal processes in emotion: Theory, methods, and research* (pp. 205–220). New York: Oxford University Press.

Lewis, M. D., & McLeod, C. (2004). Emotion regulation in the brain: Conceptual issues and directions for developmental research. *Child Development, 75,* 371–376.

Mesquita, B., & Albert, D. (2007). The cultural regulation of emotions. In J. J. Gross (Ed.), *Handbook of emotion regulation* (pp. 486–503). New York: Guilford Press.

Nolen-Hoeksema, S., & Girgus, J. S. (1994). The emergence of gender differences in depression during adolescence. *Psychological Bulletin, 115,* 424–443.

Ochsner, K. N., & Gross, J. (2008). Cognitive emotion regulation: Insights from social cognitive and affective neuroscience. *Current Directions in Psychological Science, 17,* 153–158.

Ortony, A., Clore, G. L., & Collins, A. (1988). *The cognitive structure of emotions.* New York: Cambridge University Press.

Powers, S. I., Welsh D. P., & Wright, V. (1994). Affect in families of adolescents: Investigating the meaning of behavior. *Journal of Research on Adolescence, 4*, 585–600.

Saarni, C. (1979). Children's understanding of display rules for expressive behavior. *Developmental Psychology, 15*, 424–429.

Scarr, S., & McCartney, K. (1983). How people make their own environments: A theory of genotype-environment effects. *Child Development, 54*, 424–435.

Scherer, K. R. (1984). On the nature and function of emotion: A component process approach. In K. R. Scherer & P. Ekman (Eds.), *Approaches to emotion* (pp. 293–317). Hillsdale, NJ: Erlbaum.

Scherer, K. R. (2009). The dynamic architecture of emotion: Evidence for the component process model. *Cognition and Emotion, 23*, 1307–1351.

Schulz, M. S., Cowan, P. A., Cowan, C. P., & Brennan, R. T. (2004). Coming home upset: Gender, marital satisfaction and the daily spillover of workday experience into marriage. *Journal of Family Psychology, 18*, 250–263.

Schulz, M. S., & Waldinger, R. J. (2010). Capturing the elusive: Studying emotion processes in couple relationships. In M. S. Schulz, M. K. Pruett, P. K. Kerig, & R. D. Parke (Eds.), *Strengthening couple relationships for optimal child development: Lessons from Research and intervention* (pp. 131–147). Washington, DC: American Psychological Association.

Schulz, M. S., Waldinger, R. J., Hauser, S. T., & Allen, J. P. (2005). Adolescents' behavior in the presence of interparental hostility: Developmental and emotion regulatory influences. *Development and Psychopathology, 17*, 489–507.

Silk, J. S., Steinberg, L., & Morris, A. S. (2003). Adolescents' emotion regulation in daily life: Links to depressive symptoms and problem behavior. *Child Development, 74*, 1869–1880.

Smith, C. A., & Ellsworth, P. C. (1985). Patterns of cognitive appraisal in emotion. *Journal of Personality and Social Psychology, 48*, 813–838.

Smith, C. A., & Kirby, L. D. (2009). Putting appraisal in context: Toward a relational model of appraisal and emotion. *Cognition and Emotion, 23*, 1352–1372.

Smith, C. A., & Lazarus, R. S. (2001). Appraisal components, core relational themes, and the emotions. In W. G. Parrott (Ed.), *Emotions in social psychology: Essential readings* (pp. 94–114). New York: Psychology Press.

Snyder, D. K., Simpson, J. A., & Hughes, J. N. (Eds.). (2008). *Emotion regulation in couples and families: Pathways to dysfunction and health.* Washington, DC: American Psychological Association.

Stein, J. A., Schulz, M. S., & Waldinger, R. J. (2006, November). *Connecting heart and mind: Links among beliefs about the consequences of emotion, interpersonal intentions, and affective expression in marital interactions.* Poster presented at the annual meeting of the Association for Behavioral and Cognitive Therapy, Chicago, IL.

Stein, J. A., Schulz, M. S., & Waldinger, R. J. (2011). Beliefs about emotional expression and actual emotional behaviors in couple interactions. In preparation.

Steinberg, L. (2005). Cognitive and affective development in adolescence. *Trends in Cognitive Sciences, 9*, 69–74.

Thompson, R. A., & Goodwin, R. (2007). Taming the tempest in the teapot: Emotion regulation in toddlers. In C. A. Brownell & C. B. Kopp (Eds.), *Socioemotional development in the toddler years: Transitions and transformations* (pp. 320–341). New York: Guilford Press.

Thompson, R. A., & Meyer, S. (2007). Socialization of emotion regulation in the family. In J. J. Gross (Ed.), *Handbook of emotion regulation* (pp. 249–268). New York: Guilford Press.

Timmers, M., Fischer, A. H., & Manstead, A. S. R. (1998). Gender differences in motives for regulating emotions. *Personality and Social Psychology Bulletin, 24,* 974–985.

Tong, E. M. W., Bishop, G. D., Enklemann, H. C., Why, Y. P., Diong, S. M., Khader, M. A., & Ang, J. (2007). Emotion and appraisal: A study using ecological momentary assessment. *Cognition and Emotion, 21,* 1361–1381.

Waldinger, R. J., & Schulz, M. S. (2006). Linking hearts and minds in couple interactions: Intentions, attributions and overriding sentiments. *Journal of Family Psychology, 20,* 494–504.

Waldinger, R. J., & Schulz, M. S. (2010). Facing the music or burying our heads in the sand?: Adaptive emotion regulation in mid- and late-life. *Research in Human Development, 7,* 292–306.

Welsh, D. P., & Dickson, J. (2005). Video-recall procedures for examining subjective understanding in observational data. *Journal of Family Psychology, 19,* 62–71.

Woltering, S., & Lewis, M. D. (2009). Developmental pathways of emotion regulation in childhood: A neuropsychological perspective. *Mind, Brain, and Education, 3,* 160–169.

Whitton, S. W., Waldinger, R. J., Schulz, M. S., Allen, J. P., Crowell, J., & Hauser, S. T. (2008). Prospective associations from family-of-origin interactions to adult marital interactions and relationship adjustment. *Journal of Family Psychology, 22,* 274–286.

Yap, M. B. H., Allen, N. B., Leve, C., & Katz, L. F. (2008). Maternal meta-emotion philosophy and socialization of adolescent affect: The moderating role of adolescent temperament. *Journal of Family Psychology, 22,* 688–700.

2

Risk and Protective Factors for Suicidality during the Transition to Adulthood

Parenting, Self-Regulatory Processes, and Successful Resolution of Stage-Salient Tasks

DARIA K. BOENINGER AND RAND D. CONGER

Suicide represents the third leading cause of death for those between 10 and 24 years of age in the United States (Centers for Disease Control and Prevention, 2010). Although adolescent suicide receives the most attention from media and researchers, suicide rates for emerging adults (early twenties) are actually greater than during adolescence, especially for young men; this finding underscores the importance of understanding suicide risk during the transition from adolescence to adulthood. Suicidal ideation, plans, and attempts predict completed suicide, and themselves signify intense suffering. Suicidal episodes are also the most common precipitants to psychiatric hospitalization in the United States (Institute of Medicine, 2002). Further, adolescent suicidal episodes predict young adult psychiatric disorders and impaired functioning in the realms of work, education, and social relationships (Fergusson, Horwood, Ridder, & Beautrais, 2005; Reinherz, Tanner, Berger, Beardslee, & Fitzmaurice, 2006). This personal suffering therefore translates into significant loss of productivity on the societal level (see Institute of Medicine, 2002, for the estimated costs of these problems). The whole range of *suicidality*—ideation, plans, attempts, and completions—thus deserves attention from researchers and practitioners.

This chapter casts suicide-related thoughts and behaviors in a self-regulatory framework, and delineates the implications of parenting for the development of self-regulatory capacities, as well as the relations between self-regulatory capacities, functioning in stage-salient tasks, and suicidality risk during the transition from adolescence to adulthood. We conceptualize self-regulation as the coordination of affect, cognition, and behavior in the service of long-term goals and consequences

(Dale & Baumeister, 1999), and focus especially on *coping*, which we see as self-regulation under stress. From a coping perspective, self-regulatory resources are the personal resources on which individuals draw when coordinating their affect, cognition, and behavior in the service of managing and surmounting stressful events or circumstances (see for example Carver & Scheier, 1999).

The chapter proposes two central pathways of influence from parenting to off-spring suicidality. One involves enduring vulnerabilities to suicidality created by a lack of self-regulatory resources resulting from a history of harsh or neglectful parenting. The other proposed pathway involves social role impairments in the aftermath of negative parent–child bonding experiences: harsh and uninvolved parenting, through its effects on the development of adolescents' self-systems, can hamper their ability to function well in social roles, which in turn can lead to suicidal crises. We therefore describe and empirically test how parenting influences behavioral, cognitive-affective, and conative aspects of adolescent self-regulatory resources, as well as the hypothesized links between self-regulatory resources and young adult social role functioning. We then describe and test the hypothesized associations between suicidal episodes and self-regulatory capacities and young adult functioning in work and romantic relationships.

CONCEPTUALIZING SUICIDALITY

We understand suicide and suicidal crises as responses to acute, overwhelming stress, or chronic, unbearable strain (Baechler, 1979/2001; Rudd, 2000; Shneidman, 2001). This view considers suicide as an attempt to solve a problem (whether an internal or external event or situation) that is deemed intolerable by the suicidal individual—a problem or set of problems the person believes can be resolved *only* via "taking [his or her] own life from" the situation (Baechler, 1979/2001, p. 111). What has emerged from clinical and ethnographic work (Baechler, 1979/2001; Shneidman, 2001) in this field is the episodic and qualitatively distinct nature of suicidal crises, commensurate with a stress-response view of suicidality. However, for some individuals, the suicidal response to threatening or painful circumstances becomes more and more ingrained as a coping response (see Rudd, 2000). For the kind of despair suicides we are focusing on early in the lifespan, it is clear that they usually emerge in the absence of effective coping strategies and other key self-regulatory resources such as a sense of worth and mastery (Institute of Medicine, 2002). Furthermore, noting the severe self-dysregulation involved in the emergence of suicidal crises, and the self-annihilating or self-escaping goals of suicide, some have argued that the most accurate description of suicide involves an actual collapse of the self system (Vohs & Baumeister, 2000).

DEVELOPMENT OF COPING STRATEGIES

If suicidal thoughts and behavior represent forms of coping with stress, we must understand the development of coping strategies to be able to delineate the developmental underpinnings of vulnerability to or protection from suicidality. Recent reviews of the development of coping across childhood and adolescence (Skinner & Zimmer-Gembeck, 2009) as well as across adulthood (Aldwin, Yancura, & Boeninger, 2010) have emphasized how age-related shifts in coping strategies likely emerge from the developmental progression of neurocognition, temperament and personality, and sense of self and motivation. Positive or normative development in these domains of the self system can provide the biological, social-emotional, and experiential bases for choosing effective coping strategies as individuals mature.

Assuming normative progression of cognitive and social-emotional development, important expansion of the coping repertoire and refinement of coping strategies occur during adolescence and young adulthood. For example, appropriate cognitive development during these life phases facilitates the use of more sophisticated cognitive coping strategies such as perspective-taking, humor, and positive reappraisal, as well as the emergence of proactive and anticipatory coping (that is, coping strategies that take possible future problems into consideration and work to minimize their occurrence and effects). Changes in metacognitive abilities and sense of self and identity also give rise to self reflection as a means of coping (Aldwin et al., 2010; Skinner & Zimmer-Gembek, 2007). Adolescents and young adults generally decrease their use of negative interpersonal coping strategies such as blame and hostility as they practice dyadic coping with partners other than their parents (see, for example, Nieder & Seiffge-Krenke, 2001).

However, potentially harmful coping strategies such as substance use and social withdrawal also become more prevalent during these life phases, and suicidal (self-harming) behavior in response to stress becomes markedly more common among adolescents than children (Aldwin et al., 2010). Recent theory and work in adolescent development have highlighted the potential role of brain development in creating adolescent vulnerability to risk-taking behavior via early adolescent increases in arousability occurring before full maturation of the frontal lobes (Steinberg, 2005). We believe the use of potentially destructive coping strategies likely depends heavily on individuals' developmental history in several respects, however. For example, Aldwin (2007) suggests that adolescents who, for whatever reason, have failed to move from (developmentally younger) behavioral coping strategies (e.g., escapism, physical self-soothing) to more developmentally appropriate cognitive strategies may be the most likely to turn to substances to cope with stress. This process implicates the developmental course of physiological and cognitive development within these individuals: for example, exposure to trauma or chronic stress, especially early in life, can cause alterations in various brain systems that are linked to vulnerability or difficulties with physiological regulation (De Bellis, 2001; Gunnar & Fisher, 2006). Because activation of intense stress responses generally dampens the ability of individuals to engage their executive functions (e.g., working memory, planning, and problem solving; LeDoux, 2002) it may disrupt individuals' ability to engage effectively in cognitive coping strategies such as generating multiple ideas for problem solving. Hence, such individuals may well turn to substances to help regulate their arousal, and may become more likely to see their situation as hopeless, with suicide appearing to be the only solution.

Skinner and colleagues' (Skinner, Edge, Altman, & Sherwood, 2003; Skinner & Zimmer-Gembeck, 2007) exposition of the adaptive processes underlying coping and its development reveals another way in which developmental history may influence the use of self-destructive coping strategies. As individuals engage with stressful events and circumstances, their coping efforts are focused on trying to coordinate (1) their actions with environmental contingencies, (2) their reliance on others and help-seeking with available social resources, and (3) their personal preferences with the available options (see Schulz and Lazarus, this volume, for more on the role of personal goals in coping processes). Individuals' chosen coping strategies influence the impact of the stressor, but their guiding orientation to themselves and the world (e.g., as having some control vs. being helpless) also helps determine which strategies they choose. Further, individuals' socioenviron-mental contexts shape both their coping options and outcomes. Skinner and col-leagues' proposition suggests that as individuals move through their life and cope with problems, they form foundational conclusions about their ability to manage environmental contingencies, the availability and nature of their social support, and the worth and feasibility of their desires and values. If individuals' develop-mental history with respect to coping with life challenges has left them believing that they are helpless, unloved or unlovable, and worthless or burdensome, they become vulnerable to a range of self-destructive coping strategies, including suicidal behavior (cf. Rudd, 2000).

Recent reviews of coping across adolescence and adulthood (Aldwin et al., 2010; Skinner & Zimmer-Gembeck, 2009) also highlight the central role of "social partners," or dyadic coping partners, in the development of coping across the lifespan. Early in life, we are heavily dependent on our caregivers to help us manage our stress, whether directly by meeting our basic physical needs or sooth-ing us, or more indirectly through structuring our environment to reduce stress and enhance our chances of successfully navigating challenges. As we grow older, parents and other coping partners, such as teachers, siblings, friends, and roman-tic partners, socialize us regarding "how to cope" through modeling, direct instruction or coaching, and reinforcement or punishment for certain coping strategies (Aldwin et al., 2010; Kliewer, Sandler, & Wolchik, 1994).

We also begin to engage in explicitly *dyadic* coping, in which a stressor is jointly appraised by us and a social partner (e.g., a sibling), and we pool our attention and resources to jointly cope with a given problem or challenge (Berg & Upchurch, 2007). Siblings, friends, and, especially, romantic partners become primary dyadic coping partners during adulthood. The nature and impact of dyadic coping are certainly influenced by factors such as relationship quality. Relationship quality shapes the appraisal process (as whether a dyad perceives one partner's problem as a shared problem or an individual problem) and the coping behaviors within the dyad, which can range from one spouse, sibling, or friend being uninvolved in the coping efforts of the other, to being supportive but not actively engaged, to collaboratively coping with their social partner, or to being controlling of their social partner as that person faces a stressor (Berg & Upchurch, 2007). Thus, it is not surprising that emerging research suggests that the parent–adolescent bond influences the kinds and nature of young adult dyadic coping in romantic partnerships (Seiffge-Krenke, 2006).

The influence of parent–adolescent attachment also appears to generalize to adolescent coping styles (i.e., in addition to dyadic coping patterns, specifically), with secure attachment associated with more active, problem-focused coping, and insecure attachment related to more avoidant coping strategies (Aldwin et al., 2010). The literature therefore suggests that the developmental progression of coping across adolescence and young adulthood depends on the (1) normative changes in underlying neurocognitive, social-emotional, and social cognitive capacities; (2) developmental history of coping experiences; and (3) relationship quality with close others, especially parents.

PARENTING INFLUENCES ON SELF-REGULATORY RESOURCES

Developmental research on the effects of parental socialization highlights the wide-ranging impact of parents' behavior on children's self-development and self-regulation. These parenting effects extend across all levels of the self system, playing a role in shaping the physiological (e.g., stress-response systems), behavioral (e.g., impulse control), cognitive-affective (e.g., trait anxiety), and conative-existential (e.g., conventional values, religious involvement) characteristics from which self-regulation emerges. The literature on the effects of parenting generally emphasizes the affective quality of parenting, such as how warm and supportive parents are, as well as how appropriate (versus overly harsh) and consistent they are in their discipline and how involved they are in their children's lives (this includes the monitoring behavior of the parents toward their children) (Repetti, Taylor, & Seeman, 2002). Although self-regulation involves the coordination of the different subsystems of the self (Steinberg et al., 2006), certain outcomes or adaptive processes appear to be a blend of different domains, such as effort and persistence being a blend of behavior and motivation. As we touch on some of the findings on associations between parenting and different aspects of self-development, we will focus on key outcomes within the specific domains of behavior, cognition and affect, and conation (values, goals, motivation), while acknowledging that some outcomes may span domains.

In the behavioral domain, impulse control and aggressive, oppositional behavior problems emerge as important aspects of adolescent and young adult well-being and functioning. Research on young children's ability to engage in "effortful control," such as modulating the intensity of their behavior or delaying gratification, has implicated parenting characteristics such as warmth and responsivity as a factor in the development of these regulatory capacities (Eisenberg, Valiente, & Sulik, 2009; Kochanska, Murray, & Harlan, 2000). Conversely, impulsive-aggressive children and adolescents appear to have disproportionately frequent histories of child abuse (Brent & Mann, 2005; Dodge, Pettit, Bates, & Valente, 1995; Fergusson, Woodward, & Horwood, 2000). Randomized control trials of parenting interventions have found that teaching parents how to engage in supportive, consistent behavior toward their children and adolescents reduces both symptoms and diagnoses of behavioral disorders involving aggression, hostility, and oppositional-defiant conduct (Lacourse et al., 2002; Patterson, Chamberlain, & Reid, 1982; Wolchik et al., 2002). The literature therefore indicates that how parents treat their children influences how effectively and appropriately their children can regulate their behavior.

Regarding development in the cognitive-affective domain, an increasing body of literature, including that on parenting interventions (Murry et al., 2005; Wolchik et al., 2000), reports that parenting influences child and adolescent self-appraisals such as self-esteem. Far less research has investigated potential associations between parenting and cognitive-affective personality trait development than other aspects of self-development, but the emerging literature suggests that parental warmth and consistency are linked with positive personality traits such as conscientiousness (e.g., Heaven & Ciarrochi, 2008).

The conative domain of the self includes goals, motivation, and values (Little, 1999). Most research on development in this domain investigates aspects of motivation, including persistence, often within the school context. For example, consistent with the findings in the other domains of development, support from parents is related to motivation for school, which predicts dropping out of high school (Vallerand, Fortier, & Guay, 1997). Similarly, children of parents who show greater support for their autonomy and less controlling behavior report more intrinsic motivation toward schoolwork (Gurland & Grolnick, 2005). In the realm of religion and values, much of the intergenerational transmission depends on direct teaching; however, the nature of parent–child communication and the relational quality in families also appear to influence moral values and the importance that children place on religion (Flor & Knapp, 2001; White & Matawie, 2004). Across domains of self-development, then, the literature reliably reports that supportive, warm parenting with consistent, fitting discipline is associated with children and adolescents' greater resources for regulating themselves well.

SELF-REGULATORY RESOURCES AND SOCIAL ROLE FUNCTIONING

Specific aspects of self-development or regulatory resources appear to be related to functioning in social roles. For example, the ability to regulate impulses translates into being able to follow social-contextual demands and modulate behavioral responses in school settings in response to teacher instructions or peers (Eisenberg, Spinrad, & Morris, 2002). Not surprisingly, then, young people with attention deficit hyperactivity disorder (ADHD) or symptoms such as impulsivity (apart from diagnosis) have lower rates of high school completion and postsecondary education (Loe & Feldman, 2007). Cognitive-affective characteristics such as emotional stability, conscientiousness, and agreeableness are also associated with academic performance (Poropat, 2009) and higher income and job satisfaction in young adulthood (Sutin, Costa, Miech, & Eaton, 2009). In the conative realm, motivation has clear linkages with educational achievement, including basic outcomes such as high school completion (Vallerand et al., 1997).

In the realm of romantic relationships, impulsive-aggressive behavior has obvious associations with relationship problems and dissatisfaction (cf. Caspi, 1998). In the cognitive-affective domain, neuroticism, a personality trait that includes trait anxiety and depressed mood versus emotional stability, has emerged as an important predictor of quality and satisfaction in romantic relationships (Robins et al., 2002). Extraversion, agreeableness, and conscientiousness also demonstrate associations with intimacy and satisfaction in romantic relationships (Shiner, Masten, & Roberts, 2003; White, Hendrick, & Hendrick, 2004). Finally, conative factors such as religious attendance and values are associated with greater commitment to marriage (Allgood, Harris, Skogrand, & Lee, 2009) and more positive romantic relationship quality (Wilcox & Wolfinger, 2008). Every indication suggests, therefore, that the personal resources and characteristics from which people draw in the different domains of their self-system influence their ability to achieve and function well in important social roles.

THE TRANSITION FROM ADOLESCENCE TO YOUNG ADULTHOOD: DEVELOPMENTAL TASKS AND SELF-NARRATIVES

The transition period from late adolescence to adulthood is known as *emerging adulthood* (Arnett, 2001), and generally includes the years right after high school through about the mid-20s. We view leaving high school (whether completed or unfinished) as a notable transition in social roles and societal expectations, as young people in the United States are expected to be supporting themselves in some way at that stage, or to be investing in postsecondary education or training. The demands of emerging adults' new social context and their developmental history in terms of social and personal resources create their "landscape of stressors and resources" as they enter this life phase (Aldwin et al., 2010).

Cohler and Jenuwine (1995) note the importance of considering role transitions and relevant developmental tasks in understanding suicide and suicide risk. They argue that a key influence to consider during adulthood is how individuals' achievement and functioning in their expected social roles influence their "life story," or their narrative self. Similar to Skinner and Zimmer-Gembeck's (2007) proposition that coping with life stressors influences people's sense of themselves in terms of agency, social bonds, and values and preferences, Cohler and Jenuwine (1995) argue that individuals' comparisons of their status with perceived societal expectations influences their sense of agency, worth, and future.

Emerging adulthood involves a quest for an independent identity, financial independence, and forging romantic partnerships (Arnett, 2001). Independence in identity and finances are especially salient aspects of people's views of "being an adult." As emerging adults create their narrative selves by comparing their achievement of these developmental tasks in the realm of finances and romantic relationships to perceived social standards, if they see themselves as failures and construe that as being worthless and incompetent (helpless–hopeless), this could create risk for suicidal thoughts and behavior (cf. Rudd, 2000). As we reviewed above, emerging adults' self-regulatory resources are likely linked to their ability to achieve and function well in their developmental tasks. Additionally, the influence of negative narrative selves on suicidality risk would likely be especially high among individuals who lack self-regulatory resources that could compensate for or counteract those negative self-appraisals.

EMPIRICAL EXAMPLES FROM THE FAMILY TRANSITIONS PROJECT

Next, we turn to data from the Family Transition Project to provide some initial tests of our hypothesized links among parenting, self-regulatory resources, emerging adult developmental tasks, and risk for suicidal problems. We hypothesized that harsh parenting would be negatively related to self-regulatory resources during middle adolescence, and that adolescent self-regulatory resources would be positively related to functioning in the realms of emerging adult educational–occupational status and romantic relationship status. We further hypothesized that adolescent positive self-development would predict lower likelihood of suicidal thoughts and behaviors across emerging adulthood, beyond the influence of past suicidal problems. We also hypothesized that higher educational–occupational status and more positive romantic relationship functioning would predict a lower likelihood of young adult suicidal episodes, even after accounting for past suicidal problems.

Participants and Procedures

The present study draws from a sample of 556 target adolescents (53% female) from the Family Transitions Project (FTP), initiated in 1994, which combined the Iowa Youth and Families Project (IYFP), a study of 451 rural, nondivorced families that began in 1989 and the Iowa Single-Parent Project (ISPP), a study of 105 rural, mother-headed families that had experienced divorce within the 2 years prior to the study onset in 1991. Because these studies focus on families living in rural Iowa, and because almost no racial-ethnic minorities lived in rural Iowa at the time, the sample's racial-ethnic composition was limited to families of European descent. Approximately 90% of the participants have remained in the study from its inception to the most recent wave of data collection.

The IYFP participants were recruited in 1989 via the seventh-grade classes of 34 public and private schools in eight counties in central Iowa. Families were eligible for the study if a seventh grader had a sibling within 4 years of his or her age and she or he was living with both biological parents. Approximately 78% of eligible families agreed to participate in the first wave of data collection in 1989.

The ISPP participants were first identified via lists of students provided by schools in rural areas of Iowa (excluding university communities and urban areas). Telephone calls were made to mothers who were heads of their households. Fifteen percent of those contacted met the strict criteria for inclusion in the study, which were that the families had a target child in eighth or ninth grade in 1991 with a sibling within 4 years of his or her age, and whose biological parents had divorced within the past 2 years. Of those contacted who were eligible for the study, 99% agreed to participate. The majority (94%) of the fathers maintained contact with their children; at study onset, the legal custody arrangement for the target child was joint custody (58%) or sole maternal custody (33%). Nine percent of the families reported they had no legal arrangement regarding custody.

During adolescence, families completed two interviews (scheduled within 2 weeks of each other) with a trained interviewer during each year of data collection; each interview lasted for about 2 hours and each participating family member was paid about $10 per hour for his or her time. During the first visit, each family member answered a set of questionnaires regarding demographics, mental and physical health, occupational life, and marital, family, and peer relationships. Following high school, the target adolescent continued to be interviewed; if she or he had a romantic partner, the romantic partner was interviewed as well. The interview procedures were the same, and the same types of self-report data were collected. The current study will utilize this self-report questionnaire data collected when participants were ages 13, 15, 19–20, and every 2 years thereafter through age 30.

Measures

Demographic measures in the family of origin. We used mothers' report of their education level in 1991 (average = 13.4 years). Family structure (divorced versus intact) was also assessed in 1991. Adolescent gender was reported by mothers at the study onset.

Parenting behavior. We used adolescents' reports of the affective quality of their parents' behavior toward them to assess parenting behavior of the mothers and fathers when the adolescents were age 15. The scale contains 24 items with seven response categories (1 *never* to 7 *always*). Representative items that capture negativity are "During the past month when you and your [parent] have spent time together, how often did s/he criticize you"; positivity is captured by items such as "During the past month, how often did [your parent] act loving and affectionate toward you." We used the scale averages for mothers and fathers as two indicators of a latent variable assessing parenting quality.

Self development/self-regulatory resources. To assess the self-regulatory resources on which the adolescents had to draw, we created an index of positive and negative characteristics of self-development in the behavioral, cognitive-affective, and conative domains, as well as a few cross-domain constructs. For positive characteristics, we assigned a 1 to all adolescents who scored in the top 75th percentile on a particular measure and 0 for the bottom 25%; for negative characteristics or risks, we assigned a 1 to the bottom 75th percentile and 0 for the top 25%. The averaged score for the index therefore represents personal resources relative to risks (i.e., a higher score indicates more resources) across several domains of self-development. This index includes both self-report and mother-report data on the adolescents; all data were collected when the adolescents were 15 years of age.

In the *behavioral domain* we included information from a self-reported 9-item scale of impulsive-aggressive behavior, a 22-item mother-reported scale of oppositional-defiant behavior of the adolescent, and a 4-item mother-reported assessment of the child as hard-working and helpful. In the *cognitive-affective domain,* information tapping aspects of cognitive-affective traits included 8 self-report items assessing neuroticism (trait anxiety and depression versus emotional stability); 11 self-report items on agreeableness, 6 on extraversion, and 13 mother-report items on how positive and outgoing their adolescent was. In the *conative domain* we included information related to engagement and motivation in school (1 item reported by the mother and 4 by the adolescent regarding dislike for school; 1 self-report item on GPA, 2 on time spent on schoolwork, 6 on effort in school, 3 on personal relationships with teachers, and 8 on scholastic ability, with 1 mother report on keeping up with classes) as well as adolescent reports of the importance of religious beliefs (1 item), their conventional values (14 items), and their anti-social values (16 items). We also included information regarding self-regulatory characteristics that clearly cut across domains of the self: dispositional coping styles (self-report of avoidant, problem-focused, and social support coping) and mothers' reports of their adolescents' interpersonal problem-solving styles (16-item scale).

Social role functioning. We used a similar strategy for creating the status variables related to the emerging adult developmental tasks, drawing from multiple relevant scales and assigning a 1 or 0 depending on whether they were resources or risks. All data for these indices were assessed in the first year after high school for the target adolescents. For *educational and occupational status* we included information related to education if the person reported that as their primary occupation; otherwise, we included information about their occupation and working conditions. Note that if they reported being full-time homemakers not working for pay, we assessed their happiness and satisfaction in that role (3 items total) to create this index. For educational status, we included information about type of degree or certificate being pursued (1 item), how well they were doing in classes (2 on grades plus 7 on perception of ability and school skills), and their engagement (enjoyment and keeping up) in courses (7 items). For occupation, we included information on work stress (12 items), job security and social environment (10 items), fit between job and interests/skills (10 items), safety of the job (4 items), and autonomy in their position (4 items).

For assessing *romantic relationship functioning*, we created an index of relationship quality, with a higher score indicating a more supportive, warm, and harmonious relationship. We included 17 items on perceived supportiveness of the relationship partner, 2 on satisfaction in the relationship, 24 items on partner's behavior toward the young adult (affective quality of the behavior—modeled after the parenting measure we used in 1991), 9 items on the individuals' behavior toward their partner (items adapted from same scale as previous), and the interpersonal problem-solving style of the partner (16 items). Emerging adults who were not in a steady romantic relationship were missing on this index.

Suicidal episodes. Dichotomized composite variables were created for adolescent and young adult suicidal episodes based on responses to two scales. Suicidal ideation, plans, and attempts during the past year were assessed via questions taken from the Youth Risk Behavior Survey (see Brener et al., 2004). The series of questions was framed by the statement, "Sometimes people become so unhappy with their lives that they consider suicide." Ideation was then probed via the question, "In the past 12 months, how many times have you seriously thought about committing suicide?"; plans were asked as, "In the past 12 months, how many times have you made a plan to commit suicide?"; and attempts as, "In the past 12 months, how many times have you attempted suicide?" Suicidal ideation (*How much were you bothered by thoughts of ending your life?*) in the prior week was also assessed via the SCL-90R (Derogatis & Melisaratos, 1983) depression subscale. For all analyses, response categories were reduced to 0 (*never*) or 1 (*at least once*) using information from both scales. The adolescent composite variable used information from ages 13 to 15; the young adult composite incorporated information beginning at age 19–20 and ending around age 30.

Analyses

To test our hypotheses, we conducted a series of regression analyses; missing data were handled via the full information maximum likelihood (FIML) method (see Newman, 2003). Because of the relatively low frequency of reported suicidal problems in our sample (only 43 men and 63 women reported some kind of suicidal episode between ages 19 and 30), we could not do the kind of elaborate path analyses suggested by our full theoretical framework. We therefore tested each major "link" (parenting to self-regulatory resources, self-regulatory resources to suicidal episodes, etc.) in the proposed pathway separately. We also conducted separate analyses predicting occupational and romantic relationship functioning, because the outcomes essentially involved two samples: all participants at the relevant assessment wave (506, or 91% of the original sample) were scored on educational and occupational functioning, whereas 186 participants (37% of that wave) reported that they were in a steady romantic relationship and therefore were scored on their functioning in that role.

RESULTS

The theoretical model guiding these analyses proposed that harsh and aversive parent behaviors would hamper the development of adolescent self-regulatory resources, which, in turn, were hypothesized to be important predictors of adequate role functioning as an emerging adult. Personal resources and role functioning, in turn, were expected to predict suicidal thoughts and behaviors as a young adult. In the first step in the analyses regarding these developmental pathways, the model investigating links between the affective quality of parenting and adolescent self-development provided a good fit to the data, $\chi^2 = 5(4)$, $p > 0.05$. Results indicate that (see Figure 2.1) over and above any influence of mother's education, family structure, and adolescent gender, every standard deviation increase in harsh parenting was associated with close to half a standard deviation decrement in positive self-development (or, self-regulatory resources).

Because mother's education, family structure, and adolescent sex are generally related to social role functioning and were all related to self-development in the initial model, we controlled for these demographics in models investigating effects of self-development on social role status. Regarding educational or occupational functioning in emerging adulthood, we found that every standard deviation increase in positive self-development at mid-adolescence was associated with almost a third of a standard deviation increase in functioning (see Figure 2.2A). For romantic relationship status, we found that every standard deviation increase in mid-adolescent positive self-development was linked to an increase in emerging adult romantic relationship quality of about a quarter of a standard deviation (see Figure 2.2B).

To investigate whether adolescent self-regulatory resources influence likelihood of suicidal problems in young adulthood, we controlled for gender (because females tended to report both greater personal resources and more suicidal problems) and, importantly, earlier adolescent suicidal problems. That is, we predicted relative change in suicidal thoughts and behaviors across the period from emerging adulthood to age 30. We found that positive adolescent self-development predicted young adult suicidal problems beyond a history of suicidal episodes (see Figure 2.3A). Specifically, whereas those with past problems with suicidal thinking were about 3.6 times as likely to report suicidal problems compared to those having no past suicidal episodes (controlling for sex and self-regulatory resources),

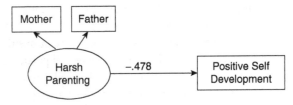

Figure 2.1. Parenting and Self Development.
NOTE: Standardized coefficient; controlling for mother's education, family structure (intact versus divorced), adolescent sex; $p < 0.001$.

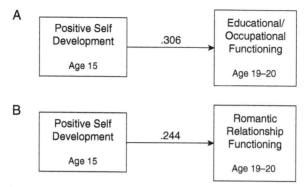

Figure 2.2. (**A**) Self-Development and Educational/Occupational Functioning.
(**B**) Self-Development and Romantic Relationship Functioning.
NOTE: Standardized coefficients; controlling for mother's education, family structure
(intact versus divorced), adolescent sex; $p < 0.01$.

moving from a complete lack of adolescent self-regulatory resources to the highest level of resources reduced the risk of suicidal problems by about 25% (controlling for sex and suicidal history). In other words, those with the highest level of personal resources were about four times less likely to report suicidal thoughts and behavior than those with the lowest level of resources, even considering prior instances of suicidal episodes. These results suggest that the personal resources on which individuals have to draw influence their vulnerability to subsequent suicidal problems as much as does their prior experience of suicidal thinking or behavior.

We followed the same procedure to test the association between achievement of emerging adult developmental tasks and young adult suicidal episodes, controlling for sex and past suicidal problems. Educational and occupational functioning at age 19–20 demonstrated a marginally significant ($p = 0.07$) effect on likelihood of suicidal problems across young adulthood (see Figure 2.3B) beyond adolescent history of suicidal problems, with a decrease in risk of 0.45 times (i.e., almost half) for those with the highest versus lowest levels of functioning. Contrary to our hypotheses, emerging adult romantic relationship functioning was not related to young adult suicidal problems over and above past suicidal problems (see Figure 2.3C). For this analysis, however, our sample dropped to 186 individuals (37% of the 19- to 20-year-old participants) who reported they were in a steady romantic relationship and then answered questions regarding the quality of that relationship. This major drop in sample size severely limited the statistical power of our model. We therefore conducted an alternative analysis using a binary indicator for whether the emerging adults were dating, to ascertain whether engaging in this normative behavior ($n = 376$) versus not dating at all ($n = 132$) would predict subsequent suicidal problems beyond suicidal history. Contrary to expectations, however, this alternative indicator of achievement of this emerging adult developmental task was not related to suicidal problems across young adulthood.

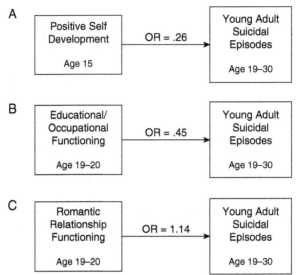

Figure 2.3. (**A**) Self-Development and Young Adult Suicidal Episodes.
NOTE: OR = odds ratio; controlling for sex and adolescent history of suicidal episode; $p < 0.05$.
(**B**) Educational/Occupational Functioning and Young Adult Suicidal Episodes.
NOTE: OR = odds ratio; controlling for sex and adolescent history of suicidal episode; $p = 0.07$.
(**C**) Romantic Relationship Functioning and Young Adult Suicidal Episodes.
NOTE: OR = odds ratio; controlling for sex and adolescent history of suicidal episode; $p = ns$.

DISCUSSION AND IMPLICATIONS

This chapter casts suicidal problems in a self-regulatory framework that views vulnerability to suicidal thoughts and behavior in response to stress as emerging from a lack of adequate self-regulatory, or coping, resources. We therefore argue that to understand the risk of suicidal thoughts and behavior during adolescence and the transition to adulthood, one must first understand aspects of the development of self-regulatory resources. Young people's ability to cope effectively depends on normative development in the domains of the self system (e.g., behavioral control, cognitive-affective personality traits), their developmental history related to coping (i.e., what they come to believe about managing contingencies, relying on others, and matching their coping efforts to their values and preferences when under stress), and on their relationships with close others, especially parents. We have focused particularly on the links between parenting and self-development and how self-development then influences vulnerability to suicidal problems.

In addition to direct effects of self-regulatory resources on suicidality risk, we discuss their potential indirect effect on suicidality through their influence on functioning in emerging adult developmental tasks. The need for financial independence and the desire for an intimate relationship represent two prominent developmental tasks during the transition to adulthood. We applied Cohler and

Jenuwine's (1995) argument that individuals' assessment of their life transitions and whether they are achieving or have achieved relevant developmental tasks becomes part of their life story. Individuals' life stories, in turn, may influence their risk of suicidality: if individuals believe they are "not matching up" or are not likely to achieve what they believe they should, they may become vulnerable to suicidal thinking or behavior, especially if they are encountering additional stress or strain. We argued that self-regulatory resources are central in this pathway of risk for suicidality, as well, because these personal resources influence individuals' ability to achieve and function well in their social roles.

We drew from the Family Transitions Project (Conger & Conger, 2002) to test hypothesized links among constructs. First, we tested the association between the affective quality of parenting (mothers and fathers) and self-development, operationalized by an index of resources and risks in the domains of behavior (e.g., impulsivity), cognition and affect (e.g., trait emotional stability), and conation (e.g., conventional values). We found a moderate relationship between these constructs, with every standard deviation increase in harsh parenting linked to a decrease of almost half a standard deviation in self-regulatory resources. These findings are consistent with the theoretical view that harsh and rejecting parenting will jeopardize the development of life-enhancing personal dispositions.

We then tested the link between mid-adolescent self-regulatory resources and emerging adult status in educational or occupational functioning and in romantic relationships. Functioning in education and employment included aspects of occupational performance, prestige, strain, enjoyment, compensation, and the like. Functioning in romantic relationships tapped relationship stability and quality, including problem-solving style. We found modest effects (standardized effects of 0.31 and 0.24, respectively) of self-development on occupational and relationship functioning beyond relevant demographic factors (mother's education, family structure, sex).

Finally, we tested the proposed associations between adolescent self-regulatory resources and young adult suicidal problems, and between functioning in emerging adult developmental tasks and suicidal episodes. The critical aspect of these investigations was whether the proposed protective factors would demonstrate an effect on likelihood of suicidal problems even after accounting for a history of suicidal thoughts or behavior in adolescence, which is by far the strongest predictor of future suicidal episodes (Joiner et al., 2005). We found mixed support for our hypotheses.

As predicted, mid-adolescent self-regulatory resources did reduce the likelihood of young adult suicidal problems even after accounting for past suicidal problems. Moving from the lowest to highest levels of personal resources demonstrated a comparable magnitude of effect on vulnerability to suicidal thoughts and behavior as did a history of suicidal episodes. Past suicidal problems increased the likelihood of future problems by 3.6 times, and being at the highest versus lowest level of self-regulatory resources decreased the likelihood of future suicidal episodes by about 4 times. Higher status on the major emerging adult task of educational and occupational achievement marginally reduced (at $p = 0.07$) the likelihood of young adult suicidal problems by a factor of almost two, beyond the effects of suicidal history. Status of emerging adult romantic relationships, however, whether investigated in terms of relationship quality or presence of dating behavior, did not predict suicidal thoughts and behavior across young adulthood, contrary to our expectations. Perhaps, given the shift in age of marriage in the United States toward the late twenties, the presence of steady romantic relationships at 19 or 20 is not as critical a developmental task for emerging adults as is pursuing an advanced education or becoming financially independent.

However, our investigation of the roles of adolescent self-regulatory resources and emerging adult functioning in the realm of education and work indicates that these resources and social role functioning play a role in vulnerability or resilience to young adult suicidal thoughts and behavior. Self-regulatory resources emerged as particularly important, both in terms of directly predicting the likelihood of subsequent suicidal episodes and in predicting the achievement of relevant emerging adult tasks, which may, in turn, play a role in suicidality risk.

Several areas emerge as important for future work, therefore. The association between quality of parenting and self-development provides a glimpse into possible intervention strategies to reduce suicide and related problems. The theoretical perspective we have described may be applied to suicide prevention by working to build effective parenting skills to foster positive self-development in their children. Ideally, evaluations of parent training programs would assess their effects on offspring suicidal problems, as well as test meditational pathways related to offspring self-regulatory capacities. This would provide invaluable information regarding the developmental processes in question in addition to offering critical guidance to suicide prevention efforts.

Second, more developmental and intervention research is warranted to understand the role of self-regulatory capacity in risk or resilience to suicidality. For example, can the link between mental illness and suicide be best explained by deficits in specific self-regulatory processes that lead to both the mental illness and the suicide risk? If so, such a reframing could help sharpen the focus of treatment and prevention for at-risk adolescents and young adults. Note, for example, that Dialectical Behavior Therapy, the gold standard treatment for adults with self-harming behavior, focuses strongly on building individuals' skill and capacity to tolerate distress and engage in effective self-soothing strategies (Lynch, Chapman, Rosenthal, Kuo, & Linehan, 2006). Although randomized, controlled trials indicate the treatment's usefulness in reducing suicidal behavior (Kliem, Kröger, & Kosfelder, 2010), meditational analyses investigating pathways via which it does so would potentially reveal fruitful "kernels"—units of behavioral influence that underlie effective intervention (Embry & Biglan, 2008)—which could be broadly applied in other settings or via other avenues. In general, research on whether and how health promotion programs that target specific self-regulatory or coping skills and resources in adolescents or young adults influence the likelihood of experiencing suicidal problems would provide potential benefit. A few such programs have already demonstrated promise for reducing suicide-related problems (see Institute of Medicine, 2002, for a review). Again, being able to specify particularly salient "kernels" or components of intervention relevant to resilience could reframe and improve suicide prevention efforts.

Finally, research should further investigate how performance in developmentally salient tasks may influence suicidality risk. Targeting older adolescents who are likely to experience difficulty in the realm of education or work in the transition to adulthood, in order to help support and build their capacity to successfully engage their opportunities in this realm may also hold promise for reducing risk of suicidal thoughts and behavior. The efficacy of vocational training or remedial educational interventions in preventing suicidal problems during the transition to adulthood should be explored.

We hope the theoretical discussion and analyses presented in this chapter can help broaden the thinking about the developmental pathways involved in suicidality during adolescence and young adulthood. Hopefully, the field will see a shift from a focus exclusively on the presence of psychological disorders and past suicide-related problems to one that emphasizes the promotion of resilience by supporting positive development in the several domains of the self system.

ACKNOWLEDGMENTS

This research is currently supported by grants from the Eunice Kennedy Shriver National Institute of Child Health and Human Development and the National Institute of Mental Health (HD064687, HD051746, and MH051361). The content is solely the responsibility of the authors and does not necessarily represent the official views of the funding agencies. Support for earlier years of the study also came from multiple sources, including the National Institute of Mental Health (MH00567, MH19734, MH43270, MH59355, MH62989, and MH48165), the National Institute on Drug Abuse (DA05347), the National Institute of Child Health and Human Development (HD027724, HD047573), the Bureau of Maternal and Child Health (MCJ-109572), and the MacArthur Foundation Research Network on Successful Adolescent Development Among Youth in High-Risk Settings. D. K. Boeninger's work on this chapter was supported by NIH Grant T32 MD018387.

References

Aldwin, C. M. (2007). *Stress, coping, and human development: An integrative perspective* (2nd ed.). New York: Guilford.

Aldwin, C. M., Yancura, L. A., & Boeninger, D. K. (2010). Coping across the life-span. In A. Freund & M. Lamb (Eds.), *Handbook of life-span development* (pp. 535–688). New York: Wiley.

Allgood, S. M., Harris, S., Skogrand, L., & Lee, T. R. (2009). Marital commitment and religiosity in a religiously homogenous population. *Marriage & Family Review, 45,* 52–67.

Arnett, J. J. (2001). Conceptions of the transition to adulthood: Perspectives from adolescence through midlife. *Journal of Adult Development, 8*, 133–143.

Baechler, J. (1979/2001). Suicides. In E. S. Shneidman (Ed.), *Comprehending suicide: Landmarks in 20th-century suicidology* (pp. 103–122). Washington, DC: American Psychological Association.

Berg, C. A., & Upchurch, R. (2007). A developmental-contextual model of couples coping with chronic illness across the adult life span. *Psychological Bulletin, 133*, 920–954.

Brener, N. D., Kann, L., Kinchen, S. A., Grunbaum, J. A., Whalen, L., Eaton, D., et al. (2004). Methodology of the youth risk behavior surveillance system. *MMWR Recommendations and Reports, 53*(RR-12), 1–13.

Brent, D. A., & Mann, J. J. (2005). Family genetic studies, suicide, and suicidal behavior. *American Journal of Medical Genetics. Part C: Seminars in Medical Genetics, 133*, 13–24.

Carver, C. S., & Scheier, M. F. (1999). Stress, coping, and self-regulatory processes. In L. A. Pervin & O. P. John (Eds.), *Handbook of personality: Theory and research*, 2nd ed. (pp. 1553–1575). New York: Guilford.

Caspi, A. (1998). Personality development across the life course. In W. Damon & N. Eisenberg (Eds.), *Handbook of child psychology, 5th ed.: Vol 3. Social, emotional, and personality development* (pp. 311–388). Hoboken, NJ: John Wiley & Sons, Inc.

Centers for Disease Control and Prevention. (2010). Web-based Injury Statistics Query and Reporting System (WISQARS) Leading Cause of Death Reports [Data file]. Retrieved August 30, 2010, from http://webappa.cdc.gov/sasweb/ncipc/leadcaus10.html.

Cohler, B. J., & Jenuwine, M. J. (1995). Suicide, life course, and life story. *International Psychogeriatrics, 7*, 199–219.

Conger, R. D., & Conger, K. J. (2002). Resilience in midwestern families: Selected findings from the first decade of a prospective, longitudinal study. *Journal of Marriage and Family, 64*, 361–373.

Dale, K. L., & Baumeister, R. F. (1999). Self-regulation and psychopathology. In R. M. Kowalski & M. R. Leary (Eds.), *The social psychology of emotional and behavioral problems: Interfaces of social and clinical psychology* (pp. 139–166). Washington, DC: American Psychological Association.

De Bellis, M. D. (2001). Developmental traumatology: The psychobiological development of maltreated children and its implications for research, treatment, and policy. *Development and Psychopathology. Special Issue: Stress and Development: Biological and Psychological Consequences, 13*, 539–564.

Derogatis, L. R., & Melisaratos, N. (1983). The Brief Symptom Inventory: An introductory report. *Psychological Medicine, 13*, 595–605.

Dodge, K. A., Pettit, G. S., Bates, J. E., & Valente, E. (1995). Social information-processing patterns partially mediate the effect of early physical abuse on later conduct problems. *Journal of Abnormal Psychology, 104*, 632–643.

Eisenberg, N., Valiente, C., & Sulik, M. J. (2009). How the study of regulation can inform the study of coping. *New Directions for the Study of Child and Adolescent Development, 124*, 75–86.

Eisenberg, N., Spinrad, T. L., & Morris, A. S. (2002). Regulation, resiliency, and quality of social functioning. *Self and Identity. Special Issue: Self and Identity, 1*, 121–128.

Embry, D. D., & Biglan, A. (2008). Evidence-based kernels: Fundamental units of behavioral influence. *Clinical Child and Family Psychology Review, 11*, 75–113.

Fergusson, D. M., Horwood, L. J., Ridder, E. M., & Beautrais, A. L. (2005). Suicidal behaviour in adolescence and subsequent mental health outcomes in young adulthood. *Psychological Medicine, 35,* 983–993.

Fergusson, D. M., Woodward, L. J., & Horwood, L. J. (2000). Risk factors and life processes associated with the onset of suicidal behaviour during adolescence and early adulthood. *Psychological Medicine, 30,* 23–39.

Flor, D. L., & Knapp, N. F. (2001). Transmission and transaction: Predicting adolescents' internalization of parental religious values. *Journal of Family Psychology, 15,* 627–645.

Gunnar, M. R., & Fisher, P. A. (2006). Bringing basic research on early experience and stress neurobiology to bear on preventive interventions for neglected and maltreated children. *Development and Psychopathology, 18,* 651–677.

Gurland, S. T., & Grolnick, W. S. (2005). Perceived threat, controlling parenting, and children's achievement orientations. *Motivation and Emotion, 29,* 103–121.

Heaven, P. C. L., & Ciarrochi, J. (2008). Parental styles, conscientiousness, and academic performance in high school: A three-wave longitudinal study. *Personality and Social Psychology Bulletin, 34,* 451–461.

Institute of Medicine. (2002). *Reducing suicide: A national imperative.* Washington, DC: National Academies Press.

Joiner, T. E., Jr., Conwell, Y., Fitzpatrick, K. K., Witte, T. K., Schmidt, N. B., Berlim, M. T., et al. (2005). Four studies on how past and current suicidality relate even when "everything but the kitchen sink" is covaried. *Journal of Abnormal Psychology, 114,* 291–303.

Kliem, S., Kröger, C., & Kosfelder, J. (2010). Dialectical behavior therapy for borderline personality disorder: A meta-analysis using mixed-effects modeling. *Journal of Consulting and Clinical Psychology, 78,* 936–951.

Kliewer, W., Sandler, I. N., & Wolchik, S. (1994). Family socialization of threat appraisal and coping: Coaching, modeling, and family context. In K. Hurrelmann & F. Festmann (Eds.), *Social networks and social support in childhood and adolescence* (pp. 271–291). Berlin: Walter de Gruyter.

Kochanska, G., Murray, K. T., & Harlan, E. T. (2000). Effortful control in early childhood: Continuity and change, antecedents, and implications for social development. *Developmental Psychology, 36,* 220–232.

Lacourse, E., Cote, S., Nagin, D. S., Vitaro, F., Brendgen, M., & Tremblay, R. E. (2002). A longitudinal-experimental approach to testing theories of antisocial behavior development. *Development and Psychopathology, 14,* 909–924.

LeDoux, J. (2002). *Synaptic self: How our brains become who we are.* New York: Penguin.

Little, B. R. (1999). Personality and motivation: Personal action and the conative evolution. In L. A. Pervin & O. P. John (Eds.), *Handbook of personality: Theory and research,* 2nd ed. (pp. 501–524). New York, NY: Guilford Press.

Loe, I. M., & Feldman, H. M. (2007). Academic and educational outcomes of children with ADHD. *Journal of Pediatric Psychology. Special Issue: Attention-Deficit/ Hyperactivity Disorder, 32,* 643–654.

Lynch, T. R., Chapman, A. L., Rosenthal, M. Z., Kuo, J. R., & Linehan, M. M. (2006). Mechanisms of change in dialectical behavior therapy: Theoretical and empirical observations. *Journal of Clinical Psychology, 62,* 459–480.

Murry, V. M., Brody, G. H., McNair, L. D., Luo, Z., Gibbons, F. X., Gerrard, M., et al. (2005). Parental involvement promotes rural African American youths' self-pride and sexual self-concepts. *Journal of Marriage and Family, 67,* 627–642.

Newman, D. A. (2003). Longitudinal modeling with randomly and systematically missing data: A simulation of ad hoc, maximum likelihood, and multiple imputation techniques. *Organizational Research Methods, 6,* 328–362.

Nieder, T., & Seiffge-Krenke, I. (2001). Coping with stress in different phases of romantic development. *Journal of Adolescence, 24,* 297–311.

Patterson, G. R., Chamberlain, P., & Reid, J. B. (1982). A comparative evaluation of a parent-training program. *Behavior Therapy, 13,* 638–650.

Poropat, A. E. (2009). A meta-analysis of the five-factor model of personality and academic performance. *Psychological Bulletin, 135,* 322–338.

Reinherz, H. Z., Tanner, J. L., Berger, S. R., Beardslee, W. R., & Fitzmaurice, G. M. (2006). Adolescent suicidal ideation as predictive of psychopathology, suicidal behavior, and compromised functioning at age 30. *American Journal of Psychiatry, 163,* 1226–1232.

Repetti, R. L., Taylor, S. E., & Seeman, T. E. (2002). Risky families: Family social environments and the mental and physical health of offspring. *Psychological Bulletin, 128,* 330–366.

Robins, R. W., Caspi, A., & Moffitt, T. E. (2002). It's not just who you're with, it's who you are: Personality and relationship experiences across multiple relationships. *Journal of Personality, 70,* 925–964.

Rudd, M. D. (2000). The suicidal mode: A cognitive-behavioral model of suicidality. *Suicide and Life-Threatening Behavior, 30,* 18–33.

Seiffge-Krenke, I. (2006). Coping with relationship stressors: The impact of different working models of attachment and links to adaptation. *Journal of Youth and Adolescence, 35,* 25–39.

Shiner, R. L., Masten, A. S., & Roberts, J. M. (2003). Childhood personality foreshadows adult personality and life outcomes two decades later. *Journal of Personality, 71,* 1145–1170.

Shneidman, E. S. (2001). Comprehending suicide: Landmarks in 20th-century suicidology. Washington, DC: American Psychological Association.

Skinner, E. A., Edge, K., Altman, J., & Sherwood, H. (2003). Searching for the structure of coping: A review and critique of category systems for classifying ways of coping. *Psychological Bulletin, 129,* 216–269.

Skinner, E. A., & Zimmer-Gembeck, M. J. (2007). The development of coping. *Annual Review of Psychology, 58,* 119–144.

Skinner, E. A., & Zimmer-Gembeck, M. J. (2009). Challenges to the developmental study of coping. *New Directions in Child and Adolescent Development, 124,* 5–17.

Steinberg, L. (2005). Cognitive and affective development in adolescence. *Trends in Cognitive Sciences, 9,* 69–74.

Steinberg, L., Dahl, R., Keating, D., Kupfer, D. J., Masten, A. S., & Pine, D. S. (2006). The study of developmental psychopathology in adolescence: Integrating affective neuroscience with the study of context. In D. Cicchetti & D. J. Cohen (Eds.), *Developmental psychopathology, 2nd ed., Vol. 2: Developmental neuroscience* (pp. 2710–2741). Hoboken, NJ: John Wiley & Sons Inc.

Sutin, A. R., Costa, P. T., Jr., Miech, R., & Eaton, W. W. (2009). Personality and career success: Concurrent and longitudinal relations. *European Journal of Personality, 23,* 71–84.

Vallerand, R. J., Fortier, M. S., & Guay, F. (1997). Self-determination and persistence in a real-life setting: Toward a motivational model of high school dropout. *Journal of Personality and Social Psychology, 72,* 1161–1176.

Vohs, K. D., & Baumeister, R. F. (2000). Escaping the self consumes regulatory resources: A self-regulatory model of suicide. In T. E. Joiner & M. D. Rudd (Eds.), *Suicide science: Expanding the boundaries* (pp. 33–41). New York: Kluwer Academic/Plenum Publishers.

White, F. A., & Matawie, K. M. (2004). Parental morality and family processes as predictors of adolescent morality. *Journal of Child and Family Studies, 13*, 219–233.

White, J. K., Hendrick, S. S., & Hendrick, C. (2004). Big five personality variables and relationship constructs. *Personality and Individual Differences, 37*, 1519–1530.

Wilcox, W. B., & Wolfinger, N. H. (2008). Living and loving "decent": Religion and relationship quality among urban parents. *Social Science Research, 37*, 828–843.

Wolchik, S. A., Sandler, I. N., Millsap, R. E., Plummer, B. A., Greene, S. M., Anderson, E. R., et al. (2002). Six-year follow-up of preventive interventions for children of divorce. A randomized controlled trial. *JAMA: Journal of the American Medical Association, 288*, 1874–1881.

Wolchik, S. A., West, S. G., Sandler, I. N., Tein, J.-Y., Coatsworth, D., Lengua, L., et al. (2000). An experimental evaluation of theory-based mother and mother-child programs for children of divorce. *Journal of Consulting and Clinical Psychology, 68*, 843–856.

3

The Status of Identity

Developments in Identity Status Research

JANE KROGER

. . . Therefore in an adolescent homelessness of self, in a time where I did not quite know my direction, I entered eagerly a nest of difference which others found for me but which I lined with my own furnishings; for after all, during the past two years I had tried many aspects of "being" . . .
—(JANET FRAME, *To the Is-land,* 1987, p. 197)

The theme of seeking one's identity has been a central focus in the study of adolescent development. In his early writings, Erikson (1963) began to lay the theoretical foundations for an understanding of adolescent identity and the identity formation process that has guided much of the research on this theme over the past 45 years. This chapter will briefly review central concepts that Erikson (1963, 1968) posits to define identity and the adolescent identity formation process. It will provide an overview of the development of one of the most popular approaches for researching questions of identity during adolescence, Marcia's (1966; Marcia, Waterman, Matteson, Archer, & Orlofsky, 1993) ego identity status model and the questions that this model has addressed. Finally the chapter will turn to review some of the newer, neo-Eriksonian directions that researchers have been undertaking with the identity status model over the past decade.

Identity is an entity that most of us, most of the time, can take for granted. For Erikson (1963), dimensions of identity first came to light in his psychoanalytic work with veterans suffering posttraumatic stress disorder from World War II; for these men, feelings of life continuity had been sorely disrupted. Thus, Erikson first began to write about identity in terms of the ego functions of sameness and continuity that identity should provide for the individual:

> What impressed me the most was the loss in these men of a sense of identity. They knew who they were; they had a personal identity. But it was as if, subjectively, their lives no longer hung together—and never would again. There was a central disturbance of what I started to call ego identity. At this point it is enough to say that this sense of identity provides the ability to experience one's self as something that has continuity and sameness, and to act accordingly. (Erikson, 1963, p. 42)

And so it was in the disturbance of ego identity that some of identity's contours and functions could more clearly be articulated. Stated simply, identity is that sense of sameness and continuity that enables one to move with a sense of well being, purpose and direction in life, and to recognize and be recognized by significant others (Erikson, 1968).

Over the ensuing years, Erikson continued to elaborate different dimensions of ego identity. He defined ego identity in terms of its tripartite nature: comprised partly of biological elements such as one's sex, one's physical features, characteristics, and limitations, partly of psychological elements such as one's needs, desires, and conscious and unconscious motivations, and partly in terms of its contextual elements and the mutual regulation between individual identity and social context. Erikson's (1968) writings on the identity crisis also became a central theme in both the scientific and popular literatures to describe a key turning point in individual psychosocial development. And his depiction of "Identity vs. Role Confusion" as the fifth key psychological task of personality development normatively met during adolescence is the foundation upon which much of the later research on identity construction and development has been based.

Perhaps the concepts of Erikson (1968) that have been most central to actual research on adolescent identity development, however, are those ego functions (e.g., rational planning, defenses against anxiety, maintaining a coherent sense of self across time and place) that enable the adolescent to "accomplish the selective accentuation of significant identifications throughout childhood and the gradual integration of self-images which culminates in a sense of identity" (Erikson, 1968, p. 209). This process and its mutual regulation by selected social contexts ideally enable the adolescent to explore and then form commitments to central, psychosocial arenas of adult functioning such as the selection of an occupational role, of meaningful ideals and values, and of important interpersonal relationships.

The Eriksonian psychosocial task of identity development, then, is one of integration. The ability to begin moving from a conferred identity—based upon identifications with the roles and ideals of significant figures of childhood—through an integrative process of exploring, reflecting upon, and reevaluating these identifications to an actual commitment to various adult psychosocial roles and values is the process of adolescent identity formation. The challenge for later identity researchers has been to operationalize this integrative process, and to examine its antecedents, consequences, and concurrent associations. I turn, now, to one of the most popular research models to take up this challenge.

JAMES MARCIA'S EGO IDENTITY STATUS MODEL

James Marcia (2007) recalls the questions he asked as he developed his very popular identity status model as a means of researching various dimensions of the adolescent identity formation process.

> What should the relationship be between a theoretical construct and the form its measurement takes? Need a measure be complex simply because the construct in question is complex? What should be the balance between reliability and validity, between expediency and thoroughness? These are the questions we faced at the inception of research on Erik Erikson's concept of ego identity. (p. 1)

Marcia's (1966, 1967) identity status model is based on Erikson's central concepts of exploration and commitment in the identity formation process. However, rather than conceptualizing identity as one's position on an identity continuum, as an entity that one had "more or less of," Marcia considered identity in terms of distinctly different qualitative styles by which one approached (or avoided) identity-defining questions. He used Erikson's concepts of identity exploration and commitment to identify four different styles (or statuses) by which one approached identity-defining decisions about what vocational choices one would pursue, and what ideological values (religious and political or social) and, later, what sexual and relational values one would hold.

Identity Achieved individuals had both undergone a meaningful exploration process regarding at least some of these issues, and they had formed commitments to future directions for their lives in these areas. The *Moratorium* individual was very much in the exploration process itself, attempting to find personally meaningful life directions, but at present, uncertain of resolutions and unable to make firm commitments. The *Foreclosed* individual had made firm identity commitments; however, these commitments were undertaken without exploration and most commonly were based on strong identifications with parents or other important childhood figures. The *Diffuse* individual had done little if any identity exploration and was unable or uninterested in making key, identity-defining commitments.

From these foundations, some 45 years of research has ensued as social scientists from many countries and backgrounds have explored questions of concurrent, antecedent, and consequent variables that may be associated with these different identity statuses. Researchers have also examined patterns of development, asking the following questions: how stable is adolescent identity status likely to be over the course of time, what trajectories of identity status change are most common, and what types of events may be linked with various identity status trajectories?

Examples of these investigations will be examined in the remainder of this chapter, and the implications of findings for theory development and future research will be addressed.

VALIDATION OF THE STATUSES: TROMSØ META-ANALYTIC STUDIES

In the early years of research on Marcia's identity status paradigm and efforts at construct validation, a number of questions were raised regarding the relationship of selected personality variables to the identity statuses. As results accrued, initial support for construct validity was found, such as high levels of separation anxiety and high levels of authoritarianism associated with the foreclosure status (Kroger, 2007). Questions then arose regarding the types of relationships with significant others (e.g., one's style of attachment and intimacy) that those in each of the identity statuses would most likely have. By the mid-1970s, questions also began to emerge about the developmental process involved in identity status changes. Over the past 45 years, a significant body of research on the identity statuses has accumulated related to these and other questions. (A recent search for "identity status" in the PsycInfo database revealed over 850 studies.) Yet major reviews of identity status findings in selected areas of research have been primarily undertaken through narrative methods.

Statistical techniques of meta-analysis are now commonly employed after a body of research literature has generated a number of findings to research questions that have been asked over the course of time (e.g., Roberts, Walton, & Viechtbauer, 2006, in the field of personality development). With the longevity of the identity status paradigm, a meta-analysis of the relationship between identity status and a number of dependent variables has been long overdue. In interpreting findings from a large body of research literature over time, techniques of meta-analysis have a number of advantages over the narrative review. Narrative reviews involve a simple counting of the frequencies of significant and nonsignificant findings (commonly termed "vote counting"). Results from vote counting methods can be very inaccurate and highly misleading over a large number of studies, especially if sample sizes are small (Hunt, 1997; Hunter & Schmidt, 2004). Vote counting, for example, does not consider the varying strength of results across studies, nor is it statistically sensitive. If a particular variable is linked with only a small positive effect, vote counting will detect it only when sample sizes are sufficiently large in the primary studies. Narrative reviews have no way of systematically resolving problems with inconsistent or conflicting findings, whereas techniques of meta-analysis overcome these difficulties.

The general goal of the Tromsø meta-analytic study of the ego identity statuses has been to examine the relationships between Marcia's four identity statuses and various personality and cognitive factors, relational patterns with significant others, as well as behavioral outcomes and developmental patterns of change over time. To date, some nine studies of the identity statuses in relation to selected variables of personality, attachment, intimacy patterns, and developmental change have been examined through meta-analysis. Some of the key findings related to questions of validation of the statuses will be briefly summarized below.

Studies included in the meta-analyses were drawn from a larger database that was assembled in the following way. All English language publications and dissertations in PsycInfo, ERIC, Sociological Abstracts, and Dissertation Abstracts International databases were searched between January 1966 and December 2005, using the following search terms: identity status, identity and Marcia, identity and Marcia's, and ego identity. Study reference details and abstracts were obtained. Eliminated first from these lists were studies that did not provide any type of statistical information (e.g., theoretical or qualitative writings). Dissertations that later appeared as publications were then eliminated from further analysis to prevent nonindependent samples. Further eliminations were made if two or more studies were based on the same data, or part of the same data, to address similar questions. The initial database of studies utilizing Marcia's (1966) identity status model consisted of 565 empirical investigations (287 publications and 278 doctoral dissertations).

For each publication or dissertation, a coding sheet was completed to provide details regarding year of publication, type of article (publication or doctoral dissertation), primary theme of study, measure of identity status and its reliability, sample size and gender distribution, mean age and age ranges for study subsamples, and other sample features. Six psychology graduate students coded all publications and dissertations, and 25% of the manuscripts were selected for a reliability check to assess agreement between two coders. Kappa values for categorical variables ranged from 0.48 to 1.00, with the agreement percentage ranging from 79% to 85%. Pearson's correlations of continuous variables ranged from 0.84 to 1.00. From this initial database, study themes were selected for further examination. All calculations were undertaken using the software program Comprehensive Meta-analysis version 2 (Borenstein, Hedges, Higgins, & Rothstein, 2007). All studies cited below were based primarily on samples of adolescents and young adults; mean ages and standard deviations will be reported for each review.

Self-esteem. Ryeng, Kroger, and Martinussen (2011a) used data from 18 studies to explore two hypotheses regarding the relationship between self-esteem and identity status. The mean age of the 4208 participants was 16.1 years (SD = 12.3). One hypothesis predicted that identity statuses involving commitment (foreclosure and achievement) would be associated with the highest levels of self-esteem, whereas the second hypothesis predicted that identity achievement alone would be associated with the highest levels of self-esteem. The first hypothesis was based on the notion that just having identity-defining commitments and hence a sense of direction in life, however attained, would likely be associated with higher levels of self-esteem than not holding commitments. The second hypothesis was based on the notion that only identity commitments attained after meaningful identity exploration would be associated with the highest levels of self-esteem. When identity status and self-esteem were assessed continuously, a moderate [according to Cohen's (1988) criteria for labeling effect sizes], positive correlation ($r = 0.35$)

was obtained between identity achievement and self-esteem; weak to medium negative correlations were found between self-esteem and the moratorium status ($r = -0.23$), the foreclosure status ($r = -0.24$), and the diffusion status ($r = -0.20$). When identity status and self-esteem were assessed categorically, some support for both hypotheses was found. However, stronger support appeared for the hypothesis that self-esteem is linked with identity commitment (achievement and foreclosure statuses) rather than identity achievement per se. The effect size difference between foreclosures and achievements was very small (Hedges's $g = 0.00$) according to Cohen's (1988) criteria, indicating no significant difference in self-esteem scores between these two statuses.

Anxiety. Lillevoll, Kroger, and Martinussen (2011a) used 12 studies to examine the hypothesis that due to the inherent discomfort of their struggle for meaningful identity commitments, moratoriums would have the highest levels of anxiety compared with remaining identity statuses. The mean age of the 1124 participants was 23.6 years (SD = 9.5). Results offered some support for the hypotheses that moratoriums did have significantly higher anxiety scores than foreclosures and foreclosures had significantly lower anxiety scores than diffusions. Effect size differences in anxiety scores for moratoriums compared with foreclosures (Hedges's $g = 0.40$) and for foreclosures compared with diffusions (Hedges's $g = -0.40$) were low to moderate; for achievements compared with moratoriums, differences were small (Hedges's $g = -0.29$). Additionally, confidence intervals surrounding these effect sizes did not include zero, indicating a significant difference between statuses. For moratoriums compared with diffusions (Hedges's $g = -0.01$) effect size differences were very small, indicating no difference. Thus, evidence primarily supports the original hypotheses, although no difference in anxiety scores was found between moratorium and diffusion statuses.

Locus of Control. Lillevoll, Kroger, and Martinussen (2011b) tested the hypothesis that the identity achieved should have a higher internal locus of control, relative to other identity statuses, whereas foreclosure and diffusions should have a higher external locus of control relative to other statuses, as they seek identity definitions from others. Only five of nine possible studies provided sufficient data on comparable locus-of-control measures for meta-analysis. The mean age of the 711 participants in this study was 23.1 (SD = 5.2). A medium positive correlation ($r = 0.26$) was found between identity achievement and internal locus of control and between identity diffusion and external locus of control ($r = 0.23$). Small positive correlations were also found between external locus of control and the moratorium status ($r = 0.17$) and the foreclosure status ($r = 0.19$). Hypotheses were partially supported; unexpected was the weak positive correlation between external locus of control and the moratorium status.

Authoritarianism. Ryeng, Kroger, and Martinussen (2011b) predicted that foreclosures would score highest on a measure of authoritarianism, relative to other identity statuses. This prediction was based on the fact that foreclosures have an identity based on identifications with significant others, and they will thus seek the values of an authority figure as the basis for forming their own identities. Nine of 13 studies contained sufficient statistical information with comparable measures of authoritarianism to be included in a meta-analysis. The mean age of the participants in this study was 21.3 years (SD = 7.9). Results supported predictions; achievements and moratoriums scored significantly lower than foreclosures on authoritarianism scales, with effect sizes that were large (Hedges's g = −0.78 and −0.67, respectively). Furthermore, foreclosures scored higher on authoritarianism than diffusions (Hedges's g = 0.42). This effect size was medium in magnitude, and the confidence intervals for both comparisons did not contain zero, indicating that these differences were significant.

Moral Reasoning. Jespersen, Kroger, and Martinussen (2011a) hypothesized that the greater introspective capacities of the identity achieved and moratorium identity statuses would be associated with higher stages of moral reasoning in Kohlberg's (1984) developmental scheme. For the 10 studies included in this meta-analysis, the mean age of the 909 participants was 21.8 (SD = 3.2). When the relationship between identity achievement/nonachievement and postconventional/nonpostconventional moral reasoning was examined, a large mean effect size was found (odds ratio = 6.85). However, contrary to expectation, no relationship was evident between foreclosed/nonforeclosed identity statuses and conventional/nonconventional levels of moral reasoning. A medium correlation (r = 0.31) was found between continuous measures of identity status and moral reasoning.

Ego Development. Jespersen, Kroger, and Martinussen (2011a) predicted that identity achievements and moratoriums should score at postconformist levels of ego development, according to Loevinger's (1976) ego development scheme. Those at more mature levels of ego development have an increased tolerance for ambiguity, a more complex awareness of inner life, and a greater concern for balancing the needs of the self with those of others, according to Loevinger; such features are particularly likely to be associated with the more mature (achievement and moratorium) identity statuses. Across 11 studies (n = 943) with all but two based primarily on undergraduate university student samples, a weak to medium relationship was found between identity achievement and postconformist levels of ego development (odds ratio = 2.11), and a medium relationship was found between "high" (achievement and moratorium) and low identity statuses and between postconformist and conformist/preconformist levels of ego development (odds ratio = 3.01). But contrary to expectation, no relationship between the foreclosure identity status and conformist level of ego development was found. A medium correlation (r = 0.35) between identity status and ego development was found when these two variables were assessed continuously. The relationship between identity status and ego development was not as strong as anticipated.

Attachment. Årseth, Kroger, Martinussen, and Marcia (2009) predicted that those in the identity achievement and foreclosure statuses would be most likely to evidence secure attachment patterns. The identity achieved presumably would need a secure attachment base from which to undertake their identity explorations, whereas the foreclosed might be defensive in their attachment style and reluctant to make negative statements about their relationships with attachment figures. For continuous measures of attachment style and identity status, correlations across 14 studies were generally small.

A small to medium correlation was found between secure attachment and identity achievement ($r = 0.21$), whereas the correlation between secure attachment and the foreclosure identity status was small ($r = 0.10$). For categorical measures of identity status and attachment style, the highest mean proportion of securely attached individuals was in the identity achieved status (0.55), whereas the lowest mean proportion of the securely attached was found in the diffusion status (0.23). Because these two statuses did not have overlapping confidence intervals, they were the only two statuses that could clearly be said to differ significantly from one another. However, the mean proportion of secure attachment among foreclosures (0.28) had an only marginally overlapping confidence interval with the identity achieved, so the mean proportions of securely attached individuals in these two statuses may also be considered to differ from one another. Support was found for a relationship between secure attachment and identity achievement; some evidence for the relationship between secure attachment and the foreclosed identity status also exists.

Intimacy. Erikson (1968) proposed that resolution of identity issues was necessary before genuine intimacy could be experienced; some theorists, however, have argued that there are important gender differences in the epigenetic relationship between "Identity vs. Role Confusion" and "Intimacy vs. Isolation" tasks in Erikson's (1968) psychosocial stage scheme of personality development. Årseth, Kroger, Martinussen, and Marcia (2009) also conducted a meta-analysis of the relationship between identity status and intimacy with 21 studies that provided sufficient data for analysis.

They found small effect size differences in intimacy scores for high (achievement and moratorium) compared with low (foreclosure and diffusion) identity statuses ranging from Hedges's g of 0.30 to 0.41 for separate analyses of men, women, and the combined sample. Among categorical assessments of identity and intimacy status (measured by Orlofsky's 1973 Intimacy Status Interview), the patterns for men and women differed. The mean odds ratio for being in both a "high" identity status and "high" intimacy status was significantly higher for men than women. Nearly half of all "low" identity status women were "high" in intimacy status, whereas only about 25% of "low" identity status men were high in intimacy status. For both men and women "high" in identity status, approximately two-thirds were also "high" in intimacy status. Support was found for the epigenetic nature of the relationship between "Identity vs. Role Confusion" and "Intimacy vs. Isolation" in Erikson's theory; however, the nature of the relationship between identity and intimacy for "low" identity status women needs further exploration.

HISTORICAL EXTENSIONS OF THE IDENTITY STATUS PARADIGM

There are a number of additional identity status research programs that are currently examining questions related to extensions of Marcia's (1966; Marcia et al., 1993) identity status paradigm, the mechanisms and processes involved in identity status change, and the types of both internal and contextual events that may be associated with various trajectories of identity status change over time.

Through the history of the identity status paradigm, there have been various attempts to elaborate Marcia's four identity statuses. One of the earliest was the proposal of possible subgroupings within the identity diffusion status (Marcia, 1989). On a theoretical basis, Marcia suggested that "self-fragmentation" diffusion would be characteristic of the borderline personality and should be differentiated from the "disturbed" diffusion that Erikson (1968) described in his comments on pathology. "Carefree" diffusions, who are socially skilled but shallow and undependable, should be distinguished from "culturally adaptive" diffusions, who are making adaptive responses to circumstances that discourage commitments. Finally, Marcia argued that the "developmental" diffusion is one who has the skills and structural potential to move on to a moratorium or identity achieved position, but is developmentally young or has temporarily suspended identity searches.

Others have also identified subgroupings within the various identity status classifications. Berzonsky (1985), in his empirical work with the identity statuses and questions of academic achievement, also suggested that diffusions may not be a homogeneous group; rather, some diffusions may be more like "passive" moratoriums, who are engaged in playful experiencing rather than the stressful struggle of classic moratoriums. Berzonsky also proposed differentiating long-term from transient foreclosures in this longitudinal study, as did Archer and Waterman (1990). And in a longitudinal study, Kroger (1995) was able to differentiate those "firm" from "developmental" foreclosures on a measure of adolescent separation-individuation processes based on object relations theory; firm foreclosures, who remained stable in identity status over the time of their university studies, were far higher in nurturance seeking both at T_1 and T_2 than developmental foreclosures, moratoriums, and achievements. Some attempts have also been made to describe phases in the moratorium process (e.g., Kroger, 1993) as well as to differentiate "open" and "closed" types of identity achievements during young adulthood (Valde, 1996).

CONTEMPORARY EXTENSIONS OF THE IDENTITY STATUS PARADIGM

Against this historical backdrop, Luyckx and his colleagues (Luyckx, Goossens, Soenens, Beyers, & Vansteenkiste, 2005; Luyckx, Goossens, Soenens, & Beyers, 2006) have undertaken perhaps the most extensive empirical refinements to the identity statuses in their studies of the intersections between identity exploration and commitment processes. In a sample of university freshman students, Luyckx et al. (2005) examined the following four identity dimensions (rather than the standard two exploration and commitment dimensions) to derive new identity statuses by means of cluster analysis: *commitment making, identification with commitment, exploration in breadth*, and *exploration in depth*. Commitment making refers to deciding upon identity-defining options. Identification with commitment denotes the extent of identification with these identity options. Exploration in breadth refers to the process of gathering information about identity-defining alternatives to guide the choices we make, while exploration in depth refers to the gathering of information about current identity-defining options to assist in the evaluation and maintenance of these choices. Results of the cluster analysis pointed to the traditional identity achieved, moratorium, and foreclosed statuses plus the differentiation of a carefree from a diffuse diffusion status.

Additionally, validation of these statuses was undertaken via measures of social adjustment, academic adjustment, depressive symptoms, substance abuse, self-esteem, openness, and conscientiousness. Links with the traditional three identity statuses were in the anticipated directions, and the diffused and carefree diffusions differed significantly on a number of these measures. The carefree diffusion, for example, scored significantly higher on social adjustment, academic adjustment, and self-esteem compared to the diffuse diffusion; the carefree diffusions also scored significantly lower than the diffuse diffusion on depressive symptoms. These distinctions suggest that at least in the initial years of university study, the carefree diffusions would not necessarily be primary targets for intervention, for they are relatively well adjusted; however, in subsequent years or beyond the university setting, the carefree diffuse identity resolution would likely be less adaptive and possibly aided by intervention.

Several years later, Luyckx and colleagues (2008) added a fifth identity dimension, ruminative exploration, to further extend their four-dimensional model of identity. This fifth maladaptive dimension was added to complement the two earlier forms of adaptive exploration (exploration in depth and exploration in breadth). They noted that although the identity exploration process has frequently been linked with variables such as openness and general curiosity in the identity status literature, distress and anxiety have also been associated with identity exploration. A separate literature has linked ruminative processes with anxiety and distress (Rood, Roelofs, Bogels, Nolen-Hoeksema, & Schouten, 2009). Thus, a means of refining the moratorium identity status into adaptive and ruminative moratorium was devised and validated using measures of self-esteem, depressive symptoms, anxiety, self-reflection, and self-rumination. Ruminative exploration status was indeed positively related to distress and to a measure of self-rumination, whereas the two forms of adaptive exploration were positively related to self-reflection. These refinements to Marcia's four-status paradigm may have important research as well as intervention implications as researchers and clinicians work to predict factors associated with both adaptive and maladaptive identity formation pathways.

Another recent attempt has been made to refine existing identity statuses. Meeus and his colleagues (Croceti, Rubini, Luyckx, & Meeus, 2008) posited that dimensions of commitment, in-depth exploration, and reconsideration underlie the identity formation process. Commitment is a strong choice that individuals have made with respect to identity-defining domains. In-depth exploration refers to the extent to which adolescents reflect on the commitments that have made, whereas reconsideration of commitment refers to one's willingness to discard commitments and search for new alternatives. This model differs from Marcia's identity status model, although this model can still be used to assign individuals to one of Marcia's identity status classifications. Using cluster analysis, Meeus, van de Schoot, Keijsers, Schwartz, and Branje (2010) identified Marcia's traditional four identity statuses plus a fifth status characterized by high commitment, high in-depth exploration, and high reconsideration of commitments. The researchers interpreted their findings to suggest that "searching" versus "classic" moratoriums can be differentiated. Searching moratoriums seek alternative commitments while already possessing meaningful identity commitments, whereas classic moratoriums do so with weak or no commitments. These two moratorium groups are likely to be at different stages of the often lengthy moratorium process; the classic moratoriums may be just beginning identity exploration, whereas the searching moratoriums may be attempting to finalize some life directions among several alternative possibilities. The moratorium process, in general, is an important developmental phenomenon that serves as the foundation for meaningful identity commitments as well as subsequent moratorium experiences. The study also differentiated an "early closure" from a "closure" (foreclosed) identity status. Early closures are those who have remained foreclosed over time, similar to the "firm" foreclosures describe in previous research. The "closure" group has considered alternative commitments but with little in-depth exploration and low reconsideration. By late adolescence, the "early closure" group had disappeared.

Thus, there have been a number of efforts to refine Marcia's identity status paradigm, and these efforts all point to some promising new directions in theory construction and implications for intervention. In addition, some of these research programs have undertaken a developmental approach to understanding issues of change and stability in identity status properties over time, and the types of events or circumstances that may be associated both with identity status change and stability. The following sections address developmental questions that have arisen through the history of the identity status paradigm, and some of the personal and contextual circumstances that have been linked with various identity status trajectories.

DEVELOPMENTAL ISSUES IN IDENTITY STATUS RESEARCH

A number of individual studies and contemporary research programs have addressed questions related to identity development in the identity status literature in the decades since its inception. Erikson (1956, p. 74) conceptualized the identity formation process as one of ongoing change and development during and beyond adolescence: "Such a sense of identity is never gained nor maintained once and for all. Like a good conscience, it is constantly lost and regained, although more lasting and more economical methods of maintenance and restoration are evolved and fortified in late adolescence." And Erikson later noted that "the return of some forms of identity crisis in the later stages of the life cycle" are to be anticipated

(Erikson, 1968, p. 135). Thus, a number of identity status researchers have been interested in the contours that identity formation may take through various trajectories of identity development during and beyond late adolescence.

Waterman (1999) raised a number of formal propositions for an eventual theory of identity status development, and several contemporary research programs have aimed to test these propositions through developmental studies. Briefly summarized, Waterman proposed the following: (1) Identity status change from adolescence to adulthood involves a preponderance of progressive developmental shifts (Diffusion to Foreclosure; Diffusion to Moratorium; Diffusion to Achievement; Foreclosure to Moratorium; Foreclosure to Achievement; and Moratorium to Achievement). Over time, there will be movement out of the diffusion status and into the achievement status. There will be some progressive shifts both into and out of the foreclosure and moratorium statuses. (2) Some forms of progressive change, specifically movement from identity diffusion, will occur at earlier ages than other forms of progressive change, specifically movement into identity achievement. (3) The moratorium status will be the least stable identity status, whereas achievement and foreclosure statuses can be quite stable. (4) Foreclosure and achievement statuses may be less stable at younger than at older ages, whereas the moratorium status is likely to be unstable across all age groups. (5) There may be some gender differences in identity status distributions for various domains of psychosocial functioning. (6) There are antecedent conditions, such as a family and school context supporting identity exploration, that may facilitate progressive identity development and other conditions that may inhibit progressive identity development.

Kroger, Martinussen, and Marcia (2010) tested a number Waterman's hypotheses in both longitudinal and cross-sectional studies drawn from the larger database of the Tromsø Meta-Analytic Studies of Ego Identity Status described earlier. Some 72 of a possible 124 investigations provided sufficient data for further analysis. Among longitudinal studies of identity status among late adolescents (18–25 years) and young adults (26–36 years) in which identity status was assessed categorically, the mean time span covered by the study was 3.0 years (SD = 2.6 years). It was predicted here that there would be a predominance of progressive (Diffusion to Foreclosure; Diffusion to Moratorium; Diffusion to Achievement; Foreclosure to Moratorium; Foreclosure to Achievement; and Moratorium to Achievement) rather than regressive changes (the reverse of these patterns). Although this hypothesis was supported (the mean proportion of progressive changes was 0.36, whereas the mean proportion of regressive changes was 0.15), there was also a large mean proportion of individuals who remained stable in their identity status over time (0.49) in both adolescence and in young adulthood. Stability over the time span of the study was also highest among committed statuses, with mean proportions of foreclosures at 0.53 and achievements at 0.66.

Among cross-sectional studies in which identity status was assessed categorically, it was anticipated that there would be decreases in mean proportions of diffusion and foreclosure statuses from mid to late adolescence, and an increase in the mean proportions of those in moratorium and achievement statuses during this time. This pattern of change was in evidence. Patterns of identity status distributions over the years of late adolescence and young adulthood were more mixed. Mean proportions of identity achievement rose to 0.34 by age 22 years (the end of university study for many), but it was not until age 36 years that the mean proportion of identity achievement rose to 0.47. In general, the mean proportions of those moving into identity achievement by young adulthood were relatively low; this finding certainly runs counter to Erikson's claim that attaining one's own identity through an exploration and commitment process is a normative task of adolescence.

With such high proportions of individuals in the general population who are likely not to have made identity commitments through meaningful identity explorations, there is certainly room for ongoing identity development during adulthood. However, the supports that are generally in place for late adolescents and young adults in many western contexts (e.g., social tolerance and institutional supports for identity exploration) are likely not to be present as people move beyond young adulthood, and there may be many obstacles in place for those beginning to explore new identity possibilities in adult life. For those not undergoing the identity formation process during late adolescence or beyond, research has suggested that there will be limits to the types of intimacy one can experience and the level of complexity in one's cognitive capacities (Kroger, 2007).

Among cross-sectional studies in which identity status was assessed continuously, it was hypothesized that moratorium and achievement scores would increase across age groups and foreclosure and diffusion scores would decrease across age groups. Although the results were in the predicted directions, all effect sizes were small. Unfortunately, there were not enough longitudinal studies of identity status assessed continuously for meaningful analysis.

Luyckx and his colleagues (Luyckx, Schwartz, Goossens, Soenens, & Beyers, 2008) examined identity status trajectories and their interplay with adjustment (depression and self-esteem) over a period of 3 years, with measurements obtained every 6 months for a group of female European college students (mean age = 18.8 years). Four trajectories of development were identified through cluster analysis, three of which had been identified in the earlier identity status literature: Pathmakers (identity achieved), Guardians (Foreclosures), Searchers (Moratoriums), and Consolidators (focused on strengthening current identity commitments at the expense of a thorough search of identity options, a possible subtype of the Consolidator class). Drifters (identity diffusions) were not identified in analyses, possibly because they drifted from the study's follow-up assessments or because they may have vacillated between searching and drifting and were classed as Searchers.

Three adjustment types were also noted in Luyckx and colleague's work (2008): Optimal adjustment, Moderate Adjustment, and Stable Maladjustment, based on measures of self-esteem and depression. Results showed that each identity group was linked with a specific adjustment profile. The Searchers were at risk for following a developmental pathway associated with maladjustment and distress, although not all Searchers demonstrated this pattern of adjustment. There may have been multiple subtypes among the Searchers. Both the Pathmaker and Consolidator trajectories were characterized by favorable adjustment profiles.

Meeus et al. (2010) have also undertaken a multiple wave study of identity status change from early to late adolescence (ages 12–20 years), based on their three-dimensional model of identity formation described in the previous section. The authors proposed a developmental continuum for their identity statuses ranging from the less mature diffusion identity status (D) through Moratorium (M) through Searching Moratorium (SM) through Early Closure (EC) or Closure (C) to Identity Achievement (A). The primary aim of their study was to determine whether the identity statuses reflect stable individual dispositions or, alternatively, states into and out of which adolescents move over time.

Results showed that progressive identity status changes clearly outnumbered regressive changes. Findings did support a nonstatic notion of identity development for about 37% of the sample. There was a general increase in high commitment statuses (ECC and A), a decrease in those not addressing identity issues (D), and a decrease in those engaged in an identity search over time (M and SM). At the same time, some 63% of adolescents were in the same identity status from T_1 through T_5. The Searching Moratorium status (seeking identity alternatives), although possessing meaningful identity commitments, was an early to mid-adolescent phenomenon and had largely disappeared by late adolescence.

Thus, from these three major developmental investigations there was support for a number of Waterman's (1999) propositions. First, when identity status movement occurs, it appears to be primarily progressive, rather than regressive. Movement from identity diffusion does appear to occur at earlier ages of adolescence, whereas movement into identity achievement does occur at later ages of late adolescence and young adulthood. The moratorium status has been demonstrated to be relatively unstable, whereas foreclosure and achievement statuses have evidenced greater stability over the adolescent and young adult time spans. And some gender differences occurred in the study by Meeus et al. (sample sizes in Kroger et al. were too small to test for gender differences and the Luyckx et al. 2008 study included only female late adolescents in the sample). What both the Kroger et al. study and the Meeus et al. study also found, however, were unpredictably high proportions of individuals not undertaking the identity formation process (not making identity status movements from foreclosure or diffusion through moratorium to achievement statuses) that Erikson (1968) described as a central task of adolescence. Possible reasons for this finding are discussed below.

FACTORS SHAPING IDENTITY STATUS CHANGE AND STABILITY

A number of researchers have begun exploring both personal and contextual factors linked with various patterns of identity status change and stability during adolescence and young adulthood. Bosma and Kunnen (2001) reviewed a number of these studies, and their review points to both proximal and distal factors associated with identity status change and stability. Distal factors include the historical and cultural context and the climates or opportunities they provide; these climates have been linked to various identity status distributions across time. In general, historical or social climates dominated by either political or social uncertainty or strong levels of authoritarian rigidity have been linked with high proportions of late adolescent foreclosures. Proximal factors include individual psychological and personality factors, life-style choices, and capacity for abstract thinking. Factors such as one's openness vs. rigidity, awareness rather than denial of psychological conflict, readiness for change, the capacity to withstand guilt and fear of disintegration, and the ability to relinquish internalized figures of identification through the second separation-individuation process have all been linked to the capacity for undertaking the identity formation process of adolescence.

In the decade since the Bosma and Kunnen (1999) review, a number of short-term developmental studies have been undertaken to explore specific factors linked with increased capacity for identity exploration. Anthis (2002a, 2002b; Anthis & LaVoie, 2006) undertook a series of studies to examine the roles that readiness for change and stressful life events may play in increasing levels of identity exploration. In short-term (5-month) longitudinal studies with late adolescent, young, and middle adulthood women, scores on a Contemplation of Change Scale (from the University of Rhode Island Change Assessment measure, URICA; McConnaughty, Prochaska, & Velicer, 1983) did indeed positively predict increased levels of identity exploration over the length of the study (Anthis & LaVoie, 2006). Additionally, scores on Action and Maintenance scales of the URICA were negatively related to increased levels of identity exploration at the end of the 5-month study interval. Certain stressful life events such as death and dying experiences of important others as well as sexist discrimination perceived by women were also associated with increases in identity exploration over time as well as decreases in identity commitments. Financial stressors, however, predicted a decrease in identity exploration (Anthis, 2002a, 2002b). For mid-adolescents, one could speculate that stressful life events would also inhibit identity exploration.

Kunnen (2006) also examined experiences of conflict as a potential driver of identity change. She suggests that not all types of conflict trigger identity change, however, and the meaning and impact of various life events as possible identity stressors are highly idiosyncratic. Kunnen undertook an intensive, 6-month study with eight participants, aged 18–23 years, using a diary method to assess identity status and strength of explorations and commitments in six identity domains. She found that strong commitments with little identity exploration were preceded by a period of minimal conflict experiences with the given identity domain. Perception of change in the content of commitments and decrease in commitment strength were related to the number of identity conflicts experienced in the 6-month interval.

Thus, individual factors such as readiness for change and the experience of stressful life events or conflicts have shown some links with decreased identity commitments and increases in identity exploration. With so many life events holding the potential for increased identity conflict and identity exploration, one issue that has intrigued me are the relatively high proportions of late adolescents and young adults in almost all longitudinal identity status researches who are not identity achieved. From an examination of longitudinal results from 11 studies conducted over these age spans, none had a mean proportion of identity achievements higher than 49% at the conclusion of the study (Kroger, 2007). To account for this phenomenon, I have presented a number of hypotheses for further exploration.

Drawing from Whitbourne's (2005) writings on identity assimilation and accommodation processes and their links with current identity, I have suggested that we strive during adolescence (and in later periods) to attain or maintain a state of identity equilibrium (Kroger, 2007). To move into the identity achievement status, some source of externally or internally induced conflict (identity disequilibrium) must first be recognized and acknowledged. Individual personality factors such as one's openness to new experiences, use of more mature defense mechanisms, level of ego resilience, information-processing style, and attachment profile are some of the factors that may be associated with one's choice of identity assimilation or accommodation responses to identity disequilibrium.

To attain identity achievement, one's contexts must also provide some "optimal level of accommodative challenge" (Helson & Roberts, 1994, p. 917), as well as environmental supports. What constitutes an optimal level of accommodative challenge will vary across individuals, according to personality factors noted above. Identity assimilation responses are more likely beyond early adulthood, as one seeks familiar life experiences and environments that confirm one's existing identity structure; this behavioral pattern maintains identity equilibrium. Identity achievement may thus become elusive beyond early adulthood, as people become less likely to choose identity accommodative responses to address new identity conflicts and less likely to choose life contexts holding optimal levels of accommodative challenge. Further research is needed to examine the nature of the reciprocal relationships between individual factors and the meaning one makes of contextual experiences in determining trajectories of identity development during adolescent and adult life.

CONCLUSIONS AND DIRECTIONS FOR FUTURE RESEARCH

Erikson (1968) postulated that the identity formation process was a normative task of adolescent development. Marcia's (1966; Marcia et al., 1993) identity status expansion of Erikson's conceptualization of identity has generated strong interest among identity researchers during its 45-year history. Support for the construct validity of the identity statuses has accrued during this interval as demonstrated by recent meta-analyses, which, in general, have provided support for hypothesized relationships. A number of refinements to the four identity statuses have also been proposed through the paradigm's history; the research program of Luyckx and his colleagues (Luyckx et al., 2006, 2008) has provided the most extensive empirical evidence for modifications to moratorium and diffusion identity statuses to date. Future research might fruitfully explore these and other refinements to the identity statuses for the purpose of identifying adaptive and nonadaptive patterns of exploration during adolescence and the young adult years and the commitments and circumstances that may be associated with them.

Longitudinal and cross-sectional studies of the ego identity statuses included in meta-analyses described here have also suggested that progressive identity status changes occur far more frequently than regressive changes, findings also confirmed by recent multiwave identity status studies of Meeus et al. (2010) and in accordance with Waterman's (1999) developmental propositions. However, a reasonably large proportion of adolescents in both the meta-analytic studies of Kroger et al. (2010) as well as the multiwave longitudinal work of Meeus et al. (2010) have shown patterns of regressive movement. Future research should aim to examine the possible patterns of regressive movement and their longer-term consequences and mental health associations. Additionally, both of the above major developmental identity status investigations point to large proportions of adolescents and young adults who have not undertaken Erikson's identity formation task of adolescence. Possible reasons for this phenomenon have been proposed by Kroger (2007) and reviewed in the previous section, but they need to be examined empirically.

Contemporary identity status researchers have also begun to explore specific intrapersonal and contextual variables associated with identity status change. Although this work is in its infancy, intrapersonal factors such as the experience rather than denial of conflict and readiness for change are linked with increases in identity exploration. Adolescent intrapsychic separation-individuation issues such as unresolved needs for nurturance and fears of abandonment have also been associated with various psychosocial manifestations (Kroger, 1995; Scharf, 2001). Contexts that provide some optimal level of accommodative challenge as well as support for change also appear to be important facilitators of progressive identity status change. It is important to probe more deeply into factors associated with not only progressive but also regressive identity statuses changes, for these factors will ultimately provide the keys to implementing successful programs of intervention.

More generally, the issues of racial and ethnic identity development have received increasing attention over the past two decades, but steps toward a comprehensive contextual theory of identity development are greatly needed. Phinney and Baldelomar (2010) offer an excellent platform for future investigations into the ways in which identity development and culture are inextricably linked. Additionally, work on the self, including changes in self-representations and self-understandings (e.g., Harter, 2006) might usefully be linked to research on the identity formation process. Marcia's (1966; Marcia et al., 1993) identity status paradigm has generated an impressive history of fruitful research into the identity formation process of adolescence; the paradigm promises, still, to hold important applications for future generations of researchers and practitioners.

References

Anthis, K. S. (2002a). On the calamity theory of growth: The relationship between stressful life events and changes in identity over time. *Identity: An International Journal of Theory and Research, 2,* 229–240.

Anthis, K. S. (2002b). The role of sexist discrimination in adult women's identity development. *Sex Roles, 47,* 477–484.

Anthis, K. S., & LaVoie, J. C. (2006). Readiness to change: A longitudinal study of changes in adult identity. *Journal of Research in Personality, 40,* 209–219.

Archer, S. L., & Waterman, A. S. (1990). Varieties of identity diffusions and foreclosures: An exploration of subcategories of the identity statuses. *Journal of Adolescent Research, 5,* 96–111.

Årseth, A. K., Kroger, J., Martinussen, M., & Marcia, J. E. (2009). Meta-analytic studies of identity status and the relational issues of attachment and intimacy. *Identity: An International Journal of Theory and Research, 9,* 1–32.

Berzonsky, M. B. (1985). Diffusion within Marcia's identity status paradigm: Does it foreshadow academic problems? *Journal of Youth and Adolescence, 14,* 527–538.

Borenstein, M., Hedges, L., Higgins, J., & Rothstein, H. (2007). *Comprehensive Meta-analysis V 2.2.046.* Englewood, NJ: Biostat.

Bosma, H. A., & Kunnen, E. S. (2001). Determinants and mechanisms in ego identity development: A review and synthesis. *Developmental Review, 21,* 39–66.

Cohen, J. (1988). *Statistical power analysis for the behavioral sciences* (2nd ed.). New York: Academic Press.

Erikson, E. H. (1956). The problem of ego identity. *Journal of the American Psychoanalytic Association, 4,* 56–121.

Erikson, E. H. (1963). *Childhood and society.* New York: W. W. Norton.

Erikson, E. H. (1968*). Identity, youth and crisis.* New York: W. W. Norton.

Frame, J. (1987). *To the island.* London: Paladin Press.

Harter, S. (2006). The self. In N. Eisenberg, W. Damon, & R. M. Lerner (Eds.), *Handbook of child psychology: Vol. 3, Social, emotional, and personality development* (6th ed., pp. 505–570). Hoboken, NJ: John Wiley & Sons.

Helson, R., & Roberts, B. W. (1994). Ego development and personality change in adulthood. *Journal of Personality and Social Psychology, 66,* 911–920.

Hunt, M. M. (1997). *How science takes stock: The story of meta-analysis* (2nd ed.). New York: Russell Sage Foundation.

Hunter, J. E., & Schmidt, F. L. (2004). *Methods of meta-analysis: Correcting error and bias in research findings* (2nd ed.). Thousand Oaks, CA: Sage Publications.

Jespersen, K., Kroger, J., & Martinussen, M. (2011a). *Identity status and ego development: A meta-analysis.* Manuscript in preparation.

Jespersen, K., Kroger, J., & Martinussen, M. (2011b). *Identity status and moral reasoning: A meta-analysis.* Manuscript in preparation.

Kohlberg, L. (1984). *Essays in moral development, Vol. 2: The psychology of moral development.* San Francisco: Harper & Row.

Kroger, J. (1993). On the nature of structural transition in the identity formation process. In J. Kroger (Ed.), *Discussions on ego identity* (pp. 205–234). Hillsdale, NJ: Lawrence Erlbaum Associates.

Kroger, J. (1995). The differentiation of "firm" from "developmental" foreclosure identity statuses: A longitudinal study. *Journal of Adolescent Research, 10,* 317–337.

Kroger, J. (2007). Why is identity achievement so elusive? *Identity: An International Journal of Theory and Research, 7,* 331–348.

Kroger, J., Martinussen, M., & Marcia, J. E. (2010). Identity status change during adolescence and young adulthood: A meta-analysis. *Journal of Adolescence, 33,* 683–698.

Kunnen, E. S. (2006). Are conflicts the motor in identity change? *Identity: An International Journal of Theory and Research, 6,* 169–186.

Lillevoll, K. R., Kroger, J., & Martinussen, M. (2011a). *Identity status and anxiety: A meta-analysis.* Manuscript in preparation.

Lillevoll, K. R., Kroger, J., & Martinussen, M. (2011b). *Identity status and locus of control: A meta-analysis.* Manuscript in preparation.

Loevinger, J. (1976). *Ego development.* San Francisco: Jossey Bass.

Luyckx, K., Goossens, L., Soenens, B., Beyers, W., & Vansteenkiste, M. (2005). Identity statuses based on 4 rather than 2 identity dimensions: Extending and refining Marcia's paradigm. *Journal of Youth and Adolescence, 34,* 605–618.

Luyckx, K., Goossens, L., Soenens, B., & Beyers, W. (2006). Unpacking commitment and exploration: Preliminary validation of an integrative model of late adolescent identity formation. *Journal of Adolescence, 29,* 361–378.

Luyckx, K., Schwartz, S. J., Berzonsky, M. D., Soenens, B., Vansteenkiste, M., Smits, I., & Goossens, L. (2008). Capturing ruminative exploration: Extending the four-dimensional model of identity formation into late adolescence. *Journal of Research in Personality, 42,* 58–82.

Luyckx, K., Schwartz, S. J., Goossens, L., Soenens, B., & Beyers, W. (2008). Developmental typologies of identity formation and adjustment in female emerging adults: A latent class growth analysis approach. *Journal of Research on Adolescence, 18,* 595–619.

Marcia, J. E. (1966). Development and validation of ego identity status. *Journal of Personality and Social Psychology, 3,* 551–558.

Marcia, J. E. (1967). Ego identity status: Relationship to change in self-esteem, "general maladjustment," and authoritarianism. *Journal of Personality, 35,* 118–133.

Marcia, J. E. (1989). Identity diffusion differentiated. In M. A. Luszez & T. Nettleback (Eds.), *Psychological development: Perspectives across the life-span* (pp. 289–318). North Holland: Elsevier Publishers.

Marcia, J. (2007). Theory and measure: The identity status interview. In A. Born & M. Watzlawik (Eds.), *Capturing identity: Quantitative and qualitative methods.* Lanham, MD: University Press of America.

Marcia, J. E., Waterman, A. S., Matteson, D. R., Archer, S. L., & Orlofsky, J. L. (1993). *Ego identity: A handbook for psychosocial research.* New York: Springer-Verlag.

Meeus, W., van de Schoot, R., Keijsers, L., Schwartz, S. J., & Branje, S. (2010). On the progression and stability of adolescent identity formation: A five-wave longitudinal study in early-to-middle and middle-to-late adolescence. *Child Development, 81,* 1565–1581.

McConnaughy, E. A., DiClemente, C. C., & Prochaska, J. O. (1989). Stages of change in psychotherapy: A follow-up report. *Psychotherapy, 26,* 494–503.

Orlofsky, J. L., Marcia, J. E., & Lesser, I. M. (1973). Ego identity status and the intimacy versus isolation crisis of young adulthood. *Journal of Personality and Social Psychology, 27,* 211–219.

Phinney, J., & Baldelomar, O. (2010). Identity development in multiple cultural contexts. In L. Jensen (Ed.), *Bridging cultural and developmental approaches to psychology: New syntheses in theory, research, and policy* (pp. 161–186). New York: Oxford University Press.

Roberts, B. W., Walton, E. K., & Viechtbauer, W. (2006). Patterns of mean-level change in personality traits across the life course: A meta-analysis of longitudinal studies. *Psychological Bulletin, 132*, 1–25.

Rood, L., Roelofs, J., Bogels, S. M., Nolen-Hoeksema, S., & Schouten, E. (2009). The influence of emotion-focused rumination and distraction on depressive symptoms in non-clinical youth: A meta-analytic review. *Clinical Psychology Review, 29*, 607–616.

Ryeng, M. S., Kroger, J., & Martinussen, M. (2011a). *Identity status and self-esteem: A meta-analysis.* Manuscript in preparation.

Ryeng, M. S., Kroger, J., & Martinussen, M. (2011b). *Identity status and authoritarianism: A meta-analysis.* Manuscript in preparation.

Scharf, M., (2001). A "natural experiment" in childrearing ecologies and adolescents' attachment and separation representations. *Child Development, 72*, 236–251.

Valde, G. A. (1996). Identity closure: A fifth identity status. *Journal of Genetic Psychology, 157*, 245–254.

Waterman, A. S. (1999). Identity, the identity statuses, and identity status development: A contemporary statement. *Developmental Review, 19*, 591–621.

Whitbourne, S. K. (2005). *Adult development and aging: Biopsychosocial perspectives* (2nd ed.). New York: Wiley.

Introduction to Section II

Friendship and Intimate Relationships

PATRICIA K. KERIG AND MARC S. SCHULZ

Section II of the volume focuses on a critical task of the adolescent-emerging adult transition, that of the formation of intimate peer relations. The body of research that exists on friendship makes a compelling case that adolescents' ability to connect with one another, give and receive social support, and provide positive modeling are important sources of resilience (e.g., Bukowski, Laursen, & Hoza, 2010). On the other hand, friendships can have a dark side as well, particularly when adolescents gravitate toward antisocial peers or succumb to the perils of peer pressure and negative influence (Parker, Rubin, Erath, Wojslawowicz, & Buskirk, 2006). In turn, adolescents who lack friendships are vulnerable to a number of troubling outcomes during adolescence, such as depression and suicidality (Harter & Marold, 1994; Prinstein, 2003). Moreover, an important point recognized by the contributors to this volume is that parents have something to do with the kinds of relationships their children form with their peers. Internal working models of self and other derived from early attachments play a part in the quality of later-life friendships (Berlin, Cassidy, & Appleyard, 2008) and intimate partnerships (Feeney, 2008). Romantic relationships similarly provide both opportunities and challenges for teens and emerging adults (Kerig, 2010), and parenting is implicated in the quality of these relations as well. The process of shifting the heart's center from the family of origin to a deep romantic attachment represents a significant step on the road toward emotional autonomy in emerging adulthood. However, should that romantic relationship recapitulate dysfunctional patterns in the parent–child dynamic, such as boundary dissolution or psychological abuse, the consequences for youth development may be dire (Kerig & Swanson, 2010).

Focusing first on the role of platonic relations, Chapter 4 by Way and Silverman provides an overview of the results of a two-decade-long series of investigations into the development of adolescent friendships through the high school years. Their work is informed by a rich array of theoretical perspectives, including Sullivan's interpersonal approach, Bronfenbrenner's (1979) ecological framework, and attachment theory. From Sullivan (1953), they derive the important observation that from the preadolescent period onward, a need for intimacy arises that plays a significant role in the development of self-worth and social skills. In addition, an important developmental milestone that both allows for the development of mutual intimacy and is informed by the quality of the friendships that ensue is the capacity for empathy and "understanding of what matters to another person." Following from Bronfenbrenner, they view adolescent development as arising from a complex interplay of nested and interconnected systems of relationships, including microcontexts such as families, peers, and schools, as well as the macrocontexts of neighborhood and culture. Way and Silverman take on this task by explicitly examining the interplay among these multiple contexts, and are rewarded by results that show that when it comes to youths' friendships, parental support and structure matter, as does school climate and the existence of racial tension. Finally, from attachment theory comes the insight that the quality of youths' friendships is influenced by the kinds of close personal relationships they have experienced earlier in life, when they internalize parental responsiveness to them and are thus able to respond to others. Furthermore, Way and Silverman take an explicitly developmental perspective and give credence to the idea that friendships not only affect development, but that development influences the ability to forge high-quality friendships. With increasing capacities for self-awareness, reasoning, and security in their identities over the course of the adolescent transition, youth are able to engage in more mutually supportive and satisfying relationships.

The methods Way and Silverman use also are rich, incorporating both quantitative and qualitative strategies. The diversity of the samples from which they derive their data also is a major strength of their work. An important theme in this chapter is the value to be gained by the interplay and dynamic tension between collecting survey data—which can tell us about the quantity of relationships—and gathering narrative and interview data, which can better capture the quality of those relationships. For example, the authors point out that qualitative data reveal more gender and ethnic similarities than have emerged from quantitative studies, particularly in regard to the universal valuing of intimacy and trust—that is, having a friend to whom one can tell "everything" and who will keep those "deep depth secrets" in utter confidence. However, a significant insight derived from their qualitative data is the finding that although friendship quality increases over the course of the adolescent transition, boys report having a harder time finding peers in whom they can entrust their more tender feelings, perhaps due to the pressure of masculine sex-role stereotyping in a homophobic culture that looks askance upon emotional closeness between males. On the other side of the coin, supplementing narrative methods with multivariate approaches such as growth curve modeling also allows them to uncover important overall trends in their data, such as the fact that whereas maternal support is related to a general increasing in friendship quality over the high school years, youth with the lowest levels of maternal support appear to compensate by investing even more heavily in their friendships. Whether that bodes well or ill for these youths' futures will be an interesting question for further longitudinal investigations, given that a precocious emancipation from the family and precipitant involvement in intensely intimate peer relationships have been associated with maladaptation and adolescent dating violence in other research (e.g., Wolfe & Wekerle, 1997).

The theme of dating relationships is taken up by the next two chapters in this section, which involve samples of youth who are progressively further along the developmental trajectory toward emerging adulthood. First, Shulman and colleagues (Chapter 5) consider the major stage-salient tasks of beginning romantic relationships and experimenting with sexuality in later adolescence, and inquire as to how these are influenced by parents' own states of mind regarding relationships. These authors make the important observation that adolescents' stage-salient tasks also represent important developmental challenges for parents. First, parents need to renegotiate the parent–child relationship to respond to new behaviors, such as dating, and parents must manage to strike a difficult balance between the desire to allow their daughters appropriate permission to explore their sexuality while at the same time protecting their daughters from the potential harm that unintegrated and negative sexual experiences can wreak. In addition, Shulman and colleagues point out that issues related to daughters' romantic intimacy also challenge parents by threatening to evoke parents' concerns about their own past (e.g., their own sexual histories, whether happy or unhappy), and their own present (e.g., recognition of their own aging and loss of reproductive status).

Inspired by attachment theory, Shulman and colleagues use Crittenden's (2006) construct of dispositional representations to organize their thinking about the ways in which Israeli mothers' internal representations of romantic relationships might "spill over" onto daughters. In addition, psychoanalytic theory contributes to their interpretive framework a number of specific mechanisms through with this intergenerational transmission might take place; for example, by emotionally "binding" daughters in an enmeshed relationship in which the boundaries and roles between them are confused (Kerig, 2005), or by engaging in projective identification (Ogden, 1979), an intersubjective process through which parents project onto daughters their own unacceptable attributes, wishes, or needs and then interact with their daughters in ways that shape the girls' inner lives and lead them to identify with those projected qualities and to experience them as indeed their own.

Their qualitative analysis of mothers' and daughters' narratives about dating relationships reveals that mothers with coherent memories characterized either by positive experiences or by resolution of difficulties encountered in their own teenage years were flexible and responsive to their daughters and were able to provide both emotional support and permission for exploration. Their daughters, in turn, described their own dating relationships in balanced and adaptive ways. In contrast, mothers who were preoccupied with their own problematic romantic histories tended to engage in overinvolvement and overidentification with their daughters, seeming to look to their daughters to rewrite the mother's own historical script; in parallel, their daughters evidenced confusion and a lack of coherence in their dating narratives. By integrating these conceptual frameworks with carefully collected and interpreted data, this study indeed sheds a unique light on the processes involved in the intergenerational transmission of intimate relationships.

Finally, Kerig and colleagues (Chapter 6) integrate family systems and attachment perspectives to investigate how parent–child boundary dissolution might influence emerging adults' capacity for mutual autonomy—in other words, the ability to engage in relationships with peers that simultaneously allow for both closeness and individuation. In a parallel to Shulman and colleagues' dilemma of parenting a child whose budding sexuality challenges a parent to both hold fast and let go, emerging adults' intimate personal relationships also require this crucial balance between closeness and separation and between accommodating to others' needs and asserting one's own. Kerig and colleagues also seek to go beyond merely establishing that "bad input = bad output" in order to demonstrate what might lead a young person to adopt an interpersonal orientation that is characterized by an overemphasis on accommodation versus an overinvestment in control. To this end, they focus on the emotional valence of the parent–child relationship by assessing whether youth perceive parents as attempting to control them psychologically in the context of warmth and emotional support, or of coldness and criticism. Intriguingly, warm but controlling parenting is associated with youths' tendency toward focusing on others' needs in relationships, whereas a rejecting parenting style is associated with a tendency toward self-focus.

Taken together, there are a number of common themes that can be derived from these three chapters. One is the importance of thinking developmentally about the relevant stage-salient issues across the adolescent transition—from friendship, particularly in early adolescence, to dating and sexual experimentation, particularly in late adolescence, to the skills needed to engage in committed and long-lasting relationships in emerging adulthood. Another key theme is the value of multiple methodologies. Whereas Shulman and colleagues point out the important insights that can be revealed by narrative research, and Kerig and colleagues show the kinds of sophisticated questions that can be addressed in multivariate analyses, Way and Silverman's chapter is exemplary for revealing the important interplay between qualitative and quantitative methods in adolescence research. Another common theme among these chapters is the way in which parental involvement shapes youths' peer relationships, for better or for worse. Although the studies presented involve diverse samples and methods, investigate different relationship functions, and derive from a range of theoretical orientations, they are remarkably consistent in finding that parental overinvolvement—whether in the form of projective identification, psychological control, or excessive monitoring—is linked to maladaptive extrafamilial relationships during the adolescent transition.

References

Berlin, L., Cassidy, J., & Appleyard, K. (2008). The influence of early attachments on other relationships. In J. Cassidy & P. R. Shaver (Eds.), *Handbook of attachment* (pp. 333–347). New York: Guilford.

Bronfenbrenner, U. (1979). *The ecology of human development: Experiments by nature and design*. Cambridge, MA: Harvard University Press.

Bukowski, W. M., Laursen, B., & Hoza, B. (2010). The snowball effect: Friendship moderates escalations in depressed affect among avoidant and excluded children. *Development and Psychopathology, 22*, 749–757.

Crittenden, P. M. (2006). Why do inadequate parents do what they do? In O. Mayseless (Ed.), *Parenting representations: Theory, research, and clinical applications* (pp. 388–433). New York: Cambridge University Press.

Feeney, J. A. (2008). Adult romantic attachment. In J. Cassidy & P. R. Shaver (Eds.), *Handbook of attachment* (pp. 456–481). New York: Guilford.

Harter, S., & Marold, D. (1994). Psychosocial risk factors contributing to adolescent suicidal ideation. In G. G. Noam & S. Borst (Eds.), *Children, youth, and suicide: Developmental perspectives* (pp. 71–92). San Francisco: Jossey-Bass.

Kerig, P. K. (2005). Revisiting the construct of boundary dissolution: A multidimensional perspective. In P. K. Kerig (Ed.), *Implications of parent-child boundary dissolution for developmental psychopathology: Who is the parent and who is the child?* (pp. 5–42). New York: Haworth.

Kerig, P. K. (2010). Relational dynamics as sources of risk and resilience in adolescent dating violence. *Journal of Aggression, Maltreatment, and Trauma, 19*, 585–586.

Kerig, P. K., & Swanson, J. A. (2010). Ties that bind: Triangulation, boundary dissolution, and the effects of interparental conflict on child development. In M. S. Schulz, M. K. Pruett, P. K. Kerig, & R. Parke (Eds.), *Strengthening couple relationships for optimal child development: Lessons from research and intervention* (pp. 59–76). Washington, DC: American Psychological Association.

Ogden, T. (1979). On projective identification. *International Journal of Psychoanalysis, 60*, 357–373.

Parker, J., Rubin, K. H., Erath, S., Wojslawowicz, J.C., & Buskirk, A. A. (2006). Peer relationships and developmental psychopathology. In D. Cicchetti & D. Cohen (Eds.), *Developmental psychopathology: Risk, disorder, and adaptation* (2nd ed.), Vol. 2. (pp. 419–493). New York: Wiley.

Prinstein, M. J. (2003). Social factors: Peer relationships. In A. Spirito & J. C. Overholser (Eds.), *Evaluating and treating adolescent suicide attempters: From research to practice* (pp. 193–215). New York: Academic Press.

Sullivan, H. S. (1953). *The interpersonal theory of psychiatry*. New York: Norton.

Wolfe, D. A., & Wekerle, C. (1997). Pathways to violence in teen dating relationships. In D. Cicchetti & S. L. Toth (Eds.), *Developmental perspectives on trauma: Theory, research, and intervention* (pp. 315–340). Rochester, NY: University of Rochester Press.

4

The Quality of Friendships during Adolescence

Patterns across Context, Culture, and Age[1]

NIOBE WAY AND LISA R. SILVERMAN

Harry Stack Sullivan, the renowned theorist who brought the topic of close friendships to the table of developmental psychology, maintained that during preadolescence (9–12 years of age) a need for intimacy arises that he defines as "that type of situation involving two people which permits validation of all components of personal worth" (Sullivan, 1953, p. 246). In response to this need, preadolescents have intimate relationships with their peers which represent "the beginning of very much like full-blown, psychiatrically defined, love" (p. 245). It is during this period that "a child begins to develop a real sensitivity to what matters to another person" (p. 245). These friendships are considered essential, according to Sullivan, for the development of self-worth, empathy, and the acquisition of social skills.

Drawing from Sullivan's work, researchers have, for decades, investigated the development, function, and consequences of close friendships during childhood and adolescence. They have found that the sharing of intimate thoughts and feelings does, in fact, increases from childhood to adolescence (Azmitia, Ittel, & Brent, 2006), that adolescent girls are more likely to have intimate same-sex friendships than adolescent boys, and that such relationships provide a wide array of social, emotional, academic, and cognitive benefits (see Rubin, Bukowski, & Laursen, 2009 for a review). Intimate (e.g., self-disclosing) and supportive friendships, for example, are associated with lower levels of depressive symptoms (Pelkonen et al., 2003) and higher levels of self-esteem (Berndt, 2004; Nangle & Erdley, 2001; Rubin, Bukowski, & Laursen, 2009; Way & Greene, 2006). A lack of close friendships, furthermore, is associated with high levels of depressive symptoms, internalizing problems, and peer victimization (Ladd & Troop-Gordon, 2003). In one study, a lack of close friends at age 16 predicted depressive symptoms at age 22, over and above previous levels of depressed mood (Pelkonen et al., 2003). The quality of close friendships, in sum, varies by age and gender and influences the emotional and social well-being of children, adolescents, and emerging adults.

Although this literature provides important information about close friendship and its correlates during adolescence, many questions have been left unanswered. We know little, for example, about the experience of friendships *during* adolescence or how the microcontexts (e.g., families, schools) *and* macrocontexts (e.g., cultural norms and expectations) shape adolescent friendships. In response to these gaps, we have conducted a series of mixed-method, longitudinal studies with adolescents over the past 15 years. The purpose of this chapter is to describe our key findings, as well as those of other researchers, regarding the experience of friendships during adolescence and the influence of micro and macrocontexts on the quality of friendships. Our studies, in sum, support Sullivan's theory regarding the need for intimate peer relations yet suggest that such a need is not limited to the preadolescent phase but extends throughout adolescence (Way, 2011). Our studies, as well as others, also underscore the critical role of macrocontexts in adolescents' experiences of their friendships (e.g., Chen, Kaspar, Zhang, Wang, & Zheng, 2004; Jia et al., 2009; Way, 2006, 2011; Way & Chen, 2000; Way & Chu, 2004; Way & Greene, 2006; Way & Pahl, 2001).

PATTERNS AND CONTEXTS OF FRIENDSHIPS

Primary limitations in the research on adolescent friendships include the almost exclusive reliance on survey methodology, the lack of studies examining how adolescents experience such friendships *during* adolescence, and the acontextual nature of the research. A focus on the frequency of a predetermined set of dimensions of friendship quality, which is the product of survey methodology, has resulted in the field knowing more about the "quantity" of friendships than its quality. Although it may be true that boys, for example, are less likely than girls to endorse survey items related to intimacy in their friendships, it is not clear how boys experience their friendships on their own terms. When qualitative research has been conducted, such research has suggested that boys and girls tend to speak about their friendships in similar ways (Radmacher & Azmitia, 2006; Way, 2011). For example, most boys speak about wanting same-sex friendships in which they can "share secrets" (Way, 2011). Without knowing about the nature of the intimacy shared between adolescents, the interpretation of the quantity of intimacy becomes difficult. Our own analytic techniques, as well as similar narrative techniques as described in this volume by Hauser, Allen, and Schulz, explore how adolescents make meaning of their experiences and, more specifically, their intimate peer relations.

In addition to an overreliance on a survey methodology, the friendship literature has been limited in its understanding of transitions with only a handful of studies examining friendships *during* adolescence. The transition from early to late adolescence produces changes in many areas of the social and emotional lives of adolescents (Kuttler & La Greca, 2004; Sippola, 1999). Thus, it is likely that adolescents also experience changes in the nature and quality of their relationships with their closest friends. Although Sullivan noted that adolescents shift from a focus on intimate same-sex friendships to a focus on "lust" relationships with opposite-sex peers during adolescence (Sullivan, 1953), he offers little in describing how the quality of intimate same-sex friendships changes during adolescence.

A third limitation in the friendship literature is the acontextual nature of the research. An ecological understanding of human development (Bronfenbrenner, 1979; Garcia Coll et al., 1996) acknowledges not only that individuals are influenced by their environments but also that environments extend beyond the events and conditions that immediately surround the person. According to this theoretical framework, a person develops within a complex system of relationships affected by multiple levels of the surrounding environment. This developing person is influenced by social systems that are nested within each other and are interconnected. In recent years, there has been a proliferation of studies based on this ecological conceptualization, designed to understand the ways in which child development is influenced by multiple relationships, settings, and contexts, such as parents and peers, homes, schools, neighborhoods, and larger political, social, and economic forces (e.g., Benner, Graham, & Mistry, 2008; Bowlby, 1969/1982; Chen & French, 2008; Coley, Morris, & Hernandez, 2004; Eccles & Roeser, 1999; Hamm, Brown, & Heck, 2005). Researchers who examine social and emotional development focus on, for example, how social skills and emotional understanding develop between children and their family members and how such interactions contribute to children's friendships (Updegraff, Madden-Derdich, Estrada, Sales, & Leonard, 2002). Additionally, empirical studies further acknowledge that children's peer relationships contribute to their school adjustment, showing links between peer acceptance and feelings of school belongingness (Ladd & Kochenderfer, 1996).

However, with few exceptions, there remains a dearth of ecologically oriented studies that pay specific attention to friendships and the ways that both microlevel and macrolevel contexts shape the quality of friendships. Yet friendships are influenced by relationships with mothers, fathers, siblings, peers, aunts, uncles, as well as by teachers and mentors, by family characteristics (e.g., SES, family structure), schools, neighborhood resources, and by cultural norms, beliefs, and practices that stem from larger political, economic, and social contexts (Bowlby, 1969/1982; Bronfenbrenner, 1979; Chen, French, & Schneider, 2006; Way, 2011). American adolescents are shaped by a culture that is infused, for example, with ideals about masculinity that are wary of intimate male friendships (Raymond, 1994; Way, 2011). They are also embedded in a culture that stereotypes black and Latino boys as "hypermasculine" or "macho" and Asian-American and white boys as "feminine" or "gay," thus making the possibilities of intimacy in male friendships more complex for each of these groups of boys (Eng, 2001; Raymond, 1994; Way, 2011). Examining friendships in the microcontexts of families, peers, and schools as well as in the larger macrocontexts of gendered expectations and racial stereotypes is

essential if we are to advance our understanding of the development of friendships during adolescence.

Studies that have included ethnic minorities, non-Americans, and/or poor and
working class populations raise questions about the generalizability of the acontextual findings that dominate the friendship literature (Chen, French, &
Schneider, 2006). Ethnic differences, for example, have been reported in friendship quality (Azmitia & Cooper, 2001; Azmitia, Ittel, & Brent, 2006; Way, 2011;
Way & Chen, 2000) and gender *similarities* in friendship intimacy have been
reported for black, Latino, and Asian-American adolescents (Way & Chen, 2000;
Radmacher & Azmitia, 2007). In addition, the importance of friendships has been
found to vary widely both within and across ethnic groups, with first generation
immigrants valuing friendships significantly less than their second generation peers, and Chinese-American immigrant parents valuing friendships less
than non-Chinese-American immigrant parents (Gupta & Sirin, 2010).

Research has also detected cultural variations in the extent to which friendships
are valued over family relationships, with less recent Latino immigrants being
more likely to value their friendships over family relationships than first generation immigrants (Azmitia & Cooper, 2001). The valuing of friendships over family
relationships, however, appears to be found among both European and African-
American adolescents (Levitt, Guacci-Franco, & Levitt, 1993). Finally, whereas
the association between friendship quality and psychological adjustment is similar across racial and ethnic groups (Azmitia et al., 2006; Way, Cowal, Gingold,
Pahl, & Bissessar, 2001; Way & Robinson, 2003), gender differences have been
found among white adolescents, with the link between friendship quality and
adjustment being stronger for boys than for girls (Nangle & Erdley, 2001). These
findings draw attention to the importance of including adolescents from a range
of contexts, cultures, and socioeconomic backgrounds in studies of friendships.
The importance of such inclusion is underscored by the fact that in recent years,
approximately 32% of the U.S. population is black, Latino, or Asian-American,
and it has been estimated that by the year 2050, "ethnic minorities" as a group will
no longer be minorities in the numerical sense (U.S. Census Bureau, 2004).
Furthermore, currently 43% of people under the age of 20 years old are ethnic
minorities and approximately 60–70% of Americans come from poor or working
class families (U.S. Census Bureau, 2007).

Responding to these gaps in the friendship literature, we have been exploring
the experience of friendships among black, Latino, Asian-American, and white
boys and girls from primarily poor and working class families for the past 15 years.
We have been interested specifically in the ways in which adolescents from different ethnic and racial groups experience friendships, how these experiences change
from early to late adolescence, and how the microcontexts of families and schools,
and the macrocontext of conventions of masculinity, shape adolescents' experiences
of friendships. (For a more detailed discussion of these studies, see Way, 2011.) To
address these goals, we have used a range of quantitative and qualitative techniques and have distinguished between *closest* friends and *general* friends (Way &
Greene, 2006). The reason for making this distinction is twofold: adolescents

themselves tend to distinguish between these types of friendships (Adler & Adler, 1998), and research has indicated that outcomes and predictors vary depending on the type of friendship that is studied (Harter, 1990). We will first briefly describe our studies and then turn to the topic of experiences of friendships during adolescence and the ways in which the microcontext of families and schools and the macrocontexts of conventions of masculinity influence the friendship quality of adolescents. We will draw from the existing body of research as well as our own studies in these discussions.

SOURCES OF DATA FOR OUR RESEARCH

Data for the Relationships Among Peers (R.A.P.) and the Connections Studies were collected over 4- to 5-year periods,[2] beginning in the participants' initial year of high school between the years of 1996 and 2004. Data collection for both studies involved administering standardized measures and semistructured interviews to primarily ethnic minority (i.e., black, Latino, Asian-American), low-income adolescents, and also conducting intensive participant observations. Each study was carried out in a public high school situated in a low-income neighborhood in an eastern city in the United States. We successfully recruited 86–95% of the freshman population during Year 1, resulting in survey components of the two studies with sample sizes that ranged from 213 (Study 1) to 225 (Study 2). For the qualitative component of each study, we interviewed a total of 242 adolescents (132 in Study 1 and 110 in Study 2) during their first year of high school and reinterviewed them each subsequent year of high school. One hundred and sixty-seven adolescents were interviewed for at least 3 years. The interview sample was chosen to reflect the student body in each of the schools with a representative sampling of girls, boys, blacks, Latinos, and Asian-Americans. Our retention rate over 4–5 years for the quantitative and qualitative components in these studies was at least 90% of those who remained in the schools in which we were collecting data and at least 60% of those in the entire study. These retention rates are standard for longitudinal studies of low-income, urban adolescents (see Seidman, 1991). Those adolescents who were retained and those who were not retained did not differ on any of our friendship variables.

Participants

The mean age of the participants at Time 1 was 14.33 years (Study 1) and 14.21 years (Study 2). A substantial majority (approximately 90%) of participants in both studies identified themselves as black (almost exclusively African-American), Latino (primarily Puerto Rican and/or Dominican), Asian-American (almost exclusively Chinese-American) or a mix of these ethnicities. The remaining adolescents either identified themselves as European-American or another ethnic or racial category (e.g., Native-American). This ethnic breakdown resembles the ethnic composition of the schools in which we collected data. Additionally, a majority of students in each of the two studies was eligible for federal assistance through the free or reduced-price lunch program.

Procedure

We recruited participants from "mainstream" English classes (i.e., not from bilingual English classes) to guarantee English fluency for the qualitative component of the study. To participate in the study, students were required to return signed parental consent forms which were available in English, Spanish, or Chinese. Questionnaires and one-to-one, semistructured interviews, in each study, were administered by a racially and ethnically diverse research team during English classes, free periods, lunch periods, or after school. Questionnaires were completed in approximately 90 minutes (two class periods), and the interviews were typically 90 minutes to 120 minutes; variations in interview time were related to year of assessment (the longer interviews took place during the latter years of the studies). Students were paid $5.00 in return for the completion of questionnaires and $10.00 for the completion of interviews in Year 1; each student was also given $5.00 for participating in each subsequent wave of data collection (i.e., Times 2–5).

Measures

All the measures that we used in our research have been utilized previously with ethnically and socioeconomically diverse urban populations and have demonstrated good to excellent internal reliability and external validity (Way & Chen, 2000). Adolescents' friendship quality with their closest same-sex friend was measured using a shortened version of the *Network of Relationships Inventory* (NRI) (Furman & Buhrmester, 1985). The shortened measure consists of 20 items with a five-point Likert scale that assess multiple dimensions of friendship quality. Five positive dimensions (i.e., intimacy, affection, reliable alliance, satisfaction, and companionship) were combined into one score that represented overall support from closest same-sex friend. The quality of general friendships, or the overall level of perceived support, was assessed with the *Perceived Social Support Scale for Friends* (PSS-FR) (Procidano & Heller, 1983). Participants were asked to respond "yes," "no," or "don't know" to 20 statements related to their experiences with their friends. Standardized scales were also used to examine psychological adjustment and family relationships (i.e., the NRI for mothers and fathers), and other variables of interest for our studies.

In each year of both studies we conducted one-to-one, semistructured interviews with our participants in order to explore their experiences of friendships and the ways in which those experiences were shaped by micro and macrocontexts. Questions on the interview protocol included general descriptions (e.g., "Tell me about your relationships with your best friend") and more specific probes (e.g., "In what ways do you trust your best friend?"). With the exception of the interview at Time 1, each interview began with the following question: "What has changed for you over the past year?" This particular question helped provide us with a clearer understanding of the adolescents' responses during the remainder of the interview. Each interview consisted of a standard set of questions; however, follow-up probes and questions related more closely to each adolescent's answers allowed us to capture his or her own descriptions of the experiences of his or her friendships.

Data Analytic Strategies

To address our questions about adolescent friendships, we employed a range of methods in the analysis of our questionnaire data. These methods included Hierarchical Regression Analysis and Growth Curve modeling (see Rogosa & Willett, 1985; Willett, Singer, & Martin, 1998). With regard to our interview data, our analytic techniques involved narrative summaries, conceptually clustered matrices (Miles & Huberman, 1995), and the Listening Guide (Brown, Tappan, Gilligan, Miller, & Argyris, 1989). The research team first read through the transcripts and created narrative summaries that condensed the interview material while retaining the essence of the stories told by the adolescents. Following that step, team members read each narrative summary independently, looking for themes in the summaries. In any 1 year of the study, a theme retained for further analysis had to be identified as a theme independently by at least two of the team members. Once themes were generated and agreed on, each team member returned to the original interviews and noted the year in the project and the specific place in the interview at which these themes emerged. They also took note if and how the themes changed during other years of the study (for more details, see Way, 2011).

QUALITY OF FRIENDSHIPS

Research on the quality of adolescent friendships typically has been grounded in Weiss' (1974) contention that children and adolescents seek social provisions in their close friendships (Furman, 1996) that include intimacy (e.g., sharing secrets together), affection, companionship (e.g., having fun together), and satisfaction (Shuman, 1993). A large body of research has focused on understanding the prevalence and correlates of these dimensions of friendship quality (see Berndt, 2004; Jia et al., 2009; Nangle & Erdley, 2001), and the extent to which they vary by gender and, more recently, ethnicity/race or nationality (see Jia et al., 2009).

Studies examining variations in friendship quality among adolescents, particularly investigations with European-American participants have repeatedly found gender differences in levels of intimacy (e.g., DuBois & Hirsch, 1990;

Furman & Buhrmester, 1985; Galambos, 2009). Adolescent females, in these studies, typically rate the quality of their same-sex friendships significantly higher than males on dimensions such as affection, companionship, and intimacy (Galambos, 2009). Our quantitative studies have also suggested gender differences in friendship quality but only among the Latino and Asian-American adolescents and not among the African-American adolescents (Way & Chen, 2000). Theorists and researchers propose that gender differences may be related to different socialization patterns (Brown & Gilligan, 1992; Maccoby, 1990; Radmacher & Azmitia, 2006). Specifically, it is posited that females prioritize interpersonal connections in their interactions whereas males focus on the enhancement of individual status (Maccoby, 1990). Yet studies of intimacy in friendships have also revealed gender similarities in the meaning and experience of intimacy and in levels of self-disclosure (Radmacher & Azmitia, 2006). Although boys and girls may report different levels of perceived support or intimacy in their friendships, the ways in which they describe these friendships and the types of friendships that they seek with their peers appear to be remarkably similar (Radmacher & Azmitia, 2006; Way, 2011).

In our studies, we find numerous gender similarities in the quality of boys' and girls' close friendships. Both boys and girls speak with great passion about their best friends with whom they share "everything" (Way et al., 2006; Way, 2011). When Amanda,[3] a participant in one of our studies, is asked what she likes about her best friend, she replies, "She keeps everything a secret, whatever I tell her." Maria responds similarly saying, "like the back of their hands, . . . I can talk to her about anything, like if I call her, I'm hysterically crying or something just happened or whatever . . . and maybe she'll be doing something, she'll stop doing that to come and talk to me and to help me." Brian states about his best friends, "I tell them anything about me and I know they won't tell anybody else unless I tell them to." When asked to define a best friend, Justin responds, "He could just tell me anything and I could tell him anything. Like I always know everything about him. . . . We always chill, like we don't hide secrets from each other." Asked what he likes about his friend, Justin replies, "If I have a problem, I can go tell him. If he has a problem, he can go tell me." Similarly, Steven states about his best friends, "We shared secrets that we don't talk about in the open." When asked to explain why he feels close to his friends, he states, "If I'm having problems at home, they'll like counsel me, I just trust them with anything, like deep secrets, anything." When Jerome is asked to describe his best friend he says: "He's like a brother, I could tell him anything, anything. If I ask him to keep it a secret, he will keep it a secret. If he tells me something, he tells me not to tell nobody. I keep it a secret. If I need him, I know he's going to be there." Expressing or wanting to express "deep depth secrets" and "private stuff" with best friends was a core theme in the boys' and girls' interviews (Way, 2011; Way et al., 2006).

Ethnic differences in friendship quality have also been reported, suggesting that socialization patterns related to ethnicity, as well as to gender, shape the quality of adolescent friendships. Jones et al. (1994), for example, explored friendship quality among Mexican-American, African-American, and European American sixth and ninth graders and found that African-American males were more likely to reveal their personal thoughts and feelings in their male friendships than were Mexican-American and European-American boys. Furthermore, significant gender differences in levels of self-disclosure in their same-sex friendships were apparent only among European-American adolescents: European-American girls were more likely to reveal their personal thoughts and feelings to their friends than were European-American boys. Similarly, in their study of black and white, socioeconomically diverse, middle school children, DuBois and Hirsch (1990) found that white girls reported having significantly more supportive friendships than white boys. No gender differences were detected among black youth. Black boys also were more likely to report having intimate conversations with their best friends than were white boys; no differences were found between black and white girls. These findings suggest that the gender socialization of white boys may be more rigid with respect to allowing for intimate same-sex friendships than such socialization among black boys. It remains unclear, however, what the processes of these socialization patterns are or if and how these patterns vary across other ethnicities and social classes.

Our research has also indicated ethnic differences with black and Latino adolescents reporting higher levels of friendship support than Asian-American adolescents (Way & Chen, 2000; Way & Greene, 2006). Kao and Joyner (2004) find that the frequency of friendship activities may be tied to friendship intimacy or support. In a quantitative analysis of a nationally representative sample of white, black, Latino, and Asian-American adolescents in grades 7–12, they find that Asian-American and Latino adolescents took part in fewer activities with their friends than did white adolescents. These findings may explain, at least in part, the ethnic differences in reports of friendship support. Our research with 700 adolescents in China finds that levels of friendship support are similar to the black, white, and Latino adolescents in our American samples but are significantly higher than the Chinese-Americans in these samples (Jia et al., 2009). The findings that Chinese adolescents are reporting higher levels of friendship support than the Chinese-American adolescents (who were exclusively children of immigrants) suggest that immigration may shift the experience of friendships. Parents who immigrate to foster the education of their children, such as the parents in many Chinese-American families, may discourage friendships for their children more than American-born parents or Chinese parents who remain in China (Way & Chen 2000). Thus the levels of friendship support among the children of these immigrants may be less than the levels of support found among the children of nonimmigrant families.

Changes in Friendship Quality during Adolescence

Most researchers who examine age-related changes in the perceived quality of friendship focus on the changes that occur from childhood to early or middle adolescence (Berndt, 2004; Furman & Buhrmester, 1992). As adolescents grow older and become more closely attached to their friends, it is also likely, however, that changes continue to occur from early to late adolescence as well (Hartup, 1993). The research that does explore changes in friendship quality during adolescence, which is primarily cross-sectional and includes only white middle-class participants, finds that perceptions of friendship support do indeed increase during adolescence (Furman & Buhrmester, 1992). Additionally, studies also find that gender differences in friendship support that surface between boys and girls during early adolescence become less differentiated as boys and girls mature (Furman & Buhrmester, 1992; Way & Greene, 2006).

In our research, we have used growth curve analysis to investigate individual trajectories of change in the perception of the quality of general and closest same-sex friendships during adolescence (Way & Greene, 2006). Our longitudinal analyses revealed an improvement in friendship quality from early to late adolescence. Such findings fall in line with existing theory suggesting that young people become increasingly capable of developing mutually supportive and satisfying friendships as they become more self-aware, cognitively skilled, and confident in their identities (McCarthy & Hoge, 1982). Our analyses also suggest no ethnic differences in the trajectories of friendship quality; perceptions of friendship quality improved at a similar rate for black, white, Latino, and Asian American adolescents. Gender differences did emerge, however, in the trajectories of friendship quality over time. Consistent with findings from past longitudinal research with mainly white participants (e.g., Rice & Mulkeen, 1995), we found that boys reported increases in friendship quality with their closest same-sex friends at a sharper rate than girls. So whereas girls and boys demonstrate significant differences in friendship quality during early adolescence, by age 16, the mean levels of friendship quality show no gender differences (Way & Greene, 2006).

Strikingly, however, our qualitative data with adolescent boys, in particular, have suggested a very different story than our quantitative data. In our qualitative data, we have found that while boys, across ethnic/racial groups, have emotionally intimate friendships with other boys during early and middle adolescence in which the emphasis is on "shared secrets," they gradually begin to lose these friendships as they grow older (Way, 2011). When asked to describe how his friendships have changed during high school, one boy in our study said in his senior year: "I don't know, maybe, not a lot, but I guess that best friends become close friends. So that's basically the only thing that changed. It's like best friends become close friends, close friends become general friends and then general friends become acquaintances. So they just. . . If there's distance whether it's, I don't know, natural or whatever. You can say that but it just happens that way." Responses such as this one was typical of our participants. Asked the same question, another boy, also in his senior year, said: "Like my friendship with my best friend is fading, but I'm saying it's still there but. . . So I mean, it's still there 'cause we still do stuff together, but only once in a while. It's sad 'cause he lives only one block away from me and I get to do stuff with him less than I get to do stuff with people who are way further so I'm like, yo. . . . It's like a DJ used his cross fader and started fading it slowly and slowly and now I'm like halfway through the crossfade." A third boy indicated in his senior year: "We used to be like close, as far as always being around each other, now it's just like we're apart, like as far as—like if I need them, they'll still be there. If they need me, I'll be there but as far as like always being together, we're not as close as we were before." Boys by their senior years, not only indicated that they were losing their closest friends, they also began to use phrases like "no homo" whenever they referred to anything remotely intimate in their friendships. Hector said, in his senior year, "I like to spend time with my boy Omar, no homo." The use of this phrase, heard repeatedly among the boys during late adolescence, suggests that the loss of close friendships is due, at least in part, to the increased pressure to act like a stereotypic man (i.e., heterosexual). This phrase, in other words, reveals the macrocontext of conventions of masculinity and the implicit homophobia that is a part of it. Yet remarkably the boys in our studies continued to express desire for intimacy with other boys and spoke about wanting to find close male friends with whom they can "share everything." This pattern, along with the prevalence of "no homo" in the interviews of boys, suggest that the macrocontext of masculinity constrains boys from having the types of friendships that they want.

The reason that the patterns in our qualitative data with boys are different from what was indicated in our quantitative data is unclear. It may be that as boys grow older in a culture that discourages same-sex friendships among boys especially as they reach manhood, their standards of "closeness" with other boys diminishes so that what was once considered a moderately close friendship is perceived during late adolescence as a very close friendship. Our semi-structured interviews, however, were able to detect a story beneath this story. While boys may report on a survey that they have close friendships during late adolescence, when interviewed about these relationships, they reveal their sense of loss and desire for more intimate friendships. Additional research is needed to more adequately explore these differences in patterns detected across methods.

THE FAMILY CONTEXT

Parental Support

Research on the links between the quality of relationships with family members and with peers has been based primarily on attachment and/or social support theories (Updegraff et al., 2001) and typically has found the quality of family relationships to be positively associated with the quality of friendships (Kerns & Stevens, 1996; Procidano & Smith, 1997). According to attachment theorists, children internalize their parents' responsiveness toward them in the form of internal working models of the self (Ainsworth & Bowlby, 1991). These internal working models in turn influence nonfamilial relationships, as children provided with security, warmth, and trust are more likely than others to seek out and experience similar qualities in their relationships with their peers (Armsden & Greenberg, 1987;

Kerns & Stevens, 1996). Attachment theorists also emphasize the enduring and stable nature of attachment styles, showing significant associations between current parent attachment and peer relationships (Armsden & Greenberg, 1987; Cauce, Mason, Gonzalez, Hiraga, & Liu, 1996). In a similar vein, social support theorists maintain that a positive association exists between adolescents' perceived support from families and from friends (Procidano & Smith, 1997).

Although the majority of attachment and social support-based research has been focused on white adolescents, a few studies have examined the links between parent–child closeness and adolescent friendships among racial/ethnic minority youth as well (see Cote, 1997; Updegraff et al., 2001) and have found that the association between parent and peer relationships varies as a function of race/ ethnicity and gender. For example, using a sample of adolescents from Latino and European-American families, Updegraff and her colleagues (2002) examined adolescents' experiences with their mothers, fathers, and best friends and found both mother and father acceptance to be significantly linked to friendship intimacy among European-American adolescents. For Latino adolescents, however, only mother acceptance was related to friendship intimacy.

Similar to Updegraff and her colleagues (2002), our longitudinal analyses, of our survey data, showed that over a 1-year period, father support was unrelated to friendship support among Latino, black, and Asian-American adolescents. Perceived support from mothers at time 1, however, was significantly associated with change over time in the quality of friendship support across ethnic/racial groups (Way & Pahl, 2001). We have found a comparable pattern in our qualitative data with those adolescents who report having emotionally intimate and self-disclosing relationships with their mothers being more likely to report similar relationships with their best friends when compared to their peers who reported being less close to their mothers (Way, 1998, 2011). Strikingly, though, our survey data have indicated that adolescents who reported the least amount of support from their mothers at time 1 showed the sharpest increases over time in reported levels of support from friends from grade 9 to 12. Although we might interpret such findings as a "ceiling effect" (i.e., those adolescents who reported initial high scores have less room to grow over time than those who initially reported low scores), the analysis indicated that there was no concurrent association between mother and friendship support. In other words, adolescents who reported the lowest mother support at Time 1 were not necessarily the same adolescents who reported the lowest levels of friendship support at Time 1. Our findings, thus, suggest a compensatory rather than a "ceiling" effect. Namely, adolescents appear to be seeking out support from their friends to compensate for a lack of support in their relationships with their mothers.

Growth curve analyses, of our survey data, examining the dynamic associations between perceptions of family support and friendship support over a 5-year period show that improvements over time in reports of family support are significantly associated with improvements over time in reports of friendship support (Way & Greene, 2006). In addition, similar to what we found in our analysis of two waves of data (Way & Pahl, 2001), adolescents who reported lower mean levels of family support (average over time) experienced sharper improvements in friendship quality over a 5-year period than those adolescents with higher mean levels of family support (Way & Greene, 2006). These associations were robust across grade and ethnicity. In sum, our longitudinal analyses of our survey and interview data have provided evidence for both attachment-like and compensatory-like patterns between family (particularly mothers) and friendship support.

Parental Practices and Attitudes

In addition to studies examining the association between the quality of family support and peer relationships, a growing body of research based on social learning theories has examined the links between adolescent friendships and parental attitudes and practices regarding friendships. According to social learning theorists, children acquire the requisite skills for friendships through modeling and observational learning (Mischel, 1966). Such research has examined primarily how parental monitoring at home influences the characteristics of peer relationships (Brown, Mounts, Lamborn, & Steinberg, 1993). The degree of parental monitoring has also been related to friendship development, with the two extremes of monitoring—excessively high and excessively low—being shown to interfere with children's abilities to establish friendships (Patterson & Southamer-Loeber, 1984). In addition, our survey data have found that those adolescents who report having parents who know their children's whereabouts and what they are doing after school and on the weekends are more likely to have supportive friendships than those who do not report having such parents (Rosenbaum, 2000).

Parental guidance, or the degree to which parents directly assist adolescents with making friends, has also been examined. Vernberg and colleagues (1993), for example, documented various strategies used by parents to help their seventh- and eighth-grade children develop friendships after moving to a new school district, such as meeting with other parents, facilitating proximity to peers, talking with their adolescent children about peer relationships, and encouraging their children to participate in activities with other adolescents. In a study of Latino and European-American adolescents and their parents, Updegraff and colleagues (2001) reported that parents—mothers in particular—often got to know and spent time with their children's friends as a way to influence these relationships. Mounts (2002, 2004) also has described various strategies parents use to influence their adolescents' friendships, such as guiding, prohibiting, and supporting.

Our studies have, in addition, indicated that parental rules and attitudes regarding their adolescents' friends are related to friendship quality. In a concurrent analysis of our questionnaire data, we found that those adolescents who perceived themselves as having parents whose attitudes toward friendships included more encouragement (e.g., "my parents think it is important have to have friends") or rules (e.g., "my parents allow me to spend time with my friends during the weekend or after school") reported having more supportive close friendships. Indeed, parenting rules and attitudes about friendships emerged as the only significant family-level predictor of closest same-sex friendship quality when included in a hierarchical regression model with adolescents' perceptions of family support and parental monitoring also included as independent predictors (Rosenbaum, 2000). In a prospective analysis, we found that parental attitudes about friendships predicted change over time in perceived close friendship quality. Adolescents who perceived their parents to have increasingly positive attitudes about friendships over time also reported having increasingly supportive close friendships (Way & Greene, 2005). Our concurrent and prospective analyses suggest that in addition to family support, parental, guidance, attitudes, and rules pertaining to friendships are critical correlates of adolescents' perceptions of the quality of their close friendships.

Our qualitative data, furthermore, suggest ethnic differences in parents' attitudes about friendships. Black and Asian American adolescents, according to the analyses of their interviews, perceive their parents to be particularly wary of non-familial friendships (Way, 1998; Way & Greene, 2005; Way & Pahl, 1999). For example, Michael, an Asian-American adolescent, says: "My mom doesn't think friends are important because they may betray you or something; they can have a bad influence on you." Like Michael, other black and Asian-American adolescents indicated that their parents, grandparents, cousins, aunts, and uncles warned them repeatedly of the possibility of being betrayed by nonfamilial friends. Previous research has suggested that many families from low-income and/or ethnic minority backgrounds maintain belief systems—due to a history of discrimination and oppression—that indicate that those who are not part of the immediate or extended family should not be trusted (Salguero & McCusker, 1996; Way, 1998). Thus, although parental attitudes and practices about friendships may influence the quality of friendships of adolescents in similar ways across ethnic/racial groups, the particular attitudes that parents have about friendships may vary.

THE SCHOOL CONTEXT

In addition to parental influences, researchers have emphasized the significance of the school environment in studies of contextual-level influences on adolescent development (Epstein & Karweit, 1983; Kuperminc, Leadbeater, Emmons, & Blatt, 1997; Roeser & Eccles, 1998). Perceptions of the school climate, or the quality of interactions and feelings of trust, respect, and support that exist within the school community, have been found to influence students' self-esteem, psychological adjustment, level of anxiety, problem behavior, academic self-concept (Kuperminc et al., 1997; Roeser & Eccles, 1998), and school behavior (Hoge, Smit, & Hanson, 1990). Theorists argue that students who perceive the school environment as respectful, supportive, equitable, safe, and dependable will find it easier, and will be more willing to make and maintain supportive friendships with their peers, than those who perceive the school as hostile (Epstein & Karweit, 1983). Epstein and Karweit (1983) note that a school environment in which there are high levels of discrimination, low expectations, and isolation may foster academic disconnection as well as disconnection from peers and adults in the school. Although the "objective reality" of the school (e.g., number of students in the school, the ethnic diversity) is likely associated with the characteristics and quality of friendships, adolescents' perceptions of the relational (e.g., teacher/student and student/student relationships) and organizational (e.g., sense of safety in the school) climate may also have a powerful influence (Roeser & Eccles, 1998).

Whereas much research has investigated the ways in which perceptions of school climate influence adolescents' psychological and academic development (Hoge et al., 1990; Kuperminc et al., 1997; Way & Robinson, 2003), substantially less attention has been directed at exploring the ways in which adolescents' perceptions of school climate shape their social development (Eccles & Roeser, 2003). To our knowledge, save for one study (see Crosnoe et al., 2003), our work is the only research to date that has specifically examined the influence of adolescents' perceptions of the climate of their school on the quality of their friendships. This absence in the research literature is particularly striking given that most adolescents spend much of their time in school, thus making and/or maintaining many of their friendships within the school context.

Findings from our quantitative and qualitative research have shown students' perceptions of school climate (i.e., teacher/student relations, student/student relations, and order, discipline, and safety in the school) to be significantly associated with changes over time in perceptions of friendship quality even after controlling for the effects of family relationships and psychological adjustment (Way & Pahl, 2001). Moreover, growth curve analyses of our 5-year survey data demonstrated that changes in two dimensions of school climate in particular (i.e., teacher/student relations and student/student relations) are significantly associated with changes over time in adolescent perceptions of friendship quality. When students reported improvements in their relationships with their teachers and high levels of support from other students, they also reported improvements in the quality of friendships in general (Way & Greene, 2006).

Our participant observation work with adolescents in schools has suggested that the racial/ethnic dynamics of the school are strongly associated with the quality and characteristics of friendships (Rosenbloom & Way, 2004). In the urban high schools in which we have conducted our studies, black and Latino students are typically in either mainstream or special education classes whereas Asian-American students are generally overrepresented in honors classrooms. According to many of the teachers we have spoken with, these divisions are made often regardless of the actual abilities of students, with Asian-American students with very low literacy skills, even in their mother tongue, being placed in honors classes so that they can "be with their peers" (Qin, Way, & Mukherjee, 2008). Such actions not only openly and actively reinforce the model minority myth of Asian-American students, they also reinforce the stereotype that black and Latino students are not smart enough for honors classes (Tatum, 1998). Our observations suggest that the peer harassment directed at Asian-American students is provoked, at least in part, by frustration and anger among black and Latino students about the preference shown by their teachers for Asian-American students (see Rosenbloom & Way, 2004). The ethnic/racial divisions created a hostile school climate in which friendships across racial/ethnic lines were discouraged and segregation was a normal part of everyday school life.

Such a hostile relational climate in the schools also appeared to make it more difficult for students to form supportive friendships even within their own racial/ ethnic group (Way et al., 2004). Our interview data indicated, for example, that those students who reported school as being a particularly hostile place (usually based on incidents of racism and discrimination) indicated having the most contentious friendships—irrespective of the ethnicity/race of their friends. On the other hand, students who recounted more positive school experiences (e.g., good teachers) tended to describe more stable, secure, and supportive friendships (Rosenbloom, 2004). Although the direction of effect for this pattern is unclear, feeling unsupported in school was clearly associated with feeling unsupported by friends (Way et al., 2005).

IMPLICATIONS FOR UNDERSTANDING THE DEVELOPMENT OF ADOLESCENT FRIENDSHIPS

The research indicates both differences and similarities across gender and ethnicity/ race in the quality of adolescent friendships. Although gender-based stereotypes of boys and of girls reinforce the belief that boys do not value intimate friendships as much as girls, studies of ethnic minority adolescents and qualitative data more generally consistently challenge those stereotypes. Whereas boys, particularly white boys, may have less intimate friendships than girls at some point in development (researchers draw varying conclusions as to when in development gender differences in friendships are evident), that does not necessarily mean that they value intimacy or friendships less than girls. Our mixed method research consistently finds that boys *and* girls, including those from China, value close friendships with same-sex peers that involve sharing "deep secrets" and emotional closeness (Jia & Way, 2009; Way, 2011; Way et al., 2006). These findings underscore the benefits of narrative approaches that allow for an exploration of how adolescents experience their worlds. Such approaches, as seen in this chapter and in Chapter 10 in this volume by Hauser and colleagues, focus on process and thus provide a rich context for understanding the frequencies found in survey-based research.

Research also has suggested that the microcontexts of parents and schools shape the quality of adolescent friendships. The unknown component, however, is the direction of effect between these contexts and the quality of friendships. It may be that having positive and supportive friendships makes it more likely that the adolescents will experience their parents and their school climate in more positive ways. In an experimental design, social psychologists at the University of Virginia found that perceptions of task difficulty were shaped by the proximity of a friend (Schnall, Harber, Stefanucci, & Proffitt, 2008). The researchers asked college students to stand at the base of a hill while carrying a weighted backpack and estimate the steepness of the hill. Some participants stood next to close friends whom they had known a long time, some stood next to friends they had not known for long, some stood next to strangers, and the rest stood alone during the exercise. The students who stood with close friends gave significantly lower estimates of the steepness of the hill than those who stood alone, next to strangers, or to newly formed friends. The longer the close friends had known each other, the less steep the hill appeared to the students involved in the study. These findings underscore the importance of the social and emotional world to perceptions. They also point to the mechanism by which friendship quality may "predict" perceptions of school climate and parental relationships as well as vice versa.

Our research on adolescent friendships also reveals the ways in which the macrocontext—specifically the conventions of masculinity—influences the quality of friendships. As the boys in our studies become men, they increasingly speak about losing their friendships and begin to use the phrase "no homo" following any statement of intimacy about another boy. Homophobia, which lies at the heart of the conventions of masculinity, leads boys away from trusting and having emotionally intimate male friendships (Raymond, 1994). Boys know that such relationships at the age of 16 or 17 will likely be interpreted as evidence of being gay, so they give up the very relationships that they appear to want the most (see Way, 2011). As others have pointed out (see Granic, Dishion, & Hollenstein, 2003), researchers of microcontexts often forget that such contexts are embedded in macrocontexts. Thus family and school level effects are a product of macrocontexts that foster or make it more difficult for boys, in particular, to have emotionally intimate friendships.

Additional research with diverse populations will help to build a more comprehensive theory of friendship development by illuminating the ways in which friendships are experienced by adolescents and the microlevel and macrolevel factors that contribute to friendship development. Although Americans represent only 4% of the world's population, they represent 98% of what we know about human development (Arnett, 2009). Thus, exploring the other 96% of the human race will not only foster more macrolevel understanding of American adolescents, but it will also enhance our understanding of friendship development more generally. With studies of friendship development among adolescents from diverse cultures and contexts, we begin to have a richer understanding of the universal and more context-specific patterns of friendships and the ways in which we can foster these critical relationships about which Harry Stack Sullivan spoke so passionately.

Notes

1. Parts of this chapter are drawn from a previous publication. See Way, Becker, and Greene, 2006.
2. In previous publications, we have referred to both studies (The R.A.P. and The Connections project) as the R.A.P. studies.
3. All names used in this article are pseudonyms to protect the confidentiality of the participants.

References

Adler, P. A., & Adler, P. (1998). *Peer power: Preadolescent culture and identity.* New Brunswick, NJ and London: Rutgers University Press.

Ainsworth, M. D., & Bowlby, J. (1991). An ethological approach to personality. *American Psychologist, 46,* 333–341.

Armsden, G., & Greenberg, M. (1987). The Inventory of Parent and Peer Attachment: Individual differences and their relation to psychological well-being in adolescence. *Journal of Youth and Adolescence, 16,* 427–454.

Arnett, J. J. (2009). The neglected 95%, a challenge to psychology. *American Psychologist, 64*(6), 571–574.

Azmitia, M., & Cooper, C. R. (2001). Good or bad? Peer influences on Latino and European American adolescents' pathways through school. *Journal of Education for Students Placed at Risk, 6,* 45–71.

Azmitia, M., Ittel, A., & Brenk, C. (2006). Latino-heritage adolescents' friendships. In X. Chen, D. C. French, & B. H. Schneider (Eds.), *Peer relationships in cultural context* (pp. 426–451). Cambridge: Cambridge University Press.

Benner, A., Graham, S., & Mistry, R. (2008). Discerning direct and mediated effects of ecological structures and processes on adolescents' educational outcomes. *Developmental Psychology, 44,* 840–854.

Berndt, T. J. (2004). Children's friendships: Shifts over a half-century in perspectives on their development and their effects. *Merrill-Palmer Quarterly, 50*(3), 206–223.

Bowlby, J. (1969/1982). *Attachment and loss, Vol. 1: Attachment* (2nd ed.). New York: Basic Books.

Bronfenbrenner, U. (1979). *The ecology of human development: Experiments by nature and design.* Cambridge, MA: Harvard University Press.

Brown, B., Mounts, N., Lamborn, S., & Steinberg, L (1993). Parenting practices and peer group affiliation in adolescence. *Child Development, 69,* 771–791.

Brown, L., Tappan, M., Gilligan, C., Miller, B., & Argyris, D. (1989). Reading for self and moral voice: A method for interpreting narratives of real-life moral conflict and choice. In M. Packer & R. Addison (Eds.), *Entering the circle: Hermeneutic investigation in psychology* (pp. 141–164). Albany: SUNY Press.

Brown, L. M., & Gilligan, C. (1992). *Meeting at the crossroads: Women's psychology and girls' development.* Cambridge, MA: Harvard University Press.

Cauce, A. M., Mason, C., Gonzales, N., Hiraga, Y. M., & Liu, G. (1996). Social support during adolescence: Methodological and theoretical considerations. In K. Hurrelmann & S. F. Hamilton (Eds.), *Social problems and social contexts in adolescence: Perspectives across boundaries* (pp. 131–151). Hawthorne, NY: Aldine de Gruyter.

Chen, X., & French, D. (2008). Children's social competence in cultural context. *Annual Review of Psychology, 59,* 591–616.

Chen, X., French, D., & Schneider, B. (2006). Culture and peer relations. In X. Chen, D. C. French, & B. H. Schneider (Eds.), *Peer relationships in cultural context* (pp. 3–20). Cambridge: Cambridge University Press.

Coley, R. L., Morris, J. E., & Hernandez, D. (2004). Out-of-school care and problem behaviors trajectories among low-income adolescents: Individual, family and neighborhood characteristics as added risks. *Child Development, 75,* 948–965.

Cote, J. E. (1997). An empirical test of the identity capital model. *Journal of Adolescence, 20,* 577–597.

Crosnoe, R., Cavanagh, S., & Elder, G. H., Jr. (2003). Adolescent friendships as academic resources: The intersection of social relationships, social structure, and institutional context. *Sociological Perspectives, 46*, 331–352.

DuBois, D., & Hirsch, B. (1990). School and neighborhood patterns of blacks and whites in early adolescence. *Child Development, 61*, 524–536.

Eccles, J. S., & Roeser, R. W. (1999). School and community influences on human development. In M. H. Bornstein & M. E. Lamb (Eds.), *Developmental psychology: An advanced textbook* (4th ed., pp. 503–554). Mahwah, NJ: Erlbaum.

Eccles, J., & Roeser, R. (2003). Schools as developmental contexts. In G. Adams & M. Berzonsky (Eds.), *Blackwell handbook of adolescence* (pp. 129–148). Maiden, MA: Blackwell.

Eng, D. L. (2001). *Racial castration: Managing masculinity in Asian America.* Durham, NC: Duke University Press.

Epstein, J. L., & Karweit, N. (1983) *Friends in school: Patterns of selection and influence in secondary schools.* New York: Academic Press.

Furman, W. (1996). The measurement of friendship perceptions: Conceptual and methodological issues. In W. M. Bukowski, A. F. Newcomb, & W. W. Hartup (Eds.), *The company they keep: Friendships in childhood and adolescence* (pp. 41–65). Cambridge: Cambridge University Press.

Furman, W., & Buhrmester, D. (1985). Children's perceptions of the personal relationships in their social networks. *Developmental Psychology, 21*, 1016–1024.

Furman, W., & Buhrmester, D. (1992). Age and sex differences in perceptions of networks of personal relationships. *Child Development, 65*, 103–115.

Galambos, N., Berenbaum, S., & McHale, S. (2009). Gender development in adolescence. In R. Lerner & L. Steinberg (Eds.), *Handbook of adolescent psychology, Vol 1: Individual bases of adolescent development* (3rd ed.) (pp. 305–357). Hoboken, NJ: John Wiley & Sons Inc.

Garcia Coll, C., Crnic, K., Lamberty, G., Wasik, B.H., Jenkins, R., Vasquez Garcia, H., & McAdoo, H.P. (1996). An integrative model for the study of developmental competencies in minority children. *Child Development, 67*(5), 1891–1914.

Granic, I., Dishion, T. J., & Hollenstein, T. (2003). The family ecology of adolescence: A dynamic systems perspective on normative development. In G. R. Adams & M. D. Berzonsky (Eds.), *Blackwell handbook of adolescence* (pp. 60–91). Oxford, UK: Blackwell Publishing Ltd.

Gupta, T., & Sirin, S. (2010). The social development of immigrant children and their families. Paper presented at the NYU Developmental Colloquia.

Hamm, J. V., Brown, B. B., & Heck, D. J. (2005). Bridging the ethnic divide: Student and school characteristics in African American, Asian-descent, Latino, and White adolescents' cross-ethnic friend nominations. *Journal of Research on Adolescence, 15*, 21–46.

Harter, S. (1990). Self and identity development. In S. S. Feldman & G. R. Elliot (Eds.), *At the threshold: The developing adolescent* (pp. 352–387). Cambridge, MA: Harvard University Press.

Hartup, W. W. (1993). Adolescents and their friends. In B. Laursen (Ed.), *Close friendships in adolescence: New Directions for Child Development,* (pp. 3–22). San Francisco: Jossey-Bass.

Hoge, D. R., Smit, E. K., & Hanson, S. L. (1990). School experiences predicting changes in self- esteem of sixth and seventh grade students. *Journal of Educational Psychology, 82*, 117–127.

Jia, Y., Way, N., Chen, X., Yoshikawa, H., Qu, Y., Hughes, D., & Lu, Z. (2009). The influence of student perceptions of school climate on socioemotional and academic adjustment: A comparison of Chinese and American adolescents. *Child Development, 80,* 1514–1530.

Jones, D. C., Costin, S. E., & Ricard, R. J. (1994, February). *Ethnic and sex differences in best friendship characteristics among African American, Mexican American, and European American adolescents.* Paper presented at the Society for Research on Adolescence, San Diego, CA.

Kao, G., & Joyner, K. (2004). Do race and ethnicity matter among friends? Activities among interracial, interethnic, and intraethnic adolescent friends. *The Sociological Quarterly, 45*(3), 557–573.

Kerns, K. A., & Stevens, A. C. (1996). Parent-child attachment in late adolescence: Links to social relations and personality. *Journal of Youth & Adolescence, 25,* 323–342.

Kuperminc, G. P., Leadbeater, B. J., Emmons, C., & Blatt, S. J. (1997). Perceived school climate and difficulties in the social adjustment of middle school students. *Applied Developmental Science, 1,* 76–88.

Kuttler, A. F., & La Greca, A. M. (2004). Linkages among adolescent girls' romantic relationships, best friendships, and peer networks. *Journal of Adolescence, 27,* 395–414.

Ladd, G. W., & Kochenderfer, B. J. (1996). Linkages between friendship and adjustment during early school transitions. In W. M. Bukowski, A. F. Newcomb, & W. W. Hartup, (Eds.), *The company they keep: Friendship in childhood and adolescence. Cambridge studies in social and emotional development* (pp. 322–345). New York: Cambridge University Press.

Ladd, G. W., & Troop-Gordon, W. (2003). The role of chronic peer difficulties in the development of children's psychological adjustment problems. *Child Development, 74,* 1325–1348.

Levitt, M. J., Guacci-Franco, N., & Levitt, J. L. (1993). Convoys of social support in childhood and early adolescence: Structure and function. *Developmental Psychology, 29,* 811–818.

Maccoby, E. (1990). Gender and relationships: A developmental account. *American Psychologist, 45,* 513–520.

McCarthy, J. D., & Hoge, D. R. (1982). Analysis of age effects in longitudinal studies of adolescent self-esteem. *Developmental Psychology, 18,* 372–379.

Mischel, W. A. (1966). A social-learning view of sex differences in behavior. In E.E. Maccoby & R.G. D'Andrade, (Eds.), *The development of sex differences.* California: Stanford University Press.

Miles, M. B., & Huberman, A. M. (1995). *Qualitative data analysis: An expanded sourcebook of new methods* (2nd ed.). Thousand Oaks, CA: Sage.

Mounts, N. S. (2002). Parental management of adolescent peer relationships in context: The role of parenting style. *Journal of Family Psychology, 16,* 58–69.

Mounts, N. S. (2004). Adolescents' perceptions of parental management of peer relationships in an ethnically diverse sample. *Journal of Adolescent Research, 19,* 446–467.

Nangle, D. W., & Erdley, C. A. (Eds.) (2001). *New directions for child and adolescent development: The role of friendship in psychological adjustment.* San Francisco: Jossey-Bass.

Pelkonen, M., Marttunen, M., & Aro, H. (2003). Risk for depression: A 6-year follow-up of Finnish adolescents. *Journal of Affective Disorders, 77,* 41–51.

Procidano, M., & Heller, K. (1983). Measure of perceived social support from friends and family. *American Journal of Psychology, 11,* 1–24.

Procidano, M. E., & Smith, W. W. (1997). Assessing perceived social support: The importance of context. In G. R. Pierce, B. Lakey, I. G. Sarason, & B. R. Sarason (Eds.), *Sourcebook of social support and personality* (pp. 93–106). New York: Plenum Press.

Qin, D., Way, N., & Muhkerjee, P. (2008). The other side of the model minority story: The familial and peer challenges faced by Chinese American adolescents. *Youth & Society, 39,* 480–506.

Radmacher, K., & Azmitia, M. (2006). Are there gendered pathways to intimacy in early adolescents' and emerging adults' friendships? *Journal of Adolescent Research, 21,* 415–448.

Raymond, D. (1994). Homophobia, identity, and the meanings of desire: Reflections on the cultural construction of gay and lesbian adolescent sexuality. In J. M. Irvine (Ed.), *Sexual cultures and the construction of adolescent identities* (pp. 115–145). Philadelphia: Temple University Press.

Rice, K., & Mulkeen, P. (1995). *Relationships with parents and peers: A longitudinal study of adolescent intimacy. Journal of Adolescent Research, 10,* 338–357.

Roeser, R., & Eccles, J. (1998). Adolescents' perceptions of middle-school: Relation to longitudinal changes in academic and psychological adjustment. *Journal of Research on Adolescence, 8,* 123–158.

Rogosa, D. R., & Willett, J. B. (1985). Understanding correlates of change by modeling individual differences in growth. *Psychometrika, 50,* 203–228.

Rosenbaum, G. (2000). *An investigation of the ecological factors associated with friendship quality in urban, low-income, racial and ethnic minority adolescents.* Unpublished doctoral dissertation, New York University.

Rosenbloom, S. R., & Way, N. (2004). Experiences of discrimination among African American, Asian American, and Latino adolescents in an urban high school. *Youth and Society, 35,* 420–451.

Rubin, K. H., Bukowski, W. M., & Laursen, B. (Eds.) (2009). *Handbook of peer interactions, relationships, and groups.* New York: Guilford Press.

Salguero, C., & McCusker, W. (1996). Symptom expression in innercity Latinas: Psychopathology or help seeking? In B. J. Leadbeater & N. Way (Eds.), *Urban girls: Resisting stereotypes, creating identities* (pp. 328–336). New York: New York University Press.

Schnall, S. S., Harber, K. D., Stefanucci, J. K., & Proffitt, D. R. (2008). Social support and the perception of geographical slant. *Journal of Experimental Social Psychology, 44,* 1246–1255.

Seidman, E. (1991). Growing up the hard way: Pathways of urban adolescents. *American Journal of Community Psychology, 19,* 169–205.

Sippola, L. K. (1999). Getting to know the "other": The characteristics and developmental significance of other-sex relationships in adolescence. *Journal of Youth and Adolescence, 28,* 407–418.

Sullivan, H. S. (1953). *The interpersonal theory of psychiatry.* New York: Norton.

Tatum, B. (1998). *Why are all the black kids sitting together in the cafeteria?* New York: Norton.

Updegraff, K., McHale, S., Crouter, A., & Kupanoff, K. (2001). Parents involvement in adolescents' peer relationships: A comparison of mothers' and fathers' roles. *Journal of Marriage & the Family, 63,* 655–668.

Updegraff, K. A., Madden-Derdich, D. A., Estrada, A. U., Sales, L. J., & Leonard, S. A. (2002). Young adolescents' experiences with parents and friends: Exploring the connections. *Family Relations: Journal of Applied Family & Child Studies, 51,* 72–80.

U.S. Census Bureau. (2004).

U.S. Census Bureau. (2007).

Vernberg, E. M., Beery, S. H., Ewell, K. K., & Abwender, D. A. (1993). Parents' use of friendship facilitation strategies and the formation of friendships in early adolescence: A prospective study. *Journal of Family Psychology, 7,* 356–369.

Way, N. (1996). Between experiences of betrayal and desire: Close friendships among urban adolescents. In B. J. Leadbeater & N. Way (Eds.), *Urban girls: Resisting stereotypes, creating identities* (pp. 173–193). New York: New York University Press.

Way, N. (1998). *Everyday courage: The lives and stories of urban teenagers.* New York: New York University Press.

Way, N. (2011). *Deep secrets: Boys' friendships and the crisis of connection.* Cambridge, MA: Harvard University Press.

Way, N., Becker, B. E., & Greene, M. L. (2006). Friendships among black, Latino, and Asian American adolescents in an urban context. In L. Balter & C. S. Tamis-LeMonda (Eds.), *Child psychology: A handbook of contemporary issues* (2nd ed.) (pp. 415–443). New York and Hove, East Sussex: Psychology Press.

Way, N., & Chen, L. (2000). Close and general friendships among African American, Latino, and Asian American adolescents from low-income families. *Journal of Adolescent Research, 15,* 274–301.

Way, N., & Chu, J. Y. (Eds.). (2004). *Adolescent boys: Exploring Diverse cultures of boyhood.* New York: New York University Press.

Way, N., Cowal, K., Gingold, R., Pahl, K., & Bissessar, N. (2001). Friendship patterns among African American, Asian American, and Latino adolescents from low-income families. *Journal of Social and Personal Relationships, 18,* 29–53.

Way, N., & Greene, M.L. (2005, April). *Adolescents' Perceptions of Their Parents' Rules and Attitudes about Friendships: Ethnic Differences and Similarities.* Paper presented at the Atlanta, Georgia Society for Research on Child Development.

Way, N., & Greene, M.L. (2006). Trajectories of perceived friendship quality during adolescence: The patterns and contextual predictors. *Journal of Research on Adolescence, 16*(2), 293–320.

Way, N., & Pahl, K. (1999). Friendship patterns among urban adolescent boys: A qualitative account. In M. Kopala & L. A. Suzuki (Eds.), *Using qualitative methods in psychology* (pp. 145–161). Thousand Oaks, CA: Sage.

Way, N., & Pahl, K. (2001). Individual and contextual predictors of perceived friendship quality among ethnic minority, low-income adolescents. *Journal of Research on Adolescence, 11*(4), 325–349.

Way, N., & Robinson, M. G. (2003). A longitudinal study of the effects of family, friends, and school experiences on the psychological adjustment of ethnic minority, low-SES adolescents. *Journal of Adolescent Research, 18,* 324–326.

Weiss, R. S. (1974). The provisions of social relationships. In Z. Rubin (Ed.), *Doing unto others* (pp. 17–26). Englewood Cliffs, NJ: Prentice Hall.

Willett, J. B., Singer, J. D., & Martin, N. C. (1998). The design and analysis of longitudinal studies of development and psychopathology in context: Statistical models and methodological recommendations. *Development and Psychopathology, 10,* 395–426.

5

The Intergenerational Transmission of Adolescent Romantic Relationships

SHMUEL SHULMAN, MIRI SCHARF, AND LITAL SHACHAR-SHAPIRA

The emergence of romantic relationships and their progression over time are important and normative developmental tasks in the transition between adolescence and young adulthood (Zimmer-Gembeck, 2002). Adolescence also marks the emergence of, and experimentation with, sexual behaviors (Furman & Shaffer, 2003) that are integrated into romantic relationships throughout adolescence. Though adolescent romantic relationships are mainly described and understood as intraindividual and peer-based phenomena (Brown, 1999), they cannot be disconnected from processes and changes within the arena of parent–child relationships (Gray & Steinberg, 1999). Increasingly independent adolescent behavior and emerging sexual interest and activity require parents to change their perceptions of their children, while also raising concerns about their own mid-life challenges. Adolescents' dating, educational choices, and achievements may trigger parents to make comparisons between themselves and their children, and may intensify doubts about themselves as individuals and as parents (Steinberg & Silk, 2002).

This chapter examines how parents' own romantic experiences as adolescents serve as models for the way they address their adolescent offspring's romance and sexuality and how this, in turn, shapes adolescent romantic behavior. In particular, emerging adolescent romantic interests and activities can reawaken parents' own relationship difficulties and doubts from the past and set the stage for their current parenting. These linkages are examined within a broader conceptual framework, influenced by attachment and psychoanalytic perspectives, that attempts to understand the dynamics of intergenerational transmission of parenting.

We first present recent understandings of adolescent romance and sexuality and review their impact on parent–child relationships. Second, the issue of inter-generational transmission of parenting will be discussed as it is pertinent to the ways parents deal with their adolescent's emerging romance and sexuality. Finally, excerpts from in-depth interviews with 72 adolescent females and their mothers will be used to demonstrate the powerful grip of parents' past experiences as adolescents on their current parenting and, in turn, on the nature of romantic relationships of their own adolescents. In addition, we discuss the conditions that facilitate more coherent reflection of the past by parents, which in turn can pave the way to a more positive impact of their past experiences on their parenting and their adolescents.

ADOLESCENT ROMANTIC RELATIONSHIPS AND SEXUAL INVOLVEMENT: A NORMATIVE BUT STRESSFUL EXPERIENCE

Romantic relationships are normative and salient during adolescence. By the age of 18 more than 70% of adolescents report having had a romantic relationship in the preceding 18 months (Carver, Joyner, & Udry, 2003). Empirical studies have demonstrated that the mean duration of relationships among 17 and 18 year olds may be 12 months or more (Carver et al., 2003; Shulman & Scharf, 2000), suggesting that by late adolescence a substantial number of adolescents have attained the capability of becoming involved in steady romantic relationships. These stable relationships are deep and intimate, accompanied by expressions of strong feelings, and are emotionally rewarding for both partners. It is important to recognize that romantic relationships and sexual attraction and desire often are experienced in concert (Furman & Shaffer, 2003), which can further explain their elevated emotionality and their increasing importance.

Despite the fact that involvement in romantic relationships is a normative part of adolescent development, there is some evidence that adolescent involvements in dating relationships and sexual behavior are associated with increased depressive symptoms, especially among females (Joyner & Udry, 2000). Research has documented that dating early (Neeman, Hubbard, & Masten, 1995) or being more involved in casual dating (Davies & Windle, 2000) can become a source of stress and be associated with problem behaviors. However, even normative dating can be stressful considering the difficulties associated with initiations, conflicts, and break-ups (Florsheim, 2003; Joyner & Udry, 2000).

Despite the documented tendency toward the increasing involvement of adolescents in stable relationships, recent findings suggest that it is also quite common for adolescents to be sexually involved in nonromantic relationships with casual partners. Among 40% of youth, loss of virginity occurs with a nonromantic partner (Giordano, Manning, & Longmore, 2006), although engagement in a sexual liaison may, in some cases, be an attempt at establishing a romantic relationship

(Giordano et al., 2006). Regardless of the underlying motive, sexual activity may also lead to the experience of some distress.

Considered together, becoming involved in romantic relationships is an important developmental marker of adolescence, and sexual behaviors within this context can be expressions of normal, healthy exploration. However, there are romantic relationships and sexual encounters that are less integrated, more stressful, and may even cause psychological turmoil (Florsheim, 2003). Moreover, the impact of these developmentally related stressors is not limited to the adolescent. The emergence of children's romantic involvement and sexuality within the family may also become a source of stress for parents, considering its medical and psychological risks for the adolescent.

ADOLESCENT ROMANTIC RELATIONSHIPS AND SEXUAL INVOLVEMENT: THE PARENTAL PERSPECTIVE

The physical, pubertal, cognitive, and social changes that adolescents undergo present parents with new challenges. Within the psychoanalytic framework, Anna Freud (1958) described the reawakening of an incestuous tension that leads to increased distance between children and parents. Blos (1967) attributed the challenges of parenting adolescents to a distancing process in which adolescents seek increased emotional independence through rebelliousness and defiance of parental rules or expectations. Research has shown that these changes are accompanied by increased conflict between parents and postpubertal children (Laursen, Coy, & Collins, 1998). Furthermore, parents may respond to their postpubertal daughters' independence-seeking by becoming increasingly protective (Paikoff & Brooks-Gunn, 1991).

Parental stress may emerge due to child-based, as well as parent-based, concerns (Deater-Deckard, 1998). Adolescents' physical and sexual maturity may incite parents' concerns about their own bodies, physical attractiveness, sexuality and reproductive ability, as well as their own sexual experiences as adolescents (Steinberg & Steinberg, 1994). This in turn may challenge the quality of parents' relationship with their children (Greenberger & O'Neil, 1990) and result in increased strain, particularly related to sexuality and themes related to separation and individuation. For example, the interaction between a daughter's menarcheal timing and her mother's reproductive status has been associated with eating problems in both mother and daughter, with daughters experiencing greater problems when they mature early and their mothers are no longer menstruating (Paikoff, Brooks-Gunn, & Carlton-Ford, 1991).

In sum, sexual development and romantic interests entail major changes for adolescents and their parents and pose new challenges for their relationships. Adolescents tend to distance themselves from parents while the peer group, close friends, and romantic partners take on greater significance in their lives. Parents face a twofold challenge: on the one hand, the increased need to protect their children while their children navigate the new territory of romance and sexuality, and on the other hand, questions, spurred by life span dilemmas, about their own achievements are raised. This combination requires parents to find their own resources, to redefine their parenthood, and adapt this to the needs of their romantically and sexually maturing adolescents. In the following section, we will discuss the concept of intergenerational transmission as a way to understand and conceptualize the means parents employ to cope with parental and personal issues in the face of the emerging romance and sexuality of their adolescents.

Intergenerational Transmission: Perspectives from Attachment Theory and Its Derivatives

The most prominent model and examination of intergenerational transmission can be found in attachment theory and its derivatives. Intergenerational transmission of attachment refers to the process through which parents' childhood experiences influence the quality of the attachment relationships developed by their children (Bowlby, 1973; Main, Kaplan, & Cassidy, 1985). Based on their experiences with caregivers, children construct mental representations termed *internal working models* (Bowlby, 1980). Models of self and other that develop from early relationship experiences influence the nature of interactions with the environment, expectations concerning availability, responsiveness and attitudes of others, as well as expectations about the self in relationships (Sroufe & Fleeson, 1986).

George and Solomon (1999) and Bretherton and her colleagues (Bretherton, Biringen, Ridgeway, Maslin, & Sherman, 1989) were among the first to show that an additional behavioral system exists, separate and unique from attachment, and is aimed at providing security and protection for the child. The *caregiving* system operates from the caregiver's point of view and is activated by the child's distress or the caregiver's perception of threat or danger to the child. Parents' past experiences with their own attachment figures influence the relationships with their children. However, it is parents' state of mind with respect to attachment, rather than the nature of past experiences, that influences parenting behaviors (Solomon & George, 2006). Activation of past experiences in a new context creates a synthesis of adults' past experiences with their own parents and their new experiences parenting their children that has the potential to lead to either repetition of past patterns or to a different set of behaviors.

Parenting an adolescent evokes parents' memories of past experiences with their own parents, as well as of their own experiences as teenagers. For example, dealing with an offspring's romantic behavior may evoke parents' memories about their own adolescent romantic experiences. It is reasonable to assume that significant past experiences and the ways an individual dealt with age-related tasks are internally represented and impact one's behavior as a parent. Crittenden, Lang, Claussen, and Partridge's (2000; Crittenden, 2006) model of Dispositional Representations (DRs) articulates ways that past experiences organize parental behavior. In Crittenden and colleagues' view, representations do not exist as mere retained static memories of past experiences, but also "dispose to action." Dispositional representations shape individuals' perception of the world and their relation thereto, and *dispose* a person to *act* in particular ways (Crittenden et al., 2000), including protectiveness toward offspring.

The central role of parents is to protect their children until they reach reproductive maturity. Parents become vigilant when they perceive their child to be in danger. However, in the midst of perceived danger, our ability to correctly assess the situation becomes limited as cognitive processing is aborted in favor of taking quick protective action (Damasio, 2003). Moreover, there are conditions in which due to parents' past similar experiences, perception of danger is exaggerated. According to Crittenden, "these ([responses] generate the neurological representation of *"the self in this context now"* (Crittenden et al., 2000, p. 392). Thus, evoked past memories affect dispositional representations and, in turn, shape parental caregiving behavior for the sake of the child's safety.

George and Solomon (1999) describe different patterns of parenting that might be employed to care for and protect children. Adaptive parenting is characterized by providing direct and flexible care that is generally positive and is based on a realistic perception of the child's needs and safety. Other patterns of parenting are also concerned with child protection but reflect skewed perceptions of the child's needs and a nonoptimal balance between the needs of the child and the needs of the parent. For example, there are parents who protect the child from a distance. They dismiss or underestimate their child's attachment needs and as a result the caregiving system is partially deactivated and represents some degree of mild rejection. In contrast, there are parents who tend to overemphasize a child's fragility and need for protection. Consequently, the parent keeps the child close and promotes dependency.

Though former experiences shape patterns of parenting, contextual conditions are also influential. Considering the innate function of parenting, which is the protection of the safety and reproduction of the next generation, it is reasonable to suggest that offspring's emerging romantic interests and sexual activity can lead to increased parental stress. Caregiving patterns that may have been expressed in milder forms during the placid years of middle childhood may intensify with the emergence of adolescent romantic interests, reflecting increased parental concern for the safety of their adolescents.

INTERGENERATIONAL TRANSMISSION: PSYCHODYNAMICALLY ORIENTED CONCEPTUALIZATIONS

Children have immense meaning for their parents. Parents may hope to perpetuate themselves through their children or fulfill dreams that have remained unrealized in their lives (Liberman, 1999). Stern (1985) described how mothers share the subjective experiences of their infants and influence these experiences in ways that correspond to the mother's internal agenda. This facilitates mothers' understanding of and empathy for their children. However, past experiences may have more pernicious influences, especially when parents have experienced traumatic events such as abuse, tyranny, or desertion (Fraiberg, Adelson, & Shapiro, 1975), and children may become the carriers of unconscious parental fears or impulses.

In his book *Separating Parents and Adolescents*, Stierlin (1981) focused specifically on intergenerational transmission in adolescence. He suggests that parents who are in their 40s may struggle with their own life-stage problems, which include whether to stay close and continue investing in the family or to start investing in their own wishes and expectations. This conflict coincides with that of their adolescent offspring, leading to a variety of interactional modes—*binding, delegating, and expelling*—that may reflect the inner conflicts of the parents more than the real needs of both generations.

The *binding* mode mainly exploits parents' dependency needs and interferes with the age-related task of adolescent individuation. By being overgratifying, the parent enhances regressive tendencies in the adolescent, whereby in fact the parent may be trying to repair his or her own past losses and deprivations. Other parents may be torn between reacting to their own wishes or the needs of the family. Through their ambivalence they may recruit their adolescent children to act out the parent's own desires. The adolescent is then *delegated* to serve parental needs, entrusted with the mission of providing the parents with experiences they missed when they were adolescents. These parents use their adolescent children as proxies to express their own unresolved conflicts and enact their past experiences. Finally, in the *expelling* mode parents are occupied with their own problems; seeing their children as obstacles in realizing their plans, they reject or neglect them.

Stierlin (1981) described how the distinctive developmental challenges of parents and adolescents might stimulate unresolved conflicts from the parent's adolescence. Sexual development and romantic involvement also play a role in the transformation that parent and child relationships undergo during adolescence (Anna Freud, 1958). Adolescent sexuality may frighten the parents when it arouses strong emotions that lead parents to question their own current and past sexuality. Moreover, these emotions may also consist of preconscious incestuous desires that parents prefer to hide (Stierlin, 1981). Even in less emotionally laden conditions, adolescent sexual development increases parental worries about the safety and well-being of their adolescents, particularly with regard to adolescent daughters.

Seeing themselves through their children can help parents to develop an empathic understanding of their children. However, when parents are still preoccupied with unresolved past experiences, the impact of the past may be carried over to the next generation in problematic ways. One of these is the process of *projective identification*, whereby unbearable experiences are projected onto the child and parents unconsciously wish their child to *reenact* their unresolved conflicts. There are instances in which parents are more preoccupied with their desire to correct their past experiences than with their own children's current and real experiences. Furthermore, parents may also be preoccupied with dilemmas related to their own mid-life issues, which may affect their parenting, particularly in sensitive domains such as separation and sexuality.

INTERGENERATIONAL TRANSMISSION: WHEN AND HOW CHANGE CAN BE EXPECTED

Attachment theories focus more on understanding the nature of caregiving, namely parenting behavior and the extent to which parental behavior protects and appropriately addresses the needs of the child. Psychoanalytic approaches emphasize the intrapsychic aspects of parenting and focus more on the way parents perceive their children as their extension or proxy (Stierlin, 1981).

The carry-over of inner working models of self and other (Sroufe & Fleeson, 1986) plays a substantial role in the way parents treat their children. Past scripts are difficult to change and are recreated in the next generation when one becomes a parent (Byng-Hall, 1995). It is common to observe individuals attempting to act in ways that are in contrast to past difficulties or intolerable experiences, as well as attempting to develop corrective scripts in their new families. However, under conditions of elevated stress, there is no time to waste on reassessment of the situation and the individual is likely to act on the basis of dispositional representations (Crittenden, 2006); thus, parents may become too protective and interfere with the child's penchant for individuation (George & Solomon, 1999).

However, despite the strong impact of past experiences there is also evidence for noncontinuity. Having experienced a difficult childhood does not necessarily lead to having an insecure state of mind or needing to reenact past experiences. Our capacity to reflect on past experiences and resolve negative feelings, or come to terms with past pain (Shabad, 1993), is the key to flexible and sensitive caregiving. Parental *reflective* functioning—that is, the parent's capacity to think reflectively about the child and their relationship—is a key factor in an adaptive caregiving (Fonagy, Gergely, Jurist, & Target, 2002; Slade, 2007). Thus, only when past scripts are open and flexible, or a parent is capable of reflecting on, or coming to terms with, painful past experiences, can more flexible and adaptive parenting be expected (Byng-Hall, 1995).

THE PRESENT STUDY

The present study represents a preliminary attempt to explore the links among parents' past romantic experiences as adolescents, their attitude and behavior toward their offspring's romantic interests and activity, and adolescents' romantic activity. Acknowledging the distinctive nature of maternal and paternal models of parenting, as well as distinctions in the parenting of sons and daughters (Shulman & Seiffge-Krenke, 1997), the current investigation focuses on the mother–daughter dyad. To gain a better understanding of this phenomenon, we present analysis of in-depth interviews with mothers and adolescent daughters with regard to mothers' past adolescent romantic experiences, and current experiences of mothers and daughters in relation to daughters' romance. Our interpretations rely on concepts from attachment theory and from the psychodynamic approaches presented above. Overall, it is our intention to highlight the diverse ways in which mothers' past experiences are related to the manner in which they parent their daughters and, in turn, play a role in daughters' romantic life.

The Sample and Procedures

The sample was composed of 72 Israeli mothers and their adolescent daughters (ages 16 to 18.5, mean age 17.17 years). Mean education level for mothers was 14 years of schooling, representing a middle-class sample. Daughters and mothers were recruited from across the country. Considering the possible impact of divorce on adolescent romantic relationships, only intact families were included in the study. The active consent of mother and daughter was required for inclusion in the study. Mothers and daughters were interviewed separately in their homes, using an adapted version of the Adolescence Experiences Interview (Scharf & Shulman, 1998) that focuses on romantic experiences. In line with the procedure used in the Adult Attachment Interview (George, Kaplan, & Main, 1985), the mothers were interviewed regarding their own romantic experiences during adolescence. They were asked to describe a significant romantic relationship and its importance to them, and to elaborate on their feelings toward the partner. If they were not involved in any romantic relationship during their adolescence, they were asked to talk about their feelings regarding not being involved in a romantic relationship. In the second part of the interview, the mothers were asked to describe their relationships with their daughters, with particular emphasis on the way they perceive and relate to their daughters' romantic activities or lack thereof. Daughters were interviewed separately in order to learn about their romantic involvements and their feelings about romance. Daughters were asked to talk about the way their mothers relate to their romantic involvements (or lack thereof). Interviews were audiotaped and then transcribed.

In the following section we provide summaries of case examples to illustrate theoretically derived patterns. These examples allow the reader to see quite vividly patterns of continuities and discontinuities between mothers' past romantic experiences as an adolescent and current representations and behavior toward their daughters.

Case Examples Highlighting Diverse Modes of Intergenerational Transmission

REPLICATION OF A FLEXIBLE SCRIPT AND ADAPTIVE PROTECTIVE BEHAVIOR

When asked about her romantic experience when she was her daughter's age, Dana, aged 43, indicated that the adolescent romantic partner she was describing was her husband. "We started dating before we were 15 years old; he was very shy and this attracted me (He is different today). He asked me out, love flourished very quickly, and it became a very strong relationship. It was, you know, adolescent love, with ups and downs. Although we had many differences, we have never separated. We could have a difference, tears; but we always part with a kiss and see you tomorrow. It never occurred to us that we would separate." Dana continued: "I remember well the age my daughter is now. I was in love, was crazy about him. When I saw him my heart would stop beating. We met a lot as we lived quite close to each other. At school I thought only of him and wrote his name millions of times in my diary. It went on. When I was 20, my mother passed away and it was natural for us to get married. But I knew all the time this would be our future."

When asked to talk about her daughter, Dana described a similar attitude toward the disagreements she sees between her daughter and her boyfriend: "Sometimes I see my daughter is stressed, is having a disagreement with her boyfriend. I almost do not say a word. *I remember myself* and I see no way to interfere. I cannot make it easier for her when she cries because of him. I can console her but no . . . this is something they have to go through. If it is a loving relationship with a future they have to go through conflicts and disagreements. It does not matter if they are young or grown up. But when you fight you should not hurt or belittle the other. We keep it in our relationship."

It is interesting to read how the mother's story is *replicated* by her 17-year-old daughter, Noa, when describing her boyfriend: "He is a very good person. One of the nicest people I have ever met. I am lucky. He is very sensitive, writes songs. Recently, I was depressed, not because of him, he tried to cheer me up. When it did not work, he became sad too. And we started to quarrel, had a difficult time. A couple of weeks ago we decided to take a break. And I became so depressed. Now it looks silly to me. I got up in the morning, thinking about him and started crying. I was afraid it was all over. But in the evening he sent me a message, was sorry, and we went to the movies and it was great. I feel that I know what love is, that I have someone very close and we are walking through life together."

As can be seen Noa, like her mother, describes a relationship that is characterized not only by love and elation, but also by an ability to accept and, above all, overcome differences and disagreements. Noa is aware of her mother's attitude: "My mother is happy for me that I have a boyfriend, last year she tried to hide that she is excited. She helps me." Interestingly, despite this perceived maternal support, Noa claims that her mother does not know everything. Thus, despite the perceived closeness and care, mother and daughter also maintain a certain level of separateness, perhaps because the mother trusts her daughter and thus encourages her autonomy.

Both mother and daughter describe their romantic relationships in terms of heightened emotionality and attraction, but also emphasize the importance of the partners' ability to resolve disagreements and become a source of support for one another (Shulman, 2003). It is evident from the mother's description that she cares about her daughter's development, but feels that the best way *to protect* her is to let her navigate through her romantic experience by herself (Crittenden, 2006). Perhaps by providing "good enough" care the mother also serves as a model for the daughter's adaptive romantic involvement. Interestingly, Noa is aware of her closeness with her mother, while at the same time she insists on her individuality.

Thus, adaptive maternal care can be provided within an atmosphere that does not interfere with the daughter developing a separate life with her partner.

ATTEMPTS FOR CORRECTION BUT IN THE FORM
OF PROTECTION FROM A DISTANCE

Rina, a 44-year-old mother, did not have any experience in a steady and serious romantic relationship during her teens. "I did not have any steady relationship before I met my husband, but I always wanted, wished for, one. Every now and then there was an 'object' on which I was focused. This was the reason for getting up in the morning, going to school; but I never had any significant relationship. I would establish contact, go out once, and lose interest." ("And how did you feel when it did not develop?") "It did not bother me. I was not depressed. I was looking for the excitement, meeting him, maybe a bit of talking and that was all." ("How do you understand that it never evolved into any relationship?") "I was very afraid of contact. I was afraid of touch. If it would evolve to touch, it would no longer interest me." ("And how did your friends, parents relate to this?") "I understand your question. It could be a reason for concern. I remember that my parents started to worry at some point. They tried to convince me to keep trying."

Later in the interview, Rina suggested that the fear of touch had passed later in life. However, in the same sentence she immediately added: "I am not sure that it really passed. I am not sure it would not be the same if I were in the same situation today. It is your nature. Luckily for me that I did not get low and depressed then. Everything was ordinary, fine."

It was quite difficult to interview Rina, in particular when asking her about her current understanding of her past behavior. We got the impression that Rina preferred to talk less and downplay her past experience revealing, to some extent, a dismissive attitude toward her past (Main et al., 1985).

This could explain Rina's attitude toward her daughter's romantic activities. On the one hand, Rina sounds supportive. On the other hand, when asked how she relates to the fact that her daughter has a boyfriend, her response sounded "diplomatic": "I am happy for her. If this suits her it is fine with me. And if it does not suit her it is also fine with me. At first I did not know who the boy was, but I was happy for her. Later on I learned that he was seven years her senior (she is 16 and he is 23), which might be a problem. But I know him, know his family; he is a nice guy. If I was against it, this would not help either. I know how much she wanted to have a boyfriend and I am happy for her. It makes no difference if he is older or younger. She will have more experiences in the future and this is what is important as at some point she might get hurt, not by this guy. I hope it will be mild, she has to learn. I hope it will not be too painful." It appears that Rina is aiming to protect her daughter from the experience of not having a boyfriend, because she believes this will have an impact on her daughter's sense of self-confidence. To achieve this she encourages her daughter to date someone older, a situation about which most other mothers would have some reservations. Despite her attempts to normalize and idealize her daughter's experiences, anxiety and negative expectations intrude on the mother's description.

Sharon, aged 16, stated that she was very happy to have a boyfriend and would break down if it was not going well. She added that they understand each other. When asked to describe her boyfriend, Sharon responds: "He knows me and knows what I love. He notices immediately when I feel bad or have a fight with my parents, and when you have a fight with your parents it is good to have somebody else with whom you can discuss issues that you do not discuss you're your parents." Sharon went on to describe how their relationship developed: "At first I did not feel that I really loved him or cared for him, but then I realized that I miss him, but still did not know what love means. After we had separated for a month I realized how much I missed him. Though my parents were supportive, I felt that they would like us to get back. Now we have quite a successful relationship. It is not that we do not have conflicts, every couple does, but they are not serious."

When asked to talk about her mother's attitude toward this relationship, Sharon described how her mother told her that knowing who the boyfriend is, she did not need to worry when she came back late. "She trusts me and him. She *never* interferes. She would *never* tell me not to go out. I can *always* rely on my mother for support and she likes my boyfriend." Sharon's accounts of her romantic experience sound appropriate though a bit idealized. She and her mother are aware of the age gap between her and her boyfriend, and, unlike her friends, do not see any possible difficulties in this relationship. Moreover, it appears that for the mother it is important that her daughter is involved in a romantic relationship, raising the possibility that Sharon serves as a proxy that might help correct for her mother's past experiences. In addition, having a daughter who is dating an older boy who is very "reliable" could help meet the mother's need for protecting her daughter though "from a distance" when more close protection might be more adequate (George & Solomon, 1999).

REENACTMENT OF PAST PAIN: LIKE MOTHER, LIKE DAUGHTER

Rachel, aged 49, describes quite a difficult experience when she was her daughter's age. She was not a popular girl but had a number of good friends and they used to go out. "Each of us had her dream about a particular boy but it did not work out. Quite often during weekends I stayed home. It was very difficult, such a feeling of despair, what to do, a feeling of dissatisfaction. *I think it still affects me today, I do not know if it is related to the message I try to convey to my daughters, good friends are important but that's not all.*" Rachel links her past difficulties to the fact that she grew up in a small place in which everybody knew everybody from early childhood and this prevented them from becoming couples. For this reason, she adds, she decided that her daughter would not study in the local high school so that she would have a better chance of meeting boys from other places.

When asked to talk about her daughter's romantic experiences, she stated that her daughter was popular at first but something changed when she became a teen. "Now she is afraid of how her friends will react if she dates somebody from school, and what will happen if it ends. I know she is giving a lot of herself and will be hurt. *I am the one who can understand her fears.* I wish she had a boyfriend despite her fears. Let me tell you, recently she had a boyfriend, five years older than her.

She was not sure how I would respond, but I did not object. I believed that it would be good for her self confidence. It is not that I was happy that he was older. She even confided to me that her friends kept asking her whether we (her parents) approve of the relationship. I thought that it was better that she went out, and that if I tried to stop her I might make the situation worse. This is good for her self confidence; going out with friends is not enough."

Dorit, 17 years old, echoing her mother's story, started the interview talking about how difficult it is not to have a boyfriend. "I need a boyfriend, but I do not want just someone so that I get what I need. I do not feel like compromising. It is better to wait than to compromise. I want a boyfriend who will spoil me, care for me; it is winter now and I feel lonely, I want somebody to hug me. It is even worse when your close friends have boyfriends and you don't. I feel as if something is wrong with me, but I am not going to compromise. If I could have a relationship now I would." When Dorit was asked whether she would elaborate on these feelings, she responded: "Hi God, do you hear me, if you are listening (laughing) I am here waiting, can you please send me a nice guy?"

Later in the interview, Dorit was asked about her mother's attitude considering that she now had a boyfriend and she responded: "I feel that my mother wants me to have a boyfriend. She would prefer that he be my age rather than older. . . . My mother, so help me God, really wants me to go out, have fun, meet people. I used to tell my close friends that if my mother could, she would have pushed somebody into my bed and said go. She is very supportive in this matter. Sometimes she is very worried, not a little worried but very worried, but despite her worries she'd never stop me or not allow me to do something. Just to tell you, my last boyfriend was 21 years old. Many mothers would not allow their daughters to date somebody this age, but she trusted me and said: If he is going to make you happy that's fine. She is open but has her limits because after all I am still her little girl."

Signs of incoherence in Dorit's story became more evident as the interview progressed. "The truth is that I do not know if she . . . (giggles). I do not think she feels bad that I do not have a boyfriend because once you have a boyfriend there are more worries. . . . But I think that she does want me to have somebody. She always asks what about this guy, that guy? Why he is not, and I say mum we are only friends. So sometimes she confuses me; on the one hand pushing me and on the other questioning, maybe not this one. But I know she does it out of love and because she *cares* for me."

Reading both interviews gives the impression that both mother and daughter describe painful experiences. Moreover, the way the mother recounts her story and the way she behaves toward her daughter raise the possibility that she still mourns her "lost" years (Shabad, 1993). To overcome her pain, Rachel is active in her efforts to write a different script for her daughter and to lead her daughter to assume a different role. She enrolled her daughter in a different school and she supported her dating an older man. Moreover, Dorit has the feeling that her mother is even willing to push somebody into her bed. It appears that Dorit is *delegated* in some ways to serve her mother's needs (Stierlin, 1981). The incoherent manner of parts of Dorit's narrative mirrors her confusion and her questioning of whether her mother protects her appropriately.

INCREASED PROTECTION AS A RESULT OF REPLICATING A DIFFICULT PAST ROMANTIC EXPERIENCE

When asked to tell about her romantic experiences when she was her daughter's age, Hadas responded: "I started a romantic relationship early, I have been with my husband since I was 15 years old." She went on to say that she was a shy girl, not somebody confident with friends who went out during weekends. "I met him when I was a ninth grader and we are the only ones who got married. It was common among my classmates to go out but I was not allowed to. I had to return home before 12, after 12 was dangerous. If I returned a minute later, it was like the end of the world. I was at school and he used to show up on his motorcycle. For whole days he would be around disturbing me at school. And once we started dating my studies deteriorated. Luckily I was later able to do something with myself."

The impression given was that Hadas was more interested in discussing her present life; so she was asked if she could talk about her relationship at that time and how she felt about having a boyfriend during those years. "I did not feel anything special. I did not show off that I had a boyfriend. I was very shy ... nowadays on the phone they (girls) tell each other we kissed, we . . . Nobody knew if we kissed. Let me tell you, it was childish love not a mature love. *You cannot consider it love.* I do not know that if I had met him at the age of 20, 25 I would have married him. It was childish love. You are not smart enough to understand what is not good for you. Therefore today *I tell my daughter not to get married.* And *when I see my girls, I do not believe that I was a girl like they are,* and even younger and made this decision. I do not understand, but you cannot turn the clock back."

When asked to explain how the relationship evolved into marriage, Hadas responded: "Do not understand me incorrectly. He was as naïve as I was. I believe that it was his first love, like mine. I was not allowed to go out, even not with friends. I had to stay home. And when I turned 18 I realized that he could go out and I had to stay home. And then I said stop, either we marry or separate, and he agreed. Maybe I am to blame."

Tzipi, 17 years old, reported that she had been in a relationship in recent months. "I had a boyfriend; I was with him for four months. Before we officially became a couple we knew that he was supposed to go abroad. So he had to leave and we fell in love and it was very difficult for him to leave. And it was difficult for me to leave him too. At the airport we were talking about how we did not have enough time together, and we decided that we would have to separate. But three days later he called saying that he loves me so much and misses me a lot. So it went on, e-mails, phone calls twice a week. Half a year passed and recently I started thinking about how to define myself (my romantic status). I am not sure whether he is faithful but I do not care; what's most important is that he loves me. I remember what kind of person he is, he gave me a different perspective on life."

As she continued, Tzipi's complex view of her relationship became even clearer. This was her first serious relationship and though she idealized her boyfriend, she was also confused. However, Tzipi was also realistic and told the interviewer that based on the fact that she had not had a boyfriend before, she knows she should live on her own, go out with friends, and enjoy parties. "I loved him, it was a great time, but now life carries on as it was in the past."

The mother's resentment of her own past adolescent romantic experience is replicated in her attitude toward Tzipi's current romantic involvement. "I will be open. To say the least, I am not satisfied with her boyfriend, and I will explain exactly why. *I see it as similar to my own mistake.* I do not think that it is right. He came and told her that he had decided to travel. I should have told him to stay with her . . . if you want to travel, that's fine, but leave and take your own way. When a guy goes out with a girl for four months, without having sex with her, that's fine. But then he leaves for six months, corresponds via the Internet, and tells her that he is going to come back but does not know for how long he will stay. He told her he would stay till she finished her finals and then they would leave together. I do not like the way he manages her life. I think a girl like her, good looking, full of life . . . *maybe she is like me but I was quite like a fish and she is pepper, I do not want somebody to take it from her*—should rather lead her own life, show she is the stronger one and not show that she is waiting. Why wait? I waited like a dummy, nobody appreciates it. *Why should she make the same mistake I did* . . . . From my point of view *I do not want them (my girls) to be like me.* I want them to understand that you have to show the man that you have your own life, he should run after you and not you after him . . . *why should she get a kick in the pants for the rest of your life* (as Hadas feels about herself). I also don't think that it is smart that she had sex with him when he returned. Why? It is stupid. Why should the first time be with someone who was a mistake? Yes, you may not know, but why not wait? You can wait a couple of months and see if the love still is as it was, but why not wait . . . you can go with your heart and later tell yourself you made a mistake. I am not old fashioned, I do not say don't have sex. But you do not have to do it right away after you have not seen him for a period of time. I am not sure that he is a saint. Why not try to meet someone else while he was away?"

Hadas' story demonstrates her projection of her own past experience onto her daughter (Stierlin, 1981). Despite the differences between their two stories, there are threads of similarities. In particular, the mother calls attention to a similar main theme of the woman being exploited by the man (that is her personal theme). Generally parents are not fully aware of the replicate script in which they are involved, but in this case the mother is aware of her past, struggles with it in her marital life, and becomes very emotional once she is afraid that her daughter is replicating her romantic history (Byng-Hall, 1995). Reading Tzipi's interview suggests that the main theme of her relationship is quite similar to that of her mother. As for the mother, she is so overwhelmed by her past that she is unable to examine whether her daughter sees matters differently. Under these circumstances, when the mother perceives her daughter in immediate danger, she is completely mobilized to protect her daughter from dangerous outcomes and from repeating the mother's personal agony (George & Solomon, 1999). The mother's behavior demonstrates close protection, with intense involvement, resulting from her own past and current difficulties and from not acknowledging the differences between herself and her daughter. Thus, not surprisingly, through her close protection, her intervention is not effective and does not help her daughter.

CENTRAL ISSUES IN THE INTERGENERATIONAL TRANSMISSION OF ADOLESCENT ROMANTIC EXPERIENCES

Theoretical conceptualizations, as well as research findings, have suggested that the romantic and sexual development of adolescents poses new challenges for both parent and child (Freud, 1958; Paikoff et al., 1991; Steinberg & Steinberg, 1994). In addition, the adolescent's sexual development raises parents' concerns about their own lives, sexuality, and way of parenting (Deater-Deckard, 1998). As seen in the cases presented, daughters' interest and involvement in romantic relationships evoked mothers' memories of their own past experiences and led mothers to draw parallels between their own past romantic experiences and their daughters' current experiences. However, despite the reactivation of past memories, different recountings and links between the two could be observed.

For mothers who report positive memories from their past, or have come to terms with their past, daughters' emerging romantic interests did not lead to preoccupation with their own adolescent romantic experiences. Their stories were coherent even when difficult memories surfaced, suggesting that a flexible script of their past has been consolidated (Byng-Hall, 1995; Pearson, Cohn, Cowan, & Cowan, 1994). However, mothers who have not resolved past conflicts described themselves as still preoccupied with their memories—"*I know it still affects me today; I see it in her and compare this with my own experience.*" Furthermore, the impression of their past experience was still vivid and they were not sure whether they would behave differently if they found themselves in the same position today. In addition, there are mothers who attribute their current misery to decisions they made at that junction of their lives. Reading the stories of these mothers creates the impression that they are still mourning the past and its consequences (Shabad, 1993). This strong link represents the intensity and closeness of the mother–daughter dyad that has been widely documented (Caplan, 1989; Chodorow, 1974). This link can be expressed in maternal empathy toward the daughter, which is adaptive, or identification with the daughter that may interfere with the latter's individuation (Jordan, 1991).

The dialectic of empathy versus identification is further evidenced in the way mothers relate to their daughters' romantic experiences. Mothers with flexible or coherent scripts are aware of the inevitable difficulties that may emerge during the development of a relationship. However, this sensitivity and empathy do not lead the mother to interfere and take an active stand. These mothers believe that their daughters need to cope with relationship difficulties in order to learn to establish a mature relationship. All that remains for the mother is to console her daughter in times of need. It was interesting to notice the way that mothers who had coped well with their own past struggles could trust their daughters' capabilities rather than interfere and attempt to manage their lives.

In contrast, the narratives of mothers who were still preoccupied with their own difficult past experiences showed intense identification with daughters. This resulted in a form of *projection* in which the mother was afraid that her daughter might replicate her past miserable experience. This could lead to two forms of behavior, one in which the mother is active in preventing her daughter from replicating her past mistake. Through a variety of measures such as playing up the daughter's need for her mother, exploiting her loyalty, or more directly by coercion of the daughter, mothers tend to *bind* their daughters (Stierlin, 1981) so that they do not make "*the same mistake I did.*" Another form is that in which the mother hopes that the daughter will correct her own difficult past. In this case the daughter is designated to serve as the mother's *proxy,* playing out the mother's unfulfilled adolescent dreams (Stierlin, 1981). Perhaps through the process of *projective identification,* the daughter in the case example presented became very eager to find a boyfriend. This was paralleled by the mother taking an active role to the extent that the daughter expressed some reservations about her mother's wishes and questioned whether the mother's expectations were appropriate.

Mothers' care for their daughters' appropriate romantic development, or concern about the daughters' vulnerability, also is an expression of maternal protective behavior (George & Solomon, 1999). Although the initial formulations of the caregiving system in attachment theory focused on mothers of young children, the need to protect offspring does not cease in adolescence, and continues at least until the stage when offspring become sexually reproductive. In fact, the emergence of sexual and romantic interests probably activates the caregiving system more strongly and, accordingly, mothers become involved and concerned about their daughters' appropriate romantic activity. Yet, as delineated in George and Solomon's (1999) description of the development of the caregiving system, maternal protective behavior is strongly associated with maternal upbringing and past. In this vein, different patterns of maternal protective behavior can be observed in the cases presented.

Accounts given by mothers with flexible scripts of their past appeared to describe strategies of providing flexible care and sympathy. First and foremost, they reflected trust in their daughters' capabilities to successfully handle the task of appropriate romantic development, despite the difficulties inherent therein. For mothers with difficult and unresolved romantic histories, their daughters' romantic relationships led to increased maternal worries and a tendency to perceive their daughters as vulnerable. The apparent result of this perception was an intensified need by the mother to protect her daughter, which could result in strict monitoring of the daughter's romantic whereabouts. These mothers had a sense that their daughters were in immediate danger and must be protected. An additional possibility resembles what George and Main (1999) described as protection from a distance. The mother encourages a relationship with a proxy, such as an older reliable boyfriend, so that she does not have to worry when her daughter is potentially unprotected (e.g., coming home late; coping with a precoscious relationship).

Interestingly, there are cases in which daughters' romantic involvement leads to an increased maternal preoccupation with mothers' own past that leaves little room for maternal protection. The mother's underlying need to correct her past through her daughter may deactivate maternal protective behavior. The desire to correct our own past experiences surpasses the need to provide care and protection, which may drive the daughter into an inappropriate romantic relationship. In our community-based, low-risk sample we did not find cases in which mothers abdicated their protective role, but this may occur in higher-risk contexts in which problematic romantic relationships and risky sexual activity among adolescents are more frequent.

Mother–daughter relationships and, in particular, reported attitudes and behaviors toward their daughter's romantic involvement were mainly understood and conceptualized with the tenets of attachment and psychodynamic theories. Incorporation of ideas presented by the life history theory (Ellis, 2004) can shed further light on the ways mothers and adolescent daughters understand and relate to romantic involvements. A central question in life history theory is: When should individuals stop converting surplus energy into growth and development, and begin converting it into reproduction? Our case examples show that although some mothers saw their daughters' romantic behavior as reflecting normative adolescent development and learning about romance, others perceived it as a step likely leading to marriage and pregnancy—reproduction. It is interesting that the less adaptive mothers were afraid that their daughters' romantic involvement could lead to "premature reproduction," which carries with it long-lasting negative impacts. In contrast, the more adaptive mothers were able to see their adolescent romance as part of adolescent growth and a gain of experience and supported it completely (Belsky, Steinberg, & Draper, 1991).

In sum, parenting adolescents and, in particular, coping with their romantic behavior can be an emotionally intense experience for parents (Steinberg & Steinberg, 1994), confronting them with the dilemma of whether their daughters are still developing or have entered the phase of reproduction that involves new demands (Ellis, 2004). It is striking how daughters' romantic activities become a mirror for mothers who see or remember themselves in the same situation. Moreover, in some cases watching their daughters becoming romantically involved, or even interested in romance, led mothers to act as if they were under similar conditions, as if they were unable to distinguish between their own and their daughters' experiences (Crittenden, 2000). This, in combination with difficult past histories, led some of these mothers to react with patterns of behavior that were not favorable either for their daughters or for themselves.

CLINICAL AND RESEARCH IMPLICATIONS

The insights gleaned from these interviews have important implications for practice and future research. Identifying parents with unresolved romantic experiences and helping them work through their difficult memories might be beneficial for them and their adolescent offspring. Intervention strategies and research suggest that teaching parents to monitor and appropriately protect their adolescents may prevent the teens from entering into risky and inadequate romantic and sexual involvements. Interestingly, these approaches suggest that this can be achieved even without parents gaining insight into their own behavior (Bakermans-Kranenburg, van IJzendoorn, & Juffer, 2003). However, despite the merits and effectiveness of such parenting interventions, it is questionable as to whether clear guidance is enough to change a parent's attitude. The conceptual framework outlined in this chapter suggests that adolescent romantic and sexual experiences are associated with the reinvoking of past parental experiences. Difficult and unresolved past experiences may lead parents to behave as if they are still involved in their own difficulties, rather than addressing their adolescent's real needs. Helping parents to reach a more integrated understanding of their own development could help them be more receptive to the experiences of their adolescents (Scharf & Shulman, 2006; Shulman, 2006).

The data presented here focused on mothers and daughters. The intensity and closeness described in our mother–daughter dyads probably reflect the distinctiveness of mother–daughter relationships (Jordan, 1991). However, the role of fathers in the development of their adolescent daughters cannot be dismissed (Shulman & Seiffge-Krenke, 1997), and fathers undoubtedly play a role in the romantic lives of their daughters, in particular, regarding issues related to daughters' sexual maturity and behavior (Tither & Ellis, 2008). In addition, it is important to learn about the role of parents in the romantic lives of adolescent boys. Research focused on other dyads in the family is thus critical. Understanding intergenerational transmission in the various dyads (e.g., father–daughter and mother–son) might extend our understanding of the mechanisms involved in persistence or change of past experiences. Research with at-risk populations and in cultures that are undergoing societal changes may shed more light on these processes. Longitudinal research following children from early adolescence to their late 20s, when romantic relationships become even more central in the lives of young people, could provide a further understanding of the dynamics of the described processes across important developmental stages.

References

Bakermans-Kranenburg, M. J., van IJzendoorn, M. H., & Juffer, F. (2003). Less is more: Meta-analyses of sensitivity and attachment interventions in early childhood. *Psychological Bulletin, 129,* 195–215.

Belsky, J., Steinberg, L. D., & Draper, P. (1991). Childhood experience, interpersonal development, and reproductive strategy: An evolutionary theory of socialization. *Child Development, 62,* 647–670.

Blos, P. (1967). The second individuation process of adolescence. *The Psychoanalytic Study of the Child, 22,* 162–186.

Bowlby, J. (1973). *Attachment and loss. Vol II. Separation and anxiety.* New York: Basic Books.

Bowlby, J. (1980). *Attachment and loss (Vol. 3): Loss*. New York: Basic Books.

Bretherton, I., Biringen, Z., Ridgeway, D., Maslin, C., & Sherman, M. (1989). Attachment: The parental perspective. *Infant Mental Health Journal, 10*, 203–221.

Brown, B. B. (1999). "You're going out with who?" Peer group influences on adolescent romantic relationships. In W. Furman, B. B. Brown, & C. Feiring (Eds.), *The development of romantic relationships in adolescence* (pp. 291–329). New York: Cambridge University Press.

Byng-Hall, J. (1995). *Rewriting family scripts: Improvisation and systems change*. New York: Guilford Press.

Caplan, P. J. (1989). *Don't blame mother: Mending the mother-daughter relationship*. New York: Harper & Row Publishers.

Carver, K., Joyner, K., & Udry, J. R. (2003). National estimates of adolescent romantic relationships. In P. Florsheim (Ed.), *Adolescent romantic relations and sexual behavior: Theory, research, and practical implications* (pp. 23–56). Mahwah, NJ: Lawrence Erlbaum Associates.

Chodorow, N. (1974). Family structure and feminine personality. In M. Z. Rosaldo & Lamphere (Eds.), *Woman, culture and society* (pp. 43–66). Stanford, CA: Stanford University Press.

Crittenden, P. M. (2006). Why do inadequate parents do what they do? In O. Mayseless (Ed.), *Parenting representations: Theory, research, and clinical applications* (pp. 388–433). New York: Cambridge University Press.

Crittenden, P. M., Lang, C., Claussen, A. H., & Partridge, M. F. (2000). Relations among mothers' procedural, semantic, and episodic internal representational models of parenting. In P. M. Crittenden & A. H. Claussen (Eds.), *The organization of attachment relationships: Maturation, culture, and context* (pp. 214–233). New York: Cambridge University Press.

Damasio, A. (2003). *Looking for Spinoza: Sorrow, and the feeling brain*. New York: Harcourt.

Davies, P. T., & Windle, M. (2000). Middle adolescents' dating pathways and psychosocial adjustment. *Merrill Palmer Quarterly, 46*, 90–118.

Deater-Deckard, K. (1998). Parenting stress and child adjustment: Some old hypotheses and new questions. *Clinical Psychology: Science and Practice, 5*, 314–332.

Ellis, B. J. (2004). Timing of pubertal maturation in girls: An integral life history approach. *Psychological Bulletin, 130*, 920–958.

Florsheim, P. (2003). Adolescent romantic and sexual behavior: What we know and where we go from here. In P. Florsheim (Ed.), *Adolescent romantic relations and sexual behavior: Theory, research, and practical implications* (pp. 371–385). Mahwah, NJ: Erlbaum.

Fonagy, P., Gergely, G., Jurist, E. E., & Target, M. (2002). *Affect regulation, mentalization, and the development of the self*. New York: Other Press.

Fraiberg, S., Adelson, E., & Shapiro, V. (1975). Ghosts in the nursery. *Journal of the American Academy and Child Psychiatry, 14*, 387–421.

Freud, A. (1958). Adolescence. *Psychoanalytic Study of the Child, 13*, 255–278.

Furman, W., & Shaffer, L. (2003). The role of romantic relationships in adolescent development. In P. Florsheim (Ed.), *Adolescent romantic relations and sexual behavior: Theory, research, and practical implications* (pp. 3–22). Mahwah, NJ: Erlbaum.

George, C., Kaplan, N., & Main, M. (1985). *An adult attachment interview*. Unpublished manuscript, University of California at Berkeley.

George, C., & Solomon, J. (1999). Attachment and caregiving: The caregiving behavioral system. In J. Cassidy & P. R. Shaver (Eds.), *Handbook of attachment: Theory, research, and clinical applications* (pp. 649–670). New York: Guilford Press.

Giordano, P. C., Manning, W. D., & Longmore, M. A. (2006). Adolescent romantic relationships: An emerging portrait of their nature and developmental significance. In A.C. Crouter & A. Booth (Eds.), *Romance and sex in adolescence and emerging adulthood* (pp. 127–150). Mahwah, NJ: Erlbaum.

Gray, M. R., & Steinberg, L. (1999). Adolescent romance and the parent-child relationship: A contextual perspective. In C. Feiring, W. Furman, & B. B. Brown (Eds.), *The development of romantic relationships in adolescence* (pp. 235–262). New York: Cambridge University Press.

Greenberger, E., & O'Neil, R. (1990). Parents' concerns about their child's development: Implications for fathers' and mothers' well-being and attitudes toward work. *Journal of Marriage and the Family, 52,* 621–635.

Jordan, J. (1991). Empathy and the mother-daughter relationship. In J. Jordan et al. (Eds.), *Women's growth and connection: Writing from the Stone Center* (pp. 28–34). New York: Guilford Press.

Joyner, K., & Udry, J. R. (2000). You don't bring me anything but down: Adolescent romance and depression. *Journal of Health and Social Behavior, 41,* 369–391.

Laursen, B., Coy, K. C., & Collins, W. A. (1998). Reconsidering changes in parent-child conflict across adolescence: A meta-analysis. *Child Development, 69,* 817–832.

Lieberman, A. F. (1999). Negative maternal attributions: Effects on toddlers' sense of self. *Psychoanalytic Inquiry, 19,* 737–756.

Main, M., Kaplan, N., & Cassidy, J. (1985). Security in infancy, childhood, and adulthood: A move to the level of representation. In I. Bretherton & E. Waters (Eds.), *Growing points of attachment theory and research. Monograph of the Society for Research in Child Development, 50,* (1–2, serial no. 209), 66–104.

Neeman, J., Hubbard, J., & Masten, A. S. (1995). The changing importance of romantic relationship involvement to competence from late childhood to late adolescence. *Development and Psychopathology, 7,* 727–750.

Paikoff, R. L., & Brooks-Gunn, J. (1991). Do parent-child relationships change during puberty? *Psychological Bulletin, 110,* 47–66.

Paikoff, R. L., Brooks-Gunn, J., & Carlton-Ford, S. (1991). Effect of reproductive status changes on family functioning and well-being of mothers and daughters. *Journal of Early Adolescence, 11,* 201–220.

Pearson, J. L., Cohn, D. A., Cowan, P. A., & Cowan, C. P. (1994). Earned- and continuous-security in adult attachment: Relation to depressive symptomatology and parenting style. *Development and Psychopathology, 6,* 359–373.

Scharf, M., & Shulman, S. (1998). *Adolescence experiences' interview.* Unpublished manuscript, University of Haifa.

Scharf, M., & Shulman, S. (2006). Intergenerational transmission of experiences in adolescence: The challenges of parenting adolescents. In O. Mayseless (Ed.), *Representations of parenting: Theory, research and clinical implications* (pp. 319–351). New York: Cambridge University Press.

Shabad, P. (1993). Repetition and incomplete mourning: The intergenerational transmission of traumatic themes. *Psychoanalytic Psychology, 10,* 61–75.

Shulman, S. (2003). Conflict and negotiation in adolescent romantic relationships. In P. Florsheim (Ed.), *Adolescent romantic relations and sexual behavior: Theory, research, and practical implications* (pp. 109–136). Mahwah, NJ: Erlbaum.

Shulman, S. (2006). Wondering" and beyond: Discussion of Arietta Slade's Reflective Parenting Programs. *Psychoanalytic Inquiry, 26,* 656–665.

Shulman, S., & Scharf, M. (2000). Adolescent romantic behaviors and perceptions: Age-related differences and links with family and peer relationships. *Journal of Research on Adolescence, 10,* 99–118.

Shulman, S., & Seiffge-Krenke, I. (1997). *Fathers and adolescents: Developmental and clinical perspectives.* Florence: Taylor & Francis/Routledge.

Slade, A. (2007). Disorganized mother, disorganized child: The mentalization of affective dysregulation and therapeutic change. In D. F. Goldsmith & D. Oppenheim (Eds.), *Attachment theory in clinical work with children bridging the gap between research and practice* (pp. 226–250). New York: Guilford Press.

Solomon, J., & George, C. (2006). Intergenerational transmission of dysregulated maternal caregiving: Mothers describe their upbringing and childrearing. In O. Mayseless (Ed.), *Parenting representations: Theory, research, and clinical implications* (pp. 265–295). New York: Cambridge University Press.

Sroufe, L. A., & Fleeson, J. (1986). Attachment and the construction of relationships. In W. Hartup & Z. Rubin (Eds.), *Relationships and development* (pp. 51–71). Hillsdale, NJ: Erlbaum.

Steinberg, L., & Silk, J. S. (2002). Parenting adolescents. In M. H. Bornstein (Ed.), *Handbook of parenting: Vol. 1: Children and parenting* (2nd ed.) (pp. 103–133). Mahwah, NJ: Lawrence Erlbaum.

Steinberg, L., & Steinberg, W. (1994). *Crossing paths: How your child's adolescence triggers your own.* New York: Simon & Schuster.

Stern, D. N. (1985). *The interpersonal world of the infant: A view from psychoanalysis and development.* New York: Basic Books.

Stierlin, H. (1981). *Separating parents and adolescents: Individuation in the family.* New York: Jason Aronson.

Tither, J. M., & Ellis, J. B. (2008). Impact of fathers' on daughters age of menarche: A genetically and environmentally controlled sibling study. *Developmental Psychology, 44,* 1409–1420.

Zimmer-Gembeck, M. J. (2002). The development of romantic relationships and adaptations in the system of peer relationships. *Journal of Adolescent Health, 31,* 216–225.

6

Autonomy with Connection

Influences of Parental Psychological Control on Mutuality in Emerging Adults' Close Relationships

**PATRICIA K. KERIG, JULIE A. SWANSON,
AND ROSE MARIE WARD**

The developmental psychopathology perspective posits that one of the primary stage-salient developmental tasks of emerging adulthood is the formation of healthy intimate relationships outside the family (Kerig & Wenar, 2006; Roisman, Masten, Coatsworth, & Tellegen, 2004). However, researchers are still trying to ascertain the specific developmental building blocks that facilitate mastery of this task, and the qualities of parent–child relationships that contribute to adaptive functioning during this transition. In this chapter, we focus on the development of the capacity for a balance of separation and connection in relationships, termed mutuality of autonomy, and investigate ways in which problems involving parent–child boundary dissolution—particularly, parental psychological control—might compromise the emergence of mutual autonomy during the transition from adolescence to adulthood.

THE DILEMMA OF AUTONOMY WITH CONNECTION

Theoretical orientations as seemingly diverse as family systems and psychoanalysis converge upon a key point, which is that one of the key tasks of human development is to balance the needs for connection and autonomy. In Salvador Minuchin's (1974) words: "Human experience of identity has two elements: a sense of belonging and a sense of being separate. The laboratory in which these ingredients are mixed and dispensed is the family, the matrix of identity" (p. 47). From an attachment theory perspective, Sroufe (1990) asserts that "The self was forged within vital relationships, within such relationships, it continues to evolve" (p. 303). By the same token, Grotevant and colleagues (1983, 1986) define identity development as a process that requires both connectedness to others and individuality of the self. Similarly, self-in-relation theory suggests that the development of the autonomous self occurs through the development of relatedness, and thus the two are intimately intertwined.

> Attachment . . . is an impulse that pushes toward a deepening awareness of the other's independent existence, the culmination of which is mutual *recognition* . . . Such recognition of the other is as much the culmination of true differentiation as is autonomy. (Benjamin, 1981, pp. 204–205)

However, as vital as the balance is between these two pulls of separateness and connection, it is not always easily achieved. Zeanah, Anders, Seifer, and Stern (1989) refer to this as the "fundamental human problem of being with others and being alone" (p. 662). One of the most well-articulated explorations of this dilemma is Bakan's (1966) philosophical treatise on the *Duality of Human Existence*. In this work, Bakan differentiated between agency—the drive toward individualism, self-assertion, and self-expansion—and communion—the tendency toward mutuality, interdependence, and the suppression of self-interest in favor of the welfare of others. Agency gives rise to competition, aggression, egocentricism, and self-validation, whereas communality inspires emotional expressiveness, sociocentrism, compromise, and an interpersonal orientation. Moreover, in Bakan's view, it is the splitting off of our agentic from our communal selves that is the cause of individual suffering and societal ills. It is imperative to mitigate agency with communion, Bakan argued, in that unmitigated agency can lead to self-serving destructiveness whereas unmodulated communality does not equip the person to meet the normative developmental challenges of childhood. The development of the person, as well as the viability of society, then, requires an integration of these two orientations. Agency must be tempered with considerations of "mutuality, interdependence, and joint welfare," whereas communality must be amended to "include aspects of agentic self-assertion and self-expression—aspects that are essential for personal integration and self-actualization" (Block, 1978, p. 515).

Mutual autonomy. More recently, Neff and Harter (2002, 2003) have offered the concept of mutual autonomy as a way of characterizing both the competencies and difficulties inherent in mastering the emerging adult's twin stage-salient tasks of individuation and connection. Mutual autonomy is defined as the attempt to "balance concerns with the self's and other's needs and feelings and to maintain both separate space and closeness in the relationship" (Neff & Harter, 2003, p. 83). Research suggests that in comparison to young adults involved in intimate relationships that are constraining of autonomy or lacking in reciprocity, those whose relationships are characterized by mutual autonomy report higher levels of both psychological health and relationship satisfaction (Neff & Harter, 2002). Relationships that are lacking in mutual autonomy can be distinguished in terms of two relational styles: those characterized predominantly by self-focused autonomy and those characterized predominantly by other-focused connection (Neff & Harter, 2002, 2003).

Self-focused autonomy. Self-focused autonomy is defined by a "greater focus on and clarity about the self's needs and feelings, a sense of separateness from one's partner, a lack of attention to relationship concerns, and dominance in decision-making" (Neff & Harter, 2002, p. 836). Research shows that young adults who are characterized by a self-focused autonomous relational style describe themselves as dominant and as having relatively more power within their intimate relationships (Neff & Harter, 2002). These defining characteristics share similarities with Horowitz, Alden, Wiggins, and Pincus' (2000) conceptualization of the interpersonal problems associated with overreliance on autonomy at the expense of connection. Those who overemphasize autonomy in their relationships with others have a tendency to behave in domineering and controlling ways and to take a stance of self-centeredness within relationships. Other characteristics of individuals who prioritize agency over connection include difficulty with perspective-taking, distrust and suspiciousness of others, a tendency to experience little concern about others' wants and needs, and a willingness to manipulate others (Horowitz et al., 2000).

Other-focused connection. In turn, the relational style of other-focused connection is described as comprising a "greater focus on and clarity about the other's needs and feelings, a sense of oneness with one's partner, preoccupation with the relationship, and subordinance in decision-making" (Neff & Harter, 2002, pp. 836–837). These defining characteristics share similarities with Horowitz and colleagues' (2000) conceptualization of the interpersonal problems experienced by individuals who overly rely on connection at the expense of autonomy. Those who overemphasize connection at the expense of autonomy tend to overaccommodate to the needs and wants of others and to sacrifice their own desires, describing themselves as excessively submissive, as easily taken advantage of, and as too forgiving and trusting (Horowitz et al., 2000). Young adults with an overly accommodating interpersonal style typically also have significant difficulty saying "no" to others, with being assertive, and with setting and maintaining boundaries in relationships (Horowitz et al., 2000). In addition, those who tend to utilize a relational style of other-focused connection have been found to describe themselves as displaying an inauthentic or false self within relationships (Neff & Harter, 2002). Jack's (1991) concept of self-silencing appears to be related to this particular characteristic of other-focused connection. The concept of self-silencing has been defined as the suppression of one's "self-expression, vitality, and perspectives" (Jack, 1991, p. 129) through outward compliance, passivity, and attempts to change one's thoughts and to adjust one's feelings to match beliefs about how one "ought" to feel. In this way, self-silencing may comprise a strategy by which emerging adults with an overly accommodating style adapt and cope in order to preserve their relationships with others.

Neff and Harter's (2003) investigations have shown that either a self-focused autonomous style or an other-focused connected style is associated with psychological distress and relationship dissatisfaction. Therefore, evidence suggests that lack of a mutually autonomous orientation at either end of the pole increases the risk that emerging adults will struggle with mastery of the key stage-salient task of developing intimate relationships. However, research to date has not yet investigated the origins of a mutually autonomous relational style. It is to a different body of literature we must turn to gather clues about the origins of relational dysfunctions in the family system.

PARENT–CHILD BOUNDARY DISSOLUTION AND LACK OF MUTUAL AUTONOMY

A clue to the origins of problems in achieving mutual autonomy is offered by Jack (1991), who proposes that one of the pathways leading to self-silencing is the childhood experience of harsh parenting. Jack suggests that children who experience harsh parenting expect negative consequences for revealing their authentic selves and therefore, as they emerge into in adulthood, they adopt the strategy of accommodating to others' perspectives in an attempt to avoid the condemnation they have come to expect. Similarly, Harter and her colleagues (1996) studied false self-behavior—defined as "acting in ways that do not reflect one's true self as a person or 'the real me'" (p. 360). Their research showed that those who experienced parental support as conditional only upon pleasing the parent were the youth who engaged in the most self-muting behavior. As Harter and colleagues (1996) suggest, lack of parental validation of one's true thoughts, feelings, and wishes may result in the development of a "socially implanted self," a false self that is vigilant to and oriented toward pleasing the other at the expense of self-assertion. Crittenden (1994) talks similarly about the development of a false self in which true expressions of feeling are subverted to the need to maintain a relationship with an invalidating or rejecting parental figure.

The literature on parent–child boundary dissolution may offer an even more refined way of understanding the processes by which maladaptive parenting undermines the child's development of a sense of autonomy within the context of connection. As Minuchin (1974) suggested, clear boundaries in the family provide its members with a sense of belonging through fostering open communication and warm connection while at the same time granting children developmentally appropriate permission for autonomy and individuality. Boundary dissolution, in contrast, interferes with healthy development through parents' failing "to acknowledge the psychological distinctiveness of the child" (Kerig, 2005, p. 8)—in other words, through a lack of mutuality of autonomy. The most well-researched form of boundary dissolution is *psychological control*, which Barber and Harmon (2002) define as "parental behaviors that are intrusive and manipulative of children's thoughts, feelings, and attachments" (p. 15) and as "parental interference in the psychological autonomy of the child" (Barber, 1992, p. 72). The psychologically controlling parent attempts to control the child's thoughts, feelings, and opinions through the use of methods such as guilt induction, withdrawal of love, and emotional abandonment. A significant body of research has emerged suggesting that psychologically controlling parenting is associated with a host of negative outcomes in childhood and adolescence (Barber, 2002; Kerig, 2005), including insecure identity (Luyckx, Soenens, Vasteenkiste, Goossens, & Berzonsky, 2007), low self-reliance (Shulman, Collins, & Dital, 1993), risky sexual behavior (Pettit, Laird,

Dodge, & Criss, 2001), and greater likelihood of involvement in peer relationships characterized by aggression and victimization (e.g., Leadbeater, Banister, Ellis, & Yeung, 2008; Morris, Silk, Steinberg, Sessa, Avanevoli, & Essex, 2002; Nelson & Crick, 2002; Olsen et al., 2002).

How might the experience of parental psychological control interfere with emerging adults' capacity to form healthy relationships with peers and romantic partners? Attachment theory (Bowlby, 1988) provides a powerful model for understanding the ways in which family of origin dynamics play a role in emerging adults' relationships with close friends and romantic partners. According to attachment theory, through their interactions with caregivers, infants develop an internal working model of relationships, or a set of beliefs and assumptions concerning the quality of care that they can expect from other people (Main, Kaplan, & Cassidy, 1985). As development continues across childhood and adolescence, this set of beliefs and assumptions, or mental representation, is believed to generalize to subsequent relationships with significant others outside of the family, thereby serving as a "cognitive map" for anticipating others' behavior as well as regulating one's own repertoire of responses (Bretherton & Munholland, 1999). In the transition to adolescence and emerging adulthood, peer and romantic relationships begin to take on the functions of attachment (Zeifman & Hazan, 2008), and youths' experiences in the family of origin are predictive of the quality of these relationships with agemates (Allen, 2008). Attachment theory also proposes that what is carried forward through development is not merely the behavior modeled by parents, but rather a model of a relationship: through their transactions with caregivers, children come to internalize both sides of the attachment dynamic (Cicchetti & Howes, 1991). As Sroufe and Fleeson (1986) put it, "Each partner 'knows' all 'parts' of the relationship and each is motivated to recreate the whole in other circumstances, however different the required roles and behavior might be" (p. 61). Thus, for example, if subjected to caregiving relationships characterized by power assertion, high degrees of control, or victimizing, children will internalize both the dominant and the subordinate roles and may enact either or both of these relational strategies in their future close relationships. In this way, then, emerging adults who have experienced the manipulative intrusion associated with parental psychological control may develop internal working models characterized by a sense of dependence and helplessness, potentially leading them to gravitate toward relationships with controlling partners who confirm these perceptions. Alternatively, emerging adults may adopt their parents' strategies as their own and model their own behavior in relationships after their parents' domineering styles. In either of these ways, whether though the development of overly accommodating or overly controlling interpersonal styles, emerging adults who have experienced psychologically controlling parenting may gravitate toward becoming involved in relationships lacking in mutual autonomy. As a consequence, youth who develop an internal working model that derives from parent–child relationships characterized by unclear boundaries may have difficulty subsequently forming healthy peer and romantic relationships in emerging adulthood.

Another construct that has utility for explaining how parent–child boundary dissolution might be linked to lack of mutual autonomy in emergent adulthood is the concept of relational aggression. Defined as "behavior that causes harm by damaging relationships or feelings of acceptance and love" (Linder, Crick, & Collins, 2002, p. 70), relational aggression includes strategies such as giving a friend or partner the silent treatment or threatening to end the relationship if the other does not comply with one's wishes (Linder et al., 2002). Although relational aggression has been studied only in the context of peer relationships, and psychological control only within the context of parent–child relationships, the resemblance between the two constructs is striking; indeed, it has recently been suggested that "relational aggression is psychological control grown up" (Kerig & Sink, 2010, pp. 207–208). In the same way that parental psychological control involves behaviors that are manipulative of children's attachments and threatening to children's feelings of security in the parent–child relationship, relational aggression involves threats to the security of an individual's relationship to a peer. Consequently, it is not surprising to find that as with other forms of boundary dissolution (Linder, Collins, & Crick, 2002), parental psychological control increases the likelihood of children becoming involved in peer relationships that are characterized by relational aggression and victimization in childhood (Crick & Grotpeter, 1995; Nelson & Crick, 2002) and college-age samples (Kerig & Swanson, 2010; Lento, 2006; Werner & Crick, 1999). Through the process of modeling, parents who engage in psychologically controlling behavior may inculcate in their children relational styles that involve a parallel lack of mutual autonomy with peers. Taken together, therefore, the existing empirical literature on the relationship between parental psychological control and later relational aggression and victimization suggests support for the idea that parents' restriction of children's psychological autonomy compromises emergent adults' ability to engage in mutually autonomous relationships with others.

Emotional valence as a moderator. Although attachment theory proposes that children internalize both sides of a maladaptive parenting relationship, and thus are equally likely to take on the victimizing or victimizer roles in their future relationships (Cicchetti & Howes, 1991), it is interesting to speculate as to what factors might determine whether children gravitate toward one or the other of the two poles of overaccommodation or overcontrol. In other words, when young adults do develop a relational style that is lacking mutual autonomy, what might account for their involvement in relationships characterized by an other-focused connection as opposed to involvement in relationships characterized by self-focused autonomy? One possibility is that the overall emotional valence of the parent–child relationship—that is, a tone of acceptance or rejection—might account for the specific relational styles that emerge over the course of childhood into adulthood. For example, Rohner (1986) proposed that children who experience intrusive parental control in the context of ostensible warmth and acceptance would develop an intensified dependence on parents, and a tendency to silence their own wants and needs and to overly accommodate to others in relationships. Barber, Stolz, and Olsen (2005) found some evidence in support of

Rohner's hypothesis in a study of adolescent depression and antisocial behavior, in that the link between psychological control and youth's maladaptive behavior was strengthened in the context of high levels of parental acceptance. Thus, previous research and conceptualizations lead to an intriguing hypothesis, that parental acceptance might moderate the relationship between parental psychological control and relational styles in young adults, such that parental acceptance might contribute to an increased likelihood of the development of an other-focused style of connection with others. In turn, parental rejection might contribute to an increased likelihood of a self-focused autonomous style with others.

WHO ARE THE "CLOSE" PARTNERS OF EMERGING ADULTS: PEERS OR ROMANTIC PARTNERS?

Before going forward, however, the following important question must be considered: who *are* the emotionally intimate partners of emerging adults? Although it often is assumed that the interpersonal relationships with the strongest emotional investments are those involving romantic partners, this is a matter of some debate in the literature. On one side of the debate, Giordano, Manning, and Longmore (2006) provide evidence for the argument that important differences exist between friendships and romantic relationships. Results of their research suggest that when compared with platonic, other-sex friendships or same-sex friendships, romantic relationships involve heightened emotionality, higher levels of social and communication awkwardness, greater asymmetry with regard to the investment in the relationship, and greater weight given to issues of exclusivity. On the other hand, Furman and Hand (2006) argue that it is important not to overemphasize the differences between romantic relationships and friendships, and point to research that suggests that the majority of adolescents view intimacy in both interpersonal contexts to be equally valued. Moreover, a developmental perspective requires that we question whether romantic relationships are particularly privileged for young people during the transition between adolescence and adulthood. For one thing, many young people may not be in committed romantic relationships during this developmental period; for example, in many of the studies we have conducted involving college freshmen, as few as one-third report being involved in a steady dating relationship. Moreover, the phenomenon of "hook-ups" currently common among college students (Paul, McManus, & Hayes, 2000) means that many sexual encounters involve brief associations with casual acquaintances, whereas the relationships that are most long-lasting and in which emotional ties are deepest are those involving platonic friendships. Moreover, recent phenomena such as "friends with benefits" (Hughes, Morrison, & Asada, 2005) suggest that the boundaries between sexual relationships and friendships are not entirely clear, and thus the labels of "friend" and "romantic partner" may not be as easily distinguished as previous research has assumed. Therefore, given the debate in the literature about the relative salience of friendships and romantic relationships, as well as developmental considerations and trends in recent popular culture, we viewed it as important to actually investigate whether parental psychological control is differentially related to emerging adults' difficulties forming mutually autonomous relationships in peer or romantic contexts.

EXAMINING THE LINK BETWEEN PSYCHOLOGICAL CONTROL AND MUTUALITY OF AUTONOMY

The goal of the present study was to take an initial step toward investigating the link between parental psychological control and emerging adults' navigation of stage-salient developmental tasks during the transition to university life, namely, the capacity to form intimate relationships characterized by mutual autonomy. We hypothesized that relational experiences within the family of origin, such as parent–child boundary dissolution and the perceived emotional valence of the parent–child relationship, play a role in emerging adults' difficulties forming relationships characterized by a balance of connection and autonomy. To investigate the hypothesis that parent–child boundary dissolution increases the risk for lack of mutuality in intimate relationships in emerging adulthood, data were gathered from 365 participants (240 females and 124 males) recruited from an introduction to psychology research pool at a midsized Midwestern university. Their average age was 18.48 ($SD = 0.54$) and the majority of the sample was female (65.8%), white (89.9%), and from affluent families.

A latent construct of parental Psychological Control was created from participants' self-reports about their relationships with mothers and fathers on three scales. The first was the Psychological Control subscale of the Parent–Child Boundaries Scale (PBS-III; Kerig, 2007; e.g., "My mother gives me the 'cold shoulder' if I don't see things her way"; "My father makes me feel guilty if I don't do what he wants me to do"). Also included were two related subscales of the Children's Report of Parental Behavior Inventory (CRPBI; Schaefer, 1965): Control through Guilt (e.g., "My mother tells me how much she has suffered for me"; "My father thinks I'm not grateful if I don't obey") and Acceptance of Individuation (e.g., "My mother allows me to tell her if I think my ideas are better than hers"; "My father likes me to choose my own way of doing things"). In addition, to assess the emotional valence of the parent–child relationship, participants were asked to complete two subscales of Schludermann and Schludermann's (1988) revision of the *Child's Report of Parental Behavior Inventory* (Schaefer, 1965). These scales were Acceptance (e.g., "My mom almost always speaks to me with a warm and friendly voice") and Rejection (e.g., "My dad makes me feel I am not loved").

Participants also were asked to report about their closest interpersonal relationship with a peer, and were asked to identify whether this relationship was with a friend or with a romantic partner. Among the participants, 36% reported that their closest relationship was with an intimate partner and 64% reported it was a friendship. A latent construct was created to assess Other-Focused Connection in this peer relationship, and was comprised of three scales. These included the Over-Accommodation scale of the Inventory of Interpersonal Problems

(IIP; Horowitz et al., 2000; e.g., "I find it hard to say 'no' to other people"; "I am too easily persuaded by other people"), the Self-Sacrificing subscale of the IIP (e.g., "I find it hard to set limits on other people"; "I trust other people too much"). In addition, the Silencing the Self scale (Jack & Dill, 1992) was included (e.g., "Instead of risking confrontations in close relationships, I would rather not rock the boat"; "I try to bury my feelings when I think they will cause trouble in my close relationship"). Similarly, a latent construct was created to measure Self-Focused Autonomy, using two subscales from the IIP: Domineering/Controlling (e.g., "I try to change other people too much"; "I find it hard to understand another person's point of view") and Vindictive/Self-Centered (e.g., "I find it hard to be supportive of another person's goals in life"; "I fight with other people too much").

As a first step, given that daughters and sons might be differentially affected by relationships with mothers and fathers (e.g., Cowan, Cowan, & Kerig, 1993), we conducted a series of independent *t*-tests to examine whether there were gender differences across the primary study variables. Female participants reported higher levels of both maternal and paternal Acceptance of Individuation, whereas male participants reported higher levels of Silencing the Self in romantic relationships. (See Table 6.1.) Second, the intercorrelations among the variables were examined. (See Table 6.2.) Results indicate that, for females, maternal and paternal psychological control were related to one another, and both forms of parent–child boundary dissolution were associated with interpersonal problems in intimate relationships, with the exception of paternal psychological control and silencing the self. Overall, the pattern of results for males differed, with both maternal and paternal psychological control having the strongest relationships with scales associated with the Self-Focused Autonomy construct.

Psychological control and mutual autonomy. To test the hypothesized relationships between parent–child boundary dissolution and mutual autonomy in romantic relationships, we ran a series of structural equation models with Mplus Version 4.21 (Muthen & Muthen, 2007) using maximum likelihood estimation. A power analysis conducted using MacCallum, Browne, and Sugawara's (1996) framework indicated adequate statistical power (>0.75). The fit of the structural equation models was evaluated with respect to four criteria. The first and most important criterion was theoretical relevance. The models were also evaluated with respect to global fit. Ideally, a model should have a nonsignificant chi-square (indicating the data were not significantly different than the hypothesized model), and a Comparative Fit index (CFI: Bentler, 1990) and Tucker–Lewis index (TLI: Bentler & Bonett, 1980) greater than 0.90 (Hu & Bentler, 1999). Although a nonsignificant chi-square is ideal, in larger sample sizes it is more difficult to obtain. The third criterion involved the microfit indices. Good fit at the microfit level was indicated by a Root Mean Square Error of Approximation (RMSEA) less than 0.05 (Browne & Cudeck, 1992), significant individual parameter loadings, and small residuals. The final criterion was parsimony. Similar to other statistical approaches, the fewer number of parameters needed to explain the relationship, the better the model.

The first model tested examined the relationship between parental psychological control and the latent constructs capturing lack of mutuality of autonomy.

Table 6.1 INDEPENDENT *T*-TESTS COMPARING REPORTS
OF MALE AND FEMALE PARTICIPANTS

	Mean Score (SD)			
	Males	Females	*t*	Cohen's *d*
Mother–Child Relationship				
PBS Psychological Control	13.66 (5.41)	12.27 (4.08)	1.37, *p* = 0.17	0.29
CRPBI Control through Guilt	9.83 (3.81)	8.69 (2.67)	1.68, *p* = 0.10	0.35
CRPBI Acceptance of Individuation	18.62 (4.04)	20.35 (3.48)	−2.14, *p* = 0.04	0.46
CRPBI Acceptance	21.19 (3.11)	21.73 (3.46)	1.52, *p* = 0.14	0.21
CRPBI Rejection	11.01 (2.91)	10.58 (3.04)	1.97, *p* = 0.19	0.14
Father–Child Relationship				
PBS Psychological Control	12.34 (4.19)	10.80 (3.31)	1.95, *p* = 0.06	0.41
CRPBI Control through Guilt	8.31 (2.51)	8.41 (2.22)	−0.19, *p* = 0.85	0.04
CRPBI Acceptance of Individuation	17.72 (4.29)	19.55 (3.84)	−2.07, *p* = 0.04	0.45
CRPBI Acceptance	20.06 (3.60)	20.56 (3.94)	1.16, *p* = 0.24	0.05
CRPBI Rejection	11.10 (2.99)	10.99 (3.30)	.33, *p* = 0.74	0.02
Dependent Variables				
IIP Overly Accommodating	9.07 (6.27)	10.70 (5.76)	−1.25, *p* = 0.21	0.27
IIP Self-Sacrificing	11.83 (6.50)	11.91 (5.16)	−.07, *p* = 0.94	0.01
IIP Silencing the Self	23.14 (5.65)	19.46 (4.99)	3.18, *p* = 0.002	0.69
IIP Domineering/ Controlling	5.52 (6.08)	3.89 (3.72)	1.63, *p* = 0.12	0.32
IIP Vindictive/Self-Centered	5.66 (4.43)	4.37 (3.72)	1.48, *p* = 0.14	0.32

NOTES: PBS = Parent-child Boundaries Scale; CRPBI = Child Report of Parental Behavior Inventory; IIP = Inventory of Interpersonal Problems.

Results suggest that the model fit the data well, CFI = 0.99, TLI = 0.97, RMSEA = 0.06, despite a significant chi-square, $\chi^2(n = 353, 11) = 23.92$, $p < 0.05$. (See Figure 6.1). As hypothesized, emerging adults' reports of psychologically controlling parenting were associated with an increased risk of being involved in intimate relationships characterized by either a relational style of self-focused autonomy or other-focused connection.

Table 6.2 Intercorrelations

Variable	1	2	3	4	5	6	7	8	9
1. Maternal PC	—	0.48***	0.22**	0.22**	0.23**	0.33***	0.31***	-0.55***	0.66***
2. Paternal PC	*0.45***	—	0.25***	0.23***	0.13	0.28***	0.36***	-0.53***	0.71***
3. IIP Overly Accommodating	*0.14*	*0.18**	—	0.71***	0.65***	0.06	0.19**	-0.19*	0.26***
4. IIP Self-Sacrificing	*0.07*	*0.19**	*0.78****	—	0.32***	0.16*	0.16*	-0.20**	0.29***
5. Silencing the Self	*-0.02*	*0.12*	*0.35****	*0.29**	—	-0.01	0.15	-0.09	0.12
6. IIP Domineering/Controlling	*0.35****	*0.33****	*0.11*	*0.23**	*-0.03*	—	0.65***	-0.31***	0.34***
7. IIP Vindictive/Self-Centered	*0.35****	*0.22**	*0.18**	*0.17*	*0.11*	*0.68****	—	-0.32***	0.35*
8. CRPBI Acceptance	*-0.53****	*-0.39****	*0.00*	*0.06*	*0.01*	*-0.19**	*-0.12*	—	-0.75***
9. CRPBI Rejection	*0.62****	*0.55****	*0.04*	*0.03*	*-0.02*	*0.25***	*0.24***	*-0.63****	—

NOTES: Correlations for females are above the diagonal; correlations for males are in italics below the diagonal. PC = Psychological Control; IIP = Inventory of Interpersonal Problems; CRPBI = Child Report of Parental Behavior Inventory.
$*p < 0.05$; $**p < 0.01$; $***p < 0.001$.

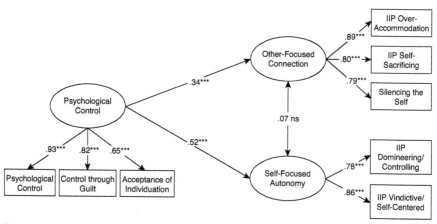

Figure 6.1. Path Diagram Showing Parent Psychological Control as a Predictor of Lack of Mutual Autonomy in Intimate Relationships.

Emotional valence as a moderator. The hypothesis that acceptance and rejection moderated the relationship between psychological control and mutual autonomy was tested following the steps outlined by Aiken and West (1991) and extended into the structural equation modeling framework by Schumacker and Marcoulides (1998). To accomplish this, participants were divided into three groups based on their relative standing on the acceptance and rejection scales: on each variable, the low group included those whose scores were equal to or lower than one-half standard deviation below the mean, the medium group included those whose scores were within one-half standard deviation above or below the mean, and the high group included those whose scores were equal to or higher than one-half standard deviation above the mean.

The invariance of the SEM models was first tested across the three levels of parental acceptance, with the parameters constrained to be equal in the three conditions (Frazier, Tix, & Barron, 2004). The results indicated that the models did differ across levels of parental acceptance, $\chi^2(n = 353, 49) = 160.00$, $p < 0.01$, CFI = 0.81, TLI = 0.76, RMSEA = 0.14, consistent with a moderating effect. Investigation of the path coefficients showed that the strongest relationship between parental psychological control and other-focused connection was for participants who reported high levels of parental acceptance. A similar procedure was followed to test for the moderating effects of parental rejection. The path coefficients indicated a significant relationship between parental psychological control and self-focused autonomy for participants who reported high levels of parental rejection.

Friendships versus romantic relationships. To investigate whether there were differences in key linkages depending on whether participants identified their closest peer relationship as involving a friend or a romantic partner, additional multigroup analyses were conducted with the participants divided into two groups on this basis. Among the participants, 227 reported about a close friend and 126 reported about a romantic partner. *t*-tests indicated that there were no systematic differences between the two groups on any of the other variables measured. In the initial model, the parameters were constrained to be equal in the two groups, and results showed that the model was not invariant across the two groups, $\chi^2(n = 353, 30) = 63.08, p < 0.001$, CFI = 0.96, TLI = 0.95, RMSEA = 0.08. Examination of the model paths indicated that the link between parental psychological control and self-focused autonomy was stronger for participants who reported about a close friend, whereas the path between psychological control and other-focused connection was stronger for participants who reported about romantic relationships.

Maternal versus paternal psychological control. To examine whether there were any differences related to parent gender, maternal and paternal psychological control were analyzed as separate latent variables. The model fit indices indicated that there were differences between the models including paternal and maternal psychological control, $\chi^2(n = 353, 29) = 185.31, p < 0.01$, CFI = 0.90, TLI = 0.84, RMSEA = 0.12. Comparison of the path coefficients in the two models indicated that the link between paternal psychological control and emerging adults' use of a relational style of other-focused connection was significant, whereas the link for maternal psychological control was not.

IMPLICATIONS OF THESE RESULTS FOR UNDERSTANDING THE EMERGING ADULT TRANSITION

The results of this initial test of the relationship between parent–child boundary dissolution and mutuality of autonomy suggests that this is a topic worthy of further inquiry. Structural equation modeling indicated that the experience of psychologically controlling parenting indeed is related to an increased risk of emerging adults' participation in intimate peer relations that are characterized by a lack of mutual autonomy, whether in the form of self-focused autonomy or other-focused connection. These findings are consistent with the supposition that by failing to "acknowledge the psychological distinctiveness of the child" (Kerig, 2005), boundary dissolution in the parent–child relationship may compromise the development of important relational functions such as the ability to comfortably balance the needs for closeness and separation. As Bowlby (1988) suggests:

> For a relationship between any two individuals to proceed harmoniously, each much be aware of the other's point-of-view, his goals, feelings, and intentions, and each must so adjust his own behaviour that some alignment of goals is negotiated. This requires that each should have reasonable accurate models of self and other which are regularly up-dated by free communication between them. (p. 131)

The results of the present study also point to a potential mechanism by which we can understand why youth who experience parental psychological control gravitate either toward overly accommodating or overly controlling strategies in their interpersonal relationships. Consistent with Rohner's (1986) hypothesis, participants whose parents engage in psychologically controlling behavior in the context of a warm and accepting relationship were those most likely to be concerned about meeting others' needs and silencing their own thoughts, wishes, and opinions when these threatened to pose conflicts in the relationship. As Barber and colleagues (2005) suggest, when the parent–child relationship is positively valenced, "adolescents—given the trust in their parents that nurturant, supportive behaviors provide—are more likely to submit to or endorse the intrusiveness of psychological control, and then internalize its violation and disrespect for their selves" (p. 37). In contrast, youth whose parents' psychologically controlling behavior emerged in the context of a negative and rejecting relationship were the youth most likely to develop relational styles that were characterized by dominance and self-centeredness. The idea that the emotional valence of the parent–child relationship might lend different meaning to the experience of boundary dissolution has been suggested elsewhere in the literature (Kerig, 2005; Kerig & Swanson, 2010). For example, parent–child role-reversal may be combined with warmth, camaraderie, and closeness and thus be experienced by the child as a gratifying kind of "specialness"—even if this comes with a cost (Hetherington, 1999). However, the results presented here suggest that guilt induction and emotional withdrawal delivered in a warm style might also foster a sense of insecurity and dependence that interferes particularly with a child's ability to individuate and develop a healthy sense of autonomy and agency. In contrast, children whose parents attempt to control their thoughts and feelings in a harsh way may be better able to pull themselves away from the parent–child bond, but at the expense of developing a sense of comfort with closeness and communion in relationships.

The results obtained here related to parent gender suggest that paternal psychological control may be particularly influential in the development of an other-focused interpersonal style. Although the small number of male participants in the current sample precluded our analyzing the models separately by gender, an additional issue that warrants consideration in future research is the possibility that there may be differences in the ways that sons and daughters are affected by their relationships with mothers and fathers (Cowan, Cowan, & Kerig, 1993; Kerig, Cowan, & Cowan, 1993; Stolz, Barber, & Olsen, 2005). Although the research on gender differences in psychological control is mixed, some studies show that adolescent sons tend to describe their mothers as more psychologically controlling than do daughters (Barber, 1996; Best, Hauser, & Allen, 1997; Shulman, Collins, & Dital, 1993). And again, although gender differences are not consistent, some research suggests that psychological control has a stronger link to daughters' than to sons' adjustment (Conger, Conger, & Scaramella, 1997). For example, Pettit, Laird, Dodge, and Criss (2001) found that adolescent girls with psychologically controlling mothers reported higher levels of anxiety, depression, and delinquency than their male peers. Intriguingly, one explanation posited for this gender difference is the tendency of girls to cope with parental control through other-focused accommodation. Because they are highly motivated to maintain harmonious relationships, daughters react to parental attempts to subjugate their feelings and opinions by internalizing and suppressing their negative responses

(Rogers et al., 2003). In contrast, sons, who are socialized to prioritize the goals of self-assertion and dominance in relationships, may be more likely than daughters to react to parental psychological control with externalizing behaviors and autonomy seeking (Rogers et al., 2003).

In addition, other research suggests that maternal and paternal psychological control may have differential effects, particularly for daughters. In general, mutuality in the mother–daughter relationship has been found to be particularly important for the development of self-esteem and social adjustment (Goldberg, 1994), whereas paternal validation is seen as critically important to daughters' ability to trust and assert themselves with males (e.g., Kalter, 1985; Southworth & Schwarz, 1987). More specifically, research suggests that paternal psychological control is differentially related to maladaptation among girls and women (Nelson & Crick, 2002; Rogers, Buchanan, & Winchell, 2003; Rowa, Kerig, & Geller, 2001). One reason for this may be that because the father–daughter relationship is characterized by less closeness than the mother–daughter bond (Steinberg, 1987), the impact of paternal psychological control is less "cushioned by other positive relational experiences compared to the effect of psychological control by mothers" (Rogers et al., 2003, p. 378). In other words, girls may react negatively to paternal psychological control because the father–daughter relationship in general is likely to be experienced as lacking in warmth, affirmation, or reciprocity (Kerig, Cowan, & Cowan, 1993). Given these hints of gender differences in the literature, it may be worth pursuing the question of whether the effects of psychological control on mutuality of autonomy differ, depending on whether we are talking about sons or daughters and mothers or fathers.

Several other limitations to this research should be considered. This was a sample of mostly female, white, and affluent youth, and therefore the results cannot be assumed to be generalizable. In addition, the cross-sectional nature of the data precludes the testing of directional relationships, and the fact that the measures were all obtained through self-report makes the results vulnerable to monoinformant biases. Furthermore, psychological control may be a subtle and covert process—especially when it occurs within the context of a positively valenced parent–child relationship—and thus may not always be accurately available to youth's perception and recall.

In conclusion, this research contributes in a small way to the ongoing debate about the roles that friendships and romantic relationships play in the lives of emerging adults. As we have found in other samples of youth in this developmental period, only a minority of the participants were involved in steady dating relationships. Therefore, most identified a close friend as the agemate with whom their personal relationships were most intimate and emotionally invested. However, for those involved in romantic partnerships, parental psychological control was most strongly related to an other-focused connection, whereas for those who reported about friendships, parental psychological control was most strongly related to self-focused autonomy. It is interesting to speculate as to whether youth who accommodate to their parents' controllingness are also more likely to foreclose on the explorations of identity, sexuality, and relational styles that being single during the transition to college would entail, and instead seek early in life the security that comes with a committed romantic relationship. For example, youth whose troubled family relationships have fostered an insecure attachment may tend to begin dating early and precociously involve themselves in intense romantic attachments with other troubled youth (Wekerle & Wolfe, 1998; Wolfe & Feiring, 2000). The resulting volatile relationships tend to be colored by anxiety about abandonment, neediness, and sensitivity to rejection (Volz & Kerig, 2010)—and thus, perhaps, to reflect an overly accommodative or overly controlling relational style. However, another significant limitation of the present data is that we were not able to compare participants' ratings across friendships versus romantic contexts. Other research has shown that individuals' relational styles do vary across contexts, with emerging adults most likely to report engaging in an other-focused connection in romantic relationships (Neff & Harter, 2003). Therefore, it is important to note that although the present findings suggest that parental psychological control increases the likelihood that emerging adults will become involved in relationships characterized by a nonmutually autonomous relational style, it also may be that the relationship context affects emerging adults' choice of relational style. This will be a valuable question to pursue in future research.

References

Aiken, L. S., & West, S. G. (1991). *Multiple regression: Testing and interpreting interactions*. Thousand Oaks, CA: Sage Publications.

Allen, J. P. (2008). The attachment system in adolescence. In J. Cassidy & P. R. Shaver (Eds.), *Handbook of attachment: Theory, research, and clinical applications* (pp. 419–435). New York: Guilford.

Bakan, D. (1966). *The duality of human existence: Isolation and communion in Western man*. Boston: Beacon Press.

Barber, B. K. (1992). Family, personality, and adolescent problem behaviors. *Journal of Marriage and the Family, 54*, 69–79.

Barber, B. K. (1996). Parental psychological control: Revisiting a neglected construct. *Child Development, 67*, 3296–3319.

Barber, B. K. (2002). Reintroducing parental psychological control. In B. K. Barber (Ed.), *Intrusive parenting: How psychological control affects children and adolescents* (pp. 3–14). Washington, D.C.: American Psychological Association.

Barber, B. K., & Harmon, E. L. (2002). Violating the self: Parental psychological control of children and adolescents. In B. K. Barber's (Ed.), *Intrusive parenting: How psychological control affects children and adolescents* (pp. 15–52). Washington, D.C.: American Psychological Association.

Barber, B. K., Stolz, H. E., & Olsen, J. A. (2005). Parental support, psychological control, and behavioral control: Assessing relevance across time, culture, and method. *Monographs of the Society for Research and Child Development, 70*, 1–151.

Benjamin, J. (1981). The Oedipal riddle: Authority, autonomy, and the new narcissism. In J. Diggins & M. Kaim (Eds.), *The problem of authority in America* (pp. 195–230). Philadelphia: Temple University Press.

Bentler, P. M. (1990). Comparative fit indexes in structural models. *Psychological Bulletin, 107(2),* 238–246.

Bentler, P. M., & Bonnet, D. G. (1980). Significance tests and goodness-of-fit in the analysis of covariance structure. *Psychological Bulletin, 88*(3), 588–606.

Best, K. M., Hauser, S. T., & Allen, J. P. (1997). Predicting young adult competencies: Adolescent era parent and individual influences. *Journal of Adolescent Research, 12,* 90–112.

Block, J. H. (1978). Another look at sex differentiation in the socialization behaviors of mothers & fathers. In J. Sherman & F. L. Denmark (Eds.), *The psychology of women: Future directions of research* (pp. 29–87). New York: Psychological Dimensions.

Bowlby, J. (1988). Developmental psychiatry comes of age. In J. Bowlby (Ed.), *A secure base: Parent-child attachment and healthy human development* (pp. 158–180). New York: Basic Books, Inc.

Bretherton, I., & Munholland, K. A. (1999). Internal working models in attachment relationships: A construct revisited. In J. Cassidy & P. R. Shaver (Eds.), *Handbook of attachment: Theory, research, and clinical applications* (pp. 89–114). New York: The Guilford Press.

Browne, M. W., & Cudeck, R. (1992). Alternative ways of assessing model fit. *Sociological Methods & Research, 21,* 230–258.

Cicchetti, D., & Howes, P. W. (1991). Developmental psychopathology in the context of family: Illustrations from the study of child maltreatment. *Canadian Journal of Behavioural Science, 23,* 257–281.

Conger, K. J., Conger, R. D., & Scaramella, L. V. (1997). Parents, siblings, psychological control, and adolescent adjustment. *Journal of Adolescent Research, 12*(1), 113–138.

Cowan, P. A., Cowan, C. P., & Kerig, P. K. (1993). Mothers, fathers, sons, and daughters: Gender differences in family formation and parenting style. In P. A. Cowan, D. Field, D. Hansen, A. Skolnick, & G. Swanson (Eds.), *Family, self and society: Toward a new agenda for family research* (pp. 165–195). Hillsdale, NJ: Erlbaum.

Crick, N. R., & Grotpeter, J. K. (1995). Relational aggression, gender, and social-psychological adjustment. *Child Development, 66,* 710–722.

Crittenden, P. M. (1994). Peering into the black box: An exploratory treatise on the development of self in young children. In D. Cicchetti & S. L. Toth (Eds.), *Rochester symposium on developmental psychopathology: Disorders and dysfunctions of the self* (pp. 79–148). New York: Rochester.

Frazier, P. A., Tix, A. P., & Barron, K. E. (2004). Testing moderator and mediator effects in counseling psychology. *Journal of Counseling Psychology, 51*(1), 115–134.

Furman, W., & Hand, L. S. (2006). The slippery nature of romantic relationships: Issues in definition and differentiation. In A. C. Crouter & A. Booth (Eds.), *Romance and sex in adolescence and emerging adulthood* (pp. 171–178). Mahwah, NJ: Erlbaum.

Giordano, P. C., Manning, W. D., & Longmore, M. A. (2006). Adolescent romantic relationships: An emerging portrait of their nature and developmental significance. In A.C. Crouter & A. Booth (Eds.), *Romance and sex in adolescence and emerging adulthood* (pp. 127–150). Mahwah, NJ: Erlbaum.

Goldberg, J. E. (1994). Mutuality in mother-daughter relationships. *Families in Society: The Journal of Contemporary Human Services, 75,* 236–242.

Grotevant, H. D., & Cooper, C. R. (1986). Individuation in family relationships: A perspective on individual differences in the development of identity and role-taking skill in adolescence. *Human Development, 29,* 82–100.

Grotevant, H. D., Cooper, C. R., & Condon, S. M. (1983). Individuality and connectedness in the family as a context for adolescent identity formation and role taking skill. *New Directions for Child Development, 22*, 43–59.

Harter, S., Marold, D. B., Whitesell, N. R., & Cobbs, G. (1996). A model of the effects of perceived parent and peer support on adolescent false self behavior. *Child Development, 67*(2), 360–374.

Hetherington, E. M. (1999). Should we stay together for the sake of the children? In E. M. Hetherington (Ed.), *Coping with divorce, single parenting, and remarriage: A risk and resiliency perspective* (pp. 93–116). Mahwah, NJ: Erlbaum.

Horowitz, L. M., Alden, L. E., Wiggins, J. S., & Pincus, A. L. (2000). *The inventory of interpersonal problems*. San Antonio, TX: The Psychological Corporation.

Hu, L. T., & Bentler, P. M. (1999). Cutoff criteria for fit indexes in covariance structure analysis: Conventional criteria versus new alternatives. *Structural Equation Modeling, 6*, 1–55.

Hughes, M. Morrison, Y, & Asada K. J. K. (2005). What's love got to do with it? Exploring the impact of maintenance rules, love attitudes, and network support on friends with benefits relationships. *Western Journal of Communication, 69*, 49–66.

Jack, D. C. (1991). *Silencing the self: Women and depression*. Cambridge, MA: Harvard University Press.

Jack, D. C., & Dill, D. (1992). The silencing the self scale: Schemas of intimacy associated with depression in women. *Psychology of Women Quarterly, 16*, 97–106.

Kalter, N., Riemer, B., Brickman, A., & Chen, J. W. (1985). Implications of parental divorce for female development. *Journal of the American Academy of Child Psychiatry, 24*, 538–544.

Kerig, P. K. (2005). Revisiting the construct of boundary dissolution: A multidimensional perspective. *Journal of Emotional Abuse, 5*, 5–42.

Kerig, P. K. (2007). *Parent-child boundaries scale-III*. Unpublished manuscript, Department of Psychology, University of Utah.

Kerig, P. K., Cowan, P. A., & Cowan, C. P. (1993). Marital quality and gender differences in parent-child interaction. *Developmental Psychology, 29*, 931–939.

Kerig, P. K., & Sink, H. E. (2010). The new scoundrel on the schoolyard: Contributions of Machiavellianism to the understanding of youth aggression. In C. T. Barry, P. K. Kerig, K. K. Stellwagen, & T. D. Barry (Eds.), *Narcissism and Machiavellianism in youth: Implications for the development of adaptive and maladaptive behavior* (pp. 193–212). Washington, D.C.: American Psychological Association Press.

Kerig, P. K., & Swanson, J. A. (2010). Ties that bind: Triangulation, boundary dissolution, and the effects of interparental conflict on child development. In M. S. Schulz, M. K. Pruett, P. K. Kerig, & R. Parke (Eds.), *Strengthening couple relationships for optimal child development: Lessons from research and intervention* (pp. 59–76). Washington, D.C.: American Psychological Association.

Kerig, P.K., & Wenar, C. (2006). *Developmental psychopathology: From infancy through adolescence* (5th ed.). New York: McGraw-Hill.

Leadbeater, B. J., Banister, E. M., Ellis, W. E., & Yeung, R. (2008). Victimization and relational aggression in adolescent romantic relationships: The influence of parental and peer behaviors, and individual adjustment. *Journal of Youth and Adolescence, 37*, 359–372.

Lento, J. (2006). Relational and physical victimization by peers and romantic partners in college students. *Journal of Social and Personal Relationships, 23*, 331–348.

Linder, J. R., Crick, N. R., & Collins, W. A. (2002). Relational aggression and victimiza-
    tion in young adults' romantic relationships: Associations with perceptions of parent,
    peer, and romantic relationship quality. *Social Development, 11,* 69–86.
Luyckx, K., Soenens, B., Vansteenkiste, M., Goossens, L., & Berzonsky, M. D. (2007).
    Parental psychological control and dimensions of identity formation in emerging
    adulthood. *Journal of Family Psychology, 21*(3), 546–550.
MacCallum, R. C., Browne, M. W., & Sugawara, H. M. (1996). Power analysis and deter-
    mination of sample size for covariance structure modeling. *Psychological Methods, 1,*
    130–149.
Main, M., Kaplan, N., & Cassidy, J. (1985). Security in infancy, childhood, and adult-
    hood: A move to the level of representation. *Monographs of the Society for Research in
    Child Development, 50,* 66–104.
Minuchin, S. (1974). *Families and family therapy.* Cambridge, MA: Harvard University
    Press.
Morris, A. S., Silk, J. S., Steinberg, L., Sessa, F. M., Avenevoli, S., & Essex, M. J. (2002).
    Temperamental vulnerability and negative parenting as interacting of child adjust-
    ment. *Journal of Marriage and Family, 64*(2), 461–471.
Muthen, B., & Muthen, L. (2007). *Mplus user's guide.* Los Angeles: Muthen & Muthen.
Neff, K. D., & Harter, S. (2002). The role of power and authenticity in relationship styles
    emphasizing autonomy, connectedness, or mutuality among adult couples. *Journal of
    Social and Personal Relationships, 19,* 835–857.
Neff, K. D., & Harter, S. (2003). Relationship styles of self-focused autonomy, other-
    focused connectedness, and mutuality across multiple relationship contexts. *Journal
    of Social and Personal Relationships, 20,* 81–99.
Nelson, D. A., & Crick, N. R. (2002). Parental psychological control: Implications for
    childhood physical and relational aggression. In B. K. Barber (Ed.), *Intrusive parenting:
    How psychological control affects children and adolescents* (pp. 161–190). Washington,
    D.C.: American Psychological Association.
Olsen, S. F., Yang, C., Hart, C. H., Robinson, C. C., Wu, P., Nelson, D. A., Nelson, L. J.,
    Jin, S., & Wo, J. (2002). Maternal psychological control and preschool children's behav-
    ioral outcomes in China, Russia, and the United States. In B. K. Barber (Ed.), *Intrusive
    parenting: How psychological control affects children and adolescents* (pp. 235–262).
    Washington, D.C.: American Psychological Association.
Paul, E. L., McManus, B., & Hayes, A. (2000). "Hookups": Characteristics and correlates
    of college students' spontaneous and anonymous sexual experiences. *Journal of Sex
    Research, 37,* 76–88.
Pettit, G. S., Laird, R. D., Dodge, K. A., & Criss, M. M. (2001). Antecedents and behavior-
    problem outcomes of parental monitoring and psychological control in early adolescence.
    Child Development, 72(2), 583–598.
Rogers, K. N., Buchanan, C. M., & Winchell, M. E. (2003). Psychological control during
    early adolescence: Links to adjustment in differing parent/adolescent dyads. *Journal
    of Early Adolescence, 23*(4), 349–383.
Rohner, R. P. (1986). *The warmth dimension: Foundations of parental acceptance-rejection
    theory.* Thousand Oaks, CA: Sage Publications.
Roisman, G. I., Masten, A. S., Coatsworth, J. D., & Tellegen, A. (2004). Salient and
    emerging developmental tasks in the transition to adulthood. *Child Development, 75,*
    123–133.

Rowa, K., Kerig, P. K., & Geller, J. (2001). The family and anorexia nervosa: Examining parent-child boundary problems. *European Eating Disorders Review, 9*(2), 97–114.

Schaefer, E. S. (1965). Children's reports of parental behavior: An inventory. *Child Development, 36,* 413–424.

Schludermann, E. H., & Schludermann, S. M. (1988). *Children's report on parent behavior (CRPBI-108, CRPBI-30) for older children and adolescents* (Tech. Rep.). Winnipeg, MB, Canada: University of Manitoba, Department of Psychology.

Schumacker, R. E., & Marcoulides, G. (1998). *Interaction and nonlinear effects in structural equation modeling.* Mahwah, NJ: Erlbaum.

Shulman, S., Collins, W. A., & Dital, M. (1993). Parent-child relationships and peer-perceived competence during middle childhood and preadolescence in Israel. *Journal of Early Adolescence, 13,* 204–218.

Southworth, S., & Schwarz, J. C. (1987). Post-divorce contact, relationship with father, and heterosexual trust in female college students. *American Journal of Orthopsychiatry, 57,* 371–381.

Sroufe, L. A. (1990). An organizational perspective on the self. In D. Cicchetti & M. Beeghly (Eds.), *The self in transition: Infancy to childhood* (pp. 281–307). Chicago: University of Chicago Press.

Sroufe, L. A., & Fleeson, J. (1986). Attachment and the construction of relationships. In W. W. Hartup & Z. Rubin (Eds.), *Relationships and development* (pp. 51–71). Mahwah, NJ: Erlbaum.

Steinberg, L. (1987). Recent research on the family at adolescence: The extent and nature of sex differences. *Journal of Youth and Adolescence, 16,* 191–197.

Stolz, H. E., Barber, B. K., & Olsen, J. A. (2005). Toward disentangling fathering and mother: An assessment of relative importance. *Journal of Marriage and Family, 67,* 1076–1092.

Volz, A. R., & Kerig, P. K. (2010). Relational dynamics associated with adolescent dating violence: The roles of rejection sensitivity and relational insecurity. *Journal of Aggression, Maltreatment, and Trauma, 19,* 587–602.

Wekerle, C., & Wolfe, D. A. (1998). The role of child maltreatment and attachment style in adolescent relationship violence. *Development and Psychopathology, 10,* 571–586.

Werner, N. E., & Crick, N. R. (1999). Relational aggression and social-psychological adjustment in a college sample. *Journal of Abnormal Psychology, 108,* 615–623.

Wolfe, D. A., & Feiring, C. (2000). Dating violence through the lens of adolescent romantic relationships. *Child Maltreatment, 5,* 360–363.

Zeanah, C. H., Anders, A. F., Seifer, R., & Stern, D. N. (1989). Implications of research on infant development for psychodynamic theory and practice. *American Academy of Child and Adolescent Psychiatry, 28,* 657–668.

Zeifman, D., & Hazan, C. (2008). Pair bonds as attachments. In J. Cassidy & P. R. Shaver (Eds.), *Handbook of attachment: Theory, research, and clinical applications* (pp. 436–455). New York: Guilford.

Introduction to Section III

Shifts in Family Roles and Relationships

MARC S. SCHULZ AND PATRICIA K. KERIG

The ability to develop and maintain close relationships is a core aspect of healthy functioning for individuals across the lifespan (L'Abate, Cusinato, Maino, Colesso, & Sciletta, 2010). In infancy and early childhood, successful connection with a caretaker is critical for physical and psychological well-being. During adolescence and the transition into adulthood there are important shifts in the nature of relationships with family members and with peers. In the second section of this book, the chapters examined the pivotal role of the development of close friendships and romantic relationships during adolescence. In this section, the chapters focus on another key relational marker of adolescence—family-based shifts in relationships and roles.

Individuation from one's parents and the attainment of greater autonomy are central developmental tasks of adolescence (Collins & Steinberg, 2006). The movement toward greater autonomy is both facilitated by and in turn drives important shifts in the adolescent's view of himself or herself, especially in regard to independence and competence. This shift toward greater autonomy is sometimes thought of as primarily involving changes in adolescent roles and self-image, but this perspective masks the fundamental relational nature of the shift toward autonomy and the complex sociocultural context in which autonomy strivings occur. Adolescents and parents are simultaneously negotiating a new way of relating to each other that leaves more room for the child's autonomy and alters the intensity of the role of parents in monitoring, directing, and protecting their child. For many parents, their child's strivings toward autonomy are threatening and they may awaken old concerns that originate in their own adolescent experiences, as Shulman, Scharf, and Shachar-Shapira document in Chapter 5 in the previous section. For adolescents, autonomy often is spoken of as a treasured goal but is experienced with significant trepidation.

McElhaney and Allen, in Chapter 7 in this section, explore how cultural and economic circumstances shape the nature, meaning, and consequences of strivings for autonomy in adolescence. Their careful review of relevant literature emphasizes the relational context of strivings for autonomy by carefully examining parental responses to bids for autonomy by children. They highlight research that demonstrates that the ways in which parents respond to adolescent strivings for autonomy have been linked to multiple aspects of adolescent adjustment. The challenge, they point out, however, is to recognize that there are variations across cultural groups in the degree to which autonomy is valued relative to loyalty and deference to the family. Much of the early research on the development of adolescent autonomy was conducted primarily from the perspective of white, middle-class American childrearing values, which limits our ability to generalize to other cultural and socioeconomic contexts. McElhaney and Allen remind us that in addition to variations across cultural groups in the degree to which autonomy is a cherished goal, some parents are likely to find themselves in circumstances in which environmental influences, such as dangerous neighborhoods, may propel them to exert greater control over their adolescent children in order to protect their well-being.

McElhaney and Allen's chapter provides a roadmap for understanding how seemingly universal goals, such as the promotion of autonomy during adolescence, may take on different meanings and be accomplished in different ways depending on context and culture. In addition to noting where additional research is needed, they highlight challenges confronting researchers in trying to understand the implications of culturally or contextually based differences in autonomy processes. For example, the impact on adolescent functioning of differences in parental promotion of autonomy or in the amount and type of parent–child conflict may depend on contextual factors such as the degree of risk a child routinely encounters in his or her neighborhood. The complexity of these interactions as well as the number and types of cultural and contextual variations that might be important suggest how much additional research needs to be conducted in this area. As McElhaney and Allen argue, basic research on the influence of culture and context on processes of autonomy is essential for informing intervention efforts designed to promote more effective parenting of adolescents.

For some adolescents, circumstances create demands that accelerate the shift toward autonomy. For example, the loss of a parent or a family economic crisis might result in adolescents taking on adult roles in their families out of necessity. Two of the contributions in this section focus on a particularly complicated context for adolescents to establish autonomy—the transition to early parenthood. At a time when most adolescents are pulling away from their families and engaging in more intense and sustained connections with peers, young mothers and fathers are establishing new and complicated family relationships. Most obvious among these new relationships is the connection with their developing child, but no less complicated is the nature of their ongoing relationship with their own parents.

Research has documented the significant challenges and stress that the transition to parenthood normatively ushers in for adults expecting their first child (Schulz, Cowan, & Cowan, 2006; Lawrence, Rothman, Cobb, & Bradbury, 2010). When the transition to parenthood occurs during adolescence, the challenges can be magnified in a number of ways. Focusing separately on young mothers and young fathers, the last two chapters in this section illuminate the nature of these challenges and the impact they have on developing parent–child relationships in these new families. Both chapters are informed by a family systems perspective that emphasizes the intricate interplay among family subsystems, family processes, and developmental processes during a major life transition.

Pittman and colleagues in Chapter 8 explore how young mothers' attempts at achieving autonomy and individuating from their own mothers may be linked to their effectiveness in parenting their children. Young mothers who can simultaneously make strides in their own sense of autonomy while still maintaining a healthy connection to their families of origin may be ideally situated to adapt to the challenges of early parenthood. The work of Pittman and colleagues points to the importance of combining striving for an autonomous identity with maintaining an effective, emotional connection with one's parents (Allen, Hauser, Bell, & O'Connor, 1994). This capacity may be a critical resource that promotes parenting competence in young mothers.

Pittman and colleagues draw data from the longstanding Baltimore Multigenerational Family Study, which has been investigating the impact of early parenthood across multiple generations for more than two decades.

Their sample is composed of African-American, primarily poor families in which young motherhood was often present across multiple generations. In this way, the Baltimore Multigenerational Family Study stands as a shining example that presents a compelling challenge to researchers who justify their work with more privileged samples by describing insurmountable obstacles to gaining access to disadvantaged and marginalized populations such as this one. In their research, Pittman and colleagues employ methodologically intensive approaches, such as careful observation of mother–grandmother interactions to assess autonomy and of mother–child interactions to assess the quality of parenting. They find that an individuated relationship between the young mother and her own mother was linked to the young mother's parenting; more individuation predicted more balanced responsiveness and appropriate maternal control with the preschooler. More autonomy also predicted the young child's ability to work more independently in challenging tasks.

Complementing these rigorous quantitative approaches is the use of rich narrative data from the interactions of grandmothers and mothers. Pittman and colleagues use these narratives to illustrate the meaning of autonomy in this sample and to elaborate on the processes underlying effective parenting in these young mothers. The integration of rigorous quantitative and qualitative methods is exceedingly rare and extremely useful.

Florsheim and Moore in Chapter 9 continue this focus on the early transition to parenthood and the integration of multiple research approaches, but focus on an even less studied group—young fathers. Their study combines observational, self-report, and narrative-based data to test a key tenet of family systems theories (e.g., Cummings, Davies, & Campbell, 2000)—the notion that behaviors in one family subsystem (e.g., the parental relationship) influence behaviors in other family subsystems (e.g., parent–child relationships). Their data are drawn from their "Young Parenthood Study" that has closely followed a sample of ethnically and socioeconomically diverse adolescents across the transition to parenthood. Beginning prior to the birth of their child, Florsheim and Moore engage the prospective parents in a videotaped conflict task that is later carefully coded. They employ a flexible approach to coding the couple interactions that can be applied to other types of dyadic interactions, including parent–child interactions. Their innovative coding approach groups both nonverbal and verbal behaviors into units that represent an interpersonally meaningful message. These units are then aggregated to obtain a summary of key interpersonal constructs for each of the dyads they consider. Another notable feature of their research approach is the thoughtful and creative use of dyadic measures, such as their assessment of mutuality in affective exchanges by estimating differences in the amount of warm interpersonal behaviors displayed by each partner.

The results of their study indicate that both the self-reported quality of the couple relationship and observed interpersonal behavior in couple interactions predict the degree of parental engagement of fathers 2 years after their child's birth. Their findings add to a burgeoning family research literature that documents connections between interpersonal functioning in multiple family contexts. Florsheim and Moore extend their analysis in important ways by identifying individuals and families that seem to be exceptions to the normative patterns identified in their variable-based approach. Echoing the work described by Hauser, Allen, and Schulz in Section IV, Florsheim and Moore demonstrate the value of identifying and studying in more depth "exceptions to a rule" such as those individuals who thrive despite difficult beginnings (Luthar, 2006; Masten & Obradovic, 2006). Careful narrative analysis of interviews with these exceptional individuals highlights the complex nature of individuals' paths through the transition to parenthood and the role of key developmental processes, such as identity development and the establishment of intimacy. Florsheim and Moore illustrate the power of narratives to capture personal meaning and self-identity during a complex transition. The narrative approaches highlighted in this chapter and in the chapter by Pittman and colleagues reflect a growing interest in narrative-based approaches across fields of psychology, particularly in lifespan and personality psychology (e.g., Lilgendahl & McAdams, 2011). As emphasized by Florsheim and Moore, the personal narratives that individuals construct reflect attempts to make sense of their experience and their place in the world. In this way they are both indicators of personality and essential developmental processes that shape identity, particularly during periods of transition.

References

Allen, J. P., Hauser, S. T., Bell, K. L., & O'Connor, T. G. (1994). Longitudinal assessment of autonomy and relatedness in adolescent-family interactions as predictors of adolescent ego development and self-esteem. *Child Development, 65*, 179–194.

Collins, W., & Steinberg, L. (2006). Adolescent development in interpersonal context. In W. Damon & R. Lerner (Series Eds.) & N. Eisenberg (Vol. Ed.), *Handbook of child psychology: Vol. 3, Social, emotional, and personality development* (6th ed.) (pp. 1003–1067). Hoboken, NJ: John Wiley & Sons Inc.

Cummings, E. M., Davies, P. T., & Campbell, S. B. (2000). *Developmental psychopathology and family process.* New York: The Guilford Press.

Lawrence, E., Rothman, A. D., Cobb, R. J., & Bradbury, T. N. (2010). Marital satisfaction across the transition to parenthood: Three eras of research. In M. S. Schulz, M. K. Pruett, P. K. Kerig, & R. D. Parke (Eds.), *Strengthening couple relationships for optimal child development: Lessons from research and intervention* (pp. 97–114). Washington, DC: American Psychological Association.

L'Abate, L., Cusinato, M., Maino, E., Colesso, W., & Sciletta, C. (2010). *Relational competence theory: Research and applications in mental health.* New York: Springer-Science.

Lilgendahl, J. P., & McAdams, D. P. (2011). Constructing stories of self-growth: How individual differences in patterns of autobiographical reasoning relate to well-being in midlife. *Journal of Personality, 78,* 391–428.

Luthar, S. S. (2006). Resilience in development: A synthesis of research across five decades. In D. Cicchetti & D. J. Cohen (Eds.), *Developmental psychopathology (2nd ed.): Vol. 3 Risk, disorder, and adaptation* (pp. 739–795). Hoboken, NJ: Wiley and Sons.

Masten, A. S., & Obradovic, J. (2006). Competence and resilience in development. *Annals of the New York Academy of Sciences, 1094,* 13–27.

Schulz, M. S., Cowan, P. A., & Cowan, C. P. (2006). Promoting healthy beginnings: A randomized controlled trial of a preventive intervention to preserve marital quality during the transition to parenthood. *Journal of Clinical and Consulting Psychology, 74,* 20–31.

7

Sociocultural Perspectives on Adolescent Autonomy

KATHLEEN BOYKIN McELHANEY AND JOSEPH P. ALLEN

The goal of achieving autonomy is a universal one, in the sense that all children begin life completely dependent on their caregivers to meet their needs, and thus must transition from relative dependence to relative independence in order to function as adults. Although the balance of autonomy and dependence across the lifespan is dictated by the developmental tasks at each life stage, these are in turn influenced by biological, psychological, and societal factors that may each carry different weight across diverse sociocultural contexts (Baltes & Silverberg, 1994; Raeff, 2006). Furthermore, the principal goal of parenting is to balance children's internal needs and capabilities against external environmental requirements. Although most goals of parenting may be seen as universal, how these goals are accomplished may vary based both on cultural context and environmental risk (Bradley, 2002; Coll & Pachter, 2002).

In traditional research and theory on family relationships during adolescence, the achievement of autonomy vis-à-vis the parent–adolescent relationship has been proposed as the key developmental task of adolescence (Collins & Steinberg, 2006; Zimmer-Gembeck & Collins, 2003; McElhaney, Allen, Stephenson, & Hare, 2009). Issues of identity development and achieving autonomy from parents are mainstays of the majority of the early theoretical work on adolescence (e.g., Blos, 1967). This focus is reflected in the large body of empirical literature investigating the nature of parent–adolescent relationships and how aspects of this relationship are linked to important outcomes for teens. Within this body of work, researchers have consistently emphasized the importance of warm, supportive parent–adolescent relationships that operate democratically, such that teens have opportunities to express themselves openly and to participate in family decision making. The ideal outcome of the autonomy process from this point of view involves a gradual realignment of the power structure of the parent–child relationship, which ultimately leads to independent functioning on the part of the adolescent.

Within American samples, the ways that parents handle adolescent strivings for autonomy have been consistently linked to numerous aspects of adolescent adjustment. For example, family discussions that allow adolescents to express their points of view openly have been linked with higher levels of social and interpersonal competence, greater self-esteem, and higher levels of ego development (Allen, Bell, & Boykin, 2000; Allen, Hauser, Bell, & O'Conner, 1994; Hall, 2002; McElhaney & Allen, 2001). In contrast, parental undermining and restriction of adolescent autonomy have been linked to a wide range of negative outcomes, including depression, poor peer relationships, greater association with deviant peers, and higher levels of externalizing behavior (Allen, Hauser, O'Connor, & Bell, 2002a; Allen et al., 2006; Fuligni & Eccles, 1993; Goldstein, Davis-Kean, & Eccles, 2005; Laible & Carlo, 2004; Lee & Bell, 2003; Soenens & Vansteenkiste, 2005). However, this research regarding the development of adolescent autonomy has been conducted primarily from the perspective of middle-class European-American child-rearing values, limiting generalization to other cultural and socioeconomic settings (referred to here as sociocultural context) (Smetana, 2002; McElhaney, Allen, Stephenson, & Hare, 2009).

A growing body of research has been devoted to exploring sociocultural influences on development, particularly with regard to approaches to parenting (Harkness & Super, 2002; Levine et al., 2008; Park & Buriel, 2006; Peterson, Steinmetz, & Wilson, 2003). This literature suggests that parenting is shaped by the broader social context, and that parents raise their children to encourage the development of those qualities that are needed for survival and success in their particular niches. When children's survival and/or subsistence are at risk, parenting practices will be tailored toward maximizing their physical well-being. Parents' goals and approaches to parenting will thus be guided both by their cultural heritage as well as by the specific challenges in their environments, and adaptive strategies for dealing with these challenges may be passed down from generation to generation (Bradley, 2002; Bornstein & Güngör, 2009; Levine et al., 2008). Factors such as social class, racism, prejudice, and discrimination, in addition to physical hazards in the environment, can create challenging social contexts that, in turn, shape parents' approaches to socialization (Coll & Pachter, 2002). However, more mainstream research on autonomy tends to overlook the notion that parental behaviors that appear restrictive and/or overly harsh in one setting may have very different (and adaptive) meanings in other contexts, and thus different consequences for child adjustment (Ho, Bluestein, & Jenkins, 2008; Deater-Deckard, Dodge, Bates, & Pettit, 1996; McElhaney & Allen, 2001).

SOCIALIZATION GOALS AND VALUES AS THEY RELATE TO AUTONOMY PROCESSES

The first step in exploring the link between sociocultural context and the autonomy process is to examine variations in values and beliefs regarding autonomy and its related constructs. Values that are particularly relevant to the autonomy process include views about the relation of individuals to larger groups, relations of children to family, and developmental expectations for gaining rights and responsibilities. Such values are closely tied to socialization goals, thus reflecting the implicit developmental theories upon which parenting behavior is based (Fuller & Garcia-Coll, 2010). The majority of this literature is comprised of cross-cultural studies comparing European-Americans with Asian and Latino groups (both within the United States and abroad) as well as with African-Americans (e.g., Chaudari, Easterbrooks, & Davis, 2009; Dodge, McLoyd, & Lansford, 2005; Russell, Crockett, & Chao, 2010). A somewhat smaller body of literature has examined values according to social class and environmental context.

Relation of the Individual to the Larger Group

One value dimension closely related to the concept of autonomy is individualism vs. collectivism. Societies that are more individualistic tend to value personal goals, with relatively less concern for the collective good, whereas more collectivist cultures are described as valuing group goals over individual goals. Middle-class European-American culture is generally regarded as highly individualistic, with a particularly strong emphasis on individual autonomy, whereas numerous other cultures have been characterized as more collectivist (Oyserman, Coon, & Kemmelmeir, 2002). For example, both Asian and Latino cultures have been characterized as more strongly emphasizing affiliation, cooperation, and harmony in interpersonal relationships (Halgunseth, Ispa, & Rudy, 2006; Kitayama, Markus, & Kurokawa, 2000). Researchers have also asserted that traditional African values also favor collectivism, with Afrocentric values centering on survival of the tribe and group commonalties (Cauce, Hiraga, Graves, Gonzales, Ryan-Finn, & Grove, 1996; Coll & Pachter, 2002).

   Some authors have noted that the collectivistic vs. individualistic dichotomy cannot completely capture complex patterns of socialization, and have emphasized that autonomy is a developmental goal even in cultures that have been characterized as more collectivistic (Peterson, Cobas, Bush, Supple, & Wilson, 2004; Smetana, 2002). Nonetheless, these cultural values can have important implications not only regarding whether and to what extent autonomy is encouraged during childhood and adolescence, but also how autonomy issues are negotiated in family relationships (Fuhrman & Holmbeck, 1995). Furthermore, cultural values can work together with a range of other contextual variables, including ethnicity, social class, education, and environmental risk to influence family relationships and the process of autonomy development (Harwood, Scholmerich, & Schulze, 2000).

Family Relationships, Children, and Child Rearing

Research examining values about family relationships across different cultures generally depicts some groups as highly valuing family solidarity and deference to parents, thus potentially deemphasizing individual autonomy. Both Latino and Chinese cultures have been described as emphasizing family solidarity and parental authority, and as particularly valuing helpfulness, obedience, and respect for elders as desirable traits in children (Chaudari et al., 2009; Fuligni & Zhang, 2004; Halgunseth, Ispa, & Rudy, 2006; Harkness & Super, 2002; Phinney, Ong, & Madden, 2000). Respect, obedience, and learning from elders in the community have also been noted as important socialization goals of African-American parenting (Coll & Pachter, 2002) and research indicates that middle-class African-American parents consider setting firm limits to be more important than encouraging independence (Smetana & Chuang, 2001). In contrast, throughout this research, both parents and teens from European backgrounds are described as emphasizing independence, self-directedness, and autonomy (Chaudari et al., 2009; Phinney, Kim-Jo, Osorio, & Vilhjalmsdottir, 2005).

Differences in child-rearing values have also been found to vary according to socioeconomic variables such as social class, income, and education. One explanation for these associations centers around the fact that such variables are markers for the types of experiences and opportunities available in a given environment (Kohn, 1969, 1979; Okagaki & Bingham, 2005). Parents from lower social classes tend to live in poorer, riskier neighborhoods, and thus their tendency to value obedience, inhibit autonomy, and socialize their children for compliance can be understood as attempts at protection–adaptive responses to the level of risk in their environment (Dearing, 2004; Garbarino, Bradshaw, & Kostelny, 2005; Magnuson & Duncan, 2002). Kohn (1963, 1979) provided an additional explanation for the association between social class and socialization goals, proposing that parental values are linked with occupational conditions. He noted that middle-class occupations are more likely to involve self-direction and individual effort, which leads to valuing these same characteristics as socialization goals (Kohn, 1963, 1979; Wilson, Wilson, & Berkeley-Caines, 2003; Wright & Wright, 1976). Working class occupations, in contrast, are subject to standardization and supervision, and depend more on collective action, all of which deemphasize individuality and emphasize conformity and obedience.

Expectations about Autonomy: Timetables

As children move towards adulthood, new rights and responsibilities are awarded to them, both by their parents and by society as a whole. Parental granting of privileges tends to be governed by judgments of maturity/readiness, and thus examination of parents' timetables provides a way to access their implicit developmental theories regarding autonomy (Goodnow & Collins, 1990). Research has revealed that families in more collectivistic cultures, including Asian-Americans and recent Asian and Latino immigrants to the United States, as well as native Asians all have later timetables for granting privileges than those of European descent in both the United States and Australia (Feldman & Quatman, 1988; Feldman & Rosenthal, 1990; Fuligni, 1998). Furthermore, timetables of middle-class African-American mothers appear to reflect specific cultural patterns and issues including concerns over health and safety, the need for adolescents to be self-sufficient at home, and more freedoms for adolescent boys vs. girls (Daddis & Smetana, 2005). In all cases, the researchers attribute these patterns to sociocultural context: variations in cultural values as well as to specific environmental challenges that families face.

COMPONENTS OF THE AUTONOMY PROCESS IN DIFFERENT CONTEXTS

Past research and theory on the autonomy process have identified several aspects of the parent–adolescent relationship as markers for how autonomy is negotiated within the family setting. Two aspects of the parent–adolescent relationship that have received substantial empirical attention include parenting style and parent–adolescent conflict. Parenting style refers to categorization of parental behavior according to two dimensions: warmth and control (e.g., Baumrind, 1991). Parents who are high in control but low in warmth have been characterized as authoritarian, an approach to parenting that is generally equated with the discouragement of individual autonomy. In contrast, authoritative parenting (high in both control and warmth) has been highlighted as optimally promoting autonomy while also setting appropriate limits. A separate body of literature has examined the presence of parent–adolescent conflict as a marker for increased bids for autonomy on the part of the adolescent; the ways in which such conflict is negotiated can indicate the degree to which autonomy is encouraged vs. discouraged within the parent–adolescent relationship (e.g., Smetana, 1988).

Parenting Style and Parental Control: Cross-Cultural Studies

With regard to cultural variations in parenting style, most studies have compared European-American parents to parents in other cultural groups. Studies have suggested that these parents tend to encourage independence and autonomy more than Asian parents, particularly Chinese parents. Chinese and Chinese-American parents have been described as more authoritarian, more frequently power assertive and restrictive, and less frequently autonomy granting and child centered than European-American parents (Chao, 2001; Dornbusch, Ritter, Leiderman, Roberts, & Fraleigh, 1987; Rosenthal & Feldman, 1990). Similarly, African-American parenting has been characterized as relatively more strict, with more emphasis on authority and discipline (particularly physical discipline) than European-American parenting, though not necessarily as compared to Latino parents (Florsheim, Tolan, & Gorman-Smith, 1996; Forehand, Miller, Dutra, & Chance, 1997; Garcia-Coll, Meyer, & Brillon, 1995; Portes, Dunham, & Williams, 1986).

Several researchers have cautioned against applying parenting typologies across cultural groups, arguing that parenting is not effectively captured by broadly generalized parenting styles (e.g., Chao, 2001). Other researchers have similarly noted that characterizing parenting solely according to ethnicity and/or cultural background is inappropriate, due to the multifaceted nature of all of these constructs (Cauce et al., 1996; Lim & Lim, 2004; Mason, Cauce, Gonzales, & Hiraga, 1996). To this point, research has demonstrated that ratings of strictness and control in both African-American and Chinese families do not covary with other indices of family functioning and/or parenting in the same manner as in other groups (Chao, 2001; Crockett, Veed, & Russell, 2010; Deater-Deckard et al., 1996; Dodge, McLoyd, & Lansford, 2005; Hill, 1995). More specifically, in families from non-European backgrounds, authoritarian parenting does not tend to covary with harsh parenting, and it is also not inversely related to parent–child closeness or to children's satisfaction with the parent–child relationship (Chao, 2001; Dornbusch et al. 1987; Hill, 1995; Kelley, Power, & Wimbush, 1992; Quoss & Zhao, 1995). Although it seems clear that approaches to parenting do vary according to cultural context, the precise nature of these variations as well as their implications for child and adolescent development are still not well understood.

Parental Control: Parenting According to Social Class and Context

In addition to variations according to cultural context, there is also evidence that parental restriction of autonomy varies according to level of environmental risk, and that strict parental control may carry different meaning in high-risk vs. low-risk settings. As noted previously, parents living in impoverished and dangerous neighborhoods tend to exert strict controls on their children's behavior, thus inhibiting their autonomy (Dearing, 2004; Garbarino, Bradshaw, & Kostelny, 2005; Magnuson & Duncan, 2002). Additional research has indicated that in high-risk families, such restrictiveness has been found to correlate *positively* with ratings of family democracy and with parental effectiveness (child compliance) (Baldwin, Baldwin, & Cole, 1990). Similarly, adolescents living in high-risk neighborhoods viewed mothers who attempted to undermine their autonomy while discussing an area of disagreement as *less* psychologically controlling, and characterized their relationship as involving higher levels of trust and acceptance (McElhaney & Allen, 2001). The opposite pattern was found for families in low-risk environments: those teens perceived the same maternal behaviors as *more* psychologically controlling, and rated their mothers as less trustworthy and less accepting.

In addition to the moderating effects of the level of community risk, researchers have examined the role of parents' experiences and opportunities in the workplace. For example, a large body of anthropological research has documented variations in parenting behaviors according to subsistence tasks, with the particular finding that parental encouragement of autonomy and self-direction varies according to such tasks (Barry, Child, & Bacon, 1959/67; Schlegel & Barry, 1991). Research within industrialized communities similarly proposes that approaches to parenting are aimed at helping children to achieve outcomes that are valued within social class (Gecas & Nye, 1974; Kohn, 1979; Luster, Rhodes, & Haas, 1989). These studies have indicated, for example, that higher socioeconomic status (SES) parents endorse valuing self-direction and tend to be both more involved with their children and less restrictive of their actions, whereas lower SES parents value conformity and demonstrate this value by being more restrictive of their children (Luster et al., 1989; Tudge, Hogan, Snezhkova, Kulakova, & Etz, 2000; Weininger & Lareau, 2009). Socioeconomic status, social class, and type of work are all clearly highly complex constructs that are likely to affect family functioning via numerous pathways (e.g., Duncan & Magnuson, 2003), and associations between these variables and approaches to parenting are not always straightforward (e.g., Tudge et al., 2000). Nonetheless, these findings are generally consistent with the notion that parental approaches to autonomy are associated with valuing self-direction vs. conformity, which in turn varies according to sociocultural context.

Parent–Adolescent Conflict

Parent–adolescent conflict has been thought to be an important component of the autonomy process within American families. It has been proposed that parent–adolescent conflict is a marker for adolescents' increasing bids for autonomy, and that the ways in which such conflict is negotiated are indicative of parents' and adolescents' general approaches to the autonomy process (Collins & Steinberg, 2006; Goossens, 2006; Smetana, 1988). However, direct expression of conflicts may be more prevalent in cultures that value individual autonomy, whereas avoidance of conflict via compliance, negotiation, or withdrawal may be favored in cultures that value harmonious relationships (Markus & Lin, 1999). Economic realities such as the necessary reliance on family members for support and survival may also serve to reduce parent–adolescent discord and increase harmony (Schlegel & Barry, 1991). Finally, in cultures in which adolescence is relatively short and youth are granted the rights and privileges of adulthood, parent–adolescent conflict may not be as necessary or relevant to the process of separation and individuation (Schlegel & Barry, 1991).

Although there may be some cultural universals with regard to parent–teen conflicts, existing data indicate that certain aspects of parent–adolescent conflict do indeed vary across both cultural and contextual lines (Gabrielidis, Stephan, Ybarram, Pearson, & Villareal, 1997; Haar & Krahe, 1999; Kapadia & Miller, 2005). With regard to similarities, both levels of parent–teen conflict and general topics of disagreement (e.g., chores) appear to be relatively consistent across cultural groups within American samples, as well as within other cultures (Cauce et al., 1996; Fuligni, 1998; Yau & Smetana, 1996). Furthermore, studies suggest that like middle-class American teens, adolescents from other cultural groups are likely to see conflicts with parents as issues of personal choice (Cauce et al., 1996; Yau & Smetana, 1996). Yet, adolescents and parents from non-European groups and/or those that adhere to more collectivistic values tend to have fewer conflicts, with parents engaging in more of the final decision making, and teens being more likely to emphasize respect and preserving harmony in their relationships with their parents (Cauce et al., 1996; Dixon, Graber, & Brooks-Gunn, 2008; Phinney et al., 2005; Qin, Pomerantz, & Wang, 2009; Yau & Smetana, 1996). Furthermore, certain patterns of conflict resolution (e.g., parental appeals to health and safety, parental power assertion) seem to be particularly characteristic of specific cultural and socioeconomic settings (Smetana, Daddis, & Chuang, 2003; Smetana & Gaines, 1999; Smetana, 2000).

NEGOTIATION OF AUTONOMY AND ADOLESCENT OUTCOMES

The above research indicates that parents value and utilize different approaches to parenting and autonomy promotion vs. restriction according to a variety of sociocultural factors. The importance of understanding group differences in approaches to autonomy becomes even clearer when the links between parenting behaviors and adolescent outcomes are considered. Research within American samples has demonstrated associations between certain styles of negotiating autonomy and a variety of important indices of adolescent adjustment (Allen et al., 2002a, 2002b, 2006; Collins & Steinberg, 2006; Zimmer-Gembeck & Collins, 2003). This research emphasizes the importance of warm, supportive parent–adolescent relationships in which parents encourage and support the adolescents' developing autonomy. Such research may be overlooking the fact that other styles of negotiating autonomy may be equally adaptive in some settings.

Parenting Style and Adolescent Outcomes

Although authoritative parenting has consistently been linked with positive outcomes in families of European-American decent, several studies have revealed that both cultural and environmental factors moderate the links between parenting style and adolescent outcomes. Some studies have indicated that authoritative parenting does not similarly benefit teens from other sociocultural backgrounds, and others have further suggested that authoritarian parenting and its correlates are linked to more adaptive outcomes in riskier settings and/or when such behavior is in line with cultural parenting values (Chao, 2001; Fung & Lau, 2009; Lamborn, Dornbusch, & Steinberg, 1996; McElhaney & Allen, 2001). For example, unilateral parent decision making that does not allow for adolescent input has been found to be associated with positive adolescent outcomes (less involvement in deviance, higher academic competence) in African-American families, whereas this same decision-making style is associated with poorer outcomes in European-American families (Lamborn et al., 1996). Thus, parenting that involves encouragement of adolescent autonomy may be beneficial for groups in which it is valued, whereas in other contexts, parenting that involves autonomy restriction appears beneficial (Lansford et al., 2005).

Parental Control and Adolescent Outcomes

Similar to the research on parenting style, in communities in which adolescents are exposed to high levels of risks (e.g., high crime rates), and also within cultural groups that highly value family solidarity and deference to parents, strict parental control has been found to be unrelated to problem behaviors, and even to predict beneficial child outcomes (Duane & Halgunseth, 2005; Lamborn, Dornbusch, & Steinberg, 1996; Rudy & Halgunseth, 2005; Simons, Lin, Gordon, Brody, Murray, & Conger, 2002). This finding has been replicated with regard to various forms of behavioral control (e.g., unilateral decision making, close parental monitoring) and, in some cases, psychological control. For example, in both low-income and high-crime settings, parental restrictiveness and close parental monitoring predict higher levels of adolescent academic competence and decreased involvement in problem behaviors (Baldwin, Baldwin, & Cole, 1990; Beyers, Bates, Pettit, & Dodge, 2003; Dearing, 2004; Gonzales, Cauce, Friedman, & Mason, 1996; O'Neil, Parke & McDowell, 2001). Furthermore, several surveys of parenting practices in primarily African-American samples have demonstrated that the level of environmental risk moderates the links between parental control and adolescent adjustment. In high-risk contexts within these samples, parental restriction of autonomy during early and middle adolescence is linked with higher levels of academic competence, decreased externalizing behaviors, and more positive self-worth (Dearing, 2004; Gonzales et al., 1996; Gutman, Sameroff, & Eccles, 2002; Mason et al., 1996; Smetana, Campione-Barr, & Daddis, 2004).

Summary and Conclusions

A growing body of research on sociocultural influences on parenting and youth development suggests that sociocultural context can shape the degree to which autonomy is valued, the ways in which it is conceptualized, and the manner in which it is negotiated within parent–adolescent relationships. Although achieving autonomy may be considered a universal developmental goal, the degree to which parents promote vs. restrict their teens' autonomy is likely to be influenced by a range of values and beliefs. Not only is there variation in the ways in which parents (and adolescents) approach the autonomy process, but the consequences of autonomy promotion vs. restriction also show variation according to sociocultural context. More specifically, whereas parental restriction of adolescent autonomy appears to be clearly linked to maladaptive outcomes in predominately European-American samples, the same is not necessarily true in other groups.

Research that aims to fully understand family processes with regard to this aspect of child and adolescent development should thus carefully consider the roles of cultural values and the constellation of variables that contribute to the level of environmental risk. Though there has been increasing attention to sociocultural context in developmental research, future research should aim to extend our understanding of the conditions under which autonomy restriction is appropriate vs. maladaptive. Furthermore, it would be useful to identify more carefully the aspects of the autonomy process that unfold similarly across settings, and those that are more particular to certain cultures or contexts. It seems premature to generalize our current theories regarding this crucial developmental process to all families until we have a more complete and nuanced understanding of the role of sociocultural context. This latter point is particularly important when designing prevention and/or intervention efforts that are aimed at altering parenting practices, presumably to improve adaptive outcomes for children and teenagers.

References

Allen, J. P., Bell, K., & Boykin, K. A. (2000, March). *Autonomy in discussions vs. autonomy in decision-making as predictors of developing close friendship competence.* Paper presented at the Biennial Meetings of the Society for Research on Adolescence, Chicago, IL.

Allen, J. P., Hauser, S. T., Bell, K. L., & O'Conner, T. G. (1994). Longitudinal assessment of autonomy and relatedness in adolescent-family interactions as predictors of adolescent ego developmental and self-esteem. *Child Development, 65,* 179–194.

Allen, J. P., Hauser, S. T., O'Connor, T. G., & Bell, K. L. (2002a). Prediction of peer-rated adult hostility from autonomy struggles in adolescent-family interactions. *Development and Psychopathology, 14,* 123–137.

Allen, J. P., Insabella, G. M., Porter, M. R., Smith, F. D., Land, D. J., & Phillips, N. (2006). A social-interactional model of the development of depressive symptoms in adolescence. *Journal of Consulting and Clinical Psychology, 74*(1), 55–65.

Allen, J. P., Marsh, P., McFarland, C., McElhaney, K. B., Land, D. J., Jodl, K. M., et al. (2002b). Attachment and autonomy as predictors of the development of social skills and delinquency during midadolescence. *Journal of Consulting & Clinical Psychology, 70*(1), 56–66.

Baldwin, A. L., Baldwin, C., & Cole, R. E. (1990). Stress-resistant families and stress-resistant children. In J. E. Rolf, A. S. Masten, D. Cicchetti, K. H. Nuechterlein & S. Weintraub (Eds.), *Risk and protective factors in the development of psychopathology* (pp. 257–280). New York: Cambridge University Press.

Baltes, M. M., & Silverberg, S. B. (1994). The dynamics between dependency and autonomy: Illustrations across the life span. In D. L. Featherman, R. M. Lerner, & M. Perlmutter (Eds.), *Life span development and behavior,* Vol. 12 (pp. 41–91). Hillsdale, NJ: Lawrence Erlbaum Associates.

Barry, H.,III, Child, I. L., & Bacon, M. K. (1967). Relation of child training to subsistence economy. In C. S. Ford (Ed.), *Cross-cultural approaches: Readings in comparative research* (pp. 246–258). New Haven, CT: HRAF Press.

Baumrind, D. (1991). The influence of parenting style on adolescent competence and substance use. *Journal of Early Adolescence, 11*(1), 56–95.

Beyers, J., Bates, J., Pettit, G., & Dodge, K. (2003). Neighborhood structure, parenting processes, and the development of youths' externalizing behaviors: A multilevel analysis. *American Journal of Community Psychology, 31*(1–2), 35–53.

Blos, P. (1967). *The second individuation process of adolescence: The psychoanalytic study of the child.* New York: International Universities Press.

Bornstein, M., & Güngör, D. (2009). Organizing principles and processes from developmental science for culture and caregiving. *Perspectives on human development, family, and culture* (pp. 69–85). New York: Cambridge University Press.

Bradley, R. (2002). Environment and parenting. *Handbook of parenting: Vol. 2: Biology and ecology of parenting* (2nd ed.) (pp. 281–314). Mahwah, NJ: Lawrence Erlbaum Associates.

Cauce, A. M., Hiraga, Y., Graves, D., Gonzales, N., Ryan-Finn, K., & Grove, K. (1996). African-American mothers and their adolescent daughters: Closeness, conflict, and control. In B. J. Ross Leadbeater & N. Way (Eds.), *Urban girls: Resisting stereotypes, creating identities* (pp. 100–116). New York: New York University Press.

Chao, R. K. (2001). Extending research on the consequences of parenting style for Chinese Americans and European Americans. *Child Development, 72*(6), 1832–1843.

Chaudhuri, J., Easterbrooks, M., & Davis, C. (2009). The relation between emotional availability and parenting style: Cultural and economic factors in a diverse sample of young mothers. *Parenting: Science and Practice, 9*(3–4), 277–299.

Coll, C., & Pachter, L. (2002). Ethnic and minority parenting. *Handbook of parenting: Vol. 4: Social conditions and applied parenting* (2nd ed., pp. 1–20). Mahwah, NJ: Lawrence Erlbaum Associates.

Collins, W., & Steinberg, L. (2006). Adolescent development in interpersonal context. *Handbook of child psychology: Vol. 3, Social, emotional, and personality development* (6th ed., pp. 1003–1067). Hoboken, NJ: John Wiley & Sons Inc.

Crockett, L., Veed, G., & Russell, S. (2010). Do measures of parenting have the same meaning for European, Chinese, and Filipino American adolescents? Tests of measurement equivalence. *Asian American parenting and parent–adolescent relationships* (pp. 17–35). New York: Springer Science + Business Media.

Daddis, C., & Smetana, J. (2005). Middle-class African American families' expectations for adolescents' behavioural autonomy. *International Journal of Behavioral Development, 29*(5), 371–381.

Dearing, E. (2004). The developmental implications of restrictive and supportive parenting across neighborhoods and ethnicities: Exceptions are the rule. *Journal of Applied Developmental Psychology, 25*(5), 555–575.

Deater-Deckard, K., Dodge, K., Bates, J., & Pettit, G. (1996). Physical discipline among African American and European American mothers: Links to children's externalizing behaviors. *Developmental Psychology, 32*(6), 1065–1072.

Dixon, S., Graber, J., & Brooks-Gunn, J. (2008). The roles of respect for parental authority and parenting practices in parent-child conflict among African American, Latino, and European American families. *Journal of Family Psychology, 22*(1), 1–10.

Dodge, K., McLoyd, V., & Lansford, J. (2005). The cultural context of physically disciplining children. *African American family life: Ecological and cultural diversity* (pp. 245–263). New York: Guilford Press.

Dornbusch, S. M., Ritter, P. L., Leiderman, P. H., Roberts, D. F., & Fraleigh, M. J. (1987). The relation of parenting style to adolescent school performance. *Child Development, 58*, 1244–1257.

Feldman, S. S., & Quatman, T. (1988). Factors influencing age expectations for adolescent autonomy: A study of early adolescents and parents. *Journal of Early Adolescence,* 8(4), 325–343.

Feldman, S. S., & Rosenthal, D. A. (1990). The acculturation of autonomy expectations in Chinese high schoolers residing in two Western nations. *International Journal of Psychology, 25,* 259–281.

Florsheim, P., Tolan, P., & Gorman-Smith, D. (1996). Family processes and risk for externalizing behavior problems among African American and Hispanic boys. *Journal of Consulting and Clinical Psychology, 64*(6), 1222–1230.

Forehand, R., Miller, K., Dutra, R., & Chance, M. (1997). Role of parenting in adolescent deviant behavior: Replication across and within two ethnic groups. *Journal of Consulting and Clinical Psychology, 65*(6), 1036–1041.

Fuhrman, T., & Holmbeck, G. (1995). A contextual-moderator analysis of emotional autonomy and adjustment in adolescence. *Child Development, 66,* 793–811.

Fuligni, A. J. (1998). Authority, autonomy and parent-adolescent conflict and cohesion: A study of adolescents from Mexican, Chinese, Filipino and European backgrounds. *Developmental Psychology, 34,* 782–792.

Fuligni, A. J., & Eccles, J. S. (1993). Perceived parent-child relationships and early adolescents' orientation toward peers. *Developmental Psychology, 29*(4), 622–632.

Fuligni, A., & Zhang, W. (2004). Attitudes toward family obligation among adolescents in contemporary urban and rural China. *Child Development, 75*(1), 180–192.

Fuller, B., & García Coll, C. (2010). Learning from Latinos: Contexts, families, and child development in motion. *Developmental Psychology, 46*(3), 559–565.

Fung, J., & Lau, A. (2009). Punitive discipline and child behavior problems in Chinese-American immigrant families: The moderating effects of indigenous child-rearing ideologies. *International Journal of Behavioral Development, 33*(6), 520–530.

Garbarino, J., Bradshaw, C., & Kostelny, K. (2005). Neighborhood and community influences on parenting. *Parenting: An ecological perspective* (2nd ed., pp. 297–318). Mahwah, NJ: Lawrence Erlbaum Associates.

Gabrielidis, C., Stephan, W., Ybarra, O., Pearson, V., & Villareal, L. (1997). Preferred styles of conflict resolution: Mexico and the United States. *Journal of Cross-Cultural Psychology, 28*(6), 661–677.

Gecas, V., & Nye, F. I. (1974). Sex and class differences in parent-child interaction: A test of Kohn's hypothesis. *Journal of Marriage and the Family, 36,* 742–749.

Goldstein, S. E., Davis-Kean, P. E., & Eccles, J. S. (2005). Parents, peers, and problem behavior: A longitudinal investigation of the impact of relationship perceptions and characteristics on the development of adolescent problem behavior. *Developmental Psychology, 41*(2), 401–413.

Gonzales, N. A., Cauce, A. M., Friedman, R. J., & Mason, C. A. (1996). Family, peer, and neighborhood influences on academic achievement among African-American adolescents: One-year prospective effects. *American Journal of Community Psychology, 24*(3), 365–387.

Goodnow, J. J., & Collins, W. A. (1990). *Development according to parents: The nature, sources and consequences of parents' ideas.* Hillsdale, NJ: Lawrence Erlbaum.

Goossens, L. (2006). The many faces of adolescent autonomy: Parent-adolescent conflict, behavioral decision-making, and emotional distancing. *Handbook of adolescent development* (pp. 135–153). New York: Psychology Press.

Gutman, L., Sameroff, A., & Eccles, J. (2002). The academic achievement of African American students during early adolescence: An examination of multiple risk, promotive, and protective factors. *American Journal of Community Psychology, 30*(3), 367–400.

Haar, B. F. & Krahe, B. (1999). Strategies for resolving interpersonal conflicts in adolescence: A German-Indonesian comparison. *Journal of Cross-Cultural Psychology, 30*(6), 667–683.

Halgunseth, L., Ispa, J., & Rudy, D. (2006). Parental control in Latino families: An integrated review of the literature. *Child Development, 77*(5), 1282–1297.

Hall, F. D. (2002, April). *African-American adolescents' observed autonomy and relatedness with their mothers as predictors of social competence.* Poster presented at the Biennial Meetings of the Society for Research on Adolescence, New Orleans, LA.

Harkness, S., & Super, C. M. (2002). Culture and parenting. In M. H. Bornstein (Ed.), *Handbook of parenting: Vol 2: Biology and ecology of parenting* (2nd ed., pp. 253–280). Mahwah, NJ: Lawrence Erlbaum.

Harwood, R. L., Scholmerich, A., & Schulze, P. A. (2000). Homogeneity and heterogeneity in cultural belief systems. In S. Harkness, C. Raeff, & C. M. Super (Eds.), *New directions for child and adolescent development: Vol. 87, Variability in the social construction of the child* (pp. 41–57). San Francisco, CA: Jossey-Bass.

Hill, N. E. (1995). The relationship between family environment and parenting style: A preliminary study of African American families. *Journal of Black Psychology, 21*(4), 408–423.

Ho, C., Bluestein, D. N., & Jenkins, J. M. (2008). Cultural differences in the relationship between parenting and children's behavior. *Developmental Psychology, 44*(2), 507–522.

Kapadia, S., & Miller, J. (2005). Parent-adolescent relationships in the context of interpersonal disagreements: View from a collectivist culture. *Psychology and Developing Societies, 17*(1), 33–50.

Kelley, M. L., Power, T. G., & Wimbush, D. D. (1992). Determinants of disciplinary practices in low-income black mothers. *Child Development, 63,* 573–582.

Kitayama, S., Markus, H., & Kurokawa, M. (2000). Culture, emotion, and well-being: Good feelings in Japan and the United States. *Cognition and Emotion, 14*(1), 93–124.

Kohn, M. L. (1963). Social class and parent-child relationships: An interpretation. *American Journal of Sociology, 68,* 471–480.

Kohn, M. L. (1979). The effects of social class on parental values and practices. In D. Reiss & H. A. Hoffman (Eds.), *The American family: Dying or developing* (pp. 45–68). New York: Plenum Press.

Laible, D., & Carlo, G. (2004). The differential relations of maternal and paternal support and control to adolescent social competence, self-worth, and sympathy. *Journal of Adolescent Research, 19*(6), 2004.

Lamborn, S. D., Dornbusch, S. M., & Steinberg, L. (1996). Ethnicity and community context as moderators of the relations between family decision making and adolescent adjustment. *Child Development, 67,* 283–301.

Lansford, J. E., Dodge, K. A., Malone, P. S., Bacchini, D., Zelli, A., Chaudhary, N., Manke, B., Chang, L., Oburu, P., Palmerus, K., Pastorelli, C., Bombi, A., Tapanya, S., Deater-Deckard, K., & Quinn, N. (2005). Physical discipline and children's adjustment: Cultural normativeness as a moderator. *Child Development, 76,* 1234–1246.

Lee, J., & Bell, N. J. (2003). Individual differences in attachment-autonomy configurations: Linkages with substance use and youth competencies. *Journal of Adolescence, 26*(3), 347–361.

LeVine, R., Dixon, S., LeVine, S., Richman, A., Keefer, C., Liederman, P., et al. (2008). The comparative study of parenting. *Anthropology and child development: A cross-cultural reader* (pp. 55–65). Malden: Blackwell Publishing.

Lim, S., & Lim, B. K. (2004). Parenting style and child outcomes in Chinese and immigrant Chinese families: Current findings and cross-cultural considerations in conceptualization and research. *Marriage and Family Review, 35,* 21–43.

Luster, T., Rhoades, K., & Haas, B. (1989). The relation between parental values and parenting behavior: A test of the Kohn hypothesis. *Journal of Marriage and the Family, 51,* 139–147.

Magnuson, K. A., & Duncan, G. J. (2002). Parents in poverty. In M. H. Bornstein (Ed.), *Handbook of parenting* (Vol. 4)*: Social conditions and applied parenting* (2nd ed.), (pp. 95–121). Mahwah, NJ: Lawrence Erlbaum.

Markus, H., & Lin, L. (1999). Conflictways: Cultural diversity in the meanings and practices of conflict. In D. Prentice & D. Miller (Eds.), *Cultural divides: Understanding and overcoming group conflict* (pp. 302–333). New York: Russell Sage.

Mason, C. A., Cauce, A. M., Gonzales, N., & Hiraga, Y. (1996). Neither too sweet nor too sour: Problem peers, maternal control, and problem behavior in African-American adolescents. *Child Development, 67,* 2115–2130.

McElhaney, K. B., & Allen, J. P. (2001). Autonomy and adolescent social functioning: The moderating effect of risk. *Child Development, 72,* 220–231.

McElhaney, K., Allen, J., Stephenson, J., & Hare, A. (2009). Attachment and autonomy during adolescence. *Handbook of adolescent psychology, Vol. 1: Individual bases of adolescent development* (3rd ed., pp. 358–403). Hoboken, NJ: John Wiley & Sons Inc.

Okagaki, L., & Bingham, G. (2005). Parents' social cognitions and their parenting behaviors. *Parenting: An ecological perspective* (2nd ed., pp. 3–33). Mahwah, NJ: Lawrence Erlbaum Associates.

O'Neil, R., Parke, R., & McDowell, D. (2001). Objective and subjective features of children's neighborhoods: Relations to parental regulatory strategies and children's social competence. *Journal of Applied Developmental Psychology, 22*(2), 135–155.

Oyserman, D., Coon, H., & Kemmelmeier, M. (2002). Rethinking individualism and collectivism: Evaluation of theoretical assumptions and meta-analyses. *Psychological Bulletin, 128*(1), 3–72.

Parke, R., & Buriel, R. (2006). Socialization in the family: Ethnic and ecological perspectives. In *Handbook of child psychology: Vol. 3, Social, emotional, and personality development* (6th ed., pp. 429–504). Hoboken, NJ: John Wiley & Sons Inc.

Peterson, G. W., Cobas, J. A., Bush K. R., Supple, A., & Wilson, S. M. (2004). Parent-youth relationships and the self-esteem of Chinese adolescents: Collectivism vs. individualism. *Marriage & Family Review, 36,* 173–200.

Peterson, G. W., Steinmetz, S. K., & Wilson, S. M. (2003). Cultural and cross-cultural perspectives on parent-youth relations. *Marriage & Family Review, 35,* 5–19.

Phinney, J., Kim-Jo, T., Osorio, S., & Vilhjalmsdottir, P. (2005). Autonomy and relatedness in adolescent-parent disagreements: Ethnic and developmental factors. *Journal of Adolescent Research, 20,* 8–39.

Phinney, J., Ong, A., & Madden, T. (2000). Cultural values and intergenerational value discrepancies in immigrant and non-immigrant families. *Child Development, 71,* 528–539.

Portes, P. R., Dunham, R. M., & Williams, S. (1986). Assessing child-rearing style in eco-logical settings: Its relation to culture, social class, early age intervention, and scholas-tic achievement. *Adolescence, 21*(83), 723–735.

Qin, L., Pomerantz, E., & Wang, Q. (2009). Are gains in decision-making autonomy during early adolescence beneficial for emotional functioning? The case of the United States and China. *Child Development, 80*(6), 1705–1721.

Quoss, B., & Zhao, W. (1995). Parenting styles and children's satisfaction with parenting in China and the United States. *Journal of Comparative Family Studies, 26,* 265–280.

Raeff, C. (2006). *Always separate, always connected: Independence and interdependence in cultural contexts of development.* Mahwah, NJ: Lawrence Erlbaum Associates.

Rosenthal, D. A., & Feldman, S. S. (1990). The acculturation of Chinese immigrants: Perceived effects on family functioning and length of residence in two cultural con-texts. *The Journal of Genetic Psychology, 151*(4), 495–514.

Rudy, D., & Halgunseth, L. (2005). Psychological control, maternal emotion and cogni-tion, and child outcomes in individualist and collectivist groups. *Journal of Emotional Abuse, 5*(4), 237–264.

Russell, S., Crockett, L., & Chao, R. (2010). *Asian American parenting and parent-adolescent relationships.* New York: Springer Science + Business Media.

Schlegel, A., & Barry, H. III (1991). *Adolescence: An anthropological inquiry.* New York: The Free Press.

Simons, R. L., Lin, K., Gordon, L. C., Brody, G. H., Murry, V., & Conger, R. D. (2002). Community differences in the association between parenting practices and child con-duct problems. *Journal of Marriage and Family, 64,* 331–345.

Smetana, J. G. (1988). Adolescents' and parents' conceptions of parental authority. *Child Development, 59,* 321–335.

Smetana, J. G. (2000). Middle-class African American adolescents' and parents' con-ceptions of parental authority and parenting practices: A longitudinal investigation. *Child Development, 71*(6), 1672–1686.

Smetana, J. G. (2002). Culture, autonomy and personal jurisdiction in adolescent-parent relationships. *Advances in Child Development, 29,* 51–87.

Smetana, J. G., Campione-Barr, N., & Daddis, C. (2004). Longitudinal development of family decision making: Defining healthy behavioral autonomy for middle-class African American adolescents. *Child Development, 75*(5), 1418–1434.

Smetana, J. G., & Chuang, S. (2001). Middle class African American parents' conceptions of parenting in early adolescence. *Journal of Research on Adolescence, 11,* 177–198.

Smetana, J. G., Daddis, C., & Chuang, S. S. (2003). "Clean your room!": A longitudi-nal investigation of adolescent-parent conflict and conflict resolution in middle-class African American families. *Journal of Adolescent Research, 18*(6), 631–650.

Smetana, J. G., & Gaines, C. (1999). Adolescent-parent conflict in middle-class African American families. *Child Development, 70*(6), 1447–1463.

Soenens, B. & Vansteenkiste, M. (2005). Antecedents and outcomes of self-determina-tion in 3 life domains: The role of parents' and teachers' autonomy support. *Journal of Youth and Adolescence, 34*(6), 589–604.

Tudge, J., Hogan, D., Snezhkova, I., Kulakova, N., & Etz, K. (2000). Parents' child-rearing values and beliefs in the United States and Russia: The impact of culture and social class. *Infant and Child Development, 9*(2), 105–121.

Weininger, E., & Lareau, A. (2009). Paradoxical pathways: An ethnographic extension of Kohn's findings on class and childrearing. *Journal of Marriage & the Family, 71*(3), 680–695.

Wilson, L. C., Wilson, C. M., & Berkeley-Caines, L. (2003). Age, gender and socio-economic differences in parental socialization preferences in Guyana. *Journal of Comparative Family Studies, 34*, 213–227.

Wright, J. D., & Wright, S. R. (1976). Social class and parental values for children: A partial replication and extension of the Kohn thesis. *American Sociological Review, 41*, 527–537.

Yau, J., & Smetana, J. G. (1996). Adolescent-parent conflict among Chinese adolescents in Hong Kong. *Child Development, 67*, 1262–1275.

Zimmer-Gembeck, M., & Collins, W. (2003). Autonomy development during adolescence. *Blackwell handbook of adolescence* (pp. 175–204). Malden: Blackwell Publishing.

8

"Mama, I'm a Person, Too!"

Individuation and Young African-American Mothers' Parenting Competence

LAURA D. PITTMAN, LAUREN S. WAKSCHLAG,
P. LINDSAY CHASE-LANSDALE, AND JEANNE BROOKS-GUNN

Mothers who transition early to parenthood are more likely to have negative outcomes as they emerge into adulthood and they are more likely to adopt more negative parenting practices in their interactions with their children (e.g., Moore & Brooks-Gunn, 2002; Wakschlag & Hans, 2000). Given that parents who are more stimulating and supportive in their parenting have children with more positive cognitive and socioemotional developmental outcomes (Bornstein, 2002), understanding what factors facilitate the development of parenting competence among young mothers is important and may inform interventions serving this population. One way in which young mothers differ from older mothers is that they are still negotiating age-appropriate developmental tasks such as individuation from one's family of origin. Thus, this chapter uses quantitative and qualitative data to examine the link between young mothers' individuation from their own mothers and their ability to parent their preschool-aged children.

DEVELOPMENTAL FRAMEWORK FOR THE STUDY OF YOUNG MOTHERHOOD

An early transition to motherhood has long been identified as a risk factor for both young mothers and their offspring (Moore & Brooks-Gunn, 2002; Wakschlag & Hans, 2000), although varying long-term trajectories have been identified (e.g., Oxford, et al., 2005). The risks that are known to be associated with teenage pregnancy (e.g., lower family socioeconomic status, low parental education) are also thought to explain many of the negative educational and vocational outcomes found among young mothers (Hotz, McElroy, & Sanders, 2005). However, those young mothers who achieve life-stage goals (e.g., high school completion), even if they are delayed in doing so, achieve better outcomes than those who do not, such as living above the poverty line, having fewer children, and not utilizing welfare (Moore & Brooks-Gunn, 2002). Similarly, although few investigators have found differences in functioning comparing infants of younger as compared to older mothers, by the preschool years consistent differences in children's cognitive and psychosocial outcomes emerge that continue into adolescence (e.g., Moore & Brooks-Gunn, 2002; Wakschlag & Hans, 2000). In addition, children whose young mothers were able to meet the demands of early adulthood (e.g., who gained further education, avoided welfare receipt) fare better as well (Furstenberg, Brooks-Gunn, & Morgan, 1987).

Young mothers who experience this "off-time" life event face multiple challenges to making a successful transition into adulthood. Taking on the parenting role in the early years may interfere with completion of other normative tasks of adolescence and young adulthood such as high school completion, employment, development of a mature identity, and financial and residential independence (Coley & Chase-Lansdale, 1998; Wakschlag & Hans, 2000). Furthermore, it is difficult to assert your independence from family members while at the same time being increasingly dependent on them for assistance with child rearing and child care. However, little research has addressed how young mothers' negotiation of these life-stage tasks affects their assumption of adult responsibilities, in general, and their parenting abilities, in particular. On the one hand, many adolescents may not be able to focus simultaneously on the normative tasks of adolescence, such as ego development and the formation of intensive peer bonds (Hauser, 1991), as well as the demands of parenting (Wakschlag & Hans, 2000). In fact, research shows that young mothers tend to be less supportive, more detached, and more intrusive in their interactions with their young children as compared to older mothers with similar demographic characteristics (Berlin, Brady-Smith, & Brooks-Gunn, 2002). On the other hand, those young mothers who have already negotiated many of these developmental tasks successfully may be better able to focus their attention on adapting to their new role as a parent.

Individuation is an important developmental task of adolescence through which adolescents differentiate themselves from the environment and recognize their own unique identities (Collins & Steinberg, 2006). It may be that the capacity to form a mature and independent identity while simultaneously remaining emotionally connected within one context (e.g., to your family of origin) is linked to relational competence in other domains such as parenting young children. Such cross-contextual linkages have already been demonstrated between relationships with family and peers, such that youth who display high levels of assertiveness and connectedness in discussions with their parents also are more likely to have cooperative peer relationships (Cooper & Cooper, 1992; Russell, Pettit, & Mize, 1998). Therefore, we reasoned that a similar correspondence in relational competence would be seen across other contexts, such as between the relationships of young mothers with their parents and young mothers with their children.

To this end, the present study was designed to integrate developmental, family, and sociodemographic perspectives in examining factors that promote parenting competence in young mothers. Although economic and sociological perspectives may be important when considering financial and educational attainment among young mothers (e.g., Moore et al., 1993; Maynard, 1997), a family systems perspective is necessary to fully understand the development of parenting competence among this group. Our data are drawn from a longitudinal study of adolescent mothers and their offspring designed to identify linkages between a mother's life course and her children's developmental outcomes (see Baydar, Brooks-Gunn, & Furstenberg, 1993; Brooks-Gunn, Guo, & Furstenberg 1993; Chase-Lansdale, Brooks-Gunn & Zamsky, 1994; Furstenberg et al., 1987; Wakschlag, Chase-Lansdale, & Brooks-Gunn. 1996). Within this sample of primarily disadvantaged, multigenerational families with young mothers, family and developmental processes that might serve as protective factors for child rearing in the next generation were examined. Specifically, we investigated the extent to which young mothers' ability to develop mature relationships within their families of origin related to a mature and appropriate parenting style with their preschooler.

INDIVIDUATION: LINKS TO ADJUSTMENT IN ADOLESCENCE AND BEYOND

During adolescence, biological, social, and psychological changes underlie the emergence of a separate and mature identity that marks the transition to adulthood. A central developmental task of this period is the achievement of "individuation," which has been defined as a balance between individuality and connectedness within a family context (Cooper, Grotevant, & Condon, 1983). The successful transition to adulthood involves the development of "greater autonomy and competence in personal decision making, problem solving, and affect regulation" (Lopez & Gover, 1993, p. 560). Theories traditionally have emphasized individuation as a process involving the relinquishment of familial attachments with an emphasis on detachment and the increasing significance of peer relationships (e.g., Blos, 1967; Erickson, 1968; Freud, 1958; Loevinger, 1976). However, the conceptualization of individuation has changed to involve a reorganization of family relationships in which adolescents develop this mature identity while, at the same time, attaining new levels of understanding and mutuality in their relationships with their parents (Bowlby, 1988; Collins & Steinberg, 2006; McElhaney, Allen, Stephenson, & Hare, 2009).

During the period of adolescence and the transition to young adulthood, multiple processes are co-occurring that influence both identity development and individuation from families. Higher level cognitive abilities that emerge during this period include the capacity to think abstractly and logically, and to consider multiple perspectives simultaneously (Kuhn, 2009) as well as the ability to engage in higher levels of moral reasoning (Eisenberg, Morris, McDaniel, & Spinrad, 2009). These competencies enable adolescents to systematically integrate complex and abstract information about the self and others while coordinating diverse social perspectives (Smetana & Villalobos, 2009). In addition, these skills allow adolescents to develop a deeper understanding of their roles in the family, to see relationships from a more sophisticated perspective, and to reason abstractly in ways that assist with problem solving and negotiating differences. Peer relation-ships also are deepened and transformed during this period, and are character-ized by new levels of commitment, genuineness, and intimacy (Brown & Larson, 2009). The more egalitarian nature of peer relationships offers a safe context for the exploration of identity and intimacy (Cooper & Cooper, 1992).

Also central to the individuation process are transformations in adolescents' relationships with their families that occur during this period. Parent–child rela-tions shift from early- to mid-adolescence toward an increase in conflict and decrease in cohesion (Conger & Ge, 1999; Smetana, Campione-Barr, & Metzger, 2006). These changes in parent–child relationships play a key role in fostering or impeding the individuation process as they provide adolescents with the opportu-nity to negotiate new patterns of independence and mutuality with their parents (Powers & Welsh, 1999). Despite this increased level and intensity of conflict in the parent–adolescent relationship, dyads whose relationships are also high in warmth and support during early adolescence continue to remain close as their relationship is transformed in mid-adolescence (Conger & Ge, 1999). Thus, par-ents play a key role in either *constraining* or *enabling* individuation via family communication processes (Hauser, 1991). Parental behaviors that are enabling include explaining, problem solving, expressing interest and curiosity, focusing, self-disclosure, empathy, and respectful listening (Hauser, 1991). Parental con-straining behaviors involve detachment, strong emotional response to expressions of disagreement, being judgmental, and devaluing (Hauser, 1991). Parental behav-iors that promote open communication and tolerance of differences foster indi-viduation through nurturing self-assertion, self-awareness, flexibility, tolerance of diverse perspectives, and mutuality.

Yet, individuation-promoting processes go beyond parental warmth and posi-tive involvement and include active support of the adolescents' assertions of autonomy. For example, adolescent daughters whose mothers are less likely to accept their arguments and claims as legitimate have lower ego development scores as well as higher anxiety and depressive affect (Brooks-Gunn & Zahaykevich, 1989; Graber & Brooks-Gunn, 1999). Furthermore, parents who demonstrate high levels of involvement but low levels of autonomy support have adolescents who are less individuated and report higher levels of symptomatology than those whose parents combine involvement with support of their adolescents' autonomy (Ryan, Deci, Grolnick, & LaGuardia, 2006). Thus, parents' communication pat-terns and parenting styles that support the adolescents' attempts to act autono-mously enhance young people's individuation and psychological adjustment.

The importance of individuation for healthy adjustment is evident in both the individual and family contexts. In terms of individual adjustment, cross-sectional research has found that college students who are more highly individuated from their parents have fewer depressive symptoms, higher levels of self-esteem, greater ego-identity development, and more positive overall emotional adjustment (e.g., Kalsner & Pistole, 2003; Mattanah, Hancock, & Brand, 2004; Ryan et al., 2006). Research examining individuation with late adolescents and young adults who are not attending college suggests a similar direction of effects (e.g., Noack & Buhl, 2004; Tanner, 2006). Furthermore, disruption in the individuation process in early adolescence has been linked to higher levels of internalizing and external-izing symptomatology in mid-adolescence (Allen et al., 2006; Allen, Hauser, Eickholt, Bell, & O'Connor, 1994). Finally, at the family level, adolescents who are individuated are more likely to engage in constructive problem solving with their parents and display less dysfunctional anger (Kobak, Cole, Ferenz-Gillies, Fleming, & Gamble, 1993).

Much of the literature on the topic of adolescent individuation has focused on White, middle-class, two-parent homes and has not examined these same dynam-ics for adolescents who live in poverty, have alternative life course trajectories (such as an early transition to parenthood), or who are members of a minority group. Preliminary evidence suggests that there are a number of similarities in individua-tion processes across ethnically and economically diverse populations (e.g., Kalsner & Pistole, 2003; Smetana, Campione-Barr, & Daddis, 2004). In addition, research has replicated with African-American late adolescents the associations found in other samples between perceived autonomy and higher levels of self-esteem, aca-demic performance, and engagement in school as well as lower levels of depressive symptoms and better academic performance (Bynum & Kotchick, 2006; Connell, Halpern-Felsher, Clifford, Crichlow, & Usinger, 1995; Smetena et al., 2004).

It is important to highlight that the social context may also influence parenting as well as family perceptions of the importance of autonomy and its function in development (see also Chapter 7 by McElhaney and Allen in this volume). In observations of 59 African-American mother–daughter dyads from low-income urban neighborhoods, Cauce and colleagues (1996) found that most mothers reported believing that fostering autonomy and self-reliance in their teenage daughters was important, but they also reported feeling the need to provide close monitoring and supervision out of concern for their children's safety and overall well-being. Similarly, Furstenberg and colleagues (2000) found that parents who were raising their adolescents in inner-city Philadelphia consistently reported the need to more closely monitor their children and to provide firm discipline in response to the dangerous neighborhoods in which they were raising their chil-dren. In fact, among high-risk families, parental behaviors that undermine ado-lescents' autonomy are positively related to mother–adolescent relationship quality, which is the pattern opposite to the one that is found among low-risk families (McElhaney & Allen, 2001). Furthermore, in these high-risk families, adolescents who are involved in more delinquent behaviors also display higher levels of autonomy when compared to their peers. Thus, the very real dangers that youth in high-risk contexts face (e.g., exposure to violence or gang involvement) may alter the relative value of facilitating autonomy in adolescence.

Hypothesized Linkages between Individuation and Parenting

It is clear that individuation is a highly salient process for adolescents during the transition to adulthood. Thus, drawing on the research described above as well as on studies that establish the central influence of mothers' relationships with their own mothers on their parenting, we hypothesized that individuation would play an important role in the adjustment to parenting in young mothers. First, a number of studies have shown that mothers' ability to reflect on their childhood experiences coherently and in a well-integrated fashion is associated with more sensitive, responsive caregiving and secure attachment in their offspring (e.g., Adam, Gunnar, & Tanaka, 2004; van Ijzendoorn, 1995). Although this research has been conducted primarily with White, middle-class women, there is some evidence that mothers' perspectives on their childhood relationships are associated with parenting competence in minority, adolescent mothers as well. For example, Ward and Carlson (1995) found that pregnant adolescents who were reflective and coherent in discussing their relationships with their own mothers were significantly more likely to be sensitive mothers and to have securely attached infants. To some extent, these data support a linkage between individuation (which, in this context, is represented by the ability to reflect on your place in the family from a mature perspective) and parenting. On the other hand, these data do not examine the *observed* quality of the relationship between mother and grandmother but are based on maternal report and they focus primarily on the mother's relationship with her mother *during childhood*, rather than during adolescence and the transition to adulthood. A starting premise in our research was that the transformation of the mother–daughter relationship that occurs during adolescence and young adulthood affects mothers' parenting abilities. Thus, a direct assessment of current mother–daughter interactions seemed especially important in understanding multigenerational family processes in young, African-American families, as in this context, mothers and grandmothers often coreside or share child-rearing responsibilities (Pittman & Boswell, 2007).

Additional literature identifies kinship social support in general, and social support from grandmothers in particular, as a protective factor for the mental health and parenting competence of African-American mothers under circumstances of stress and disadvantage (e.g., Ceballo & McLoyd, 2002; Hunter & Taylor, 1998) as well as among adolescent mothers with infants (Oberlander, Black, & Starr, 2007). These data also provide some support for the idea that there are links between autonomy processes and a young woman's parenting abilities. In particular, in comparison to mothers who receive either "too much" or "too little" support from their own mothers, mothers who receive grandmother support that balances assistance with respect for the young mothers' autonomous functioning are less likely to allow their mothers to step into the primary caregiver role by the time their children are 6 years old (Apfel & Seitz, 1996). However, several studies have shown these positive effects of emotional support for young mothers only when mothers and grandmothers are not coresiding (Contreras, 2004; Speiker & Bensley, 1994; Wakschlag et al., 1996). It has been suggested that these somewhat paradoxical effects can best be explained within a developmental framework (Speiker & Bensley, 1994). That is, grandmothers who support the young mothers' independence while remaining emotionally available facilitate their daughters' assumption of adult roles. However, the specific dimensions of a supportive relationship between mothers and grandmothers that are linked to positive parenting have not been well-delineated. In addition, support often has been confounded with mother–grandmother coresidence despite the fact that coresidence and mother–grandmother closeness may be inversely related (Speiker & Bensley, 1994; Wakschlag et al., 1996).

To address these shortcomings in the previous literature, our research team became interested in determining the dimensions of the mother–grandmother relationship that would be particularly salient predictors of young mothers' parenting. Specifically, for young women who became parents during adolescence or the transition to young adulthood, we hypothesized that the individuation process would be centrally linked to their parenting competence. That is, we posited that the interpersonal skills that young women acquire through successful negotiation of the individuation process are precisely those skills that are central to the provision of developmentally sensitive and appropriate parenting. In fact, the continuities between the relational skills involved in the adolescent individuation process and in the parenting of toddlers, who also are developing their own autonomy, are striking (see Table 8.1). As described above, a well-individuated

Table 8.1 Hypothesized Continuities between Individuation and Young Mothers' Parenting

Individuation during Adolescence and the Transition to Young Adulthood		Parenting during the Preschool Period	
Core Individuation Dimension	Adolescent learns to:	Core Parenting Dimension	Facilitates Young Mother's ability to:
Self-Assertion[1,2]	Express her point of view and communicate it clearly	Demandingness[3]	Set firm limits using reasoning and explanations
Perspective Taking[1,2]	See things from another's point of view and coordinate multiple perspectives	Decentering[4]	Negotiate joint plans and accommodate to child's point of view
Separateness[1]	Tolerate disagreement	Autonomy support[3]	Provide structure to facilitate child's independence
Mutuality[1,2]	Responsiveness to other's needs and feelings	Emotional connectedness[3,4]	Flexible availability based on child's cues

[1]Cooper et al. (1983).
[2]Hauser (1991).
[3]Greenberg and Speltz (1988).
[4]Belsky (1999).

relationship in adolescence has been defined as one that balances individuality and connectedness within the parent–adolescent relationship (Cooper et al., 1983). Thus, parents' flexible capacity to tolerate differences and foster adolescent perspective taking while remaining emotionally available to their adolescent is central to successful individuation. Similarly, developmentally sensitive parenting with young children relies on a combination of parental flexibility, capacity for decentering and perspective taking, and emotional responsiveness (Belsky, 1999). For example, the adolescent's capacity to assert her own point of view despite disagreement with her mother may support her ability to set limits in the face of her preschooler's protest and to articulate the reasons behind her decision. Similarly, a young mother who is comfortable with separateness from her own mother may be better able to tolerate and support her child's burgeoning independence. The capacity for perspective taking, such as the ability to consider alternative points of view, may help young mothers to allow their preschoolers to share in decision making and solve problems through mutual negotiation. It has been noted that young mothers seem to have particular difficulty during the preschool period as child independence increases (Borkowski et al., 2002). In contrast, mothers who can maintain a sense of closeness with their own mothers, despite their differences, may also be more likely to feel emotionally connected to their children as their children become increasingly independent.

Just as individuation has been characterized as a dyadic process involving comfort with differences, validation of others' needs and feelings, and the coordination of multiple perspectives (Cooper et al., 1983), the focal point of the parent–child relationship during the preschool years is the negotiation of a "goal-corrected partnership" (Greenberg & Speltz, 1988). Parallel to the adolescent individuation process, the emergence of a goal-corrected partnership rests on supporting autonomy, assisting the child to develop an increasingly differentiated self-awareness, and increasing mutuality in the regulation of relationship processes. Behavioral expectations are also increased in adolescence (Smetana et al., 2006) and the preschool years (Campbell, 2002), requiring a concomitant shift in parental use of discipline, reasoning, and negotiation. This dovetails with parallel cognitive shifts that occur during both of these periods. The emergence of higher level abilities to symbolize and think abstractly serves as a cornerstone of the developmental transformation in the parent–child relationship in both of these developmental stages (Campbell, 2002; Laursen & Collins, 2009).

THE BALTIMORE MULTIGENERATIONAL FAMILY STUDY: MATERNAL LIFE COURSE AND CHILD OUTCOME IN MULTIGENERATIONAL YOUNG CHILDBEARING FAMILIES

The original Baltimore study was designed to evaluate a comprehensive prenatal care program for adolescent mothers in the late 1960s. The study followed a sample of 400 teenage mothers, their mothers, and their firstborn children and compared their transition to adulthood to that of their classmates who had delayed childbearing (Furstenberg, 1976). At the 17-year follow-up, several findings were striking. First, although many of the mothers had fared better than expected, their offspring generally had fared poorly (Brooks-Gunn, 1990). On the other hand, there was significant variability in adolescent outcomes, with those young mothers who had improved their life trajectories over the course of the study (e.g., gained further education, avoided welfare receipt) being significantly more likely to have children with positive adjustment at adolescence as compared to those mothers who did not overcome the obstacles presented by an early transition to parenthood (Furstenberg et al., 1987). To take an in-depth look at the processes that might serve a protective function for the offspring of young mothers, the 20-year follow-up (from which the data presented here are derived) used a family systems perspective to examine multigenerational family processes as a pathway to understanding variability in parenting and child outcome.

The present sample, referred to as the Baltimore Multigenerational Family Study, consisted of 96 multigenerational, African-American families (mothers, grandmothers, and 3-year-old children). Close to half of the sample were original Baltimore study participants (with the children representing Generation IV) with the remainder of the sample recruited from Baltimore area prenatal clinics ($N = 35$) and referrals from participants ($N = 17$) (for details see Chase-Lansdale, Gordon, Coley, Wakschlag, & Brooks-Gunn, 1999). Mothers' mean age at first birth was 18 and 71% of the mothers were 19 years or younger at first birth. However, the study was designed to include not only adolescents but also young adult mothers (age at first birth ranging from 13 to 25 years) since we believed that the social ecologies of the two groups would be similar (Chase-Lansdale et al., 1994). Slightly more than half of the sample was coresiding with the grandmothers. For approximately one-fourth of the sample, the biological grandmother was deceased or unavailable. In these families, the person most like a grandmother to the child (generally great-grandmothers, aunts, or paternal relatives) was included.[1]

Conceptualization and Measurement of the Mother–Daughter Relationship: The Scale of Intergenerational Relationship Quality

Our conceptualization of the salient dimensions of the mother–grandmother relationship was derived from theory and methods from developmental and family research (Clark, 1985; Cooper et al., 1983; Hetherington & Clingempeel, 1988) as well as from research on the social ecology of African-American family life (Boyd-Franklin, 1989; Kochman, 1981; Lewis & Looney, 1983; Scott-Jones, 1991). To assess discourse patterns central to the individuation process, at the end of the second of two home visits young mothers and grandmothers were asked to select topics of disagreement with each other and to discuss these for about 5 minutes each. Rather than asking the dyads to choose from a preexisting list of topics, these self-selected disagreements presumably more accurately reflected the concerns of their daily lives, which may have differed from those of nonparent, middle-class, White adolescents studied in previous research. These discussions were videotaped and coded using the Scale of Intergenerational Relationship Quality (SIRQ) developed for this purpose (Wakschlag, Chase-Lansdale, & Brooks-Gunn, 1991). The SIRQ is a global coding system that includes both individual and dyadic ratings (for details see Wakschlag et al., 1996; Wakschlag, Chase-Lansdale, & Brooks-Gunn, 2001). The SIRQ has since been validated in other studies of adolescent mothers (e.g., Hess, Papas, & Black, 2002).

Factor analysis of the SIRQ ratings extracted four meaningful dimensions. First, *Emotional Closeness* reflected healthy emotional connectedness within the dyad such as warmth and concern for the partner, validation, mutuality in conflict resolution, and emotional openness. The second factor, *Positive Affect,* assessed the degree to which interactions were characterized by an upbeat, animated tone. *Grandmother Directness,* the third factor, reflected the degree to which grandmothers expressed maturity demands for their daughters in an assertive, nonconfrontational manner. The fourth factor, *Individuation,* is central to our present discussion. Three observations codes loaded on this factor: (1) young mothers' emotional maturity as witnessed by her ability to assert her separateness positively and nondefensively while maintaining a sense of mutuality; (2) young mothers' communication clarity, with higher scores reflecting her ability to make herself understood through elaborating her position clearly; and (3) dyadic comfort during the disagreement process, where higher scores reflected dyads who appeared open and relaxed in their interactions. Thus, those who had higher levels of individuation were better able to engage in the conversation with their mother regarding the topic selected, both listening to their mothers' point of view and also sharing their thoughts.

Individuation was not correlated with the mother's age at the transition to parenthood ($r = 0.14$, NS) or to living with the grandmother ($r = 0.05$, NS) or with a male partner ($r = 0.11$, NS). Thus, individuation was not merely a proxy for chronological age or achievement of residential independence. On the other hand, *Individuation* was correlated with mothers' life course achievements. *Individuation* was significantly correlated with high school completion ($r = 0.37$, $p < 0.001$) and whether they were ever employed ($r = 0.23$, $p < 0.05$) and was marginally associated with a measure of mothers' verbal intelligence ($r = 0.18$, $p < 0.10$). The modest nature of these correlations, however, suggests that individuation was not merely a reflection of mothers' verbal fluency or educational achievement but rather captured an independent relational dimension.

The Mother–Daughter Relationship and Parenting

First, the associations between individuation and mother's parenting behavior with her preschooler were examined. The mother–child interaction was assessed using independent observations of the mothers with their preschoolers in a videotaped Puzzle Task (adapted from Goldberg & Easterbrooks, 1984; Matas,

Arend, & Sroufe, 1978). Four puzzles of increasing difficulty were presented, with the mother instructed to let the child work as independently as possible, but to give any help she felt was needed (for details see Chase-Lansdale et al., 1994; Wakschlag et al., 1996). Based on observations of these puzzle tasks, two dimensions of parenting were derived, termed *Competent Parenting* and *Problematic Parenting*. Mothers' *Competent Parenting* reflected the provision of emotional support, setting reasonable controls on the child's behavior and giving anticipatory guidance that minimized upset while fostering maximal autonomy. Mothers who were high in *Competent Parenting* created a positive learning experience for their child, encouraging them to work on the puzzle independently initially (e.g., praising their successful placement of puzzle pieces) and then providing guided assistance as the task became more difficulty (e.g., giving hints to look at the colors of the pieces). Mothers who were low in *Competent Parenting* were not engaged in the task with their child, appearing passive or lethargic during the interactions. Mothers' *Problematic Parenting* reflected mothers' inconsistency, harshness, emotional disengagement, and difficulty monitoring. Mothers who scored high on *Problematic Parenting* often were disengaged during the interactions, did not control their child's behaviors, and often exhibited intense displeasure or disapproval of their child. As would be expected, *Competent Parenting* and *Problem Parenting* were negatively correlated with each other ($r = -0.57$, $p < 0.001$)

Regression models were used to test the associations between *Individuation* and *Competent Parenting* and *Problematic Parenting*, respectively, when other aspects of the mother–grandmother relationship and demographic factors were controlled. The continuity between individuation and mothers' parenting behavior was confirmed. *Individuation* was the only SIRQ factor that consistently and strongly predicted mothers' *Competent* ($\beta = 0.35$, $p < 0.001$) and *Problematic* ($\beta = -0.22$, $p < 0.05$) *Parenting* (Wakschlag et al., 1996). An individuated relationship between the young mother and her own mother was linked to the young mother's parenting; more individuation predicted more balanced responsiveness and appropriate maternal control with the preschooler. This association held true regardless of maternal age, education, and receptive language abilities. However, further analyses showed that individuation exerted its strongest effects when mothers were younger at the time of first birth and did not currently coreside with the grandmother. Conversely, older mothers benefited most from being highly individuated when they were living with the grandmother. With relatively older mothers, living with their own mothers likely creates multiple situations in which they need to negotiate shared parenting and other responsibilities; thus, mothers who can articulate their concerns and resolve differences effectively with their own mothers (i.e., skills associated with individuation) are more likely to be doing better overall and be effective in their parenting. With younger mothers, living independently may be the more challenging task. The ability of younger mothers to articulate their needs for assistance and support from their own mothers when not living with their mothers is likely linked to being able to communicate better and work with their own child as well. These findings highlight the complex interplay between timing of developmental transitions, family structure, and family processes.

Interestingly, the influence of the mothers' individuation extended to the third generation as well. *Individuation* was significantly correlated with an independent observed measure of the child's approach to a problem-solving task ($r = 0.25$, $p < 0.05$). Children whose mothers were high on *Individuation* were significantly more likely to be able to work independently on a challenging task while at the same time being responsive to maternal directives. However, this association appeared to be mediated by the mother's parenting. Regression analyses showed that mothers' *Individuation* was no longer a significant predictor when mothers' *Competent Parenting* was included in the equation. Similarly, the inclusion of *Problematic Parenting* was associated with a reduction in the contribution made by mothers' *Individuation* (to only marginal significance). Thus, the association between mothers' individuation and the child's autonomous behaviors seems to be driven, at least in part, by mothers' parenting. This is consistent with recent cross-sectional research that has found that adolescent mothers who have successfully negotiated their identity development and have been able to separate from their family of origin are more effective in their parenting roles and have infants with more advanced cognitive development (Aiello & Lancaster, 2007).

In Their Own Voices

To supplement the quantitative data presented above, several excerpts from the disagreement task for two families are presented here to highlight differences in the process of the discussions that occurred in young mother–grandmother dyads as a function of high versus low individuation. Like the narrative approach utilized by Hauser, Allen, and Schulz (Chapter 10, this volume), examination of the way in which young mothers express their concerns during the disagreement task with their own mothers provides insights into their ability to reflect on their own experiences, illustrating their level of individuation. Whereas both young mothers were confronted with a very serious concern by the grandmothers in regard to their parenting, Kendra[2] (who scored more than one SD above the mean on *Individuation*) was able to "take in" her mother's comments, think about them, and integrate them into her point of view by the end of the discussion, while, at the same time, being able to share her own point of view quite eloquently. In contrast, Shanequa (who scored more than 0.5 SD below the mean on *Individuation*) merely reacted to her mother's statements and had trouble understanding the broader issue or articulating her own point of view. In essence, the process for the dyad high on *Individuation* was marked by a sense of flexibility, openness, and reflection for both partners in contrast to the more static and less mutual process in the low *Individuation* dyad.

Family 1: Shanequa (age at first birth: 14.8 years; current age: 20.6 years; lives with maternal aunt and two daughters, Tayla, age 5.5 years, and Tamika, age 3 years; highest grade completed: 10th).

GM: There's something on my mind and it's concerning Tayla. . . Tayla. . . is really fighting, or striving for your attention some. Now I know that Tayla's been with me for quite a while and. . . um. . . I mostly do, mostly, everything as far as she concerned. But I think her feelings is that you pay Tamika more attention than you do her. And that worries me a whole lot because, I mean, sometimes it seems to me that you push Tayla off a little. . . . I think that's why you and Tayla don't get along so because she feel as though you cater to Tamika and this is one thing that I would like to see improve. . .

Shanequa: (head down, shoulders hunched, gaze averted). . . She don't listen. She don't listen.

GM: She's just rebelling because you pay Tamika more attention. . . . she knows that I'm there for her all the time, you know, but I don't think she has that feeling that you're there all the time. She knows she can always come to me. I mean, I have seen you push her off a little, many a time. You know I have talked to you about this so, um, this is one wish that you would get together with her and maybe be more, maybe show her more attention. I know she don't listen, she can be a problem child, sometime but I deal with that all the time. But I can see that she loves you. . . . I think maybe if you get together with her and show a little more affection toward her, you know. Cause I know Tamika's been with you all the time. Tayla's been with me the majority of the time when you moved out, but I think she wants more attention and love from her mommy.

Shanequa: (crying softly, silent) You mean like when I go out, take Tayla with me instead of Tamika?

GM: Maybe, one day if you just get together with you and Tayla both, just you all alone and leave Tamika with me. . . just have a day together to show her that, you know, and even when she goes on trips on the school like tomorrow. . . you can maybe make time to go with her on her trip tomorrow to the park.

Shanequa: (Nods slightly in silence.)

Family 2: Kendra (age at first birth: 16.5 years; current age: 19.7 years; lives with her own mother, older sister, and 3-year-old son, Quintin; highest grade completed: 10th).

GM: (very sharply) I don't think you spend enough time with Quintin. I think you oughta, I mean it's alright to go out at night, but I think you should involve him in some of your trips. . . I do not think it's fair for Quintin to be left with his gramma or aunt. There is no communication between you and Quintin. . . You're always without Quintin, and I do not think it's fair. . . I had four children, I ain't never left you home alone, I never had time to go run on the streets and, if so, there's no place I went without my kids. You're going to have to do something about this. . . Quintin is completely lost.

Kendra: (crying) First of all, I do spend time with him, second of all, he always want to go with [his aunt], because she always with him even when I had to go to school and finish. And third of all, when we go places, I take him a million places, I take him to Keesiya's house, we go for walks and talk about things. (pause) But, maybe you're right, I'm gonna have to change and spend a little more time with him and less with my friends. But, you have to realize that I missed out on a lot of things when I first had him. . . . (crying more) You know when a part of your life is just gone. And you wanna make up for it, even though you're too old, and that's the way I feel, . . . because I was too young and I felt as though I missed out on three years of my life and I'm ready to make them up (hugs GM, both are tearful).

GM: I understand. Well, I think you have expressed yourself and I'm glad we had this talk.

Kendra: Me, too.

GM: (warmly) I just would like for you to spend a little more time with Quintin to learn [about] your son and find out yourself that you will be a very lovely mother to your son.

As discussed above, the observational coding of *Individuation* considered three underlying dimensions: the young mother's emotional maturity, her communication clarity, and the dyad's comfort during the process. Kendra, whose scores reflected high levels of individuation, clearly displayed her emotional maturity through her nondefensive style in listening and responding to her mother's concerns. At first she countered her mother, indicating that her son had not wanted to go with her, but then she integrated her mothers' point of view and agreed that she should do more with him. In addition, she worked to help her mother understand her perspective, explaining how difficult it was for her at this stage in her life to not be able to do things that others her age were doing. Shanequa on the other hand, showed a lack of individuation from her aunt. She was not expressive, used few words, and quickly agreed with her aunt without sharing her point of view. Furthermore, her body language, in which she was hunched over with her head down, displayed her discomfort in disagreeing with her aunt. Kendra, in comparison, although crying initially, appeared to have connected with her mother by the end of the conversation, when both stated that they understood the other's point of view and that talking about these things was helpful.

These differences in emotional maturity and mutuality and perspective taking associated with *Individuation* displayed in the disagreement task by Shanequa and Kendra were then paralleled in their interactions with their preschoolers. Shanequa was disengaged, appearing rather bored and saying little during the Puzzle Task with her daughter. She seemed unable to see things from her daughter's perspective, focusing on task completion rather than fostering mastery through encouragement and helpful hints. When her daughter got "stuck," rather than providing clues to help her see what to try next, Shanequa simply took over and completed the puzzle herself rather than facilitating her daughter's independent problem-solving ability. In contrast, Kendra was actively engaged with her son during the Puzzle Task, using verbal and physical encouragement, graded assistance, and modeling. She seemed to understand intuitively the level of assistance her son would need and provided this as a means to foster his independence. She took steps to make the task manageable for him by organizing the pieces, but then stepped back and allowed him to put the pieces in himself. For example, when her son was unable to figure out where a piece went, she demonstrated for him, but then took it out again and told him, "You do it," so that he would feel a sense of mastery.

Similar to those illustrated by Kendra and Shanequa, differences can be observed in the discussions between two other mother–daughter pairs in our study. Both disagreements focused on the young mother's relationship with her romantic partner. These contrasting vignettes highlight the separateness and self-assertion dimensions of the individuation process. Atisha (who scored one standard deviation above the mean on *Individuation*) was better able to express a distinct point of view in disagreement with her mother in contrast to Monique (who scored one standard deviation below the mean on *Individuation)* who had difficulty expressing differences with her mother. Atisha initiated a discussion about her mother favoring her partner. Throughout the discussion Atisha's behavior reflected a sense of assertiveness and self-confidence. She faced her mother when speaking, she spoke distinctly and forcefully, and she was able to build a case for her point of view despite her mother's disagreement. In contrast, Monique presented herself quite differently, often mumbling responses and merely reacting to her mother's concerns that the child's father, with whom Monique is living, had not been taking his responsibility seriously. In addition, unlike Atisha, who initiated this serious conversation about her partner, Monique seemed unable to express her own point of view. When it was her turn to raise a disagreement, she was unable to do so, putting her head down, laughing, and stating "I don't disagree about nothing—what she tells me to do, I do."

Family 3: Atisha (age at first birth: 20.5 years; current age: 24 years; lives with her husband, mother, father, and 2-year-old daughter, Melody; highest grade completed: 12th).

> *Atisha:* Why does it seem like no matter what Joe do, you always take his side? He always right.
>
> *GM:* (laughing) Because (of) the way you are.

Atisha:	What you mean the way I am? What do I do? . . . . Some things you fuss at me about when I do, like, when I tell Melody, "Oh, stop crying to everybody cuz you just want somebody to pet you up;" Now when I yell, when I say that, you go, "Well, she just wants some attention" and when Joe say it, [you say],"Do what your father says."
GM:	No, I don't say that.
Atisha:	Yes, you did. You did it yesterday. . .
GM:	When?
Atisha:	When she was crying about a splinter in her finger.
GM:	. . . It was a screw she was using, it's something that she did that he should have corrected her.
Atisha:	Alright, now how come when Joe never came and picked me up, you said, you asked me why didn't I call him? And he's been picking me up. . .
GM:	(interrupting) That's right because. . .
Atisha:	. . . for the past seven months. . .
GM:	(interrupting) Let me answer.
Atisha:	I want to finish. (Both laugh.) He's been picking me up for the past seven months at 12:00 to take me to the bank. (She continues describing her example.)

Family 4: Monique (age at first birth: 18 years; current age: 21 years; lives with the father of her child and 3-year-old son; highest grade completed: 10th).

GM:	You got to make him go get a job. . .
Monique:	I do.
GM:	I worry about the way his life's headed. . . Tell him you ain't gonna give him a key, tell him he has to go home to his mother "til he gets a job." Don't shrug like that. I ain't kidding, threaten him.
Monique:	(laughs)
GM:	Make that boy get a job, he done had two good jobs. . . . And don't give him no more money.
Monique:	I won't.
GM:	No more, you keep on saying that, no money.
Monique:	I'm not.

This difference in level of individuation also was reflected in the contrasting levels of autonomy support the two young mothers provided to their own children. Atisha worked hard to make the task interesting and enjoyable to her daughter. She was playful and asked questions to help her daughter develop an approach to the task that would enable her to complete it independently. She gave hints that matched the difficulty of the task, being less directive during easier puzzles (e.g., "What does this piece look like?") and more directive as the task difficulty increased (e.g., directing her daughter to try pieces with more clear cut visual cues first so that she could use pictorial aspects of the puzzle as a guide). Atisha also responded warmly to her daughter's successful completion of the puzzles. On the other hand, Monique was rather disengaged and did not seem to know how to foster her son's engagement with the puzzles. In contrast to Atisha's steady stream of cues, which were responsive to the level of the task difficulty and her child's level of interest and skill, Monique became involved only when her son found the task too difficult and started to give up, at which point she physically forced him to work on the puzzle (i.e., pulling his arm and placing him between her legs).

CONCLUSIONS AND CLINICAL IMPLICATIONS

The quantitative and qualitative findings presented in this chapter highlight linkages between developmental processes and parenting competence in young mothers as well as the way in which psychological and social-ecological factors intersect in influencing developmental pathways. Young mothers who displayed higher levels of individuation during their interactions with their own mothers also displayed more competent parenting, including autonomy-supporting behaviors (e.g., facilitation of their child's completion of puzzles that were too hard). The continuities we found in individuation across three generations are quite striking and provide a potential window into processes that promote healthy development in both mothers and their children. In particular, these processes suggest intriguing avenues for intervention with young mothers. For example, multigenerational interventions that promote young mothers' capacities for independent decision making and problem solving within a family context may support positive adaptation to the parenting role (e.g., Cherniss & Herzog, 1996). In addition, interventions may need to focus on specific tasks that are particularly challenging for young mothers because of their development stage. For example, Osofsky and Thompson (2000) report that in their parenting intervention for teenage mothers, they targeted helping young mothers increase their empathy for their infants because they observed that these young mothers tended to be focused on themselves, as would be expected with someone trying to develop her own identity during late adolescence. Although many prevention programs for young mothers focus on enhancing education and employability in order to delay subsequent pregnancies, model programs should target the underlying psychological processes that lead young mothers to be cognitively and emotionally better prepared for parenthood (Borkowski, Farris, & Weed, 2007). Similarly, programs targeting increased involvement of adolescent fathers in the lives of their young children would do well to consider how developmental and psychological processes may contribute to these men's effectiveness as parents. The quality of the father's relationship with the young mother has been identified by several as contributing to the quality of their parenting involvement (e.g., Florsheim & Moore, Chapter 9, this volume; Pittman & Coley, 2011). However, fewer have considered how young men may not be developmentally prepared for this early transition to parenthood (but see Florsheim & Moore, Chapter 9, this volume). Overall, consideration of these developmental processes is likely to enhance the well-being of both young parents and their children. Specifically, this research suggests that young mothers' individuation from their family of origin is one such process that may make a difference in the mothers' parenting and, thus, their children's subsequent functioning.

ACKNOWLEDGMENTS

The Baltimore Multigenerational Family Study was supported by the Office of Adolescent Pregnancy Programs, the National Institute of Child Health and Development (HD25398), NORC, the Chapin Hall Center for Children, and the Educational Testing Service. This article is based, in part, on Dr. Wakschlag's dissertation, work supported in part by funding from the Walden and Jean Young Shaw Foundation. We also appreciate the support from NIMH through the Family Research Consortium to Dr. Pittman, through a postdoctoral fellowship (MH19734) as well as their support to Dr. Chase-Lansdale and Dr. Brooks-Gunn (MH49694). This research was also influenced by the Working Group on Communities, Neighborhoods, Family Processes, and Individual Development of the Social Science Research Council, in particular the members of the Phenomenon-Based Cluster on Young Multigenerational Family Processes. The Social Science Research Council working group was funded by the William T. Grant Foundation, the Smith Richardson Foundation, and the Russell Sage Foundation. Finally, we are deeply grateful to the study staff for their careful data collection and the generous contribution of time and insights from study families.

Notes

1. For simplicity's sake, both grandmothers and grandmother figures will be referred to as grandmothers here.
2. Names are changed to maintain confidentiality.

References

Adam, E. K., Gunnar, M. R., & Tanaka, A. (2004). Adult attachment, parent emotion, and observed parenting behavior: Mediator and moderator models. *Child Development, 75*, 110–122.

Aiello, R., & Lancaster, S. (2007). Influence of adolescent maternal characteristics on infant development. *Infant Mental Health Journal, 28*, 496–516.

Allen, J. P., Hauser, S. T., Eickholt, C., Bell, K. L., & O'Connor, T. G. (1994). Autonomy and relatedness in family interactions as predictors of expressions of negative adolescent affect. *Journal of Research on Adolescence, 4*, 535–552.

Allen, J. P., Insabella, G., Porter, M. R., Smith, F. D., Land, D., & Phillips, N. (2006). A social-interactional model of the development of depressive symptoms in adolescence. *Journal of Consulting and Clinical Psychology, 74*, 55–65.

Apfel, N., & Seitz, V. (1996). African American adolescent mothers, their families, and their daughters: A longitudinal perspective over twelve years. In B. J. R. Leadbeater & N. Way (Eds.), *Urban girls: Resisting stereotypes, creating identities* (pp. 149–170). New York: New York University Press.

Baydar, N., Brooks-Gunn, J., & Furstenberg, F. F. (1993). Early warning signs of functional illiteracy: Predictors in childhood and adolescence. *Child Development, 64*, 815–829.

Belsky, J. (1999). Interactional and contextual determinants of attachment security. In J. Cassidy & P. R. Shaver (Eds.), *Handbook of attachment: Theory, research, and clinical applications* (pp. 249–264). New York: Guilford.

Berlin, L. J., Brady-Smith, C., & Brooks-Gunn, J. (2002). Links between childbearing age and observed maternal behaviors with 14-month-olds in the Early Head Start Research and Evaluation Project. *Infant Mental Health Journal, 23*, 104–129.

Blos, P. (1967). The second individuation process of adolescence. In R. Eissler & H. Hartmann (Eds.), *Psychoanalytic study of the child* (pp. 162–186). New York: International Universities Press.

Borkowski, J. G., Bisconti, T., Weed, K., Willard, C., Keogh, D. A., & Whitman, T. L. (2002). The adolescent as parent: Influences on children's intellectual, academic, and socioemotional development. In J. G. Borkowski, S. L. Ramey, & M. Bristol-Power (Eds.), *Parenting and the child's world: Influences on academic, intellectual, and social-emotional development* (pp. 161–184). Mahwah, NJ: Lawrence Erlbaum.

Borkowski, J. G., Farris, J. R., & Weed, K. (2007). Toward resilience: Designing effective prevention programs . In J. G. Borkowski, J. R. Farris, T. L. Whitman, S. S. Carothers, K. Weed, & D. A. Keogh (Eds.), *Risk and resilience: Adolescent mothers and their children grow up* (pp. 259–278). Mahwah, NJ: Lawrence Erlbaum.

Bornstein, M. H. (Ed.). (2002). *Handbook of parenting: Vol. 1. Children and parenting* (2nd ed.). Mahwah, NJ: Lawrence Erlbaum.

Bowlby, J. (1988). *A secure base.* New York: Basic Books.

Boyd-Franklin, N. (1989). *Black families in therapy: A multi-systems approach.* New York: Guilford.

Brooks-Gunn, J. (1990). Adolescents as daughters and as mothers: A developmental perspective. In I. Sigel & G. Brody (Eds.), *Methods of family research: Biographies of research projects: Vol. 1: Normal families* (pp. 213–248). Hillsdale, NJ: Lawrence Erlbaum.

Brooks-Gunn, J., Guo, G., & Furstenberg, F. F. (1993). Who drops out of and who continues beyond high school? A 20-year follow-up of Black urban youth. *Journal of Research on Adolescence, 3*, 271–294.

Brooks-Gunn, J., & Zahaykevich, M. (1989). Parent-daughter relationships in early adolescence: A developmental perspective. In K. Kreppner & R. M. Lerner (Eds.), *Family systems and life-span development* (pp. 223–246). Hillsdale, NJ: Lawrence Erlbaum.

Brown, B. B., & Larson, J. (2009). Peer relationships in adolescence. In R. M. Lerner & L. Steinberg (Eds.), *Handbook of adolescent psychology, Vol. 2 Contextual influences on adolescent development* (3rd ed., pp. 74–103). Hoboken, NJ: John Wiley & Sons.

Bynum, M. S., & Kotchick, B. A. (2006). Mother-adolescent relationship quality and autonomy as predictors of psychosocial adjustment among African American adolescents. *Journal of Child and Family Studies, 15,* 529–542.

Campbell, S. (2002). *Behavior problems in preschool children: Clinical and developmental issues* (2nd ed.). New York: Guilford.

Cauce, A. M., Hiraga, Y., Graves, D., Gonzales, N., Ryan-Finn, K., & Grove, K. (1996). African American mothers and their adolescent daughters: Closeness, conflict, and control. In B. J. R. Leadbeater & N. Way (Eds.), *Urban girls: Resisting stereotypes, creating identities* (pp. 100–116). New York: New York University Press.

Ceballo, R., & McLoyd, V. C. (2002). Social support and parenting in poor, dangerous neighborhoods. *Child Development, 73,* 1310–1321.

Chase-Lansdale, P. L., Brooks-Gunn, J., & Zamsky, E. S. (1994). Young African-American multigenerational families in poverty: Quality of mothering and grandmothering. *Child Development, 65,* 373–393.

Chase-Lansdale, P. L., Gordon, R. A., Coley, R. L., Wakschlag, L. S., & Brooks-Gunn, J. (1999). Young African-American multigenerational families in poverty: The contexts, exchanges, and processes of their lives. In E. M. Hetherington (Ed.), *Coping with divorce, single parenting, and remarriage: A risk and resiliency perspective* (pp. 165–191). Mahwah, NJ: Lawrence Erlbaum.

Cherniss, C., & Herzog, E. (1996). Impact of home-based family therapy on maternal and child outcomes in disadvantaged adolescent mothers. *Family Relations, 45,* 72–79.

Clark, R. (1985). *Parent-child early relational assessment.* Madison: Department of Psychiatry, University of Wisconsin Medical School.

Coley, R., & Chase-Lansdale, P. L. (1998). Adolescent pregnancy and parenthood: Recent evidence and future directions. *American Psychologist, 53,* 152–166.

Collins, W. A., & Steinberg, L. (2006). Adolescent development in interpersonal context. In N. Eisenberg, W. Damon, & R. M. Lerner (Eds.), *Handbook of child psychology, Vol. 3.* (6th ed., pp. 1003–1067). Hoboken, NJ: John Wiley & Sons.

Conger, R. D., & Ge, X. (1999). Conflict and cohesion in parent-adolescent relations: Changes in emotional expression from early to midadolescence. In M. J. Cox & J. Brooks-Gunn (Eds.), *Conflict and cohesion in families: Causes and consequences* (pp. 185–206). Mahwah, NJ: Lawrence Erlbaum.

Connell, J. P., Halpern-Felsher, B. L., Clifford, E., Crichlow, W., & Usinger, P. (1995). Hanging in there: Behavioral, psychological, and contextual factors affecting whether African American adolescents stay in high school. *Journal of Adolescent Research, 10,* 41–63.

Contreras, J. M. (2004). Parenting behaviors among mainland Puerto Rican adolescent mothers: The role of grandmother and partner involvement. *Journal of Research on Adolescence, 14,* 341–368.

Cooper, C., & Cooper, R. (1992). Links between adolescents' relationships with their parents and peers: Models, evidence and mechanisms. In R. Parke & G. Ladd (Eds.), *Family-peer relationships: Modes of linkage* (pp. 135–158). Hillsdale, NJ: Lawrence Erlbaum.

Cooper, C., Grotevant, G., & Condon, S. (1983). Individuality and connectedness in the family as a context for adolescent identity formation and role-taking skill. In H. Grotevant & C. Cooper (Eds.), *Adolescent development in the family* (pp. 43–59). San Francisco: Jossey-Bass.

Eisenberg, N., Morris, A.S., McDaniel, B., & Spinrad, T. L. (2009). Moral cognitions and prosocial responding in adolescence. In R. M. Lerner & L. Steinberg (Eds.), *Handbook of adolescent psychology, Vol. 1 Individual based of adolescent development* (3rd ed., pp. 229–265). Hoboken, NJ: John Wiley & Sons.

Erickson, E. H. (1968). *Identity: Youth and crisis*. New York: Norton.

Freud, A. (1958). Adolescence. *The Psychoanalytic Study of the Child, 13*, 255–278.

Furstenberg, F. F. (1976). *Unplanned parenthood: The social consequences of teenage childbearing*. New York: Free Press.

Furstenberg, F. F., Brooks-Gunn, J., & Morgan, S. P. (1987). *Adolescent mothers later life*. Cambridge, MA: Cambridge University Press.

Furstenberg, F. F., Cook, T. D., Eccles, J., & Elder, G. E. (2000). *Managing to make it: Urban families and adolescent success*. Chicago: University of Chicago Press.

Goldberg, W., & Easterbrooks, M. (1984). The role of marital quality in toddler development. *Developmental Psychology, 20*, 504–514.

Graber, J. A., & Brooks-Gunn, J. (1999). "Sometimes I think that you don't like me": How mothers and daughters negotiate the transition into adolescence. In M. J. Cox & J. Brooks-Gunn (Eds.), *Conflict and cohesion in families: Causes and consequences* (pp. 207–242). Mahwah, NJ: Lawrence Erlbaum.

Greenberg, M., & Speltz, M. (1988). Attachment and the ontogeny of conduct problems. In J. Belsky & T. Nezworski (Eds.), *Clinical implications of attachment* (pp. 177–218). Hillsdale, NJ: Lawrence Erlbaum.

Hauser, S. T. (1991). *Adolescents and their families: Paths of ego development*. New York: The Free Press.

Hess, C. R., Papas, M. A., & Black, M. M. (2002). Resilience among African American adolescent mothers: Predictors of positive parenting in early infancy. *Journal of Pediatric Psychology, 27*, 619–629.

Hetherington, M., & Clingempeel, G. (1988). *Longitudinal study of adjustment to remarriage: Family interaction global coding manual*. Charlottesville: University of Virginia.

Hotz, V., McElroy, S., & Sanders, S. (2005). Teenage childbearing and its life cycle consequences: Exploiting a natural experiment. *The Journal of Human Resources, 40*, 683–715.

Hunter, A. G., & Taylor, R. J. (1998). Grandparenthood in African American families. In M. E. Szinovacz (Ed.), *Handbook on grandparenthood* (pp. 70–86). Westport, CT: Greenwood Press/Greenwood Publishing Group, Inc.

Kalsner, L., & Pistole, M. C. (2003). College adjustment in a multiethnic sample: Attachment, separation-individuation, and ethnic identity. *Journal of College Student Development, 44*, 92–109.

Kobak, R. R., Cole, H. E., Ferenz-Gillies, R., Fleming, W. S., & Gamble, W. (1993). Attachment and emotion regulation during mother-teen problem solving: A control theory analysis. *Child Development, 64*, 231–245.

Kochman, T. (1981). *Black and White styles of conflict*. Chicago: University of Chicago Press.

Kuhn, D. (2009). Adolescent thinking. In R. M. Lerner & L. Steinberg (Eds.), *Handbook of adolescent psychology, Vol. 1 Individual based of adolescent development* (3rd ed., pp. 152–186). Hoboken, NJ: John Wiley & Sons.

Laursen, B., & Collins, W. A. (2009). Parent-child relationships during adolescence. In R. M. Lerner & L. Steinberg (Eds.), *Handbook of adolescent psychology, Vol. 2 Contextual influences on adolescent development* (3rd ed., pp. 3–42). Hoboken, NJ: John Wiley & Sons.

Lewis, J., & Looney, J. (1983). *The long struggle: Well-functioning working-class black families.* New York: Brunner-Mazel.

Loevinger, J. (1976). *Ego development: Conceptions and theories.* San Francisco: Jossey-Bass.

Lopez, F. G., & Gover, M. R. (1993). Self-report measures of parent-adolescent attachment and separation-individuation: A selective review. *Journal of Counseling and Development, 71,* 560–569.

Matas, L., Arend, R. A., & Sroufe, L. A. (1978). Continuity of adaptation in the second year: The relationship between quality of attachment and later competence. *Child Development, 49,* 547–556.

Mattanah, J. F., Hancock, G. R., & Brand, B. L. (2004). Parental attachment, separation-individuation, and college student adjustment: A structural equation analysis of mediational effects. *Journal of Counseling Psychology, 51,* 213–225.

Maynard, R. (Ed.) (1997). *Kids having kids: Economic costs and social consequences of teen pregnancy.* Washington, DC: Urban Institute Press.

McElhaney, K. B., & Allen, J. P. (2001). Autonomy and adolescent social functioning: The moderating effect of risk. *Child Development, 72,* 220–235.

McElhaney, K. B., Allen, J. P., Stephenson, J. C., & Hare, A. L. (2009). Attachment and autonomy during adolescence. In R. M. Lerner & L. Steinberg (Eds.), *Handbook of adolescent psychology, Vol. 1: Individual based of adolescent development* (3rd ed., pp. 358–403). Hoboken, NJ: John Wiley & Sons.

Moore, K., Myers, D., Morrison, D., Winquist, N., Brown, B., & Edmonston, B. (1993). Age at first childbirth and later poverty. *Journal of Research on Adolescence, 3,* 393–422.

Moore, M. R., & Brooks-Gunn, J. (2002). Adolescent parenthood. In M. H. Bornstein (Ed.), *Handbook of parenting: Vol. 3: Being and becoming a parent* (2nd ed., pp. 173–214). Mahwah, NJ: Lawrence Erlbaum.

Noack, P., & Buhl, H. M. (2004). Relations with parents and friends during adolescence and early adulthood. *Marriage & Family Review, 36,* 31–51.

Oberlander, S. E., Black, M. M., & Starr, R. H., Jr. (2007). African American adolescent mothers and grandmothers: A multigenerational approach to parenting. *American Journal of Community Psychology, 39,* 37–46.

Osofsky, J. D., & Thompson, M. (2000). Adaptive and maladaptive parenting: Perspectives on risk and protective factors. In J. P. Shonkoff & S. J. Meisels (Eds.), *Handbook of early childhood intervention* (2nd ed., pp. 54–75). New York: Cambridge University Press.

Oxford, M. L., Gilchrist, L. D., Lohr, M. J., Gillmore, M. R., Morrison, D. M., & Spieker, S. J. (2005). Life course heterogeneity in the transition from adolescence to adulthood among adolescent mothers. *Journal of Research on Adolescence, 15,* 479–504.

Pittman, L. D., & Boswell, M. K. (2007). The role of grandmothers in the lives of preschoolers growing up in urban poverty. *Applied Developmental Science, 11,* 20–42.

Pittman, L. D., & Coley, R. L. (2011). Coparenting in families with adolescent mothers. In J. McHale & K. M. Lindahl (Eds.), *Co-parenting: Theory, research and clinical applications* (pp. 105–126). Washington, DC: APA Press.

Powers, S. I., & Welsh, D. P. (1999). Mother-daughter interactions and adolescent girls' depression. In M. J. Cox & J. Brooks-Gunn (Eds.), *Conflict and cohesion in families: Causes and consequences* (pp. 243–281). Mahwah, NJ: Lawrence Erlbaum.

Russell, A., Pettit, G. S., & Mize, J. (1998). Horizontal qualities in parent-child relationships: Parallels with and possible consequences for children's peer relationships. *Developmental Review, 18*, 313–352.

Ryan, R. M., Deci, E. L., Grolnick, W. S., & La Guardia, J. G. (2006). The significance of autonomy and autonomy support in psychological development and psychopathology. In D. Cicchetti & D. J. Cohen (Eds.), *Developmental psychopathology, Vol. 1. Theory and methods* (2nd ed., pp. 795–849). New York: John Wiley & Sons.

Scott-Jones, D. (1991). Adolescent childbearing: Risks and resilience. *Education and Urban Society, 24*, 53–64.

Smetana, J. G., Campione-Barr, N., & Daddis, C. (2004). Longitudinal development of family decision making: Defining healthy behavioral autonomy for middle-class African American adolescents. *Child Development, 75*, 1418–1434.

Smetana, J. G., Campione-Barr, N., & Metzger, A. (2006). Adolescent development in interpersonal and societal contexts. *Annual Review of Psychology, 57*, 255–284.

Smetana, J. G., & Villalobos, M. (2009). Social cognitive development in adolescence. In R. M. Lerner & L. Steinberg (Eds.), *Handbook of adolescent psychology, Vol. 1: Individual based of adolescent development* (3rd ed., pp. 187–228). Hoboken, NJ: John Wiley & Sons.

Speiker, S., & Bensley, L. (1994). Roles of living arrangements and grandmother social support in adolescent mothering and infant attachment. *Developmental Psychology, 30*, 102–111.

Tanner, J. L. (2006). Recentering during emerging adulthood: A critical turning point in life span human development. In J. J. Arnett & J. L. Tanner (Eds.), *Emerging adults in America: Coming of age in the 21st century* (pp. 21–55). Washington, DC: American Psychological Association.

van Ijzendoorn, M. H. (1995). Adult attachment representations, parental responsiveness, and infant attachment: A meta-analysis on the predictive validity of the adult attachment interview. *Psychological Bulletin, 117*, 387–403.

Wakschlag, L. S., Chase-Lansdale, P. L., & Brooks-Gunn, J. (1991). *Manual for the Scale of Intergenerational Relationship Quality.* Unpublished manuscript, University of Chicago.

Wakschlag, L. S., Chase-Lansdale, P. L., & Brooks-Gunn, J. (1996). Not just ghosts "Ghosts in the Nursery": Contemporaneous intergenerational relationships and parenting in African-American families. *Child Development, 67*, 2132–2147.

Wakschlag, L. S., Chase-Lansdale, P. L., & Brooks-Gunn, J. (2001). Scale of intergenerational relationship quality. In J. Touliatos, B. F. Perlmutter, & G. W. Holden (Eds.), *Handbook of family measurement techniques, Vol. 2* (pp. 70–71). Thousand Oaks, CA: Sage.

Wakschlag, L. S., & Hans, S. L. (2000). Early parenthood in context: Implications for development and intervention. In C. Zeanah (Ed.), *Handbook of infant mental health* (2nd ed., pp. 129–144). New York: Guilford.

Ward, M., & Carlson, E. (1995). Associations among adult attachment representations, maternal sensitivity and infant-mother attachment in a sample of adolescent mothers. *Child Development, 66*, 69–79.

9

Young Fathers and the Transition to Parenthood

An Interpersonal Analysis of Paternal Outcomes

PAUL FLORSHEIM AND DAVID R. MOORE

INTRODUCTION: YOUNG FATHERS IN DEVELOPMENTAL PERSPECTIVE

The transition to parenthood is regarded as a critical developmental milestone, posing a number of new challenges associated with dramatic increases in responsibility, new demands for emotional attunement and stability, and profound shifts in the nature and parameters of intimacy. Indeed, many young couples report significant declines in marital satisfaction, directly related to the emotional and physical strain of caring for a newborn as well as diminished time and energy for romance (Lawrence et al., 2008). The typical difficulties of early parenthood usually are compensated for by a parent's psychological preparation for child rearing, a durable relationship between the coparents, and love for the child. Although most parents are able to manage temporary declines in relationship satisfaction by drawing on their interpersonal reserves, some couples become increasingly hostile and pervasively distressed. This problematic adjustment to parenthood can be particularly dire when it "spills over" onto the parent–child relationship (Katz & Gottman, 1996; Katz & Woodin, 2002; Kitzmann, 2000; Laurent et al., 2008; Margolin et al., 2001).

Adolescent parents in general, and adolescent fathers in particular, are thought to be especially susceptible to coparenting relationship problems (Cabrera, Fagan, & Farrie, 2008; Fagan, Bernd & Whiteman, 2007). In addition to being more likely to have unstable relationships with their coparenting partners, young fathers are often psychologically unprepared for fatherhood and interpersonally ill-equipped to provide the sort of nurturance and care that an infant needs. Despite having generally optimistic views of marriage before childbirth, less than 20% of adolescent coparenting couples are married when their child is born (Ryan, Manlove, & Moore, 2004). In addition, there is evidence that over time, committed romantic relationships between young parents tend to dissolve and young fathers become increasingly disengaged as parents, contributing to the high rates of impoverished children among households headed by single mothers (Carlson, McLanahan, & Brooks-Gunn, 2008).

The social and public health concerns associated with the decline in stable two-parent families have generated some debate about how to support marriage or promote engaged parenthood among young fathers and their partners (Halford, Markman, & Scott, 2008). Concerns about the impact of unstable coparenting relations on child development have also led to an increased interest in young couples who are able to successfully navigate the transition to parenthood and surmount the significant risk factors that they encounter along the way. In regards to this last point, it is important to note that despite the well-documented risks associated with early parenthood, not all young fathers fail as relationship partners or as parents; some are in fact able to manage the frustration, anxiety, and demands that accompany the monumental responsibility of parenthood and maintain (or establish for the first time) positive relations with both their partners and children (Carlson & McLanahan, 2006; Fagan, Palkovitz, Roy & Farrie, 2009).

In this chapter, we use an interpersonal framework to develop an understanding of how adolescent males manage the transition to parenthood, highlighting different pathways and outcomes that can emerge during this process. We employ complementary methods and analytic strategies to provide a comprehensive understanding of the development and functioning of young fathers. More specifically, a combination of observational and self-report data helps provide a broad perspective on interpersonal trends associated with the adjustment to parenthood, while interview-based narrative data from two young fathers help anchor these trends in the concrete life experiences of individuals.

PART I: EXAMINING INTERPERSONAL CONSISTENCIES AND INCONSISTENCIES

The Young Parenthood Study (YPS) is a longitudinal investigation of adolescent mothers and their partners, which was designed to test two primary hypotheses: (1) The observed quality of young couples' interactions, assessed prior to childbirth, would predict paternal functioning; and (2) Changes in couples' quality of relationship scores would predict paternal functioning and engagement (Florsheim et al., 2003; Moore & Florsheim, 2008). With respect to both hypotheses, paternal functioning was defined in terms of whether the father was still involved in coparenting and if still involved, the quality of his behavior while interacting with his child. As described below, we focused on the parenting behavior of young men, identifying consistencies between couple relations and paternal functioning across the transition to parenthood. In general, we anticipated that positive dyadic relations prior to childbirth would predict positive parenting 2 years later.

Identifying consistencies across developmental stages and interpersonal contexts contributes to the discovery and articulation of developmental principles, including the principle of interpersonal spillover. Such principles are useful in the design of preventive and intervention programs for parents because identifying predictors of positive parenting can assist health and mental health professionals in providing at-risk parents with relevant, useful support. In this study, however, we were also interested in moving beyond an exclusive focus on statistically significant consistencies. More specifically, we hoped to identify subgroups of young fathers that did not follow the normative or predictable patterns. For example, similar to the resilient adolescents described by Hauser and colleagues in this volume (Hauser, Allen, & Schulz, Chapter 10) who "bounced back" after experiencing significant psychopathology in their youth, we have found that some fathers manage to rise above their difficult, problem-ridden beginnings and function more positively than anyone might have guessed (Florsheim & Ngu, 2006). Conversely, other fathers appear to have positive relations with their partners during the pregnancy but go on to experience significant problems during the transition to parenthood, despite their efforts to remain engaged as fathers. Both of these subgroups of young fathers—those with unexpected positive and negative trajectories across the transition to parenthood—are important to understand because their achievements and struggles may provide important insight into the psychological and interpersonal challenges that many young fathers face; they can also illuminate the factors that determine how young fathers respond to these challenges.

THE YOUNG PARENTHOOD STUDY

Participants

Participants in this study included 179 young expectant couples. At the time of recruitment, the pregnant adolescents were 14 to 18 years old and their partners, the young expectant fathers, were 14 to 24 years old. The mean age of expectant fathers in the study was 18.3 (SD = 2.1), and the mean age of expectant mothers was 16.4 (SD = 1.3). Thirty percent of the expectant fathers and 13.3% of the expectant mothers had dropped out of high school. The remaining participants were either in school or had graduated. The ethnic composition of the sample was 59% African-American, 28% Latino, and 13% white. Hollingshead SES scores ranged from 5 (*impoverished*) to 63 (*upper middle class*), with both the overall median (*Mdn* = 28.8) and mean (*M* = 28.4, *SD* = 7.6) scores in the lower middle-class range (see Moore & Florsheim, 2008, for details).

Participants were recruited through schools and clinics for pregnant/parenting teens in the Metropolitan Chicago area. Because this was a study of relations between young mothers and fathers, we required that both partners be willing to participate together, regardless of whether they were romantically involved. Pregnant adolescents were invited to participate through prenatal classes. We were usually able to determine which students were eligible for the study, based on age, age of partner, parent status, and number of weeks pregnant; however, we could not verify the eligibility of all potential recruits. We estimate that our recruitment rate for eligible couples was approximately 50%.

Many of the fathers who did not participate were no longer involved in a romantic relationship with the pregnant adolescent. In an effort to address our concern that this sampling strategy may have led to an atypical sample of young parents due to its reliance on young fathers' willingness to be interviewed, we collected data on a small group of pregnant adolescents ($n = 19$) whose partners refused participation in the study. Analyses of variance (ANOVAs) and chi-square tests indicated that there were no significant differences between this group of single mothers and the expectant mothers whose partners participated in the study on any of the demographic variables measured [including age, socioeconomic status (SES), length of relationship with partner, education, marital status, and ethnicity].

Procedure

After obtaining informed consent and parental consent for all teens under the age of 18, researchers administered a semistructured interview with each young expectant father and mother separately. This interview, which was audiotaped, focused on a wide range of topics, from basic background information to an in-depth exploration of the participant's relationship history, sense of self, and experience of the impending transition to parenthood. Following the semistructured interview, couples engaged in a videotaped conflict task in which they were asked to discuss and resolve a recent conflict or disagreement and to try to come to some resolution on the issue. After explaining the task, the interviewers left the room to allow the participants to talk privately. Participants were primed for this discussion during their interviews, as they were asked several questions regarding a recent disagreement. Couples were also administered a questionnaire to assess self-reported quality of their relationship with their partner. We refer to baseline data collection as Time 1 or T1.

Couples were followed up twice. One year after their child's birth (Time 2 or T2), couples were administered the interview and quality of relationship measure again. At the 2-year postbirth follow-up (Time 3 or T3), another interview was conducted, which focused primarily on the coparenting relationship, the adjustment to parenthood, and the young parent's experience as a father or mother. Additionally, father–child interactions were observed during a semistructured puzzle task in which the parent was instructed to interact as naturally as possible with his child and assist his toddler in assembling a developmentally appropriate jigsaw puzzle. As with the prebirth mother–father interaction task, the father–child interactions were videotaped for later observational coding. For each meeting, participants were paid $40 each ($80 per couple) as reimbursement for their time.

Measures

Relationship quality at Time 1 and Time 2. Young parents' perceived quality of their own relationship was assessed by the Quality of Relationship Inventory (QRI; Pierce et al., 1997), a structured self-report measure designed to assess perceived conflict, depth/investment, and support in dyadic relationships. The QRI is a 25-item self-report measure based on a 4-point scale ranging from *not at all* to *a lot.* Higher scores on the QRI indicate more positive appraisals of the relationship. Sample questions include "To what extent can you trust this person not to hurt your feelings?" and "To what extent can you count on this person to help if you were in a crisis situation, even if he or she had to go out of his or her way?" The bivariate correlation between male and female scores was moderately strong and statistically significant, $r(167) = 0.48, p < 0.001$.

Observed interpersonal behavior. The Structural Analysis of Social Behavior (SASB; Benjamin, 1974) was used to code the 10-minute videotaped interactions in which couples discussed a recent disagreement (at T1) as well as the observed interactions of the young fathers and their children (at T3). SASB is a circumplex model that can be used to describe interpersonal behavior in terms of simple and complex combinations of hostility, warmth, control, submission, autonomy-giving, and autonomy-taking/assertiveness. The *affiliation* dimension of the SASB model describes the degree of warmth or hostility in any given interpersonal exchange (e.g., a hug would typically be considered high in affiliation; a slap or insult would be rated high in hostility). The *interdependence* dimension represents the degree of enmeshment (controlling or submitting) or autonomy (giving or taking) observed in dyadic behavior (e.g., a command would be considered high in control; the refusal to obey a command would be high in autonomy taking; soliciting approval would be highly submissive).

The SASB model is ideal for the purposes of examining interpersonal spillover because it is flexible enough to be used to code dyadic interactions across distinct interpersonal contexts (e.g., mother–father and parent–child interactions). Several variations of SASB coding schemes have been developed (Florsheim & Benjamin, 2001). The SASB–Composite observational coding scheme (Moore & Florsheim, 1999) was selected for this study, facilitating the coders' ability to work directly from the videotaped interaction and record the frequency of specific SASB behaviors during the 10-minute interactions. In the SASB coding scheme, a "unit" of interpersonal behavior is defined as a single interpersonally meaningful message. The message may be nonverbal (e.g., a gesture, facial expression) or verbal (as brief as a single word or as long as a meandering sentence), or a combination of verbal and nonverbal behavior (e.g., both what is said and the tone with which it is said are taken into account when coding a given unit of behavior).

The process of coding a single unit of behavior according to the SASB-coding method involves three steps. First, the coder decides whether a behavior is self-focused, other-focused, or both self- and other-focused. Once the focus of the behavior has been determined, the second step is to rate the unit of behavior for its degree of interdependence using a scale ranging from *highly enmeshed* to *highly differentiated*. Finally, the degree of affiliation is rated on a scale ranging from *extremely hostile* to *extremely warm*.

For the purposes of this study, we used two different indexes to operationally define the quality of mother–father interactions assessed at T1 (before birth) and the quality of father's interactions with his child at the 2-year follow-up (T3). For couples' behavior at Time 1, the SASB index was based on the sum of both partner's warmth/affiliation scores minus the absolute value of the difference between partners' warmth/hostility. This formula was used to adjust for the fact that couples' behavior can appear high in warmth or hostility based solely on a single partner's behavior. We subtracted the absolute value of the difference to help ensure that high scores reflect some degree of balance between partners (Moore & Florsheim, 2001). Values were standardized to facilitate comparisons across mother–father and father–child interactions. Thus, higher scores on this index indicated that a couple demonstrated a high degree of net warmth (relative to hostility) and that there was a high degree of balance (or mutuality) between partners in their independent warmth scores.

The index for assessing the quality of father's parenting behavior toward his child at the 2-year follow-up was also based on a ratio of SASB-coded warmth-to-hostility scores. However, there were two specific differences in this index, which was designed to more accurately measure the quality of parent–child interactions. First, we excluded self-focused codes because the base rates of self-focused behavior were close to zero. This was largely due to the fact that the play activity "pulled for" other-focused parenting behavior. The second difference was that controlling behaviors were included in our index of parenting in order to effectively distinguish parents who used benevolent forms of influence (i.e., nurturance and guidance) from those who relied on strict or hostile methods of control. High rates of strict controlling behavior are a potential problem within the context of a parent–child play activity, and we wanted to make sure that our measure of parenting behavior reflected this behavior, in addition to hostility alone. Hence, the index of the quality of father's interactions with his child reflects net warmth (in autonomy-giving, loving expressions, and benevolent control/guidance) relative to hostility (e.g., neglect, blame) *plus* strict control. The resulting index, which was also standardized, was a continuous measure with higher scores indicating higher parental warmth relative to parental hostility and strict control.

Videotaped discussion tasks were rated by coders who had received a minimum of 75 hours of training in the original SASB system, plus an additional 20 hours of training with the SASB–Composite. Intraclass correlations were used to estimate the rate of agreement between coders across specific SASB codes (Shrout & Fleiss, 1979). Intraclass correlation coefficients ranged from 0.71 to 0.98, with a mean of 0.87. For a detailed description of the SASB coding systems including information regarding validity, see Florsheim and Benjamin (2001).

RESULTS

Retention

At the first follow-up, 147 (82%) young fathers and 164 (91%) young mothers completed the QRI for a second time. At the second follow-up, we were able to obtain videotaped father–child interaction data from only 90 of the original 179 fathers. An additional 33 participated in the follow-up data collection, but were unable to bring their child to the laboratory for the play activity. Forty fathers (24%) were entirely disengaged from parenting at the second follow-up and were unavailable or unwilling to be interviewed. We were unable to find or determine the status of 16 fathers.

Statistical Analyses of Consistencies across
the Transition to Parenthood

In the first set of analyses, multiple regression analysis was used to test the hypotheses that observed quality of couples' interactions and change in couples' quality of relationship scores would predict paternal engagement, defined in terms of (1) whether the father was still involved in coparenting and (2) the quality of observed father–child interactions. In these two analyses, observed father–mother interactions (as assessed by SASB scores) and couples' QRI residual change scores (assessed at both T1 and T2) were included as predictors, and fathers' observed parenting (assessed at 2 years postbirth) was included as the dependent variable. Father's SES and age were included as demographic controls. All predictor and control variables were simultaneously entered into the regression equation. As indicated in Table 9.1, results of the multiple linear regression analysis with father–child SASB scores as the dependent variable indicated that couples' interactions (assessed before birth) significantly predicted fathers' behavior with their children at follow-up. Father's age was also a significant predictor of father–child behavior, with older fathers observed to be more warmly engaged.

Logistic regression analysis targeted mothers' report of fathers' engagement in coparenting (0 = engaged, 1 = disengaged) as the criterion variable. Results indicated that both couples' interpersonal behavior and couples' change in QRI scores predicted paternal disengagement. Specifically, fathers exhibiting greater net warmth toward their partners before the transition to parenthood were more likely to remain engaged in parenting over time.

Examination of Inconsistencies across
the Transition to Parenthood

In the second set of analyses we used the same data set, but took a different statistical approach in order to highlight those fathers whose patterns are not represented by

Table 9.1 MULTIPLE REGRESSION ANALYSES: COUPLES BEHAVIOR
AND CHANGE IN RELATIONSHIP QUALITY AS A PREDICTOR
OF PATERNAL BEHAVIOR AND PATERNAL ENGAGEMENT

| | Linear Regression | | | Logistic Regression | | |
| | Paternal Warmth | | | Paternal Disengagement | | |
Independent Variables	SE	β	B	SE	Wald	Exp (B)
Father's SES	0.010	0.180	−0.017	0.020	0.709	0.983
Father's Age	0.053	0.325*	0.067	0.101	0.438	1.069
Couple's Warmth	0.056	0.244*	−0.231	0.119	3.806*	0.793
Couple's QRI T1	0.014	0.179	0.009	0.025	0.127	1.009
Couple's QRI T2	0.012	−0.023	−0.072	0.020	13.342**	0.931

NOTE: Father's parenting behavior (assessed 2 years postbirth) was measured by the standardized score of net warmth (relative to hostility and strict control). Father's behavior with partner (assessed prenatally) was measured by the standardized score for net warmth (relative to hostility). See the Method section for a detailed description of these indexes. SES was assessed using Hollingshead's (1974) Four-Factor Index. All variables were entered simultaneously in the model. Both models (based on R^2 and Nagelkerke's R^2, respectively) accounted for 22.5% of the variance in paternal behavior and paternal disengagement. Effect sizes for both models, as indexed by Cohen's f^2, were 0.29, indicating a moderate effect (Cohen, 1988).

*$p < 0.05$; **$p < 0.01$.

the statistical analyses presented in Table 9.1. For this analysis, we split our couples into three discrete groups based on their SASB interactions: warm, hostile, and neutral. "Warm" couples had standardized warmth/hostility scores above 1.0 (i.e., greater than 1 SD above the mean), based on the formula described above. "Hostile" couples had combined warmth/hostility scores below −1.0. "Neutral" couples had warmth/hostility scores between −1.0 and 1.0.

Next, we wanted to further divide these three affiliation groups based on changes in their QRI scores between T1 and T2. To accomplish this goal, we calculated residual change scores to differentiate between fathers whose QRI scores had increased or declined between T1 and T2, relative to other fathers in the sample (Cronbach & Furby, 1970). Residual change scores, in which scores at one point in time are regressed against scores at another point in time for the purpose of obtaining a value that reflects relative differences over time, are regarded as more reliable indictors of change than raw difference scores. A positive residual score indicates that a score's value has increased over time, while accounting for time-dependent differences in group means and standard deviations. A negative residual score indicates that values are decreasing over time. Because the average QRI score at T2 was significantly lower than the average QRI score at T1, a positive residual change score might represent a set of QRI scores that was actually relatively stable over time (e.g., not losing ground). Fathers with a standardized residual change scores below 0 were grouped into the "declining QRI" group and fathers with a standardized residual change scores above 0 were grouped into the "stable/increasing QRI" group.

Finally, using both the SASB-based parenting scores (described above) and mothers' report of paternal involvement, fathers were divided into four discrete groups, based on their engagement with their child: (1) positively engaged fathers had standardized SASB scores above 0.5; (2) neutral fathers had standardized SASB scores in the range between 0.5 and –0.5; (3) negatively engaged fathers had standardized SASB scores below –0.5; and (4) disengaged fathers were no longer involved in parenting, as reported by mothers. Using these categories, we created 6 × 4 tables (below) to describe the distribution of fathers across these groups. Visual inspection of the distribution of cases across the 24 categories suggests that fathers in hostile couples (at T1) tended to become disengaged or engaged in hostile parenting 2 years postbirth and that fathers in warm couples (at T1) tended to become more warmly engaged with their children. However, the distribution of cases across cells was quite broad. As such, the chi-square analyses yielded nonsignificant results, $\chi^2(15) = 20.33$, $p = 0.11$. The point of presenting the data in this format is to help identify individual cases (and clusters) that are not well represented by statistically significant regression coefficients. In this particular set of analyses, the numbers of cases that were clearly "off the regression line" included a sizable minority.

The regression analyses outlined in Table 9.1 highlight interpersonal consistencies across the transition to parenthood, but Table 9.2 indicates a somewhat

Table 9.2 SUBGROUPS OF YOUNG FATHERS BASED ON COUPLES' INTERACTIONS AT T1, QUALITY OF RELATIONSHIP CHANGE BETWEEN T1 AND T2, AND PATERNAL BEHAVIOR AT T3

| | Paternal Functioning | | | |
Couples' Functioning	Disengaged	Hostile	Neutral	Warm
Hostile Interaction/Declining QRI	11	7	3	2
Hostile Interaction/Stable–Increasing QRI	4	8	6	7
Neutral Interaction/Declining QRI	5	4	4	4
Neutral Interaction/Stable–Increasing QRI	5	4	7	7
Warm Interaction/Declining QRI	3	3	1	7
Warm Interaction/Stable–Increasing QRI	1	3	5	7

NOTE: Numbers in cells reflect total number of participants in each subgroup.

different story. By reconfiguring the same dataset, we draw attention to those young men whose prebirth (T1) couples' functioning did *not* predict their 2-year postbirth parenting outcomes (assessed at T3). Some of these fathers appeared to be functioning well at T1, but were disengaged or negatively engaged with their children at T3. By contrast, some young men appeared to be engaged in relatively hostile relationships with their partners at T1, but were positively engaged with their child at T3. From our perspective, the data in Table 9.2 complement the findings reported in Table 9.1, underscoring the notion that the experiences of a sizable minority of young fathers are not necessarily well represented by statistically significant regression coefficients that capture normative patterns in the data. These underrepresented patterns are critical to understand because they have important implications for the development of preventive and intervention programs. In the next section, we introduce two young fathers, Robert and Steven, whose narratives illustrate different paths through the key developmental event of parenthood and highlight the rich and complex nature of this transition.

PART II: A TALE OF TWO TRANSITIONS TO FATHERHOOD

The Case of Robert

Robert is an articulate 17-year-old high school senior whose data located him on the lower right corner of Table 9.2, one of seven to have positive relations at T1 and positive parenting at T2. His girlfriend, Sarah, was 5 months pregnant when both agreed to participate in our longitudinal study of young couples. After some introductory questions, focusing on his school, work, and family situation, the interviewer turned to Robert's relationship with Sarah, whom he had been dating for about a year.

> Interviewer: "Tell me about your relationship with Sarah."
> Robert: "Right now it's solid. I mean we try . . . I try to do as much as I can. We just went baby shopping for the baby, already, and I spent about over a hundred dollars. And I guess . . . I go and see her every day. If she needs me, I'm there, I told her that, if she needs me I'm there no matter what. And she's . . . it's like we have no problems."
> Interviewer: "How do you feel about Sarah?"
> Robert: "I love her. I do, there's nothing I wouldn't do for her. It's like, if she needs me, whatever it is, I don't care what it is. If we break up, I'll still be friends with her. That's the way I feel 'cause I still want to have that friendship though. And in a relationship, I still want to be friends, too, at the same time. 'Cause you can't just be lovers, you got to be friends too; in order to love somebody you have to be friends with them too. So you have to know how to speak

to them as a friend and as a lover too. That's the way
I see it."

Interviewer: "How has the relationship changed since you found out
Sarah is pregnant?"

Robert: "Actually, it got more intense, 'cause when I found out that
she was pregnant, I was happy. And the only thing I was
worried about was what my mother was going to say. I knew
my father was going to say that he was going to take care of
the baby. But once I found out that my mother was cool
about it, it was like, I have no problems. It's like everything
has been smooth ever since I found out that she was
pregnant . . . it's like . . . but the attitude changes. That I know
I have to deal with, but it don't bother me, 'cause I know that
it's just a part of pregnancy, so I was like, it don't bother me."

Eighteen months later, Robert was in trade school, working as an electrician's
assistant, and living with Sarah and his 1-year-old daughter, Stacy. Sarah was
pregnant again, expecting a second daughter. Robert agreed to meet for a second
interview, and again the interview focused on the relationship with Sarah.

Interviewer: "How has the relationship changed since Stacy's birth?"

Robert: "It's been more of a mind, a mind game. I mean, 'cause
before we was goin' through problems with each other.
I was lying and she was feeling very on edge,
overprotective. I don't know why I was lying. It was all
about stupid things, about money, about where I'm going.
It was a lot of stupid things that I don't even remember,
remember right now [laughs]."

Interviewer: "Why do you think that you were doing that?"

Robert: "Scared."

Interviewer: "Scared of what?"

Robert: "The fatherly responsibilities . . . I was honestly scared.
I mean it was like, I was in school, I had all these doubts.
That was one of my downfalls. I had a lot of doubts.
Because I would come home and she would be mad
because Stacy would be getting into all this stuff and I'm
not there, and she would start arguing with me. Before
long, we . . . I would have to sit back, we'd sit back and talk
and I'd ask what's been going on through the day. I would
take care of Stacy when I come home. You know, she's
taken care of her all day, she's tired, she's just like 'Aaah,
I can't take it no more,' and I just come up there and I take
care of her. It's basically, we just trying to balance out
everything. I come home from work, I may be tired but
I will still try to do my part as a father and a husband."

As indicated earlier, many fathers experience a decline in relationship satisfaction across the transition to parenthood, as the family system undergoes an often dramatic shift to make room for the needs of the newborn (Belsky & Pensky, 1988; Shapiro, Gottman, & Carrere, 2000). In the case of Robert and Sarah, the strain of early parenthood and a diminishing level of relationship satisfaction eventually led to a brief episode of infidelity. According to Sarah, she was feeling lonely, isolated, and overlooked, and had a brief affair with an old boyfriend, in part to make Robert jealous. Infidelity is not uncommon among young couples and its occurrence often ends in separation (Previti & Amato, 2004). Robert did not mention the infidelity in his interview at the T3 follow-up, but he reflects upon the context in which it occurred and (implicitly) his effort to move past it.

Interviewer: "Has your relationship changed at all since the last time we talked?"

Robert: "Yeah, some things have changed. You know, we've had another daughter. We have to depend more on each other more than depending on other people. We've become our own little family and that is basically the thing that we still strive for. I'm learning how to have my own family, how to raise my kids, how to be a husband. I mean it was a challenge having one daughter, and now I have two. Sophie, the baby, she likes to be hugged a lot, she plays a lot, she likes to run around. You have to keep your eyes open everywhere."

Interviewer: "How would you like for things to be different?"

Robert: "I want more trust, and well, you always want more love. More trust, more understanding, more security. We are secure with our relationship, but I want it to be even more. 'Cause right now, the fact that I'm traveling a lot, I worry about what she is doing. But I want to go to the point where you're not worried about that anymore . . . just feel relaxed."

Interviewer: "Has Sarah changed?"

Robert: "Yeah, she's changed. She's stressed out and wants more affection 'cause the babies, I have to give my affection to them too. She wants more, and they want more. Just basic little stuff. Ain't nothing really big. I have to share everything with three people and she has to do the same so."

Robert remains coherent, direct, and self-assured throughout the interview. Although he chooses not to share information about Sarah's infidelity, he is open enough to talk around it, letting us know that things are not perfect. He reflects upon his struggles with family, including issues of trust and love, with a remarkable degree of balance and perspective. Throughout his narrative, he emphasizes his attachment to Sarah, and his deep investment in making the relationship work. He seems able to organize himself and his relationships around a fairly well-defined role as a father and husband. Although the intimacy issues with Sarah are prominent, it is interesting to note that Robert also casually alludes to Sophie's intimacy needs—that she likes to be hugged a lot. Robert seems to recognize that Sophie's need for love is part of the fabric of his life, both joyful and challenging. Eventually, the interview turned to issues of parenthood, asking Robert about his adjustment to becoming a father. Robert's responses demonstrate that he appears to have adjusted well, despite the difficulties in his relationship with Sarah.

Interviewer: "How do you feel about being a father?"

Robert: "I love it. I wouldn't trade it. I think I would've done it differently . . . to establish the money and everything first instead of raising the child and doing the money thing at the same time. I think I would have waited a little longer than I did. Would I give it up? No, I wouldn't give it up."

Interviewer: "Can you describe yourself as a father?"

Robert: "I think every parent wants their child to have things that they didn't have. You know, the only way to do that is raise them right, bring them up the way that you feel is right, make sure that they get their education, make sure that they stay healthy, make sure they eat their vegetables, make sure they stay reading, or you know, keep learning more and more. Like, we get her the ABC toys and the counting toys. You know, trying to show her what to do and what not to do. Tell her the difference between right and wrong. That's the way I feel like a parent should be, you know. Teach them the right from the wrong, the good from the bad. Just teach them how you feel like they should be raised, you know."

Interviewer: "What do you think is the best thing about being a father?"

Robert: "Watching them grow. Ya know, this is something, my babies are mine. It's not nobody else's. That is something that I have a chance to raise, you know. Nobody can tell me you have to do this, you have to do that. I don't have to do nothing I don't want to do. This is my child. I raise them how I want them to be raised, ya know. What I think is right, what I think is wrong, not what you think. Ya know, when I was raised I had to do what my Mom and Dad told me. Now it is like I'm grown and I have to implant that to them, ya know. This is something I love."

Robert's narrative reflects two somewhat contradictory themes that are noted in the research literature on the transition to parenthood. On the one hand,

Robert describes a positive relationship with Sarah, particularly when she is pregnant, and a positive adjustment to parenthood. However, like many young fathers, Robert has struggled with some serious problems in his relationship with Sarah, and some initial doubts about his ability to function as father. Despite his youth, Robert's narrative is remarkably similar to the stories of adult fathers, who experience strain in their marital relations but are nonetheless able to function well as parents and coparents. In Robert's case, several factors seem to help define his resilience across the transition to parenthood. These include his ability to integrate contradictory emotions into a coherent experience of self and other, a sense of agency and direction, and the clear motivation and capacity for establishing and sustaining relationships with his partner and child, despite the challenges that they pose (Hauser et al., Chapter 10, this volume).

THE CASE OF STEVEN

Like Robert, Steven was 17 years old when he was first interviewed. When asked how he felt about his girlfriend, Rita, his response in this prenatal interview was similar to Robert's.

Steven:	"I feel good because I love her a lot. She had a miscarriage before, you know, that brought us down a lot, and that's when we started arguing more, but now I know she's pregnant again, I feel like we got a little closer. She was, like, everything I wanted . . . everything. This is the longest [relationship] I've ever had, going on like four years, and the longest I ever had before her, is eight months, you know, and back then, I was young; now I know what I'm doing."
Interviewer:	"Okay. Has your relationship changed at all since you found out that she was pregnant?"
Steven:	"Umm, yeah we got a little closer, we started talking more about it, you know, started spending more of our time together."

At the second follow-up (2 years following the baby's birth), when we asked about the relationship with Rita, Steven was somewhat circumspect.

Interviewer:	"How would you describe your current relationship now with Rita?"
Steven:	"Maybe a little better, but we still have problems, you know. I noticed that every time we live together, we always seem to argue more. And when we're separated, when we're not living together but we're still dating and stuff, we seem to get along more."

Interviewer: "Okay. And you say that you still have problems.
               What kind of problems?"

Steven: "I guess we're, we're still too young. Wanna go, wanna be
               out, wanna go out with our friends. Probably 'cause how
               young we are. But you know, hard to do that 'cause, we
               both can't go out, you know. Like if I go out, she got to stay
               in. And if she goes out then I gotta stay in."

Interviewer: "How would you say that you, you feel about her?"

Steven: "I mean like, I care about her a lot. I care about her, 'cause
               we been together for about like it's gonna be six years now.
               But only two off and on, you know. So we've been together
               four years straight, and the last two off and on. And I,
               I think that's a long time, you know. Six, I think six years is
               a long time. 'Cause I've known people who've been together
               for like two years, but there there already talking about
               getting married. But you know, I mean, I don't see myself
               getting married yet. Or even getting married at all 'cause
               I know, like 50% of marriages always end up in divorce."

Steven gets caught up in his own ambivalence about the relationship, and never
gets to describe how he feels about Rita or describe the quality of his relationship
with her. In this sense, he appears less emotionally focused than Robert, but also
much more self-focused, which does not bode well for his investment in parenting and coparenting. Rita was more direct about the problems she and Steven
were experiencing at the time:

Rita: "It's not . . . it's not good, it's rocky. We have arguments.
               Before, I would really try not to argue with him. Actually,
               I'd try to talk to him about it. And lately it's like I don't care
               anymore, you know; if we argue, I don't deal with it. I just
               hang up and I won't call him anymore. It's like I don't
               wanna, I'm not gonna argue with him, I used to stress out
               over it all the time. And I can't do it no more. I just let it
               fall. And now it seems like if I just kinda leave him, like if
               I kinda just let it, leave it alone, you know, he'll come, you
               know. I kinda try to talk to him about it and all this stuff.
               So it seems like it's working out better recently."

Interviewer: "What kinds of things do you usually argue about?"

Rita: "Umm, just the time he spends with my son. Like, he
               works from 1 to 9 right now, so it's like all day really, you
               know. And, so . . . when he comes out of work, you know,
               he doesn't worry about spending time with me. He's like,
               worried about being still with his friends, you know? And
               I don't, like, I just tell him, if you're gonna do it, you know,
               just go. 'Cause I have the baby mostly all day, you know.

And I just tell him like, go, I'm not gonna beg you to spend time with him. That's all. So just go and do what you gotta do. And then I'll hang up, you know. And then he'll come to my dad's house and talk to me about it. And sometimes, you know, sometimes he'll go, and sometimes I just deal with it. That's what I keep telling him lately. I don't think we're gonna be together long."

When the interviewer asked Steven about his adjustment to fatherhood, he seemed confused and had a hard time focusing on his relationship with his child.

Interviewer: "What are your feelings about being a father?"
Steven: "I think being a father is . . . at an early age, I think it wasn't, umm, I mean, I don't regret it, but it, you know. . . It wasn't planned, but I, I won't, I mean, I'm never gonna regret it, you know. I mean, it takes two, I know it was my fault. So, when we had him, I was only 18. You know, I mean I was scared, like I'm sure everybody is, you know, when they first have a son. I mean I didn't have no high school diploma. I mean, you know, I wasn't working at the time, so I was like, you know, I was a little scared. Like, I didn't know what to do."
Interviewer: "Okay. How would you describe yourself as a father?"
Steven: "I wouldn't say bad . . . I wouldn't say like, I mean, I'm a good father. Ummm, I know I haven't been there all, all, all the time, you know. But I've been there long enough for him to know that I'm his father. He calls me Dada. He recognizes me as his father. That's good. I am helpful . . . helpful. I think, I think I'm a good father. I mean I, I, I don't think I'm doing nothin' wrong."
Interviewer: "Yeah, what would be an example of how you think you're a good father?"
Steven: "Like partly supporting him, you know. You gotta, you gotta support them. He's your son, you know. You gotta, you gotta buy him, you gotta buy him his food. You gotta buy him his clothes. You gotta buy him his diapers, you know. You gotta take him to here, you gotta take him there."
Interviewer: "Okay. What's the best thing about being a father?"
Steven: "I guess the time when I'm with him, you know, like I said, I'm always acting, I'm, I'm always happy when I'm with him. 'Cause that's my son, you know. I look at him and I, and I see, I see me when I was like two years old. So, I see the way I was acting. So, I think being with him is just, I don't know . . . when, once you have a child, you're gonna be like, 'wow.'"

Both Robert and Steven report declines in the quality of their relationships, but Steven's is more extreme, and when asked how he feels about being a father, Steven does not answer directly. He notes the unplanned nature of the pregnancy and is able to reflect somewhat about the difficulties related to being a teen father, but he does not come back around to describing his feelings as a father. Like many of the young fathers interviewed, he describes himself as a father primarily in terms of the financial support he provides. He seems distant and disconnected as a father, and surprised that his son, who is 2 years old at the time of the interview, knows him to be his father. Although he indicates that he is "always happy" when he is with his son, Steven's narrative account of the father–child relationship lacks emotional substance or relevant details that would help make his account more coherent and compelling.

Robert's and Steven's narratives present a challenge for researchers because despite similar starting points, they have divergent trajectories across the transition to fatherhood. We know that in the larger sample, some participants have stories that support our hypotheses, but others do not. Several young men represented in Table 9.2 are either doing better or worse than one might expect, based on their circumstances and background factors assessed at T1. Many researchers regard these individuals as anomalies who distract from the main point of statistically significant findings, as the objective of most research is to identify consistencies and predictable patterns in the data. In this chapter, we illustrate the importance and utility of examining both continuities and discontinuities across the transition to fatherhood in order to attain a more complete understanding of young fathers' adjustment to the critical life transition of fatherhood.

DISCUSSION

In this chapter, we addressed the issue of how young fathers manage—or fail to manage—the transition to parenthood. We approached the topic from different methodological perspectives, highlighting both trends in interpersonal spillover across the transition to parenthood and divergences from these trends. In addition, we included samples of narrative data excerpted from interviews conducted with two young fathers to help anchor the quantitative analyses in the concrete experiences of study participants. After having studied the lives of young fathers over a number of years, we have become increasingly aware of the limitations of any single methodological approach to data analyses and have adopted this mixed method approach because we believe it helps tell a more complete story (Pittman, Wakschlag, Chase-Landale, & Brooks-Gunn, Chapter 8, this volume). In this discussion, we attempt to weave together the strands of data presented, providing a more comprehensive perspective on the interpersonal development of young fathers across the transition to parenthood.

The finding that the quality of couples' relations prior to childbirth predicted the quality of fathers' behavior with their 2-year-old children is largely consistent with previous research on the spillover phenomenon observed among adult couples (Katz & Woodin, 2002; Kitzmann, 2000; Laurent et al., 2008). This finding underscores the stability of interpersonal functioning over time and across interpersonal domains, and contributes to the literature on interpersonal spillover in two important ways. First, it confirms that the spillover phenomenon occurs in young, unmarried couples. This is relevant to current public interest in supporting "fragile" families, particularly those families in which fathers are at risk for disengagement (Cabrera et al., 2008; Carlson et al., 2008). Despite understandable skepticism about the capacity of many young men to meet the challenges of paternity, these findings suggest the possibility that programs designed to help couples communicate more positively and warmly might facilitate improved paternal engagement (Carlson & McLanahan, 2006; Schulz, Cowan, & Cowan, 2006). Second, many previous studies of interpersonal spillover have not examined couples/parents *across* the transition to parenthood; in particular, few researchers have investigated the links between prebirth couples' relations and postbirth paternal engagement. The finding that the spillover phenomenon is evident across this transition suggests that programs designed to support positive coparenting relations prior to childbirth—when young men might be most amenable to intervention—could help facilitate a positive transition even among at-risk fathers. It is particularly interesting to note that the quality of couples' relations prior to childbirth predicted paternal functioning, *even after* controlling for the effect of declining couples' relationship satisfaction on parenting. This suggests that even if we assume that relationship quality and satisfaction will decline for most young coparenting couples, it may still make sense to support the development of their interpersonal skills in order to facilitate more positive coparenting alliances and improved father–child interactions.

In an effort to make sense of these divergent pathways, we looked to Erik Erikson and Robert Kegan, two lifespan developmental theorists who addressed the challenges involved in moving from adolescent to adult roles. According to Erikson's (1968) theory of psychosocial development, adolescence is first and foremost a period of identity development, which requires personal exploration and experimentation. Erikson proposed that although adolescents are highly motivated to develop intense relations with friends and romantic partners, their relationships serve the primary purpose of identity development. The achievement of a coherent and cohesive self is a prerequisite for true intimacy achievement, which typically occurs in early adulthood, and involves establishing deep, enduring connections with others, often within the context of forming a family. It seems likely that for many adolescents, becoming a father too soon could force a young man to confront the challenge of commitment and intimacy without adequate time for exploration, experimentation, or the development of interpersonal skills needed for adult relationships. Adolescent mothers face similar developmental struggles, but their functioning may be more dependent on their capacity to find new, more individuated ways of being connected with their own mothers as they simultaneously develop their own identities as mothers (Pittman et al., Chapter 8, this volume).

Drawing from Erikson's theory of psychosocial development, Robert and Steven could be characterized as torn between the developmental demands of identity and intimacy concerns. Steven's uncertainty about his relationship with Rita and his deep ambivalence about whether to spend time with his family or his friends is developmentally expectable, despite its unfortunate consequences. One of the developmental problems posed by adolescent fatherhood is that typical concerns about identity and intimacy are often in conflict. Identity requires distinction and separation, whereas intimacy requires commitment and connection. Although adolescents clearly struggle with issues of intimacy while engaged in the task of identity formation, the developmental sequencing suggests that identity issues will usually take precedence over intimacy concerns. Young fathers are challenged to function "as if" they had achieved a stable identity and to develop the capacity to at least feign intimacy prior to resolving identity concerns. This heightens the risk of becoming overwhelmed by the demands of both stages, and failing to resolve either. In this respect, Robert is an exception to the "developmental rule" insofar as he appears to be able to balance the challenges of both identity and intimacy, and find meaning in his life as a father.

In his constructivist-developmental theory, Robert Kegan (1982) emphasized a set of stage-based challenges different from those proposed by Erikson. Kegan suggested that adolescents tend to be deeply embedded in interpersonal concerns, defining themselves in term of their relationships, whereas adults define themselves to a greater extent as institutional beings, occupying specific roles and operating within social structures. Drawing from Piaget's theory of cognitive development, Kegan (1982) proposed that one of the most important developmental achievements in life involves the capacity to organize and make sense of one's experience within some larger context. As adults, we struggle to find meaning within the structure of work life and family life, which comprise our most fundamental institutions. Furthermore, young men and women develop an "institutional self," meaning they begin to identify with social roles and function in ways that contribute to social institutions. Kegan's theory helps make some sense of how Robert managed to remain focused and balanced, despite the interpersonal turmoil that he and Sarah have experienced along the way. Despite his youth, Robert was able to meaningfully situate himself in the institutional role of father and husband, and construct a narrative of fatherhood that is personally compelling and consistent with the expectations and needs of his daughters. By way of contrast, Steven appears to be searching for but failing to find a way to make sense of his experience as a father. His inability to see himself as fully occupying the role of father suggests that he is still engaged in the exploration phase of development, a point that is clearly frustrating for Rita, who seems to anticipate that his level of engagement is waning.

Considered in tandem, these narrative accounts of the transition to fatherhood seem to underscore the importance of personal meaning and role definitions in the developmental process (Hauser et al., Chapter 10, this volume). The quality of a young father's relationship and his interpersonal behavior toward his partner and child are clearly important to the development of his identity as a father.

However, because these relationships are often tumultuous across the transition to parenthood, a clear sense of purpose and meaning seems like a necessary additional ingredient. Robert seems deeply connected to Sarah and his daughters. In addition, his narrative suggests that despite his early uncertainties about his capacity to function as a father, he is nonetheless able to invest in this role. Steven, on the other hand, is unable to construct a meaningful role for himself as a father, and seems interpersonally adrift, uncertain as to where he belongs.

Although Steven seems like a failure in contrast to Robert, it is important to remember that both young men were only 18 when they became fathers; Steven's shortcomings are more expected than Robert's developmental achievements. The contrast between them raises questions about individual differences in development; how can young men from similar backgrounds respond so differently to becoming fathers? Whereas Erikson and Kegan help us understand fatherhood from stage-based development models, it is also informative to consider the adjustment to fatherhood from the perspective of personality psychology. In a recent paper, Dan McAdams and Bradley Olson (2010) proposed a personality theory-based model for understanding individual differences in adjustment, suggesting three independent layers of personality development. The first layer of personality is based on "traits" or dispositional tendencies. The second layer of personality pertains to how individuals cope with life's increasingly complex challenges and competing demands. The third layer of personality development involves creating an internal narrative.

If we define personality development as a complex, multifaceted process, it is easy to understand how individuals respond to life stages in different ways, as the pace of development varies across the different layers and quality of coping depends on individual circumstances and characteristics. For example, despite the tendency to regard personality traits as stable over time, there is research indicating that many adolescents become more conscientious and agreeable as they transition to early adulthood (Roberts et al., 2006). This shift in orientation (and personality) is often commensurate with increased levels of intimacy, as they become more attentive to the needs and concerns of others. However, some adolescents are not well equipped to meet the interpersonal challenges of intimacy and are resistant to becoming fully engaged in close relationships. The absence of successful intimate relations during adolescence and early adulthood can inhibit or thwart personality development because our experience (of self and others) becomes constrained.

In addition, as young men and women fulfill adult roles, including parenthood, most become more goal directed and deliberative, but do so in varying degrees and with different approaches to life's challenges. How the "agentic" self develops during this phase of life becomes an emblematic component of personality development (Hauser et al., Chapter 10, this volume). There are many different ways to successfully manage and direct our lives, just as there are many ways to become lost, disempowered, and ineffective. Robert's responses illustrate the particular way that he balances competing demands and negotiates his various roles. For Robert, his sense of agency seems tied to a well-defined set of values and priorities.

In contrast, Steven's absence of agency seems profound, disrupting his relationship with both Rita and his child.

The third layer of personality—development of a narrative self—involves the process of actively constructing a coherent, meaningful storyline from the elements of one's life. According to McAdams and Olson (2010), the stories we tell ourselves about ourselves are critical to the developmental process because through this process we become "authors" of our lives and more fully engaged in determining what happens next. Steven's difficulty articulating a coherent description of himself as a father reflects a profound absence of "authorship" in the living of his life, especially in regards to parenthood. Robert, on the other hand, is able to construct a narrative in which he is simultaneously engaged in both intimacy and identity concerns. Despite the potential for becoming torn between conflicting demands, Robert focuses on his children as primary characters in the story of his life. This focus helps him manage the inherent developmental conflict in a manner that seems mature beyond his years.

CONCLUSIONS

One obvious solution to the challenges of adolescent fatherhood is pregnancy prevention. However, prevention is not always successful and so clinicians and educators must consider the question of how to help young fathers (and their partners) manage the daunting task of simultaneously navigating through two developmental stages. Constructing an enduring, meaningful role as a father and remaining emotionally connected with one's children are difficult adult achievements, beyond the grasp of many young men. The differences observed between Robert and Steven underscore the need for tailoring programs to meet the particular needs of young fathers, which will vary, depending on developmental status, personal assets and liabilities, social circumstances, and interpersonal skills.

In recent years, several family researchers have created models for helping at-risk couples develop interpersonal skills needed to manage conflict and maintain connection (Halford et al., 2008; Schulz et al., 2006). These programs, which are designed to help prepare parents for the interpersonal difficulties related to coparenting, are important but probably not sufficient to prepare *young* fathers for the challenges of parenthood. We believe it is also important to provide psychoeducational programs to support the social-cognitive development of young men, including their capacity for clarifying personal values and goals, organizing and following through on tasks, and managing competing expectations and responsibilities. Additionally, individual- or couples-based counseling services may help young men construct a coherent narrative of the self as a father. Such a narrative could serve as a road map for navigating through difficult times without losing track of personal bearings (values, goals, priorities). For many young men, the process of developing a personal narrative involves having a context for discussing and reflecting upon plans, wishes, and feelings; a narrative self often emerges through dialogue with trusted significant others (Hauser et al., Chapter 10, this volume). Although it make sense to use psychoeducational approaches to provide fathers with some support, many young fathers may need a relationship with a counselor or mentor who can encourage them to tell their story in a manner that facilitates psychological coherence and interpersonal connection. Finally, some young men may need basic case management services to assist in the development of life skills necessary to fill adult roles, particularly employment.

As we have discussed in this chapter, the interpersonal and personal concerns of young fathers can seem contradictory in the sense that it can be difficult for them to reconcile personal needs and wishes with what is best for their partner and child. Such interpersonal challenges are also relevant to young mothers, but are played out somewhat differently (Pittman et al., Chapter 8, this volume). Young mothers tend to struggle with finding a positive balance between autonomy and connection with their own mothers, who are often the primary source of parenting support. For both young mothers and fathers, these interpersonal struggles can lead to role confusion, relationship problems, and deep feelings of self-doubt and defeat (Erikson, 1968; Kegan, 1982). However, it can also lead to an increased sense of interpersonal connection and personal integrity, depending on the availability of external supports and internal resources (Pittman & Coley, 2011).

Like others who use a mixed-method approach to examine the developmental process (e.g., Hauser et al., Chapter 10, this volume), we have found that honing in on fatherhood from different angles through the use of different methodologies has deepened our appreciation for both the interpersonal and intrapersonal challenges involved in becoming a positively engaged father. Although we are not yet in a position to make any proclamations or specific recommendations about how best to help young men stretch themselves and mature beyond their years, we are hopeful that this chapter will assist in developing models of support for young fathers that consider a fuller range of developmental pathways.

ACKNOWLEDGMENTS

This research was supported by the Office of Adolescent Pregnancy Programs (APR 000965) and the Robert Woods Johnson Foundation (RWJF-036768). All names and identifying information used in this chapter have been altered to protect the confidentiality of research participants.

References

Belsky, J., & Pensky, E. (1988). Marital change across the transition to parenthood. *Marriage and Family Review, 12*, 133–156.

Benjamin, L (1974). Structural analysis of social behavior. *Psychological Review, 81*, 392–425.

Cabrera, N., Fagan, J., & Farrie, D. (2008). Explaining the long reach of fathers? Prenatal involvement on later paternal engagement. *Journal of Marriage and Family*, *70*(5), 1094–1107.

Carlson, M., & McLanahan, S. (2006). Strengthening unmarried families: Could enhancing couple relationships also improve parenting? *Social Service Review*, *80*(2), 297–321.

Carlson, M., McLanahan, S., & Brooks-Gunn, J. (2008). Coparenting and nonresident fathers' involvement with young children after a nonmarital birth. *Demography*, *45*(2), 461–488.

Cohen, J. (1988). *Statistical power analysis for the behavioral sciences*. New York: Erlbaum.

Cronbach, L., & Furby, L. (1970). How we should measure "change": Or should we? *Psychological Bulletin*, *74*(1), 68–80.

Erikson, E. (1968). *Identity: youth and crisis*. Oxford, England: Norton & Co.

Fagan, J., Bernd, E., & Whiteman, V. (2007). Adolescent fathers' parenting stress, social support, and involvement with infants. *Journal of Research on Adolescence*, *17*(1), 1–22.

Fagan, J., Palkovitz, R., Roy, K., & Farrie, D. (2009). Pathways to paternal engagement: Longitudinal effects of risk and resilience on nonresident fathers. *Developmental Psychology*, *45*(5), 1389–1405.

Florsheim, P., & Benjamin, L. S. (2001). The structural analysis of social behavior observational coding scheme. In P. K. Kerig & M. Lindahl (Eds.), *Family observational coding schemes: Resources for systemic research* (pp. 127–150). Hillsdale, NJ: Laurence Erlbaum & Associates.

Florsheim, P., & Ngu, L. Q. (2006). Fatherhood as a Transformative Process: Unexpected Successes among High Risk Fathers. In L. Kowaleski-Jones, N. H. Wolfinger, L. Kowaleski-Jones, N. H. Wolfinger (Eds.), *Fragile families and the marriage agenda* (pp. 211–232). New York, NY US: Springer Science + Business Media.

Florsheim, P., Sumida, E., McCann, C. Winstanley, M., Fukui, R. Seefeldt, T., & Moore, D. (2003). Adjustment to parenthood among young African American and Latino couples: Relational predictors of risk for parental dysfunction. *Journal of Family Psychology*, *17*, 65–79.

Halford, W., Markman, H., & Stanley, S. (2008). Strengthening couples' relationships with education: Social policy and public health perspectives. *Journal of Family Psychology*, *22*(4), 497–505.

Katz, L., & Gottman, J. M. (1996). Spillover effects of marital conflict: In search of parenting and coparenting mechanisms. In J. P. McHale, P. A. Cowan, J. P. McHale, P. A. Cowan (Eds.), *Understanding how family-level dynamics affect children's development: Studies of two-parent families* (pp. 57–76). San Francisco, CA US: Jossey-Bass.

Katz, L., & Woodin, E. M. (2002). Hostility, hostile detachment, and conflict engagement in marriages: Effects on child and family functioning. *Child Development*, *73*(2), 636–651.

Kegan, R. (1982). *The evolving self*. Cambridge, MA: Harvard University Press.

Kitzmann, K. (2000). Effects of marital conflict on subsequent triadic family interactions and parenting. *Developmental Psychology*, *36*(1), 3–13.

Laurent, H. K., Kim, H. K., & Capaldi, D. M. (2008). Prospective effects of interparental conflict on child attachment security and the moderating role of parents' romantic attachment. *Journal of Family Psychology*, *22*(3), 377–388.

Lawrence, E., Rothman, A., Cobb, R., Rothman, M., & Bradbury, T. (2008). Marital satisfaction across the transition to parenthood. *Journal of Family Psychology, 22*(1), 41–50.

Margolin, G., Gordis, E. B., & John, R. S. (2001). Coparenting: A link between marital conflict and parenting in two-parent families. *Journal of Family Psychology, 15*(1), 3–21.

McAdams, D., & Olson, B. (2010). Personality development: Continuity and change over the life course. *Annual Review of Psychology, 61,* 517–542.

Moore, D. R., & Florsheim, P. (1999). *Structural analysis of social behavior—Composite observational coding scheme.* Unpublished manuscript. University of Utah.

Moore, D. R., & Florsheim, P. (2001). Interpersonal processes and psychopathology among expectant and nonexpectant adolescent couples. *Journal of Consulting and Clinical Psychology, 69*(1), 101–113.

Moore, D., & Florsheim, P, (2008). Interpersonal process and risk for child abuse among young mothers and fathers. *Child Abuse and Neglect, 32,* 463–475.

Pierce, G. R., Sarason, I. G., Sarason, B. R., Solky-Betzel, J. A., & Nagel, L. C. (1997). Assessing the quality of personal relationships. *Journal of Social and Personal Relationships, 14,* 339–356.

Pittman, L. D., & Coley, R. (2011). Coparenting in families with adolescent mothers. In J. P. McHale, K. M. Lindahl, J. P. McHale, K. M. Lindahl (Eds.), *Coparenting: A conceptual and clinical examination of family systems* (pp. 105–126). Washington, DC US: American Psychological Association.

Previti, D., & Amato, P. (2004). Is infidelity a cause or a consequence of poor marital quality? *Journal of Social and Personal Relationships, 21*(2), 217–230.

Roberts, B. W., Walton, K. E., & Viechtbauer, W. (2006). Patterns of mean-level change in personality traits across the life course: A meta-analysis of longitudinal studies. *Psychological Bulletin, 132*(1), 1–25.

Ryan, S., Manlove, J., & Moore, K. A. (2004). The relationship between teenage motherhood and marriage. *Child Trends* (www.childtrends.org).

Schulz, M. S., Cowan, C. P., & Cowan, P. A. (2006). Promoting healthy beginnings: A randomized controlled trial of a preventive intervention to preserve marital quality during the transition to parenthood. *Journal of Consulting and Clinical Psychology, 74*(1), 20–31.

Shapiro, A. F., Gottman, J. M., & Carrere, S. (2000). The baby and the marriage: Identifying factors that buffer against decline in marital satisfaction after the first baby arrives. *Journal of Family Psychology, 14*(1), 59–70.

Shrout, P. E., & Fleiss, J. L. (1979). Intraclass correlations: Uses in assessing rater reliability. *Psychological Bulletin, 86*(2), 420–428.

Introduction to Section IV

Life Events and Coping with Challenges

PATRICIA K. KERIG AND MARC S. SCHULZ

n the last section of this volume, contributors address ways in which stressful life events and extraordinary challenges may affect development during the adolescent transition. The study of adolescent and young adult development and functioning under challenging circumstances can help identify adaptive strategies that can become the focus of intervention efforts designed to foster adjustment. Such studies also highlight how normative developmental progressions can be altered by challenging events and circumstances (Hinshaw, 2008).

This section of the volume begins, fittingly, with the work of Stuart Hauser, who, along with his colleagues Joseph Allen and Marc Schulz, reports, in Chapter 10, the results of an extraordinary 14-year follow-up of a group of young adults who had been psychiatrically hospitalized in early adolescence. Inspired initially by the observation that some of these youth achieved unexpectedly positive outcomes in adulthood, Hauser and colleagues gave careful thought to the conceptual and methodological questions involved in defining and studying the concept of resilience. As Luthar and colleagues (1993) have argued, resilience is not a unidimensional construct, and Hauser and colleagues take this admonition to heart and construct a multidimensional model of resilience involving evidence of superior functioning in the domains of ego functioning, close relationships, attachment representations, and social competence. Furthermore, they give careful consideration to the developmental context, pointing out that following their participants over time could not be a matter of simply readministering the same measures, but rather had to take into account the changing developmental tasks during the transition to adulthood, including the need to achieve new forms of independence from parents while maintaining a connection with them.

The investigators' bar for defining resilience is high, and only four men and five women qualified for the "exceptional functioning" designation. Their eloquently presented life stories and internal dialogues reveal much that is important about the psychological processes involved in the successful transition from adolescence to young adulthood. A major theme the investigators derive from the narratives of exceptional youth is that of the importance of coherence: in their understanding of their histories and why they were psychiatrically hospitalized, in their representations of relationships and understanding of their importance, in their reflections about their own inner processes and those of others, and in their clarity about how the institution itself played a role in their development. Their self-images are vibrant, even if negative, and their relationships with others are numerous and vital—again, even if negative. Impressively, Hauser, Allen, and Schulz complement these in-depth person-oriented analyses with observations of parent–child interactions during adolescence. Again, they walk us thoughtfully through the methodological considerations they made and their struggles to derive categories and units of analysis that meaningfully capture participants' personal meanings and internal representations without sacrificing either investigative precision or the true richness of the phenomenon at hand. Among their findings, one of the most striking and thought-provoking is that it was *adolescents'* enabling of *parents'* autonomous and differentiated functioning that most clearly distinguished the family interactions of the youth who went on to become resilient adults. As Hauser and colleagues note, even though these youth were full of anger and resentment toward their parents, they still showed signs of reaching out to them. These findings are reminiscent of Rutter's (1990) description of the protective process of "reduction of negative chain reactions" and Katz's (1997) characterization of resilience as "playing a poor hand well." Even in the absence of psychological health and "good-enough" parenting, resilient youth are those who can find ways of cultivating what they need from the interpersonal environment—perhaps by themselves becoming the ones to sow the seeds. The authors' sensitive and insightful reading of these young people's lives truly brings them to life.

Following this, in Chapter 11, Diamond and colleagues review and critique the state of the art in research on sexual minority development in the family context.

They make the compelling argument that from a systemic perspective, a youth's sexual orientation and the coming-out process are *family* experiences that play out as a function of complex transactions. Although often conceptualized as a challenge or stressor, as indeed for many it is, Diamond and colleagues point out that a child's revealing his or her sexual minority status is also a profound experience for the other members of the family. Coming to terms with the sexual minority status of a family member acts as a catalyst for the entire family to readjust, realign, and transform, and may even create an opportunity for growth and the promotion of psychological health for all family members. Viewed as a process rather than a discrete event, even the most hostile and rejecting parental reactions, such as expulsion of the youth from the family home, may represent the initial point of a relational shift that in fact leads to reconciliation and increased intimacy.

The theme of bidirectionality of influences, which emerges repeatedly in this chapter, has important implications for developmental research. For example, although perceived family support may help to buffer youth from the stresses associated with societal homophobia, resilient youth may be those who are most adept at *eliciting* support and affirmation from their families, such as by emphasizing their own acceptance of and positive attitude toward their sexual orientation. However, research regarding such bidirectional effects is rare, and the authors make a persuasive case for the need for investigators to challenge themselves methodologically in order to create study designs that allow the detection of these reciprocal and dynamic systemic relationships as they unfold over time. Diamond and colleagues also give careful consideration to relationship dynamics and cultural beliefs in ethnic minority families that can further complicate and contextualize the coming-out process and the manner in which youth choose to express, inhibit, or adapt their same-sex attraction and behavior.

Picking up on this theme of ethnic diversity, Conger and colleagues in Chapter 12 present an important extension of their family system model for understanding risk and resilience in adolescent development by considering the unique cultural and economic context of Mexican-origin families. The importance of understanding adolescent development among ethnic minorities in the United States cannot be understated, given that it is this most rapidly growing group of young people in the United States (U.S. Census Bureau, 2010) and the one at the highest risk for exposure to the kinds of stresses that could interfere with a successful transition from adolescence and adulthood (e.g., Coker et al., 2009; Spencer et al., 2006). In their model, Conger and colleagues study the interplay of economic stress, interparental conflict, and parent–child relations as they affect child competence. The authors add to their well-replicated family stress model considerations that are specific to Mexican-origin families in the United States, including the common experiences of poverty, residence in high-risk neighborhoods, and exposure to racial discrimination. At each stage of the model, these culture-specific factors act as potentiators of the processes by which economic strain leads to disruptions in parent's emotional functioning, increases in interparental conflict, negative parenting, and less competent youth development. The authors also make the critical point that it is important to look at these processes early in development, given that youths' entry into the adolescent phase sets the tone for much of what is to come.

Conger and colleagues' chapter also represents a model of how a clear well-elaborated theoretical model can be tested empirically using multivariate methods to create latent constructs and test the structural relationships among them. A particular strength of their structural equation modeling approach is its ability to differentiate between direct and mediated effects in complex systems, such as families. This differentiation can inform theory and intervention development in important ways. For example, their analyses suggested that for Mexican-origin families, mothers' parenting behavior was particularly influential in determining whether children were resilient; however, mothers' child management strategies themselves were affected by the father's emotional well-being; thus, even if it is the mother who delivers the message, the father has a role in shaping its tone. By the same token, the investigators' models also reveal the unexpected finding that neighborhood riskiness had a direct effect on youth that was not mediated by family variables—thus, it is important to keep in mind that across the course of adolescence youth increasingly inhabit a world of peers and extrafamilial influences from which no amount of parental structuring and support can fully protect them.

Conger and colleagues explain with clarity and precision the techniques that they employ to gather the prospective interview and self-report data they use for their longitudinal investigations. However, there are also rich sources of data lying unrecognized and underutilized in the archives of the institutions with which young people have come into contact.

To this end, Best and Hauser's concluding chapter in this section, Chapter 13, sheds light on an important methodological approach for mining archival data to understand the unfolding of the lives of young people who have undergone psychiatric hospitalization. With the inquisitiveness, ingenuity, and indefatigability of detectives, Best and Hauser describe how they explored these records to get them to give up their secrets and reveal the lives hidden within them. A particularly innovative technique employed by the researchers is the Life Chart method, which allows for a moving picture of each participants' life course that is quantitatively informative (how many symptoms were present?), qualitatively suggestive (is the life chart full and dense or sparsely populated?), developmentally sensitive (when was the symptom's onset and what was its course?), and contextually informed (were there precipitating life stressors?). Another innovative strategy the authors demonstrate is the application to archival data of an empirically validated child functioning rating scale that hereto had previously never been used for this purpose. By describing these methodological innovations, Best and Hauser promise to open the eyes of other researchers to sources of rich information about adolescent lives that we had not realized indeed were mineable "data."

References

Coker, T. R., Elliott, M. N., Kanouse, D. E., Grunbaum, J. A., Schwebel, D. C., Gilliland, M. J., Tortolero, S. R., Peskin, M. F., & Schuster, M. A. (2009). Perceived racial/ethnic discrimination among fifth-grade students and its association with mental health. *American Journal of Public Health, 99,* 878–884.

Hinshaw, S. P. (2008) Developmental psychopathology as a scientific discipline: Relevance to behavioral and emotional disorders of childhood and adolescence. In T. P. Beauchaine & S. P. Hinshaw (Eds.), *Child and adolescent psychopathology* (pp. 3–26). Hoboken, NJ: John Wiley & Sons.

Katz, M. (1997). *On playing a poor hand well: Insights from the lives of those who have overcome childhood risks and adversities.* New York: Norton.

Luthar, S. S., Doernberger, C. H., & Zigler, E. (1993). Resilience is not a unidimensional construct: Insights from a prospective study of inner-city adolescents. *Development and Psychopathology, 5,* 703–717

Rutter, M. (1990). Psychosocial resilience and protective mechanisms. In J. Rolf, A. S. Masten, D. Cicchetti, K. H. Nuechterlein, & S. Weintraub (Eds.), *Risk and protective factors in the development of psychopathology* (pp. 181–214). Cambridge, UK: Cambridge University Press.

Spencer, M. B., Harpalani, V., Cassidy, E., Jacobs, C. Y., Donde, S., Goss, T. N., Munoz-Miller, M., Charles, N., & Wilson, S. (2006). Understanding vulnerability and resilience from a normative developmental perspective: Implications for ethnically and racially diverse youth. In D. Cicchetti & D. J. Cohen (Eds.), *Developmental psychopathology. Vol. I: Theory and method* (2nd ed., pp. 627–672). New York: Wiley.

U.S. Census Bureau. (2010). *Current population reports: 2009.* Washington, DC: U.S. Government Printing Office.

10

Exceptional Outcomes

Using Narratives and Family Observations
to Understand Resilience

STUART T. HAUSER, JOSEPH P. ALLEN,
AND MARC S. SCHULZ

I know I could try . . . I know if I try I will know how to go back. . . . In between you can go up or you can go down. You go up and somebody pushes you down, you're gonna be bummed. And if you go down and nobody helps you back up, you're gonna be bummed. So you should just sit in the middle for now . . . see how things work out. And if I feel like I'm gonna talk, I'm gonna. If I don't feel like it, then I'm gonna sink down. And right now I'm sinking. But I think I might be able to work things out. (Eve, at age 15.)[1]

Eve, a 15-year-old girl, thinks aloud about changing, a year after mutilating her face and arms. A decade later we found that she and several other young men and women, seriously troubled in their teenage years, were leading healthy and productive lives. The questions raised by such transformations are numerous. How did they occur? What characterized these individuals as adolescents? If we just listen to their stories, might it be possible to draw conclusions that speak to the fundamental nature of resilience? These are some of the topics we sought to address in this study, while seeking to develop and utilize a time-tested but often overlooked approach in psychological research: the study of individual narratives.

Our work draws from our long-term study of young adults who, during their adolescence, were hospitalized as psychiatric patients. Whatever the stresses that led to their interlude in the hospital of months, and sometimes more than a year, the hospital itself was problematic for these teens. They were separated from their families and abruptly placed in unusual surroundings. At the hospital they had to respond to unfamiliar adults, whom they never asked to be their caretakers, a new collection of peers, many of whom presented in frightening ways, and a special school program that most found repugnant.

Writing about her adolescent years in a psychiatric hospital, Kaysen (1993) characterizes this stage of her life as *Girl Interrupted*. Was this period also a major interruption in the lives of these former patients in our study who are now leading fulfilling, nonimpaired lives? How do they perceive, and understand, their time in the hospital from the vantage point of young adulthood? Along with understanding the development and adaptation of a larger group of adolescents whom we continue to follow in their adult years we have been intensively studying the families and tracing the pathways of this special subgroup of former patients. Our goal has been quite simple: to see what we might learn about the paths that led them from their troubled teen years to young adult lives characterized by remarkable competencies and minimal evidence of major social and psychiatric problems.

IDENTIFYING AND STUDYING RESILIENCE

Fourteen years after they first participated in our project, we found *all* of the original participants we had first met as young adolescents, now spread across the country and world. Our original goal in following our participants through to young adulthood was to identify adolescent individual *and* family predictors of adaptation and experience in the early adult years. As we proceeded, a new and compelling question quickly surfaced: How could we account for unexpectedly competent outcomes in the group of young men and women whose lives had been deflected during their adolescence? Often called *resilience,* similar discontinuities were recognized in early programs of research on schizophrenia (Garmezy, 1973) and are currently a focus of much scholarly and scientific activity (e.g., Davis, Luecken, & Chalfant, 2009; Luthar, 2006; Masten & Obradovic, 2006).

We approached the study of resilience using a person-centered approach (Bergman, Eye, & Magnusson, 2006) rather than a traditional variable-centered approach. We view resilience as a multidimensional construct; thus we assembled outcome profiles using multiple domains to identify resilient young adults. We then carefully examined data collected prospectively during adolescence to identify predictors of these unusually positive outcomes. In this chapter we focus primarily on data derived from yearly interviews first begun in the hospital then continued over the next 2 years. Through these interview texts we consider how the former patients gave meaning to the troubling circumstances leading to hospitalization, and to their experiences in the ensuing years. We also examine functioning in their families using systematic family observations obtained soon after our individual interviews.

At the start of the study, we met with 146 middle adolescents and their families. Equal numbers were drawn from two groups: nonpsychotic in-patient adolescents from a private teaching hospital and adolescents from the freshman class of a local high school. The patients included three major diagnostic groups: disruptive behavior disorders, mood disorders, and personality disorders. Patients with psychosis, evidence of mental retardation, or medical conditions with psychiatric sequelae were excluded from the study. The samples were comparable in age, race, and family type, and were predominantly white middle and upper middle class.

Over the following 2 years, we continued to meet with 80% of these adolescents and their families. The adolescent participants responded to specific developmental and personality measures, and participated in annual clinical research interviews, usually with the same clinically trained interviewer (for more details, see Hauser, Allen, & Golden, 2006). The interviews were semistructured and always included inquiries about past family and individual history, current peer and family experience, school life, the handling of intense feelings, and future visions. We have used the interviews to assess coping strategies, elements of self-image, and constructs related to affective communications. In this report and other related ones (e.g., Hauser et al., 2006) we use the interviews as a source of narrative data.

The participants and their parents also engaged in a family discussion task, based on a revealed difference procedure (Strodtbeck, 1951) using Kohlberg moral dilemmas (Kohlberg, 1981). Our family analyses are based on these recorded discussions (described in greater detail in Hauser et al., 1984). We located 100% of the original participants when they were in their mid-twenties, and met with 98% of those still alive. Using conceptually relevant measures and diverse methods, we assessed dimensions of ego development, close relationships, attachment representations, and aspects of social competence.

This new direction in our work was sparked by several interviews calling our attention to former patients who appeared to be functioning exceptionally well. To systematically study these young adults with remarkable recoveries from their adolescent years we operationalized the definition of "exceptional functioning" by applying two thresholds to the full range of our new measures. First, we identified former patients with development and relationship scores above the 50th percentile for the entire sample (including both the high school and patient samples). We used friends of the participants to assess their ability to reflect, their adaptive functioning, and their ego resilience (Kobak & Sceery, 1988). Relationship closeness was assessed by self-report (Berscheid et al., 1987) and attachment coherence ratings derived from an age 25 interview (Main & Goldwyn, 1998); a traditional sentence completion task was used to assess ego development (Loevinger, 1976). The second threshold involved indications of social deviance and psychopathology. To be identified as exceptional on these markers of *dysfunctional behaviors,* former patients needed to have scores below the 50th percentile for the entire sample on measures of dysfunctional behavior. Here we used three indices: hard drug use in the past 6 months (Elliot et al.,1983), criminal behavior in the past 6 months (Elliot et al., 1983), and global psychiatric symptomatology (Derogatis, 1983). Four men and five women, 13.4% of the 67 former patients, fit this definition of exceptional outcomes. This group of nine young men and women were demographically similar to the other 56 former patients in terms of age, percentage that were female, and diagnosis, although they were almost twice as likely to have experienced parental divorce prior to age 14.

Using Ward's cluster and transposed principal components analyses of the patients with these sources of data, we found these nine young men and women in the same cluster and loading on the same component. We then proceeded to compare the nine exceptional former patients with a group of former patients whose adult outcomes were neither outstanding nor unusually dysfunctional for individuals with similar histories (i.e., they had outcome scores between the 40th and 60th percentiles for the *entire* former patient group).

STUDYING RESILIENT NARRATIVES

Many successive readings and rereadings of adolescent interviews obtained across multiple years led to the development of a Narrative Guide for their analysis as texts (for more detail, see Table 10.1 in Hauser et al., 2006). The Narrative Guide highlights the specific content and structural dimensions expressed in the individual interviews of the exceptional former patients.[2] We began by demarcating two stories: the patient's path to the hospital and life within the hospital. We focused on the following questions: Were the stories told coherently? Was there evidence of self-interruptions, digressions, and overt refusals to continue and to disclose? Were multiple events included or was the story that was told woven around a single overriding episode? Embedded in these stories were representations of self and interpersonal relationships. For representations of self, we considered coherence, ways of disclosure and privacy, self-reflection, self-efficacy, self-esteem, aspirations, mastery, helplessness, and long-term visions. Relational representation dimensions included the extent to which the adolescent spoke of relationships as interconnected, the presence of seeking and eliciting relationships, and the discussion of sustaining and changing relationships.

We did not intend our Narrative Guide to serve as a rigid template, imposing categories onto these rich texts. Its purpose was to sensitize the reader to important themes, while not interfering with awareness of unanticipated meanings. We analyzed each year's interview texts with the same basic Guide, now applied to new stories about the participants' current life and self-described changes. But when a participant's path returned to the hospital, we paid particular attention, since we believe that such successive accounts will illuminate how these adolescents were making sense of a most distressing time in their young lives.

Following each participant through adolescence, we tracked enduring themes, connections, and new meanings attributed to past events. Do some adolescents, for example, express a dominant voice in the very first interview that is elaborated with increasing complexity over time? Do the adolescents' relationships evolve over time on dimensions of trust, confidence, and closeness? Ideas about enduring themes led to thoughts about how pathways of development can be discerned in these narratives. Did the resilient patients show pathways different from comparison groups—patients with average outcomes or high-functioning nonpatients? Findings based on Year 1 interviews from the nine exceptional participants and from the seven participants whose outcome scores fell between the 40th and 60th percentile of the entire patient group point to intriguing differences between these two groups.

Four themes ultimately emerged that characterized the narratives of the exceptional adolescents: narrative coherence, self-reflection/self-complexity, sense of agency, and continual gravitational pull toward forming relationships, however problematic and challenging these might be at first. It was only through careful attunement to recurring patterns in individual narratives that these themes emerged. These themes were often buried in innumerable chaotic and emotion-charged events that swept up both our exceptional and our more typical patient groups.

For both the exceptional and the average former patients, cascading family and individual events that had gone awry, leaving the individual feeling helpless and overwhelmed, were central in *Paths to the Hospital* stories. Participants spoke of many losses, school failures, paralyzing fears about attending school, accelerating self-hatred, and pervasive social unease often linked with painful isolation. Their actions, which usually propelled others to recommend hospital admission, included serious overdose, self-mutilation, and violent outbursts. Yet for all but one of the exceptional adolescents, stories were easily elicited and coherent; they were not surprised that the course of events led to the hospital. This was not so for the average outcome patients. Their views of how they came to the hospital were vague and strongly colored by surprise, rage, and betrayal.

Exceptional patients' *Life in the Hospital* narratives showed great variation, ranging from disturbing nightmares and continuous angry actions to forceful verbal protests about not being taken seriously. They shared a complex view of a confusing and rapidly changing world, in which they took leading, and quite active, roles. Several described how they became more open with others during their hospitalization, often coupled with their positive psychotherapy experiences and feeling more secure about their growing self-restraint. Exceptional participants also spoke of the hospital as being a "terrible" and unacceptable place. One participant spoke of her terror as she watched a friend placed in restraints. In brief, these patients, who had displayed such successful adult adaptation, initially perceived and constructed many sides to this extraordinary time in their lives. In stark contrast, adolescent narratives of the patients with average outcomes were almost unidimensional: the hospital was useless, an incredible waste of time; or it was extremely helpful, where everyone was "nice."

The exceptional patients also expressed a spectrum of self-representations: self-hatred, failed self-restraint, and feeling overwhelmed. They frequently reflected about their experiences, how they elicited certain events, and how they were reacting to people and activities over which they seemed to have no control. Several described dramatic swings in their confidence and self-esteem within a single day, and then over the course of their hospital stay. Accompanying these fluctuations in self-esteem were changing self-images of their bodies, which they initially found repulsive; love of being the center of attention; and feeling "boxed up." The average patients communicated fewer self-images, and the ones they did describe were usually characterized by low self-esteem, helplessness, and resentment over their unbearable plight.

The exceptional patients described many relationships, especially troubling ones that erupted before arriving at the hospital. For all but one exceptional

patient, these preexisting relationships were angry, frightening, and often confusing. As adolescents, all brought up their near-constant loneliness and haunting
rejections from past relationships that had gone sour. Yet, at the same time, these
boys and girls were constantly seeking, and finding, new individuals they might
trust—a parent, sibling, peer, hospital staff member, or psychotherapist. The average patients portrayed more consistent isolation and chaos in past and present
relationships.

The narratives of one exceptional patient, Sandy, illustrate and elaborate many
of these themes. Sandy was 14 years old when we first met her, arriving at the
hospital soon after her serious and unexpected suicide attempt. Clear about being
desperately unhappy for many hours immediately before trying to kill herself with
an overdose, she erupted angrily when the interviewer asked too many questions
about her sadness: "I just get depressed. . . I don't talk to no one. If anyone talks to
me, I get really mad at them. I can't describe it." And Sandy doesn't want to dwell
on this state:

> I don't want to think about it, but people keep bringing it back up. I don't
> know the answers to the questions. I don't even want to think about it. I don't
> even ask myself why I tried to kill myself because I'm not going to think
> about it.
>
> *Interviewer:* You want to keep it out of your mind?
>
> Yup. Just like when I get out of this place, I'm gonna keep this place out of
> my mind. . . I don't like being locked up here. I don't like people telling me
> what to do, when to do it, why to do it, how to do it, where to do it, and things
> like that. I don't like being locked up.

Other than taking occasional pleasure in drawing, Sandy's 2 months in the hospital were filled with unhappy, angry, resentful, and discouraged moments. She
reported that "This place depresses me. It's screwing me up. It hasn't been any help
to me. . . I just hate everything about this place." Sandy wasn't doing well, but she
was exquisitely coherent in describing her difficulties, and mentally active in her
attempts (sometimes functional and sometimes not so) to cope with the problems
she faced.

Sandy and her family kept her hospitalization a secret from all but one or two
close friends. Others were told that Sandy had gone away for a couple of months.
In the weeks and years leading up to her hospitalization, many people had died or
otherwise left her—a favorite grandfather, then a grandmother, an aunt, and an
uncle. Her boyfriend's sister was killed in a car accident. Two days before her suicide attempt, her steady boyfriend withdrew from her, without warning, after
recovering from a flare up of his chronic illness. One further stirring loss was her
mother. Because Sandy and her mother were having so many fights, Sandy's
mother moved out of the house 2 months before Sandy's overdose and her father
moved in.

In the hospital, Sandy was troubled by her volatile relationships with other girls
in her hospital unit. Relationships mattered to her. Feeling controlled by the staff,

and sometimes by other patients, Sandy also wrestled with how to regulate her own emotions and impulses:

> I feel controlled in here and there's nothing I can do about it. . . . I keep my anger in . . . I have it all boxed up inside of me. I'm not gonna get mad because I don't feel like getting put in four comers [restraints] . . . Maybe I'll let it out when I get out of here. But I don't feel like getting locked up and tied down.

Again, we see Sandy's strong efforts to be *in control*. Agency was her recurring meme. Sandy described typical adolescent yearnings for independence alongside her confusion: "I don't ask anybody for advice. I figure things out for myself. I don't know what to ask people for advice right now." Sandy was uneasy and annoyed with the possibility of being sent against her will, following discharge, to a restrictive residential school that the hospital was recommending. She hated the plan, seeing it as confirming the hospital's belief that "I can't cope with the problems myself and shit like that." Sandy was flailing, but she knew she ultimately wanted to be in charge of her own life and destiny.

One year later, Sandy was in a profoundly different relationship with a new institution. Sandy's new stepfather, an alumnus of a nearby liberal coed private secondary school, suggested she apply there. To her surprise, she was accepted. Interviewed while she was living at this new school, Sandy's mood and connection to the interviewer were markedly different from the previous year. Sandy attributed the positive changes to her new school:

> I was made more aware of things. . . . It's made me more mature than I was last year. . . A lot of positive things. I'm more confident in myself. Last year I was not confident in myself. I was self-conscious . . . and if someone looked at me, I'd think they were thinking something bad about me and I'm not that way anymore. I've changed that way.

For the first time, Sandy speaks at length about her depression:

> I was getting depressed . . . very, very depressed and having trouble with my mother, we weren't even speaking to each other . . . and the fact my parents had gotten divorced. Things like that.

Sandy was able to provide a more complex account of her relationship with her mother. She noted that there were many ongoing strains connected with their struggles and felt that her mother kept belittling her, treating her like a little girl. She blamed her mother for her parents' divorce, having for years heard her "daily bitching" at her father, who was always away. Sandy's descriptions of her relationship with her mother were quite different from those of the more typical adolescent patients—who often either minimized the painful aspects of those relationships or angrily and quickly wrote them off. In her interview, Sandy indicated that she now regretted hurting her mother's feelings by accusing her mother of causing the divorce. But life with her mother continued to be volatile. Sandy exploded when her stepfather, concerned about his own biological child, announced Sandy was "screwing up his daughter's mind." Feeling unprotected by her mother, who took her new husband's side, Sandy stopped talking to her mother for the next 6 months. Sandy's intense focus on relationships and her desire to take an agentic role were both vying for central roles in the emerging play of her life.

Sandy's relationship with her psychiatrist was also changing in notable ways. No longer disdainful and distant, she referred appreciatively to Dr. Thompson. Sandy reported that after she spoke with Dr. Thompson about both her parents, Dr. Thompson told her, "you should look at it from both sides. And I tried it out and it worked." At the same time, Sandy's yearnings for greater independence sprung back. Immediately after praising her psychiatrist's help, Sandy announced she was ending therapy.

Sandy remained acutely aware of her strong fears of being open and exposed, of being fragile, and of being overcontrolled. After first leaving the hospital, she was frightened that "if I talked about myself and my feelings and what was going on in my head, that they'd think I needed to come back. And I was really scared about that . . . After a while I figured out . . . they're not going to send me back, if they let me out. Why would they send me back?" Then Sandy became more engaged in her therapy, thinking more about who she was, struggling to bring order to what she sometimes thought of as her personal chaos. Gradually, Sandy was carving out the mental space in her life to allow herself to turn to taking on some of the normative tasks of adolescent psychosocial development, tasks that had been put on hold previously.

Sandy continued to experience dramatic swings in mood, her actions, and close relationships. Soon after we met with her, 1 year after leaving the hospital, school authorities found her smoking marijuana in the dormitory. The school responded by restricting Sandy's activities and giving her extra work details. Her father and his new wife became enraged, adding additional punishments. Offended by what she saw as their unfairness, Sandy ceased visiting them, deciding to live with her mother only during school vacations. In the midst of describing these new quarrels with her father, Sandy remembered her life-long troubles with him over his severe and arbitrary use of power with her and her brothers. Importantly, Sandy's stories indicated that she *cared* about these relationships, and wasn't afraid to express this caring, via a desire for connection when relationships went well or clear anger and frustration when they did not.

A few months after our interview, Sandy admitted herself to the psychiatric ward of a local hospital because she was "doing a lot of drugs" and crying all of the time. After "doing downers" every day for 15 days, she suddenly stopped. "I got totally crashed. . . I was like floating for two weeks." Two weeks later, she discharged herself. "I sort of straightened myself out by myself, because they really didn't do anything for me. I mean it was more like I had to help myself and I couldn't have done it at home because I really have a lot of trouble living at home. . . I couldn't have handled it." Sandy's self-awareness is striking for a late adolescent.

Bill, a new boyfriend from her residential school, entered Sandy's life about this time. She spent much time with Bill's family, dazzled by their lively intellectual exchanges about politics and social issues. She loved being with this family, amazed by how much it differed from her own in its constant stress on achievement, social action, and understanding. Sandy was now thinking about how she resembled her father, along the lines of his concealing feelings and having to appear strong. Recalling his frightening violent episodes toward her mother and sister, she reflected more about herself and her desires to be different in her relationships:

I find it really hard to show emotions in front of people like crying. . . . It is very hard to show weakness and I know that is like him, because he just has to be strong. And I don't trust many people, friends, which is really bad, because that is why I don't have too many close friends. And, I have always wanted to be on top. I always wanted to be ahead of everybody and the best in everything I did. Like competitiveness, I guess.

At the time of her final adolescent interview, Sandy was looking toward entering a large university, where her older brother was enrolled. She had ended her relationship with Bill, having decided that his close but complicated connection with his family and his father's preoccupation with work were "weird." She continued to refine and sharpen her view of herself and her control over her life, and began to show signs of patience with her own development:

I'm pretty sure of myself . . . I don't know if I've found my . . . true self or anything . . . but I don't like sit in my room for hours and say, "OK what am I and who am I and what am I going to be" . . . it'll come after awhile. . . After . . . lots of experience and stuff, I'll finally be someone. It's not like I'm wanting to go out looking for myself.

Sandy corrects the interviewer's simplistic question about whether she believes that life "unfolds beyond your will or you create the person you are," as always, wanting to acknowledge the complexity of self and of life (and to be in control of the interview):

I think it's like everything altogether. Like you create . . . what you like and what you want to do . . . and then stuff happens around you, that you have . . . no control over . . . influences from the outside . . . everything added altogether . . . I think I have more control . . . I mean like decide what kind of outside influences are going to be around you like . . . say if you really went to a high pressure school . . . then you might come out a really paranoid insecure person . . . like really neurotic and stuff . . . You get to pick what school you go to, what kind of school is going to have the kind of influence.

She was also thinking more clearly and complexly about how she affected others:

> When I get in a bad mood, I can really make things awful for people even . . .
> I regret it after and say I'm really, really sorry, I didn't mean to do that; but
> when I'm in a bad mood I don't care . . . it's just that everything's really bad
> for me at that time . . . and I hate that, I hate that part of me.

Although wary of rejection and worried about being hurt, Sandy was hopeful about the coming years and was now emphasizing her parents' assets—her father's "really great mind" and her mother's "classiness."

Seven years following this late adolescent interview, we again met with Sandy who was now in her mid-twenties. Her interviewer's impressions, dictated immediately after spending several hours talking with Sandy, give a lucid summary of Sandy as a young adult.

> Sandy was very attractive, physically and personality-wise. She had just come
> in from work and looked very nice, in a pretty red dress and high heels and
> was a very pleasant person to interview, very personable . . . She seems to
> have a very strong marriage, to be very committed to a career and very intent
> on finishing her college degree . . . She seems to have . . . some good friend-
> ships. Most of her friends are her husband's, except for her friend Karen, who
> she has known since high school. She was very engaged with all of the tasks.
> She also shared how much she enjoyed doing the interview and that she
> really didn't do it so much for the money, although she was going to buy
> herself an outfit. She was very interested and enjoyed sharing these things
> with us. She was a very pleasant person to have come to know.

EMERGING NARRATIVE THEMES

Returning to the four themes we noted earlier, we can see how clearly they emerged from Sandy's narratives, even in the midst of so many confusing experiences and relationships in her life.

The overall coherence of Sandy's narratives is perhaps the most striking feature we see. What Sandy describes is confusing—her life *is* confusing—but her descriptions convey the chaos, and the complex sense of self that she is developing within this chaos, with exceptional clarity and force. From the very start, we have been struck with the ease of discerning the exceptional participants' stories—at first about their paths to the hospital and then about their experience there. In these early accounts and in subsequent years, these patients offer coherent stories filled with intelligible responses to their recent and remote history of personal successes and failures. Sometimes these "ups and downs" are turbulent. Yet the interviewer, and later the reader, can readily grasp and comprehend much of the alternating disappointments and successes. Changes and connections to the past were often the very first elements in a resilient participant's account upon again meeting the interviewer. Their stories existed in a larger context and they knew it and made it clear.

The second theme that clearly emerges in Sandy's narrative as well as those of the other exceptional patients we interviewed was a capacity for self-reflection and an ability to hold in mind a complex, nuanced view of self. Sandy can see herself as helpless (in the face of drug use at one point), as in control (even while threatened with four point restraints), as strong, and as afraid to show weakness. These characteristics are not contradictory for Sandy, but simply part of the complexity of her human experience, which she accepts implicitly. We've consistently seen similar patterns in the narratives of other exceptional patients. For example, each year, with much pride, one exceptional patient brought up what he called his "many life styles." He expressed this theme through his appreciation of different kinds of music: "I want to go to school and learn more and more and more. I have a lot of different kinds of music and sometimes I am really contradicting of how I think . . . because sometimes I am really violent and sometimes I am very passive."

Ever apparent were the resilient participant's vacillating appraisals of themselves. By no means were these evaluations increasingly positive over the years. More typically, they were marked by swings of confidence and disappointment accompanied by optimism and pessimism about life's chances. More important was participants' *awareness* of these changing self-evaluations and movement in the direction of kinder self-regard each year. Asked what was the key to how much she had changed in the last year, Rachel explained that she felt so good about herself because of her newly found independence:

> All of a sudden you say, "I've had enough" . . . I think it comes with independence . . . as you learn to stand on your own two feet, you learn to like yourself a lot more, because you are doing things for yourself and not letting other people do them for you . . . I think that's it. I'm really pleased that that is what I did.

Tolerance of ambiguity and negative facets of the self characterize this and our other exceptional patients' narratives. Self-awareness flows from this ability to view the self in all its richness and unevenness.

A strong sense of agency, or what Bandura (1989) has termed self-efficacy, was a third theme that characterized the narratives of Sandy and the other exceptional patients. As evidenced by Sandy's discerning observations at the end of her young adult interview about how her role in life unfolds, the narratives of the resilient participants in our study show increases in a sense of self-efficacy, a belief in one's ability to influence one's course in life. A second exceptional patient, Rachel, began to express such a view after leaving the psychiatric hospital in adolescence. At first dismayed, and then relieved, Rachel began to see herself differently:

> I didn't know where to turn . . . all these people had been doing everything for me and they sent me out and they said, "Well, here you are" . . . and I just had to start looking for my own life . . . and so after a few weeks I started realizing that things had to be done and that I was the only one that had

to do them. It was easier after I started thinking that way . . . I'd never been able to do things on my own and then that started changing. I could control my own life; it was something else. I enjoyed it.

The following year, sad about her parents' reaction to her becoming pregnant and planning to marry, Rachel "pulled out" of her sadness:

I stood up and said to myself, "Hey, this is my life, and this is what I want to do. I wish you could accept it. If you can't, that's too bad . . . that's how I stood up and said it. And they started to come around. Once they knew I was going to finish school, they knew I could get it together then. Then they felt better."

Related to this belief in agency are the resilient participants' detailed visions of their futures and the roles they see for themselves in effecting these aspirations. For Rachel, this future contained her views of becoming, in rapid succession, a wife and mother.

Each of the exceptional participants described how he or she sometimes refused to settle for a specific solution—from the hospital, therapist, or family. Several, like Sandy, found new schools for themselves, refusing to attend the school recommended by the hospital and finding a school in which their academic and social development prospered. They had a sense that *they*, and not others, would be in charge of their own lives, and while typically ill-equipped to put this into practice as adolescents, it was a goal toward which they moved unerringly as development progressed.

Finally, an intense focus upon developing relationships was a theme that emerged forcefully through all of the exceptional patients' narratives. The exceptional patients reflect often about others' motives, feelings, and thoughts. Then there is the immense importance that these individuals attribute to close friends. They persistently think about and invest in maintaining relationships. Rachel, marrying at 16, spoke of her life unraveling when she runs away from school for 2 weeks. And she recalled feeling "all messed up" after she and her boyfriend ended a relationship in which they both felt too dependent on each other. Soon after meeting her future husband she became more hopeful and energized, deciding then that she was "going to pick up where I left off and not get so dependent on other people."

The exceptional participants also frequently remind us of the many intersections among representations of self, representations of relationships, and actions. Rachel, for example, spoke of the ways in which her growing good feelings about herself led her to find new friends; and how these friends, in turn, confirmed and amplified these positive views of herself.

INTERFACE WITH SYSTEMATIC FAMILY OBSERVATIONS

Our emphasis in this chapter on personal narratives in no way negates the value of information gleaned from more traditional, quantitative methods such as systematic family observations. We expect each approach will enhance the other. In part, observations of family interactions may help in identifying the source of some of the remarkable traits displayed by our exceptional patients. Family systems theory and research has documented the role of families in protecting children and adolescents from psychopathology or poor developmental outcomes (e.g., Davies & Cicchetti, 2004; Rutter, 1998). Research by Anthony (1974) found that the parents of resilient children were less possessive and anxious than those of the "average" child, and more likely to allow their child greater autonomy. Although much thought and research have been devoted to identifying these broad attitudes and values, fewer investigators have examined the specific ways in which parents and children may interact so as to promote resilient outcomes. In developing our approach to family observation, we were influenced by Lieber (1977) and Wynne, Jones, and Al-Khayyal (1982), who argued that healthy patterns of communication could provide the high-risk child with the resources and coping strategies that underlie subsequent resilient functioning.

Three family interaction variables were tentatively identified by Wynne and colleagues as being associated with greater competence in high-risk children: maternal warmth; a warm, active, and balanced family interaction; and healthy and benign parental attributions toward the child. Building on this argument, Lieber observed that "positive focusing behaviors" (one parent taking a leadership role, clarifying and encouraging further exploration) were associated with familial "low-risk" status. Through independent analyses, families' "positive behavior" predicted risk more strongly than the absence of disturbance in communication. Lieber concluded that *parental facilitation* of communication was worthy of further exploration.

Parental facilitation, or in our terms, "enabling," is likely an important family component, perhaps particularly so during adolescence. We were initially motivated by an interest in examining whether families of disturbed adolescents can be distinguished by parents' attempts to interfere with the autonomous and agentic functioning of their children. Among these impediments to independent perceptions and actions are "binding" (constraining) interactions through which parents actively resist the differentiation of their children. Building on Lieber, we expanded this theory to account for *enabling* interactions, through which family members encourage or support the expression of more independent perceptions or thoughts. In addition to the detailed study of parental constraining and enabling, our work emphasizes bidirectionality, as we examine interactions from adolescent to parent as well as those from parent to adolescent.

Shortly after each year's individual assessments from which our narrative analyses were drawn, patients and parents also participated in a revealed differences procedure (Strodtbeck, 1951). Each family member met separately with one experimenter and responded to the same set of Kohlberg (1981) moral dilemmas (Hauser et al., 1984; Hauser, 1991). The family then reassembled to defend and attempt to resolve their differences for three different coalitions that we identified in advance based on their answers to the dilemmas: adolescent and mother versus father, adolescent and father versus mother, and adolescent versus mother *and* father. The intent of this procedure was to probe how adolescents and their parents resolved differences around deep moral questions—such as the morality of robbing to save a wife's life; or how a son should respond to his father's breaking a long-term promise when the father impulsively takes his son's newspaper boy earnings to use for his own fishing trip. Driven by theoretical and clinical considerations, we designed a microanalytic approach, the Constraining and Enabling Coding System (CECS), to identify the presence of behaviors (e.g., acceptance, curiosity) that *enable* interactions and those (e.g., devaluing, distracting) that *constrain* interactions (see Hauser et al., 1984 for more details). The CECS also captures whether the complexity and clarity of the family's discourse improve across speech turns or degrades.

In previous studies (e.g., Hauser et al., 1984; Hauser, 1991) we found a greater prevalence of enabling interactions in families whose adolescents function at higher levels of ego development, as contrasted with the increased frequency of constraining within those families whose adolescents are functioning at lower ego development levels. More recent analyses indicate that the exceptional adolescents, while hospitalized, were consistently more enabling toward both parents. In other words, during a particularly stressful period these boys and girls were more accepting and empathic toward their parents in conversations about difficult moral dilemmas. Moreover, both parents expressed higher levels of enabling toward these exceptional boys and girls. Were their enabling behaviors reflecting the robust ways that these patients were coping with this chaotic time in their lives? Or could it be that the hospital was providing a welcome "time out" from a distressing, perhaps even destructive, family and school environment? Coming together, reunited again with their parents, although no longer living together on a daily basis, might potentially facilitate the development of renewed interest in productive interactions not diminished by daily hassles. These two interpretations are *not* mutually exclusive.

The unique interaction patterns in the families of the patients who turned out to lead exceptional lives in the early adult years—higher levels of many kinds of affective enabling expressed by the exceptional adolescents and specific kinds of cognitive and affective enabling expressed by their parents (i.e., curiosity, empathy)—suggest that this group of patients may have been able to maintain adaptive relationships with their parents, in which their attempts at connection were reciprocated in ways that facilitate family discourse. These mutually positive engaging interactions are especially striking in that they were occurring during a time that was turbulent for the adolescents and their parents, as their sons and daughters were resentful and disappointed. Do these interactions contain the seeds of the coherence, sense of self, agency, and relationship focus that were displayed by our exceptional patients? This is a question we must await future research to answer, although the linkages we observed suggest this is a promising avenue to pursue.

THE ROLE OF NARRATIVE IN RESILIENCE

In the long run, detailed readings of these narratives may help us address questions about the ways in which they may have contributed to these patients' subsequent young adult development. How, for example, do self-narrative complexity and coherence lead to recovery and psychological health? Does the patient's recognition and expression of these accounts enhance ongoing and later adaptation?

As we think about the direction of influence between narratives and adaptation, it is important to recognize the strong possibility that causal paths may not necessarily move from narratives to outcomes. These narratives could be markers of adaptation, reflecting changing life circumstances and optimism. In this view improved adaptation is reflected in more reflective and coherent narratives. Alternatively, reflection and narrative construction may be critical coping resources that help the individual thrive in the face of adversity. New visions and life plans along with renewed motivation may be the product of sustained reflection that is reflected in narratives.

Longitudinal analyses of the interviews of these nine former patients, combined with parallel analyses of more typically functioning patients, can help elucidate some of these potentially complex causal pathways. For instance, our analyses suggest that average outcome patients experienced greater helplessness, rage, and diminished self-esteem as adolescents than exceptional adolescents. Fewer steadily supportive and protective relationships with friends and family were available. Delineating key dimensions through these qualitative analyses should make it possible for others to take the next steps of defining new variables that can be systematically coded in these and other adolescent interviews. These constructs can then be examined in relation to other theoretically relevant adolescent variables, such as ego development and self-esteem. Most importantly, future work might clarify how narratives such as these might predict the development of young adult close relationships, attachment, and psychopathology.

Understanding generated via narrative analysis can also shed light on the ways in which exceptional adolescents adapted to trying circumstances during a stressful period in their development. Tracing the flow of meanings adolescents give to the self and to relationships points to mechanisms that might underlie exceptional outcomes. Formal characteristics of their teenage narratives, such as increasing coherence over the years and emerging self-reflection, may be among the special features that distinguish these young adults from their more typical peers. Through such developing skills, these adolescents may have compensated for serious psychopathology and adverse hospital and home circumstances, as well as exploited available resources such as psychotherapy, special teachers, and schools. Traditional pencil and paper measures and even careful observations of behavior may not be attuned to the subtle manifestations of these inner strengths.

IMPLICATIONS AND FUTURE DIRECTIONS

The narrative and family observation data raise many issues and questions. The central question, to be sure, is what they add to our knowledge of resilience. The narrative approach we have taken has several methodological and substantive implications that extend well beyond research on resilience. In terms of methods, it represents a shift from a traditional focus on small, isolated elements of interviews to a more integrated and contextualized focus on larger narratives. Our previous analyses of interviews were based on dimensions (e.g., expressed affect, defenses, adaptive strengths) reflected in one or two speech segments. In the narrative work presented here, we have deliberately shifted to distinctions requiring larger texts to detect their presence. As we worked with our previous methods, we often had the impression that we were *not* capturing fundamental aspects of a participant's experience or grasping his or her past and present representations. And when coders would point out these limitations, we would usually speak, somewhat dismissively, about the compromises involved in carrying out empirical research; how we could not possibly study all the important, and unique, features embodied in one individual's rich interview, since our analyses were not "clinical" ones. Looking back, we can now see that these compelling questions, raised by sensitive students, were tied to two problems. First, the units we were analyzing were too constricted. Fuller portions of text are required to see and identify certain nuances of form and meaning. But more importantly, our eyes were focused on categories derived from our own theoretical lens. Defenses, adaptive strengths, and specific emotions all come from theoretical perspectives that we assumed were relevant to answering our questions and led us to a variable-focused approach that captured elements of these constructs. Concerns about the limitations of these variable-centered approaches led to our constructing a new way to analyze narratives within adolescent and young adult interviews, our Narrative Guide for interview texts.

Our focus in this study has been on identifying sources of resilience, but we believe the lessons we have learned have implications for many areas of research relevant to adolescent and lifespan development. For example, recently, personality psychologists have championed the potential of narrative analysis for understanding adaptation and personality functioning across the life cycle (Lilgendahl & McAdams, 2011; Pals, 2006). The chapters in this volume focusing on friendship (Way and Silverman, Chapter 4) and adolescent parents (Florsheim & Moore, Chapter 9; Pittman, Wakschlag, Chase-Lansdale, & Brooks-Gunn, Chapter 8) illustrate the benefits of narrative analysis for informing these literatures.

What can we learn about resilience through looking at the interviews and narratives? Cohler (e.g., Cohler et al., 1995) has most consistently argued for incorporating this approach in the study of resilient development, but more recently personality psychologists have championed the potential of narrative analysis for understanding adaptation across the life cycle (Lilgendahl & McAdams, 2011; Pals, 2006). Cohler (1987) has argued that narratives offer "information about the manner in which persons understand or interpret misfortune. For some persons . . . particular forms of adversity are experienced as insurmountable obstacles; others are able to use these misfortunes as the basis for renewed efforts at coping, leading to continued resilience" (p. 397). And he reminds us that "little is known about the manner in which persons create particular narratives and become committed to particular strategies for resolving problems that are most consistent with their sense of self and the totality of their life histories" (p. 398).

Through the narrative analyses presented here, we already have a better grasp of how our exceptional participants perceived and understood themselves and their interpersonal worlds at the time of major disturbance, and ways these constructions changed over time.

Notes

1. All names of participants in this chapter are not their actual names. In addition, we further protect confidentiality by changing any other possible identifying information such as hospital names, geographic locations, or type of work.
2. The ideas for this Narrative Guide were strongly influenced by the work of Brown and Gilligan (1992) and Main and Goldwyn (1998).

References

Anthony, E. J. (1974). The syndrome of the psychologically invulnerable child. In E. J. Anthony & C. Koupernik (Eds.), *The child in his family: Vol. 3, Children at psychiatric risk* (pp. 529–544). New York: Wiley.

Bandura, A. (1989). Regulation of cognitive processes through perceived self-efficacy. *Developmental Psychology, 25*, 729–773.

Bergman, L. R., von Eye, A., & Magnusson, D. (2006). Person-oriented research strategies in developmental psychopathology. In D. Cicchetti & D. Cohen (Eds.), *Developmental psychopathology, Vol. 1: Theory and method* (2nd ed., pp. 850–888). Hoboken, NJ: John Wiley.

Berscheid, E., Snyder, M., & Omoto, A. M. (1987). The relationship closeness inventory: Assessing the closeness of interpersonal relationships. *Journal of Personality and Social Psychology, 57*(5), 792–807.

Brown, L., & Gilligan, C. (1992). *Meeting at the crossroads: Women's psychology and girls' development.* Cambridge, MA: Harvard University Press.

Cohler, B. J. (1987). Adversity, resilience, and the study of lives. In E. J. Anthony & B. J. Cohler (Eds.), *The invulnerable child* (pp. 363–424). New York: Guilford Press.

Cohler, B. J., Stott, F. M., & Musick, I. S. (1995). Adversity, vulnerability, and resilience: Cultural and developmental perspectives. In D. Cicchetti & D. J. Cohen (Eds.), *Developmental psychopathology* (Vol. 2, pp. 753–800). New York: John Wiley and Sons.

Davies, P. T., & Cicchetti, D. (Eds.). (2004). Special Issue: Family systems and developmental psychopathology [Special Issue]. *Development and Psychopathology, 16*(3).

Davis, M. C., Luecken, L., & Lemery-Chalfant, K. (2009). Resilience in common life: Introduction to the special issue. *Journal of Personality, 77*, 1637–1644.

Derogatis, L. R. (1983). *SCL-90 administration and scoring manual.* Towson, MD: Clinical Psychometric Research.

Elliot, D. S., Ageton, S. S., Huizinga, D., Knowles, B. A., & Canter, R. (1983). *The prevalence and incidence of delinquent behavior: 1976–1980.* Boulder, CO: Behavioral Research Institute.

Garmezy, N. (1973). Competence and adaptation in adult schizophrenic patients and children at risk. In S. R. Dean (Ed.), Schizophrenia: The first ten Dean Award Lectures (pp. 163–204). New York: MSS Information Corp.

Hauser, S. T., Allen, J. P., & Golden, E. (2006). *Out of the woods: Tales of resilient teens.* Cambridge, MA: Harvard University Press.

Hauser, S. T., Powers, S. I., Noam, G., Jacobson, M., Weiss, B., and Follansbee, D. (1984). Familial contexts of adolescent ego development. *Child Development, 55,* 195–213.

Hauser, S. T., with Powers, S. & Noam, G. (1991). *Adolescents and their families: Paths of ego development.* New York: Free Press.

Kaysen, S. (1993). *Girl interrupted.* New York: Random House.

Kobak, R., & Sceery, A. (1988). Attachment in late adolescence: Working models, affect regulation, and representations of self and others. *Child Development, 59,* 135–146.

Kohlberg, L. (1981). *The meaning and measurement of moral development.* Worcester, MA: Clark University Press.

Lieber, D. (1977). Parental focus of attention in a videotape feedback task as a function of a hypothesized risk for offspring schizophrenia. *Family Process, 16,* 467–475.

Lilgendahl, J. P., & McAdams, D. P. (2011). Constructing stories of self-growth: How individual differences in patterns of autobiographical reasoning relate to well-being in midlife. *Journal of Personality, 79,* 391–428.

Loevinger, J. (1976). *Ego development: Conceptions and theories.* San Francisco: Jossey-Bass.

Luthar, S. S. (2006). Resilience in development: A synthesis of research across five decades. In D. Cicchetti and D. J. Cohen (Eds.), *Developmental psychopathology* (2nd ed.): *Vol. 3: Risk, disorder, and adaptation* (pp. 739–795). Hoboken, NJ: John Wiley and Sons.

Main, M., & Goldwyn, R. (1998). Attachment scoring and classification systems. Manual in Drafts, Version 6.1. University of California, Berkeley. Unpublished manual.

Masten, A. S., & Obradovic, J. (2006). Competence and resilience in development. *Annals of the New York Academy of Sciences, 1094,* 13–27.

Pals, J. L. (2006). Narrative identity processing of difficult life experiences: Pathways of personality development and positive self-transformation in adulthood. *Journal of Personality, 74,* 1079–1110.

Strodtbeck, F. (1951). Husband-wife interaction over revealed differences. *American Sociology Review, 16,* 463–473.

Wynne, L. C., Jones, J. E., & Al-Khayyal, M. (1982). Healthy family communication patterns: Observations in families "at risk" for psychopathology. In F. Walsh (Ed.), *Normal family processes* (pp. 142–164). New York: Guilford Press.

11

Sexual-Minority Development in the Family Context

LISA M. DIAMOND, MOLLY R. BUTTERWORTH,
AND KENDRICK ALLEN

The psychosocial development of sexual-minority (i.e., lesbian, gay, and bisexual) adolescents and young adults has been a topic of rigorous study since the early 1980s (reviewed in D'Augelli, 2006a). This body of research has yielded important information about the normative developmental processes through which sexual minorities begin to question their sexual orientation, to accept their nonheterosexual identity and disclose it to others, and to develop strategies for coping with social marginalization, harassment, social stigma, and internalized shame and homonegativity. At the same time, research has increasingly demonstrated the incredible diversity of the sexual-minority population (Diamond, 2008; Savin-Williams, 2001, 2005). Hence, studies attempting to chart normative pathways of sexual-minority development have increasingly been supplanted by studies documenting the *multiple* pathways of healthy sexual-minority development (see Savin-Williams, 2001; Savin-Williams & Cohen, 2004; Savin-Williams & Diamond, 1998). This approach is particularly relevant to examining the influence of familial factors on sexual-minority development, given that the dazzling diversity of sexual-minority youths' person-level characteristics (i.e., temperament, social competence, interpersonal history, access to social support, intellect, attitudes, mental health) is matched by similar diversity in *family-level* characteristics and functioning (i.e., family structure, cohesion, openness, communication skills, emotional climate, etc.).

Such family-level factors are critical to healthy adjustment. Research increasingly demonstrates that high-quality close relationships are fundamental to sexual-minority youths' healthy adjustment (Diamond & Savin-Williams, 2003; Savin-Williams, 1998b), and family ties remain among the most important of such relationships (reviewed in Crosbie-Burnett, Foster, Murray, & Bowen, 1996; Savin-Williams, 2001). Of course, in the distant past a child's sexual orientation was actually "blamed" on his or her family—specifically on dysfunctionally distant fathers and smothering mothers—but this theory has been resoundingly disproven (see Ellis, 1996; Freund & Blanchard, 1983). Nor is it true (as popular media often appear to suggest) that sexual minorities are uniformly alienated or ostracized from their families of origin. Rather, research has demonstrated incredible diversity in sexual-minority individuals' family experiences; perhaps the only generalization that can safely be made is that a youth's same-sex orientation poses a unique set of challenges for the *entire* family, even when some family members do not even know (or do not *yet* know) about the youth's sexual identity. Overall, the family ties of sexual-minority adolescents and young adults can be sources of support *or* shame, acceptance *or* rejection, joy *or* distress, comfort *or* alienation. The manner in which sexual minorities and their relatives reshape and redefine their bonds to one another in light of the issues raised by same-sex sexuality can have important influences on *each* family member's adjustment.

Hence, our goal in this chapter is to review current research on the role of the family in fostering (or hindering) psychosocial development among sexual-minority adolescents and young adults. Notably, we follow the lead of recent work that has increasingly adopted a family systems approach to understanding sexual-minority development (Crosbie-Burnett et al., 1996; Heatherington & Lavner, 2008; Willoughby, Doty, & Malik, 2008). This approach seeks to understand the dynamic, changing interplay between youths and their family members as they *all* undergo different adaptational challenges as part of the youths' identity development and psychosocial adjustment, and how family-level variables interact with individual-level variables to shape the entire family's trajectory of growth and development. Hence, whereas the "first generation" of research on sexual-minority youths' family relationships typically considered unidirectional chains of influence (*from* family members *to* the youths), more recent research has attended to *bidirectional* chains of influence, exploring processes through which the entire family system embarks on a long-term trajectory of growth, realignment, and transformation as a result of the challenges introduced by having a sexual-minority family member. From this perspective, the outcome of interest is not the sexual-minority individual's development in and of itself, but rather the complex set of adjustments and realignments within the entire family system that ideally function to promote the well-being of the sexual-minority youth *and* to sustain healthy, nurturing dynamics among all family members.

DEVELOPMENTAL CHALLENGES

We begin by clarifying the population of youths under study: *Sexual-minority* refers to any individual with same-sex attractions or relationships, as these attractions and relationships automatically render him or her a minority with respect to conventional societal norms and expectations regarding heterosexuality. The reason for using this term is that of all adolescents with same-sex attractions and/ or behavior (who constitute approximately 6–12% of American adolescents), the majority do *not* identify themselves as lesbian-gay-bisexual (Garofalo, Wolf, Wissow, Woods, & Goodman, 1999; Mosher, Chandra, & Jones, 2005). It is to capably represent the experiences of these youths that we emphasize sexual-minority status rather than lesbian-gay-bisexual identification. Regardless of the cause and consistency of youths' same-sex attractions or behavior, and their reluctance versus willingness to identify as lesbian, gay, or bisexual, same-sex experiences place youths in a precarious position with respect to social norms, exposing them to stigmatization and social marginalization. Although attitudes toward same-sex sexuality have grown more tolerant in recent years (reviewed in Loftus, 2001), and although the visibility of lesbian-gay-bisexual individuals in mass media and popular culture has surged (Walters, 2001), considerable stigma and intolerance remain pervasive, especially for sexual-minority youths who do not live in large urban centers with large and visible lesbian-gay-bisexual populations or who have highly stigmatizing school environments that offer few protective resources (Russell & McGuire, 2008). Studies using large, representative samples have consistently found that youths with histories of same-sex attraction or behavior are disproportionately likely to report being threatened or injured with a weapon, being involved in fights requiring medical attention, and witnessing violence more generally (Faulkner & Cranston, 1998). Hence, their sexual-minority status poses serious mental and physical health challenges on a day-to-day basis.

The psychological stress emanating from the chronic stigmatization, denigration, and harassment of a marginalized social group has been called *minority stress* (or *gay-related stress* in the specific context of sexual minorities), and has been advanced as an explanation for the fact that sexual minorities show consistently higher rates of anxiety and mood disorders, particularly those who report the greatest exposure to prejudice and stigmatization (Meyer, 2003). Minority stress appears to take a particularly heavy toll on adolescents: Sexual-minority youths face higher risks of numerous mental and physical health problems, including anxiety, depression, suicidality, eating disorders, substance use, sexual risk behaviors, and conduct problems, and many of these risk factors are related to sexual-minority youths' disproportionate exposure to psychological stress owing to their sexual-minority status (Cochran & Mays, 2007; Frisell, Lichtenstein, Rahman, & Langstrom, 2010; Meyer, 2003; Rosario, Schrimshaw, Hunter, & Gwadz, 2002; Russell, 2006). These stressors include external factors such as violence, victimization, stigmatization, and harassment (Balsam, Rothblum, & Beauchaine, 2005; Horn & Nucci, 2006; National Coalition of Anti-Violence Programs, 2007), as well as internal factors such as internalized shame, discomfort, and fear associated with one's same-sex sexuality (Igartua, Gill, & Montoro, 2003; Meyer & Dean, 1998).

The key factor to remember, when considering the influence of minority status and minority stress on sexual-minority youths' daily lives and relationships, is that the *global* climate of marginalization, stigmatization, and denigration of same-sex sexuality has a diverse range of *local* effects on specific youths in specific environments, with different ages, backgrounds, and–importantly–different family contexts. It is similarly important, however, to avoid oversimplified notions of causality, in which all of a sexual-minority youth's adjustment problems flow directly from his or her exposure to stigmatization and social rejection. In some cases, a youth's preexisting adjustment difficulties may actually *elicit* particularly

negative social responses (from family members as well as peers and acquaintances) and may end up exacerbating his or her experiences of marginalization
and self-denigration. For example, one of the few longitudinal examinations of
sexual-minority youths' experiences with gay-related stress (Rosario et al., 2002)
found that although some forms of gay-related stress were directly and uniquely
associated with increases (over a 1-year period) in adjustment problems, other
adjustment problems actually proved to be independent predictors of 1-year
increases in gay-related stressors. Hence, in understanding why sexual-minority
youths face increased risks for mental and physical health problems, and how
their family contexts might moderate these risks, we must remember to take into
account such intersecting, bidirectional causal pathways. Some sexual-minority
youths enter into their sexual-developmental trajectories with a host of preexisting problems, which make them particularly vulnerable to the maladaptive consequences of social denigration and marginalization.

FAMILY SYSTEMS AS STRESSORS AND SUPPORTS

The family context can obviously play a critical role in mediating and moderating
these complex effects. Numerous studies have documented global correlations
between familial support and acceptance and sexual-minority youths' psychological adjustment, self-acceptance, social competence, and overall well-being
(reviewed in D'Augelli, 2006b; Heatherington & Lavner, 2008; Savin-Williams,
2001; Willoughby et al., 2008). To provide just one example, a representative study
of Minnesota youths found that youths' perceptions of family connectedness
functioned as a protective factor buffering sexual-minority youths from suicidal
ideation and behavior (Eisenberg & Resnick, 2006).

The difficulty, however, remains in identifying the specific processes and mechanisms underlying these links. "Support" and "acceptance" are relatively global
constructs, and research conducted among adults has long indicated that individuals' *perceptions* of support from spouses, friends, and family members are
more powerful predictors of adjustment than concrete supportive *acts* (Helgeson,
1993). In fact, several studies indicate that obvious displays of support may actually *exacerbate* distress under stressful circumstances by reminding individuals of
their vulnerability and needfulness (Bolger & Amarel, 2007). According to this
research, the most psychologically beneficial family contexts for sexual-minority
youths might be those in which parents and siblings subtlety support and affirm
the youths' sexual identity and intervene to protect him or her from minority
stress, *but without the youth being explicitly aware of this*. Given that practically all
of the research on familial influences on sexual-minority youths' adjustment has
relied exclusively on the reports of youths themselves, we simply do not have the
data to determine whether this is the case.

Bidirectional causal pathways provide yet another complication when it comes
to pinpointing beneficial processes of family support. Does familial support
directly influence sexual-minority youths' adjustment, or do supportive families

simply "come with" a confluence of *other* characteristics that foster youths' well-being (such as sensitive and responsive caregiving, financial stability, access to high-quality schools, a positive emotional climate, and stable parental marriage)? Also, "reverse" chains of causality must be considered. Specifically, well-adjusted sexual-minority youths may do a better job of *eliciting* support and affirmation from their family members than youths struggling with depression, anxiety, and conduct problems. In the latter case, parents might not conclude "Boy, this child really needs my help and support," but instead might think "Why should I endorse or approve of this lifestyle? Whether it is causing or resulting from my child's distress, it is clearly *bad*." Research on family responses to sexual-minority youths' disclosure of sexual orientation bears this out: Ben-Ari (1995) found that parents adjusted more easily to their youths' same-sex orientation when the youth presented this revelation along with *positive* information about his or her overall happiness and well-being. To some degree, this presents sexual-minority youths with a Catch-22 situation: Those struggling with uncertainty, confusion, and fear about their sexual orientation—and who therefore may have the most to gain from familial expressions of unconditional love and support—may be the least likely to receive such assurances, since their parents might want to avoid "encouraging" what they view as an unhealthy lifestyle.

Also, when familial support and cohesion *do* appear to serve adaptive functions, these functions may have more to do with youths' overall emotional adjustment than with their specific adjustment to their sexual-minority status. For example, Darby-Mullins and Murdock (2007) examined perceptions of global family climate among sexual-minority youths recruited from lesbian-gay-bisexual support groups. They found that although youths who perceived higher levels of familiar cohesion and expressiveness were better adjusted, these effects were neither mediated nor moderated by the youths' self-acceptance of their sexual orientation. Hence, many youths may turn to peers (specifically fellow sexual-minority peers) to bolster their confidence and acceptance of their same-sex sexuality, and to learn how to cope with the specific day-to-day challenges of their sexual-minority status, while turning to family members for global reassurances of love, affection, and self-worth, which provide potent sources of generalized resiliency.

"MOM, DAD, I HAVE SOMETHING TO TELL YOU. . ."

All of these processes and negotiations begin, however, with the moment that a youth's family becomes aware of his or her sexual-minority status, and in fact the way that families handle this transition—both in the immediate aftermath of the disclosure and also over time, as they collectively adjust to their "new reality"—reveals much about the family's ability to cope constructively and provide a stable foundation for the sexual-minority youth's future development. Before exploring some of these dynamics, it is worth beginning with the question, "Why disclose at all?" Certainly, many sexual minorities report that telling their parents about their same-sex sexuality was one of the most difficult and frightening milestones of identity development (Savin-Williams, 1998a, 2001). Youths making these disclosures typically fear permanent damage to the familial relationship (Heatherington & Lavner, 2008). In addition to abject disapproval and scorn, youths must often witness and cope with their parents' expressions of deep sadness and disappointment about relinquishing their conventional dreams and fantasies about their child's future (Herdt & Beeler, 1998). Given these disincentives, many youths delay disclosing their sexual identity to parents until the college years, when they are out of the house and no longer have to deal with the emotional and interpersonal repercussions on a day-to-day basis (Savin-Williams, 2001).

Others choose never to tell: Is this necessarily maladaptive? It is easy to reflexively assume that family openness is always preferable to secrecy, and those youths who choose *never* to share their identity with their parents and siblings will suffer long-term consequences both with respect to their individual adjustment and also with respect to the quality of their family relationships. Yet researchers have increasingly called this assumption into question (Green, 2000; Laird, 2003; LaSala, 2000). Although many sexual-minority youths and adults *do* report distinct benefits associated with being open about their sexuality with family members, such as increased intimacy, communication, connectedness, and support (Herdt & Beeler, 1998; LaSala, 2000; Weston, 1991), this is not always the case. Such beneficial consequences are highly dependent upon the type of family relationships that existed prior to the disclosure. For youths whose families have a history of hostile conflict and poor communication, and who have expressed open denigration of lesbian, gay, and bisexual individuals, secrecy might actually prove psychologically adaptive, allowing them to protect and cherish their own personal truth and integrity and—perhaps most pressingly—preventing expulsion from the home. Hence, the most adaptive strategy may be for youths to carefully *evaluate* their goals and expectations regarding disclosure to the family and to realistically assess whether—given their own particular family dynamics—these expectations are likely to be met (Green, 2000).

Also, in many cases a youth's family might already suspect his or her same-sex orientation, and may have tacitly accepted it. Hence, although the family may not have reckoned with this information *as a family*, and might never have discussed it with one another, it may be an "elephant in the room," obvious to everybody involved despite the collective silence. In these cases, initiating a direct conversation about the issue may or may not deepen intimacy or support, and the downsides might actually outweigh the benefits.

As Herdt and Beeler (1998, p. 179) cautioned:

[it is not that disclosure] necessarily leads to a qualitatively better life, nor necessarily to better psychological adjustment or development, but that it certainly leads to a *different* life and to *different* psychological development and adjustment. . . . surely, disclosure is likely to affect the way in which one *enacts* one's identity in relation to others. . . . there are the possibilities of developing new roles for themselves within the family, of changing the quality and nature of their relationships, and of forging a new sense of self and place in the world.

Accordingly, researchers and clinicians should not assume that disclosure to family members is always the most psychologically adaptive route, but should instead consider a more complicated set of questions about the *specific meaning and implications* of disclosure for different youths, with different family histories, in different social contexts. Such questions have remained underinvestigated, and constitute important directions for future research.

MOTIVES FOR DISCLOSURE

Overall, however, the most recent historical trends have been toward *more and earlier* disclosure, compared with earlier generations (Peplau & Beals, 2004; Savin-Williams, 2001). Reliable data on the total proportion of contemporary sexual-minority youths who have disclosed their sexual orientation to their families are practically impossible to obtain, and previous estimates have been found to vary quite dramatically depending on how samples were recruited (Green, 2000). For example, studies of openly identified lesbian-gay-bisexual adults recruited from lesbian-gay-bisexual community events tend to report relatively higher rates of family disclosure than individuals recruited from support groups, or those who remain somewhat closeted more generally. It is also important to remember that many sexual minorities disclose to *some* family members, but not to all. Overall however, studies suggest that about 80% of openly identified lesbian-gay-bisexual adults are open about their sexuality to at least some family members (Kaiser Foundation, 2001), with about 60–77% of respondents reporting that they are "out" to their parents (Bryant & Demian, 1994).

The increasing rates of disclosure at earlier ages among current cohorts of sexual-minority youth likely represents the fact that these youths are also coming into awareness of their same-sex sexuality at progressively earlier ages, due to increased visibility and discussion about issues related to sexual orientation in the popular media, on the internet, and in the culture at large. Hence, contemporary youths struggling with nascent same-sex attractions have a historically unprecedented amount of information at their disposal to help them understand their feelings, and can make direct contact with a wealth of supportive resources. The more they know and understand about their sexual orientation, and the more they begin to develop a robust self-concept as a lesbian, gay, or bisexual individual, the more difficult it may be to keep their developing identity (and developing lesbian-gay-bisexual social networks) from their parents. Even youths who do not report having extremely intimate family ties indicate that they deeply desire a sense of authenticity in the family, wanting to share their true selves with their parents and siblings and wanting to stop investing so much time and exhausting energy into hiding the "evidence" of their sexual-minority status (Savin-Williams, 2001).

Another reason for youths to disclose to family members, despite the risks, is to seek their support and help. Although numerous studies over the years have found that sexual-minority individuals often develop intensely close networks of friends, sometimes called "families of choice" (Weston, 1991), which serve "familial" functions of day-to-day support, intimacy, and security, research suggests that there is something nonetheless unique and irreplaceable about family ties. Elizur and Ziv (2001), for example, found significant positive effects of family support—and specifically family acceptance of their child's sexual orientation—on Israeli sexual-minority youths' psychological adjustment, and these effects were independent of the support and acceptance that youths received from their friends. The fact that their research was conducted in Israel is worth noting: Family support and acceptance might prove particularly important in cultural, geographic, and community contexts that place extremely strong emphasis on family cohesion, and in which family members spend a great deal of time together (Elizur & Mintzer, 2001). In such cases, keeping such a deeply important secret may prove particularly burdensome for youths.

Importantly, disclosure does not necessarily mean disclosure *to everyone*. In many cases, family members are told one at a time, in staggered fashion (reviewed in Green, 2000), starting with individuals expected to be most accepting (usually mothers and sisters, as reviewed by Savin-Williams, 2001). Family members expected to be highly rejecting may never be told. Such patchwork approaches to disclosure can establish complicated dynamics and tensions within the family as a whole, with different subsets of the family inadvertently cast as "ingroup" and "outgroup" members, each group maintaining starkly different perceptions and expectations of the sexual-minority youth (and with "ingroup" members often feeling burdened by the secret they carry, as noted by Crosbie-Burnett et al., 1996).

HOW DO PARENTS TYPICALLY REACT?

Much of the early research (as most popular literature) on parental reactions to their adolescent children's disclosure of same-sex sexuality portrayed a fairly uniform picture of catastrophic sadness, anger, and rejection (reviewed in Savin-Williams, 2001). Yet this global portrait does not do justice to the diversity of parental responses, and to the complex array of factors that shape parents' psychological journey through the discovery, understanding, and hopefully acceptance of their child's sexual orientation. Certainly it is important to differentiate between the family's overall emotional *acceptance* of the sexual-minority youth and their willingness to establish an open and honest dialogue about it. Overall, the former is often far easier for families to achieve than the latter. Even among adults who are completely "out" to their parents, many report *never* discussing the issue directly with their families (Kaiser Foundation, 2001), and the same is often true for youths.

Many parents quietly tolerate their adolescent child's same-sex sexuality, continuing to express love and affection toward their child without ever explicitly acknowledging his or her sexual-minority identity or disclosing it outside the family (D'Augelli, Grossman, & Starks, 2005; Herdt & Beeler, 1998). Muller (1987) called this pattern (detected during qualitative interviews with parents of lesbians) "loving denial," and he contrasted these parents with those who made an open and honest effort to engage their children in an ongoing, authentic dialog about their sexual questioning and identification. Another pattern detected by Muller was *resentful denial,* characterized by a refusal to discuss or acknowledge the child's sexual orientation, lack of acknowledgment of the child's same-sex romantic partners or sexual-minority friends, and an increasing sense of emotional and interpersonal distancing. The worst-case scenario was open and unequivocal rejection, which Muller called *hostile recognition.*

Clearly, we cannot simplistically dichotomize families into "accepting" or "rejecting" categories. Rather familial response is a dynamic process influenced by the context in which the disclosure takes place, the family's own interpersonal history and sense of cohesion, their collective skills and habits regarding disclosure, problem-solving, emotion regulation, and the temperamental traits of all family members. Additionally, there is the critical dimension of time. Practically all studies of parental responses find that parents' *initial* reactions are rarely their *permanent* reactions (Beals & Peplau, 2006; Savin-Williams, 1998a, 2001). Even the most dire parental responses can usually be repaired: In one qualitative study (Potoczniak, Crosbie-Burnett, & Saltzburg, 2009) the authors found that *all* of the adolescents who were initially expelled from their homes after disclosing their same-sex sexuality reported that their parents eventually recanted the expulsion and invited them back. In some cases, family relationships eventually *improved* after the disclosure (Beals & Peplau, 2006; Cramer & Roach, 1988), presumably because the process of coping with the disclosure helps the family to reach new levels of mutual intimacy and acceptance. Overall, however, the specific processes through which such gradual transformations and realignments take place remain poorly understood (Heatherington & Lavner, 2008). Although we know that the process of responding and reacting to an adolescent child's "coming out" is a journey rather than a discrete event, we know little about the pace and topography of this journey.

Perhaps the most important predictor of familial adjustment to a child's disclosure of a same-sex sexual orientation is the quality of familial ties prior to the disclosure. Contrary to the notion (disseminated in the media and in some popular literature) that parents' inability to accept their child's sexuality can immediately and permanently rupture previously harmonious relationships, in reality the predisclosure relationship provides a critical foundation for the entire family's subsequent adjustment (Savin-Williams, 2001). In some cases, the role of preexisting relationship quality is mediated by youths' overall approach to the disclosure process. When the preexisting bond is strong and secure, youths are more likely to be motivated to disclose in order to reinforce and maintain closeness with their parents (Savin-Williams & Ream, 2003). Conversely, youths often report that the *absence* of closeness with their parent is a sufficient reason to avoid disclosure.

Yet high-quality familial ties do not always motivate youths to disclose; in some cases the depth and supportiveness of youths' family ties may simply exacerbate their fears of *losing* these ties upon disclosure. For example, Waldner and Magruder (1999) found that youths with strong family relationships were actually less likely to publicly express their sexual identity and to seek out gay-supportive resources in their community, which the authors speculated might result from the youths' concern that such displays of openness might jeopardize these valuable ties. This demonstrates that no simplistic relationship exists between relationship quality and subsequent strategies for openness and adjustment: Understanding how the different members of the family *appraise* the "news" and its implications is critically important.

UNIQUE ISSUES FOR ETHNIC-MINORITY FAMILIES

Culture and ethnicity play important roles in structuring sexual minorities' family relationships. As noted earlier, reliable estimates are difficult to obtain, but extant research suggests that ethnic minorities are often less likely to disclose their sexuality to family members, largely because they expect more negative responses (reviewed in Green, 2000). Same-sex sexuality obviously has drastically different meanings in different cultures (Blackwood, 2000; Murray, 2000; Williams, 1998), and families with highly traditional or religious backgrounds might have more negative conceptions of same-sex sexuality—or less knowledge about it altogether—than more mainstream Western families (Espin, 1997; Greene, 1998; Morales, 1992). For example, some languages do not even *have* positive or neutral terms for "lesbian," "gay," or "bisexual" (Espin, 1997).

Importantly, the nature, parameters, and underlying reasons for the stigmatization of same-sex sexuality vary considerably across different ethnic groups, and these differences have correspondingly distinct implications for sexual-minority individuals' experiences, both in terms of initial decisions to disclose and also with respect to long-term adjustment. For example, Latino, African-American, Asian-Pacific Islander, and South Asian communities typically place considerable emphasis on family ties, and same-sex sexuality is often construed to be a violation and betrayal of familial cohesion and loyalty (Espin, 1987; Jayakar, 1994; Smith, 1997; Wooden, Kawasaki, & Mayeda, 1983).

For example, many South Asian families continue to arrange their children's marriages (Jayakar, 1994), and the social ties created by these marriages may have important implications for the family's integration into other social networks. Men and women whose same-sex sexuality leads them to withdraw from this tradition may be viewed by their parents as making a selfish choice that impacts negatively upon the family's entire social system. In these cases, sexual minorities may feel impossibly torn between familial loyalty and their desire to seek same-sex romantic ties.

In ethnic groups that have sharply demarcated gender roles, same-sex sexuality carries the additional stigma of gender role deviation (Carrier, 1989; Ramos, 1994). For example, many Latino communities expect men to display the exaggerated masculine characteristics of "machismo" (courage, aggressiveness, power, and invulnerability), whereas women must display appropriate "etiqueta" (patience, nurturance, passivity, and subservience). Because these cultures typically construe same-sex sexuality as gender nonconformity, sexual minorities are often viewed by their families and communities as having fundamentally failed as men or women, never having quite attained appropriate maturity and adult status. Within African-American communities, same-sex sexuality is often associated with long-standing cultural stereotypes of African-Americans as hypersexual and morally bankrupt (Clarke, 1983; Greene, 1986). Thus, sexual minorities often feel pressured to hide their same-sex sexuality in order present an image of normalcy to larger Anglo society and contradict these racist stereotypes (Clarke, 1983; Gomez & Smith, 1990).

For all of these reasons, ethnic-minority youths and young adults may express their sexuality in distinctive ways that run counter to common conceptions of "the lesbian-gay-bisexual experience." For example, some ethnic-minority men might pursue exclusively sexual same-sex behavior with strangers to avoid identifying as gay, and maintain their most important romantic ties to women (Carballo-Dieguez & Dolezal, 1994). Others might identify as lesbian or gay and regularly pursue same-sex behavior, but might resist larger participation in gay culture, choosing to emphasize the cultural component of their identity in order to maintain their strong cultural and family ties (Mays, Cochran, & Rhue, 1993). These factors must be carefully considered by researchers investigating how sexual-minority youths from different ethnic groups manage their sexual-minority identity in the context of broader family and community ties.

FROM THE FAMILY'S POINT OF VIEW

In considering how sexual-minority adolescents and young adults maintain functioning relationships with their families, it is important not to lose sight of the fact that adjustment to a family member's disclosure of same-sex sexuality may be experienced quite differently from the *family's* point of view than the point of view of the sexual-minority individual. Overall, there has been far more research from the latter perspective than from the former (Crosbie-Burnett et al., 1996). Of course from a clinical perspective, it might be argued that a youth's *perception* of his or her parents' reaction to disclosure is more important than the objective "truth" of that reaction; this might well be the case if the "outcome of interest" is the youth's own adjustment, given the vast body of research demonstrating that individuals' construals of their close relationships may be more predictive of well-being than objective features of those relationships (reviewed in Diamond, Fagundes, & Butterworth, 2010).

Yet if we are interested (as we are) in the *entire family's* adjustment and collective development in response to the youth's sexual-minority identity, then it is not sufficient to assess only the sexual-minority youth's perspective. Hence, although previous research suggests important general patterns and developmental processes in the overall disclosure and adjustment process, much work remains to be done in applying what we have learned from this individualistic perspective to draw conclusions about coordinated *family-wide* processes of adjustment. To provide just one example, discrepancies between *youths'* perspectives on "how it went" when they told their parents about their sexual orientation and how *their parents* thought it went might be particularly telling in revealing how the family as a whole grapples with this new reality in the days, weeks, and years after that transformative moment.

What we do know from the small amount of qualitative, clinically oriented accounts available (Beeler & DiProva, 1999; Griffin, Wirth, & Wirth, 1986) is that many of the psychological hurdles faced by sexual-minority youths—feelings of invisibility, fears of marginalization and social stigmatization, uncertainty and confusion about the future—are *shared* by their parents, siblings, aunts, uncles, and grandparents. Family members also face many of the same practical decisions: Should they hide this information from colleagues? Can anyone "tell"? Which friends of the family are likely to be supportive, and which are likely to be judgmental and rejecting? Will people think that it is the family's "fault," and that they somehow provided a dysfunctional childhood environment that "caused" this to happen? It is also not uncommon for some family members—especially siblings—to question their *own* sexuality. Given the public visibility of scientific findings about the potential genetic underpinnings of same-sex sexuality, it is perhaps natural for siblings and even parents to wonder if they are carrying the much-touted "gay gene," and what that might mean for them.

Overall, then, one way to summarize these issues is to note that such families face an extended period of *vulnerability* during which they gradually reconstruct a new sense of themselves as a unit, and during which they must revise their own individual relationships with the sexual-minority family member (Beeler & DiProva, 1999). This vulnerability, as noted earlier, need not be interpreted as necessarily dramatic or negative. Some families experience these transitions as positive events that bring them together, whereas others wrestle with significant feelings of anger, resentment, and betrayal (Crosbie-Burnett et al., 1996; Savin-Williams, 2001). Perhaps the only reliable predictions that can be made are that (1) families with high-quality ties *before* the disclosure, characterized by mutual intimacy, support, cohesion, and warmth, generally fare better (Patterson, 2000; Savin-Williams, 2001), and (2) the family's adjustment must be considered in light of contextual factors such as their local community, values, religious background, economic status, and cultural beliefs (Crosbie-Burnett et al., 1996; Rostosky et al., 2004; Savin-Williams, 2001).

Much, however, remains unknown. Given how little research has taken a long-range perspective on sexual-minority individuals' relationships with their families of origin, we know little about how these relationships continue to evolve and change over the course of adolescent and adult development, and how normative developmental transitions—in the life of the sexual-minority individual as well as his or her kin—are affected by these issues.

DIRECTIONS FOR THE FUTURE: FAMILY SYSTEMS
RATHER THAN MEMBERS

Throughout this chapter, we have attempted to show that many straightforward assumptions about unidirectional family influences (i.e., flowing *from* parents and siblings *to* the sexual-minority adolescent or young adult) provide an inadequate representation of the overall role of familial factors in sexual-minority youths' developmental trajectories. We now want to further explore the implications of this perspective, specifically highlighting the value of adopting a *family systems* perspective on sexual-minority development (as exemplified by Heatherington & Lavner, 2008; Willoughby et al., 2008). According to this perspective, "trigger events" such as a child's disclosure of same-sex sexuality can be understood only with respect to a broad series of cascading realignments that take place among *all* family members. The manner in which each individual family member copes, and the ways in which they cope *together* as an intersecting, dynamic system, is shaped by each member's own individual characteristics as well as the long-standing patterns of interaction they have developed with one another over the years. Equally important, each step in the family's journey influences the next one, repeatedly remaking the emotional terrain that the sexual-minority youth finds himself or herself carefully navigating.

In applying a family systems approach to understanding familial adjustment to an adolescent's same-sex orientation, it is useful to consider the existing literature on how families cope collectively with stressful events more generally. Walsh (2003), for example, has emphasized that familial adaptations can be understood as occurring within three key domains of resilience: *organizational patterns, communication and problem-solving,* and *making meaning of adversity.* Each of these domains is highly relevant to the psychological and emotional challenges that families confront after a child reveals a same-sex orientation, and family-wide processes and strategies within each domain are likely to have significant effects on the youths' subsequent development. Consider, for example, the domain of communication. As noted earlier when discussing parents who adopt a pattern of "loving denial" in response to their child's sexuality (Muller, 1987), some families may show disjointed and contradictory patterns of communication with their sexual-minority child, openly expressing warmth and love while simultaneously shutting down any discussion of the youth's actual day-to-day life as a member of a sexual minority. Given how many families show improvements in their responses to a child's sexual orientation over time, it is intriguing to consider the processes through which youths might eventually chip away at their parents' denial, using the foundation of mutual warmth and intimacy to progressively open a tentative dialog that might break through the parents' resistance. Hence this scenario provides an example of why a family systems approach is valuable: The key realignments that need to be made to promote optimal adolescent adjustment are "multisided," involving changes in both the youths' and the family members' behavior and expectations.

In considering how these changes take place, Willoughby and colleagues (2008) emphasized the twin characteristics of *family adaptability* and *family cohesion*. They defined adaptability as the family's ability to flexibly change and adjust when confronted with new and challenging situations, whereas cohesion was defined as the overall sense of emotional connectedness and emotional bonding within the family. They reviewed evidence suggesting that adaptability and cohesion are dynamically related to one another over time; families with strengths in one domain find it easier to enact and engage the other domain when confronted with the stress of a child's disclosure of same-sex sexuality.

One reason that future research should devote increased attention to such systemic processes and determinants of adaptation is that they may help to explain important sources of variation in sexual-minority youths' overall adjustment. As noted by Heatherington and Lavner, linkages between certain family characteristics and youths' adjustment outcomes "may be strong and negative in chaotic, conflictual families but weak or even positive in highly cohesive families. *This is because family processes provide the means for making meaning out of events, problem-solving, and adapting to change*" (Heatherington & Lavner, 2008, p. 337, emphasis added). Importantly, these adaptive processes are just as important for the *family's* eventual well-being as for the *adolescent's* well-being. Accordingly, perhaps the most valuable potential contribution of a family systems approach is that it prompts us to ask broader, more complex questions about how different family members' trajectories of adjustment are fundamentally interconnected, and the ways in which each member's adaptation (or the lack thereof) "pulls" on the system as a whole. Investigating these processes is a critical direction for future research.

However, such investigative goals entail notable methodological challenges. First and foremost, we must do a better job of assessing familial reactions to youths' sexual orientation *over time*, and from the perspective of *multiple* family members. This will no doubt prove difficult: One of the reasons that most existing research on sexual-minority youth is based exclusively on the reports of youths is that their parents often have no interest in "laying bare" their family dynamics and challenges at a time of such acute stress and uncertainty. Hence, research protocols must be structured in such a way as to maximize family member's subjective experiences of safety and reassurance and to minimize their feelings of vulnerability and anxiety. Ideally, the more family members can be drawn into such research projects (including not only siblings, but extended family members), the more willing each individual member might be to maintain their participation over time, viewing such participation as a *family* commitment rather than an individual donation of time.

CONCLUSIONS

Perhaps the single most defining characteristic of sexual-minority youths' family relationships is that they *have* no single defining characteristic. The family processes and dynamics of sexual-minority youths are as diverse as these individuals themselves. Thus, in investigating the family context of sexual-minority adolescent development, we must remember to cast aside our preconceptions about which family ties and experiences "matter," and instead consider *all* of a sexual-minority youth's family experiences as potentially developmentally significant. Although prior research has clearly treated the youth's initial disclosure of same-sex sexuality as a critical turning point, this is by no means the most significant event. Rather, the complex interpersonal dynamics that unfold at a quiet family dinner may prove just as meaningful and influential. The task for the next generation of research on sexual-minority youths' adjustment is to parse the specific dynamics of these diverse experiences to understand their adaptive significance. This requires greater awareness of the unique features linking and distinguishing between different familial bonds, and the different processes through which they meet family members' psychosocial needs. Along the same lines, we must also remember that family experiences are always embedded within specific sociocultural contexts, which must be carefully analyzed to accurately discern why particular subsets of sexual minorities have distinctive familial experiences and developmental pathways. Whereas early research on sexual minorities tended to emphasize their shared experience of stigmatization, researchers now face the more difficult but compelling task of charting the multiple, interacting factors producing diversity in long-term developmental pathways. Greater understanding of such diversity will clearly not only advance our knowledge about sexual minorities, but will deepen our knowledge of how *all* individuals benefit from family ties over the life course.

References

Balsam, K. F., Rothblum, E. D., & Beauchaine, T. P. (2005). Victimization over the life span: A comparison of lesbian, gay, bisexual, and heterosexual siblings. *Journal of Consulting and Clinical Psychology, 73*, 477–487.

Beals, K. P., & Peplau, L. A. (2006). Disclosure patterns within social networks of gay men and lesbians. *Journal of Homosexuality, 51*, 101–120.

Beeler, J., & DiProva, V. (1999). Family adjustment following disclosure of homosexuality by a member: Themes discerned in narrative accounts. *Journal of Marital & Family Therapy, 25*, 443–459.

Ben-Ari, A. (1995). The discovery that an offspring is gay: Parents', gay men's, and lesbians' perspectives. *Journal of Homosexuality, 30*, 89–112.

Blackwood, E. (2000). Culture and women's sexualities. *Journal of Social Issues, 56*, 223–238.

Bolger, N., & Amarel, D. (2007). Effects of social support visibility on adjustment to stress: Experimental evidence. *Journal of Personality and Social Psychology, 92*, 458–475.

Bryant, A. S., & Demian. (1994). Relationship characteristics of American gay and lesbian couples: Findings from a national survey. *Journal of Gay and Lesbian Social Services, 1*, 101–117.

Carballo-Dieguez, A., & Dolezal, C. (1994). Contrasting types of Puerto Rican men who have sex with men (MSM). *Journal of Psychology and Human Sexuality, 6*, 41–67.

Carrier, J. M. (1989). Gay liberation and coming out in Mexico. *Journal of Homosexuality,*
17, 225–252.

Clarke, C. (1983). The failure to transform: Homophobia in the black community. In
B. Smith (Ed.), *Home girls: A black feminist anthology* (pp. 197–208). New York:
Kitchen Table Press.

Cochran, S. D., & Mays, V. M. (2007). Physical health complaints among lesbians, gay
men, and bisexual and homosexually experienced heterosexual individuals: Results
from the California Quality of Life Survey. *American Journal of Public Health, 97*,
2048–2055.

Cramer, D. W., & Roach, A. J. (1988). Coming out to mom and dad: A study of gay males
and their relationships with their parents. *Journal of Homosexuality, 15*, 79–91.

Crosbie-Burnett, M., Foster, T. L., Murray, C. I., & Bowen, G. L. (1996). Gays' and lesbians' families-of-origin: A social-cognitive behavioral model of adjustment. *Family*
Relations, 45, 397–403.

Darby-Mullins, P., & Murdock, T. B. (2007). The influence of family environment factors on self-acceptance and emotional adjustment among gay, lesbian, and bisexual
adolescents. *Journal of GLBT Family Studies, 3*, 75–91.

D'Augelli, A. R. (2006a). Developmental and contextual factors and mental health among
lesbian, gay, and bisexual youths. In A. M. Omoto & H. S. Kurtzman (Eds.), *Sexual*
orientation and mental health: Examining identity and development in lesbian, gay, and
bisexual people (pp. 37–53). Washington, DC: American Psychological Association.

D'Augelli, A. R. (2006b). Stress and adaptation among families of lesbian, gay, and bisexual youth: Research challenges. In J. J. Bigner (Ed.), *An introduction to GLBT family*
studies (pp. 135–157). New York: Haworth Press.

D'Augelli, A. R., Grossman, A. H., & Starks, M. T. (2005). Parents' awareness of lesbian, gay, and bisexual youths' sexual orientation. *Journal of Marriage & Family, 67*,
474–482.

Diamond, L. M. (2008). *Sexual fluidity: Understanding women's love and desire.*
Cambridge, MA: Harvard University Press.

Diamond, L. M., Fagundes, C. P., & Butterworth, M. R. (2010). Intimate relationships
across the lifespan. In M. E. Lamb, L. White, & A. Freund (Eds.), *Handbook of lifespan*
(Vol. 2, pp. 379–433). New York: Wiley.

Diamond, L. M., & Savin-Williams, R. C. (2003). The intimate relationships of sexual-
minority youths. In G. R. Adams & M. Berzonsky (Eds.), *The Blackwell handbook of*
adolescence (pp. 393–412). Oxford, UK: Blackwell.

Eisenberg, M. E., & Resnick, M. D. (2006). Suicidality among gay, lesbian, and bisexual
youth: The role of protective factors. *Journal of Adolescent Health, 39*, 662–668.

Elizur, Y., & Mintzer, A. (2001). A framework for the formation of gay male identity:
Processes associated with adult attachment style and support from family and friends.
Archives of Sexual Behavior, 30, 143–167.

Elizur, Y., & Ziv, M. (2001). Family support and acceptance, gay male identity, and psychological adjustment: A path model. *Family Process, 40*, 125–144.

Ellis, L. (1996). Theories of homosexuality. In R. C. Savin-Williams & K. M. Cohen
(Eds.), *The lives of lesbians, gays, and bisexuals: Children to adults* (pp. 11–34). Fort
Worth, TX: Harcourt Brace.

Espin, O. M. (1987). Issues of identity in the psychology of Latina lesbians. In Boston
Lesbian Psychologies Collective (Ed.), *Lesbian psychologies: Explorations and chal-*
lenges (pp. 35–51). Urbana: University of Illinois Press.

Espin, O. M. (1997). Crossing borders and boundaries: The life narratives of immigrant lesbians. In B. Greene (Ed.), *Ethnic and cultural diversity among lesbians and gay men* (pp. 191–215). Thousand Oaks, CA: Sage.

Faulkner, A. H., & Cranston, K. (1998). Correlates of same-sex sexual behavior in a random sample of Massachusetts high school students. *American Journal of Public Health, 88*, 262–266.

Freund, K., & Blanchard, R. (1983). Is the distant relationship of fathers and homosexual sons related to the sons' erotic preference for male partners, or to the sons' atypical gender identity, or to both? *Journal of Homosexuality, 9*, 7–25.

Frisell, T., Lichtenstein, P., Rahman, Q., & Langstrom, N. (2010). Psychiatric morbidity associated with same-sex sexual behaviour: Influence of minority stress and familial factors. *Psychological Medicine: A Journal of Research in Psychiatry and the Allied Sciences, 40*, 315–324.

Garofalo, R., Wolf, R. C., Wissow, L. S., Woods, E. R., & Goodman, E. (1999). Sexual orientation and risk of suicide attempts among a representative sample of youth. *Archives of Pediatrics and Adolescent Medicine, 153*, 487–493.

Gomez, J., & Smith, B. (1990). Taking the home out of homophobia: Black lesbian health. In E. C. White (Ed.), *The black women's health book: Speaking for ourselves* (pp. 198–213). Seattle, WA: Seal.

Green, R. J. (2000). "Lesbians, gay men, and their parents": A critique of LaSala and the prevailing clinical "wisdom." *Family Process, 39*, 257–266.

Greene, B. (1986). When the therapist is white and the patient is black: Considerations for psychotherapy in the feminist heterosexual and lesbian communities. *Women and Therapy, 5*, 41–66.

Greene, B. (1998). Family, ethnic identity, and sexual orientation: African-American lesbians and gay men. In C. Patterson & A. R. D'Augelli (Eds.), *Lesbian, gay, and bisexual identities in families: Psychological perspectives* (pp. 40–52). New York: Oxford University Press.

Griffin, C. W., Wirth, M. J., & Wirth, A. G. (1986). *Beyond acceptance: Parents of lesbians and gays talk about their experience.* New York: St. Martin's Press.

Heatherington, L., & Lavner, J. A. (2008). Coming to terms with coming out: Review and recommendations for family systems-focused research. *Journal of Family Psychology, 22*, 329–343.

Helgeson, V. S. (1993). Two important distinctions in social support: Kind of support and perceived versus received. *Journal of Applied Social Psychology, 23*, 825–845.

Herdt, G., & Beeler, J. (1998). Older gay men and lesbians in families. In C. Patterson & A. R. D' Augelli (Eds.), *Lesbian, gay, and bisexual identities in families: Psychological perspectives* (pp. 177–196). New York: Oxford University Press.

Horn, S. S., & Nucci, L. (2006). Harassment of gay and lesbian youth and school violence in America: An analysis and directions for intervention. In C. Daiute, Z. Beykont, C. Higson-Smith, & L. Nucci (Eds.), *International perspectives on youth conflict and development* (pp. 139–155). New York: Oxford University Press.

Igartua, K. J., Gill, K., & Montoro, R. (2003). Internalized homophobia: A factor in depression, anxiety, and suicide in the gay and lesbian population. *Canadian Journal of Community Mental Health, 22*, 15–30.

Jayakar, K. (1994). Women of the Indian subcontinent. In L. Comas-Diaz & B. Greene (Eds.), *Women of color: Integrating ethnic and gender identities in psychotherapy* (pp. 161–181). New York: Guilford Press.

Kaiser Foundation. (2001). *Inside-out: Report on the experiences of lesbians, gays and bisexuals in America and the public's view on issues and policies related to sexual orientation*. Mento Park, CA: Kaiser Foundation.

Laird, J. (2003). Lesbian and gay families. In F. Walsh (Ed.), *Normal family processes: Growing diversity and complexity* (3rd ed., pp. 176–209). New York: Guilford Press.

LaSala, M. C. (2000). Lesbians, gay men, and their parents: Family therapy for the coming-out crisis. *Family Process, 39*, 67–81.

Loftus, J. (2001). America's liberalization in attitudes toward homosexuality. *American Sociological Review, 66*, 762–782.

Mays, V. M., Cochran, S. D., & Rhue, S. (1993). The impact of perceived discrimination on the intimate relationships of black lesbians. *Journal of Homosexuality, 25*, 1–14.

Meyer, I. H. (2003). Prejudice, social stress, and mental health in lesbian, gay, and bisexual populations: Conceptual issues and research evidence. *Psychological Bulletin, 129*, 674–697.

Meyer, I. H., & Dean, L. (1998). Internalized homophobia, intimacy, and sexual behavior among gay and bisexual men. In G. M. Herek (Ed.), *Stigma and sexual orientation: Understanding prejudice against lesbians, gay men, and bisexuals* (pp. 160–186). Thousand Oaks, CA: Sage.

Morales, E. (1992). Latino gays and Latina lesbians. In S. H. Dworkin & F. J. Gutierrez (Eds.), *Counseling gay men and lesbians: Journey to the end of the rainbow* (pp. 125–139). Alexandria, VA: American Association for Counseling and Development.

Mosher, W. D., Chandra, A., & Jones, J. (2005). *Sexual behavior and selected health measures: Men and women 15–44 years of age, United States, 2002*. Advance data from vital and health statistics, no. 362. Hyattsville, MD: National Center for Health Statistics.

Muller, A. (1987). *Parents matter: Parents' relationships with lesbian daughters*. Tallahassee, FL: Naiad Press.

Murray, S. O. (2000). *Homosexualities*. Chicago: University of Chicago Press.

National Coalition of Anti-Violence Programs. (2007). *Anti-lesbian, gay, transgender, and bisexual violence in 2007: A report of the National Coalition of Anti-Violence Programs*. Retrieved June 1, 2008, from www.ncavp.org/publications/NationalPubs.aspx.

Patterson, C. J. (2000). Family relationships of lesbians and gay men. *Journal of Marriage and the Family, 62*, 1052–1069.

Peplau, L. A., & Beals, K. P. (2004). The family lives of lesbians and gay men. In A. L. Vangelisti (Ed.), *Handbook of family communication* (pp. 233–248). Mahwah, NJ: Lawrence Erlbaum Associates.

Potoczniak, D., Crosbie-Burnett, M., & Saltzburg, N. (2009). Experiences regarding coming out to parents among African American, Hispanic, and White gay, lesbian, bisexual, transgender, and questioning adolescents. *Journal of Gay & Lesbian Social Services: Issues in Practice, Policy & Research, 21*, 189–205.

Ramos, J. (Ed.). (1994). *Companeras: Latina lesbians*. New York: Routledge.

Rosario, M., Schrimshaw, E. W., Hunter, J., & Gwadz, M. (2002). Gay-related stress and emotional distress among gay, lesbian and bisexual youths: A longitudinal examination. *Journal of Consulting & Clinical Psychology, 70*, 967–975.

Rostosky, S. S., Korfhage, B. A., Duhigg, J. M., Stern, A. J., Bennett, L., & Riggle, E. D. B. (2004). Same-sex couple perceptions of family support: A consensual qualitative study. *Family Process, 43*, 43–57.

Russell, S. T. (2006). Substance use and abuse and mental health among sexual-minority youths: Evidence from Add Health. In A. M. Omoto & H. S. Kurtzman (Eds.), *Sexual orientation and mental health: Examining identity and development in lesbian, gay, and bisexual people* (pp. 13–35). Washington, DC: American Psychological Association.

Russell, S. T., & McGuire, J. K. (2008). The school climate for lesbian, gay, bisexual, and transgender (LGBT) students. In M. Shinn & H. Yoshikawa (Eds.), *Toward positive youth development: Transforming schools and community programs* (pp. 133–149). New York: Oxford University Press.

Savin-Williams, R. C. (1998a). "... *And then I became gay": Young men's stories.* New York: Routledge.

Savin-Williams, R. C. (1998b). Lesbian, gay and bisexual youths' relationships with their parents. In C. Patterson & A. R. D'Augelli (Eds.), *Lesbian, gay, and bisexual identities in families: Psychological perspectives* (pp. 75–98). New York: Oxford University Press.

Savin-Williams, R. C. (2001). *Mom, Dad. I'm gay.* Washington, DC: APA Press.

Savin-Williams, R. C. (2005). *The new gay teenager.* Cambridge, MA: Harvard University Press.

Savin-Williams, R. C., & Cohen, K. M. (2004). Homoerotic development during childhood and adolescence. *Child and Adolescent Psychiatric Clinics of North America, 13,* 529–549.

Savin-Williams, R. C., & Diamond, L. M. (1998). Sexual orientation. In W. K. Silverman & T. H. Ollendick (Eds.), *Developmental issues in the clinical treatment of children and adolescents* (pp. 241–258). Boston: Allyn & Bacon.

Savin-Williams, R. C., & Ream, G. L. (2003). Sex variations in the disclosure to parents of same-sex attractions. *Journal of Family Psychology, 17,* 429–438.

Smith, A. (1997). Cultural diversity and the coming-out process: Implications for clinical practice. In B. Greene (Ed.), *Ethnic and cultural diversity among lesbians and gay men* (pp. 279–300). Thousand Oaks, CA: Sage.

Waldner, L. K., & Magruder, B. (1999). Coming out to parents: Perceptions of family relations, perceived resources and identity expression as predictors of identity disclosure for gay and lesbian adolescents. *Journal of Homosexuality, 37,* 83–100.

Walsh, F. (2003). Family resilience: A framework for clinical practice. *Family Process, 42,* 1–18.

Walters, S. D. (2001). *All the rage: The story of gay visibility in America.* Chicago: University of Chicago Press.

Weston, K. (1991). *Families we choose: Lesbians, gays, kinship.* New York: Columbia University Press.

Williams, W. L. (1998). Social acceptance of same-sex relationships in families: Models from other cultures. In C. Patterson & A. R. D' Augelli (Eds.), *Lesbian, gay, and bisexual identities in families: Psychological perspectives* (pp. 53–71). New York: Oxford University Press.

Willoughby, B. L. B., Doty, N. D., & Malik, N. M. (2008). Parental reactions to their child's sexual orientation disclosure: A family stress perspective. *Parenting: Science and Practice, 8,* 70–91.

Wooden, W. S., Kawasaki, H., & Mayeda, R. (1983). Lifestyles and identity maintenance among gay Japanese-American males. *Alternative Lifestyles, 5,* 236–243.

12

Resilience and Vulnerability of Mexican Origin Youth and Their Families

A Test of a Culturally Informed Model of Family Economic Stress

RAND D. CONGER, HAIRONG SONG, GARY D. STOCKDALE, EMILIO FERRER, KEITH F. WIDAMAN, AND ANA M. CAUCE

The United States continues to undergo dramatic changes regarding the ethnic distribution of young people in the population (see Cauce, Cruz, Corona, & Conger, 2011). Demographic data reveal that minority youth make up an increasing portion of the overall citizenry of the United States and this trend is expected to continue until there is no longer a clear ethnic majority group in the country as a whole. These population shifts bring to the fore both scientific interest and policy concerns related to minority youth. Especially important will be new theoretical insights, research findings, social programs, and informed policies that promote the successful development of this segment of the population. These new initiatives are particularly important inasmuch as ethnic minority youth are at relatively high risk for a variety of negative developmental outcomes. These difficulties include increased risk for antisocial behavior and involvement with the criminal justice system, emotional problems, early initiation into sexual activities and childbirth, obesity and physical illness, early death, and school drop-out (Cauce et al., 2011). Simply put, the most rapidly increasing portion of the under 20 population in the United States faces serious challenges in the process of transitioning from adolescence to a successful adulthood. Finding ways to cope more effectively with these challenges will generate major benefits for minority youth, their families, and the country as a whole.

In this chapter we focus on two aspects of these issues. First, we report early findings from a study of Mexican-origin youth and their families that examine pathways to successful development despite the significant adversities often faced by Latinos. Second, we recognize that a successful transition from adolescence to adulthood typically begins during the early teen years. That is, we expect that the supports and stresses experienced by young people as they begin their adolescent years often set the tone for the next decade of their lives and beyond. For example, Scaramella, Conger, and Simons (1999) found that nurturing and supportive parenting during early adolescence reduced risk for increases in problems with conduct during the next several years. On the other hand, Feldman, Conger, and Burzette (2004) showed that traumas suffered during early adolescence predicted greater risk for clinically significant psychiatric problems during the transition to adulthood. Indeed, previous research on human development across the life course demonstrates that multiple dimensions of risk and resilience emerge during childhood, become intensified during the rapid social and biological changes of adolescence, and, in that process, impact success or failure during the transition to adulthood (e.g., Laub & Sampson, 2003; Luthar, 2003). These findings emphasize the importance of identifying mechanisms of risk and resilience during early or emerging adolescence as a basis for understanding the processes through which adolescents do or do not make a successful transition to the adult years.

To address these issues we use data from the California Families Project (CFP), a study of Mexican-origin children and their families living in California. This ethnic group is especially important inasmuch as the majority of Latinos or Hispanics in the United States are of Mexican descent; in California, they represent 77% of the Latino population (U.S. Census Bureau, 2000). Because Mexican-Americans currently constitute 25% of California's population, the State serves as a bellwether for national trends. For the CFP, we define Mexican-Americans as people of Mexican origin, including both recent immigrants to the United States as well as citizens who were born in this country.

An important emphasis in the CFP is the identification of developmental processes associated with risk and resilience. To a significant degree, risk for maladjustment emerges over time as part of a developmental process beginning during childhood (Cicchetti, 1999; Conger, 1997; Glantz & Leshner, 2000). In addition to its theoretical importance, this developmental perspective on psychopathology has enormous practical significance, inasmuch as a better understanding of these early risk processes could lead to the creation of more effective interventions designed to prevent both emotional and behavioral problems during adolescence and into the adult years (Cicchetti, 1999; Sloboda, 1999). Moreover, the developmental psychopathology perspective also considers early factors that promote competent or successful adjustment as well as threats to emotional, behavioral, or physical well-being (Masten et al., 2005). Despite the strengths of this approach, the studies beginning in childhood that do exist typically have not addressed either the Latino experience in general or the Mexican-American experience in particular (see Burton & Jarrett, 2000; McLoyd, Cauce, Takeuchi, & Wilson, 2000). Consistent with the work of Hauser (1999) and the themes of the present volume, the primary goal of the CFP is to help address these important gaps in previous research on risk and resilience across the years of adolescence and into adulthood.

THE CONCEPTUAL MODEL

As shown in Figure 12.1, the conceptual model for this report is particularly concerned with the role that the family plays in youth development and how general family context and parent functioning affect both competent behavior (i.e., attachment to school, educational expectations or aspirations, and grade point average) and problematic youth development (i.e., conduct problems in school). The model derives from earlier research on family economic stress (e.g., Conger & Conger, 2002) and has been extended to capture unique influences on the lives of Mexican-American and other minority youth. The original family stress model traced the specific processes through which economic hardship and other life stresses affect family relationships and the development of children and adolescents (e.g., Conger & Conger, 2002; Conger et al., 2002). The inclusion of economic pressure as a key element of our conceptual model (see Figure 12.1) reflects this emphasis in the current study. The economic aspect of family stress processes is especially salient for families of Mexican origin inasmuch as these families frequently experience extremely low incomes that often fall below the official poverty line (approximately 30% of Mexican-Americans in 1996 compared to about 12% for the nation as a whole; Baca Zinn & Wells, 2000). Consistent with these earlier findings, the U.S. Census Bureau (2010) reports that 25.3% of Hispanics were below the poverty line in 2009 compared to 9.4% of non-Hispanic whites.

The conceptual framework guiding the CFP extends this earlier model by delineating specific, stressful conditions to which many Mexican-American parents and children may be exposed, such as living in risky neighborhoods or experiencing ethnic discrimination (Figure 12.1). Consistent with findings from earlier research, the model proposes that economic pressure, such as the inability to meet basic material needs involving food, adequate clothing and housing, and medical care,

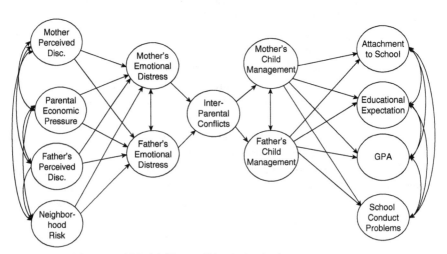

Figure 12.1. Theoretical Model (Disc. = Discrimination).

will increase the emotional distress of both mothers and fathers (Conger & Donnellan, 2007). Economic pressure also increases the likelihood that a family will be forced to reside in a high-risk living environment with a history "of violence, poor educational systems, few ladders of opportunity, and where intensive drug distribution and sales, gang activity, and other forms of criminal deviance are rampant" (Vega & Gil, 1999, p. 62). Thus, neighborhood risk is included as an additional marker of family stress in Figure 12.1.

The theoretical model also incorporates stress related to occupying a minority role in the dominant culture through the experience of actual or perceived discrimination by both mothers and fathers (Portes & Rumbaut, 2001; Vega et al., 1998). For example, Vega and his colleagues found that perceived discrimination was associated with depressed mood in Mexican-American adults (Finch, Kolody, & Vega, 2000). Similarly, discrimination related to minority status has been related to emotional distress for Latinos in general (e.g., Salgado de Snyder, 1987; Amaro, Russo, & Johnson, 1987).

The model in Figure 12.1 predicts that these three markers of stressful life experiences or conditions—economic pressure, living in a risky neighborhood environment, and experiencing discrimination because of race or ethnicity—will increase parental emotional distress, such as depressed mood and anxiety. Earlier research supports these predictions for economic stress (Conger & Donnellan, 2007; Conger, Conger, & Martin, 2010), for stressful events and conditions in general (Conger, Patterson, & Ge, 1995; Ge, Lorenz, Conger, & Elder, 1994), and for majority as well as minority families, including Mexican-Americans (Brody, McBride, Kim, & Brown, 2002; Conger et al., 2002; Parke et al., 2004). Consistent with the family stress model, we predict that stress-related disruptions in caregivers' emotional functioning will exacerbate interparental conflict, which, in turn, will negatively affect parenting practices (e.g., Conger et al., 2002; Conger & Donnellan, 2007; Cummings, Goeke-Morey, & Dukewich, 2001; Fincham, 1998; Gonzales, Pitts, Hill, & Roosa, 2000; Harold & Conger, 1997). That is, we predict that conflicts between caregivers will "spill-over" into parent–child relationships by disrupting effective parenting behaviors. In the present analyses, we are especially concerned with the positive management of child behaviors through practices such as explanation, positive reinforcement of desired behaviors, and monitoring of children's activities.

Figure 12.1 indicates that the exogenous and earlier mediating constructs in the family stress model are expected to influence child development only indirectly through child management practices. Specifically, we expect that effective management practices will promote competent development in terms of school attachments, expectations, and performance and will reduce the risk for the development of conduct problems in school such as fighting or skipping school. The process through which this set of events occurs has to do with the types of parenting behaviors evaluated in this study. Parents who monitor their children's activities, reinforce their positive accomplishments, and provide relevant explanations for the rules they enforce should have children who are less likely to develop conduct problems and who are more likely to succeed in social and academic environments.

These predictions are consistent with the family stress model and findings from previous research (Conger & Donnellan, 2007; Conger et al., 2010). Thus, when parents are able to maintain these constructive approaches to child rearing even when they live in stressful environments, children should be more resilient and adaptive in their daily lives. We evaluate these predictions in the following analyses. Especially important, we concentrate our analyses on a cohort of fifth-grade children who are just entering adolescence. Consistent with a growing literature on the development of competence and maladjustment across the life course, the success with which they transition to adolescence is expected to significantly affect their future competence during their entry into the adult years (see Burt, Obradovic, Long, & Masten, 2008).

THE PRESENT STUDY

Participants and Procedures

Participants in the CFP included over 650 fifth-grade, emerging adolescents and their families. All families were of Mexican origin and the focal fifth-grade student was a nonhandicapped, normally functioning child who attended the fifth grade in a public or Catholic school in one of two cities in northern California. Children were drawn at random from the student rosters for the school districts of these two cities. For the present analyses, only two-parent families ($N = 548$) were included because of the focus on interparental conflict and on both mother and father effects on the child.

Families were recruited by telephone or, for cases in which there was no listed phone number, by a recruiter who went to their home. Among the eligible families, 68.6% of them agreed to participate in the study. All family members were of Mexican origin as determined by their ancestry and their self-identification as being of Mexican heritage. First, second, and third generation children of Mexican origin were eligible for the study. Also, the focal child had to be living with his or her biological mother. Either two-parent (82% of the sample) or single-parent (18% of the sample) families were eligible to participate. In two-parent families, the father had to be the child's biological father.

Trained research staff interviewed the participants (child, mother, and, in most cases, father) in their homes. Interviewers were all bilingual and most were of Mexican heritage. They received 2 weeks of training and continuing supervision in the field by the interviewer coordinator. Continuing checks were made to ensure that interviewers complied with a standardized set of interviewing procedures. During the child's tenure in fifth grade, interviewers visited the families on two separate occasions, usually within a 1-week period. Each visit lasted between 2 and 3 hours and each participant was interviewed separately by one of the two interviewers. Every effort was made to ensure that the interviews were conducted so that other family members could not hear the questions or answers for mother, father, or focal child. The mother provided demographic information about the family and household members. Interviews were conducted in Spanish or English based on the preference of each participant.

MEASURES

All measures were available in both Spanish and English for parents and children to complete. The Spanish versions of all measures were translated from English by native Spanish speakers who were members of the project research staff. An independent group of bilingual staff members translated the measures from Spanish to English to ensure that the original meaning of each item was maintained. All measures were evaluated during the fifth grade.

Parent-reported economic pressure. To measure economic pressure, parents independently completed three subscales adapted from the economic hardship measures developed by Conger and colleagues (e.g., Conger & Elder, 1994). Mother and father reports on these subscales were averaged to generate three separate indicators for a latent construct assessing economic pressure. The first subscale is composed of two items concerned with whether the parents felt that they could not "make ends meet" during the past 3 months. The two items specifically asked whether there was enough income to pay monthly bills and if there was any money left over at the end of the month. Higher scores on this scale indicate more difficulty making ends meet. The second subscale measured whether the family could meet its basic material needs related to clothing, a car, a home, furniture and household appliances, food, and medical services. The responses used a four-point Likert-type scale (1 = *not at all true*, 4 = *very true*). The responses were reverse coded such that higher scores indicate a higher degree of unmet material needs. The third subscale queried whether the family had made significant financial cutbacks in many areas, such as food and utilities, because of economic hardship. These responses were dichotomously scored (1 = *yes*, 0 = *no*) and summed to create a subscale. Indicator loadings for the latent construct ranged from 0.763 to 0.856 indicating that the indicators were reliable measures of the latent construct.

Perceived discrimination. This 17-item instrument was used to measure the mother's and father's experiences with and perceptions of discrimination or prejudices against Mexicans/Mexican-Americans in the workplace, neighborhood, and schools (Johnston & Delgado, 2004). Participants responded to a four-point Likert-type scale (1 = *almost never or never*, 4 = *almost always or always*). To derive indicators for the latent construct of discrimination, we randomly assigned each of the 17 items into one of four subscales, or parcels, yielding three four-item parcels and one five-item parcel as indicators of discrimination. Past research (e.g., Kishton & Widaman, 1994; Little, Cunningham, Shahar, & Widaman, 2002) supports parceling items to create indictors for latent variables because it decreases the effect of measurement error and produces indicators with high reliability, which in turn better define the latent variable. A high score on the construct indicates higher levels of discrimination. Factor loadings ranged from 0.58 to 0.84.

Neighborhood risk. The target children and their mothers completed two scales assessing the degree of environmental risk existing in their neighborhoods. One scale contains 10 items adapted from existing measures developed by Aneshensel and Sucoff (1996) and by Bowen and Chapman (1996) indicating how often criminal events (e.g., violent crimes, theft, gang fights, and public uses of alcohol and drugs) occur in the neighborhood. Responses were made on a four-point Likert-type scale (1 = *almost never or never*, 4 = *almost always or always*). Another questionnaire elicits personal evaluations of the attractiveness of the neighborhood using a four-point Likert-type scale (1 = *not at all true*, 4 = *very true*) (Lansing & Marans, 1969). All the items in this scale were reverse coded; correspondingly, higher scores indicated lower neighborhood quality. Sample items explore neighborhood characteristics such as aesthetic appeal, safety, and supportiveness of neighbors. We averaged across mother and child reports on each scale to create two indicators for a latent factor of neighborhood risk. Factor loadings were 0.77 and 0.80. A high score indicates a high risk for criminal activities and low environmental quality in the neighborhood.

Mother and father emotional distress. To measure emotional distress, the short form of the Center for Epidemiologic Studies Depression Scale (CES-D; Radloff, 1977) and the Mini Mood and Anxiety Symptom Questionnaire (MASQ; Clark & Watson, 1995) were completed by each child's mother and father. The short form of the CES-D was developed by Cole, Rabin, Smith, and Kaufman (2004). It contains 10 items designed to measure depressive symptomatology in the general population. The response format is a four-point Likert scale (1 = *almost never or never*, 4 = *almost always or always*). The MASQ includes 90 items related to symptoms of anxiety and mood disorders. The Mini-MASQ is a shortened version that includes 26 items (Casillas & Clark, 2001). In this study, the response categories were modified from the original five-point to a four-point Likert-type scale (1 = *not at all*, 4 = *very much*). For mothers, the alphas were 0.73 and 0.77 for the CES-D and MASQ, respectively, and for fathers they were 0.70 and 0.84. These two scales were used to create a two-indicator latent factor evaluating emotional distress for the mother and a separate factor for the father. Factor loadings ranged from 0.77 to 0.85.

Interparental conflicts. Each parent completed the Behavioral Affect Rating Scale (BARS) that was developed by Conger from diverse sources (see Matthews, Wickrama, & Conger, 1996). The BARS evaluates the expression of warmth and hostility in close relationships (e.g., the marital relationship or parent–child relationship). For this study, items from the two hostility subscales were used to create indicators of interparental hostility. Responses were made using a four-point Likert-type scale (1 = *not at all*, 4 = *very much*). The 13 items assessing the father's hostility toward the mother (reported by the mother) were randomly assigned to four parcels. The 13 items assessing the mother's hostility toward the father (reported by the father) were parceled in the same manner. Four composite parcels of three, three, three, and four items were used as indicators of interparental conflict. The indicators were created by averaging the corresponding parcels from the father's hostility to the mother and the mother's hostility to the father. Factor loadings ranged from 0.67 to 0.83.

Child management. Each parent answered a questionnaire on parenting practices using measures from the Iowa Youth and Families Project (Conger & Elder, 1994). The scores from the subscales for Inductive Reasoning (IR) and Positive Reinforcement (PR) were used for the analysis in this study. Both subscales use a four-point Likert-type response format (1 = *almost never or never*, 4 = *almost always or always*). The IR measures the degree to which parents both care about their their children's opinions and feelings and also explain decisions on family matters that involve the child. The PR subscale (containing three items) measures how often the parent positively reinforces the child's good behaviors in situations such as earning good grades, doing chores, and participating in sports at school. Each parent also completed a questionnaire reporting the degree to which he or she monitored the child in daily life (Small & Kerns, 1993; Small & Luster, 1994). Items from this scale asked whether the parent knew what was going on in most aspects of the child's life, including schoolwork and play activities. The monitoring scale and the two subscales for parenting practices were used to create three indicators for the child management latent variable. Factor loadings ranged from 0.71 to 0.78.

Child's attachment to school. The target child completed a school attachment questionnaire that assessed the child's attachment to school (see Roeser, Lord, & Eccles, 1994) and also attachment to teachers (Armsden & Greenberg, 1987). A sample question representative of this scale is, "you look forward to going to school." All questions were answered using a four-point Likert-type scale (1 = *not at all true*, 4 = *very true*). Three indicators for the school attachment latent construct were created from this measure by randomly assigning items to three parcels, two with seven items and one with six items. Factor loadings ranged from 0.73 to 0.80.

Child's educational expectations. This instrument contains two items investigating the target child's educational aspirations and expectations. These items are, "How far would you like to go in school?" and "How far do you expect to go in school?" The responses ranged from 1 = 8th grade or less to 8 = Ph.D. or professional degree (e.g., law, medicine, dentistry). The sum of these two items was used as the single indicator for the construct.

Child's GPA. The focal child's grade point average (GPA) during the fifth grade was a factor with three indicators: (1) the child's self-report of his or her GPA, (2) the mother's report of the child's GPA, and (3) the father's report of the child's GPA. Factor loadings ranged from 0.53 to 0.71.

Child's conduct problems at school. Both the mother and father reported on the child's conduct problems at school using three questions from the School Performance Scale (Conger & Elder, 1994). These questions tapped the following behaviors occurring in the school environment: (1) nonattendance, (2) fighting and arguing, and (3) suspensions. Responses to these questions were averaged across fathers and mothers and then summed and used as two indicators for the conduct problems factor. Factor loadings were both 0.76.

Analyses

The purpose of this study was to test predictions from the theoretical model (Figure 12.1). This model has four exogenous latent variables (i.e., Mother's Perceived Discrimination, Father's Perceived Discrimination, Parental Economic Pressure, and Neighborhood Risk) that were hypothesized to act as external stressors. The model also has five mediating variables: two primary mediators (Mother's Emotional Distress and Father's Emotional Distress), one secondary mediator (Interparental Conflicts), and two tertiary mediators (Mother's Child Management and Father's Child Management). The four outcome variables of interest were Attachment to School, Educational Expectation, GPA, and School Conduct Problems. These outcome variables assessed child adaptation to school.

Model estimation. Variations of this model were fit to the data using structural equation modeling (SEM) with Mplus 5.21 (Muthén & Muthén, 2007). First, a fully saturated model was established as a baseline model in which all factors within a column (e.g., exogenous stress variables, tertiary mediators) were regressed on all preceding factors in the model. Next, nonsignificant paths (direct effects) were eliminated in ordered processes of four phases, described as follows. In phase one, all nonsignificant paths from the tertiary mediators to the child outcomes were eliminated (e.g., Father's Child Management to GPA). Next, all nonsignificant paths from the secondary mediator to the child outcomes were eliminated. Then, all nonsignificant paths from the primary mediators to the child outcomes were eliminated. Finally (for this, the first phase), all nonsignificant paths from the exogenous variables to the child outcomes were eliminated. In phase two, nonsignificant paths from the secondary mediator to the tertiary mediators were eliminated (none). Then, all nonsignificant paths from the primary mediators to the secondary mediator were eliminated. Finally, all nonsignificant paths from the exogenous variables to the primary mediators were eliminated, completing phase two. This process was repeated for the secondary mediator (phase three) and the primary mediators (phase four). For all these model estimations, factors within each column were allowed to correlate freely.

Model fit indexes. For our analyses, we used the chi-square statistic associated with full information maximum likelihood (FIML) estimation to account for missing data, which are present in almost all longitudinal studies. FIML estimation uses all available information in the moment matrix to estimate model parameters even when some data are missing (Enders, 2001). Previous research shows that FIML provides a more accurate estimate of model parameters than ad hoc procedures such as listwise or pairwise deletion (Enders, 2001). Several standard fit indices were used to evaluate competing, or nested, models, all of which are based on the chi-square statistic. Because the chi-square value is sensitive to sample size, three alternative fit indexes are also reported. The root mean square error of approximation (RMSEA) indicates close fit when values are less than 0.05 and reasonable fit when values are between 0.05 and 0.08 (Browne & Cudeck, 1993). The other two indexes are the Tucker–Lewis index (TLI; Tucker & Lewis, 1973) and the comparative fit index (CFI; Bentler, 1990), both indicating acceptable fit for values above 0.90.

RESULTS

Correlations

Table 12.1 provides the correlations among the variables used in the structural equation models (SEMs). As expected, most of the exogenous stress variables predicted parent emotional distress. For example, economic pressure was positively and significantly correlated with both mother (0.31) and father (0.36) emotional distress. Also, as expected, mother and father emotional distress were positively related to interparental conflicts. In turn, conflicts between parents were negatively related to child management skills for both parents. Mothers' child management skills were positively related to three school outcomes (attachment to school, educational expectations, and GPA) but they did not predict school conduct problems. On the other hand, fathers' parenting behaviors predicted all of the child outcome variables except for educational expectations. In general, then, the correlations among study constructs were consistent with predictions from the theoretical model (Figure 12.1). These findings suggested the usefulness of more formal and comprehensive tests of the theoretical model.

Test of the Theoretical Model

The model estimation steps described earlier produced the final model provided in Figure 12.2. In this model, only statistically significant direct effects (standardized regression coefficients) for the predicted paths from one variable to another are presented; however, both significant (solid lines) and nonsignificant (dotted lines) associations are shown. The fit of this final model was acceptable with a $\chi^2(563, N = 548) = 758.34$, $p < 0.001$; CFI = 0.966; TLI = 0.962; and RMSEA = 0.025. With some important exceptions, the results were generally supportive of predictions from the theoretical model.

First, both perceived discrimination and economic pressure were associated with higher levels of emotional distress for both mothers and fathers. For example, the standardized regression weight from father's perceived discrimination to father's emotional distress was 0.43 and statistically significant. Despite the fact that neighborhood risk was positively correlated with emotional distress for mothers (see Table 12.1), this path was not significant in the final model, suggesting that the earlier correlation was produced by the significant association between neighborhood risk and the other exogenous variables in the model. Also consistent with expectations, both mothers' and fathers' emotional distress predicted interparental conflicts. The results were also supportive of the prediction that the exogenous stress variables would be related only indirectly to interparental conflicts through the emotional distress variables. That is, there were no significant direct paths from the stress variables to interparental conflict even though two of the stressors (the mother's perceived discrimination and economic pressure) were significantly correlated with interparental conflict (see Table 12.1). These results

Table 12.1 Correlations among Factors Used in SEM Path Analysis

Factor	1	2	3	4	5	6	7	8	9	10	11	12
1. Perceived Discrimination (M)												
2. Perceived Discrimination (F)	0.132*											
3. Economic Pressure (M, F)	0.186*	0.217*										
4. Neighborhood Risk	0.270*	0.061	0.179*									
5. Emotional Distress (M)	0.351*	0.113	0.310*	0.217*								
6. Emotional Distress (F)	0.035	0.498*	0.364*	0.125	0.201*							
7. Interparental Conflicts (M, F)	0.125*	0.058	0.130*	0.109	0.377*	0.323*						
8. Child Management (M)	0.029	−0.140*	−0.081	−0.147*	−0.143*	−0.276*	−0.275*					
9. Child Management (F)	−0.089	−0.111	−0.130*	−0.215*	−0.211*	−0.153*	−0.449*	0.692*				
10. Attachment to School (C)	−0.054	−0.133*	−0.164*	−0.246*	0.008	−0.058	−0.126*	0.442*	0.449*			
11. Educational Expectation (C)	0.044	−0.076	−0.168*	−0.032	−0.035	−0.181*	−0.060	0.274*	0.091	0.199*		
12. Grade Point Average (GPA) (C)	−0.074	−0.188*	−0.134	−0.112	−0.174*	−0.266*	−0.109	0.430*	0.360*	0.301*	0.249*	
13. School Conduct Problems (C)	0.097	0.062	0.190*	0.260*	0.136*	0.212*	0.118	−0.114	−0.176*	−0.186*	−0.151*	−0.477*

NOTE: M = Mother, F = Father, and C = Child.

*Indicates correlation is significant: $p < 0.05$, z-test, two-tail.

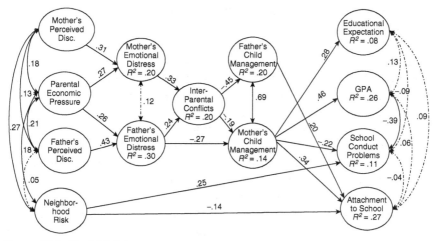

Figure 12.2. Final Model.

are consistent with a mediated process from external stressors to interparental conflict through emotional distress as proposed in the theoretical model.

Also important, the association between emotional distress and child management was mediated through interparental conflict. For example, the zero-order correlation between mothers' emotional distress and mothers' child management was negative and statistically significant (see Table 12.1); however, this association was not statistically significant in the SEM, consistent with the mediating hypothesis in the theoretical model. The same pattern of findings occurred for fathers' distress and parenting behavior. Interestingly and unexpected, fathers' emotional distress directly predicted mothers' child management in the SEM. Fathers' distress may act as a significant stressor for the mother and disrupt her parenting behavior in a fashion similar to interparental conflicts. Also as predicted by the theoretical model, with a single exception, only child management skills directly predicted child developmental outcomes. Mothers' parenting was positively associated with GPA, educational expectations, and attachment to school and negatively related to school conduct problems. The last finding is especially interesting because mothers' child-rearing style did not demonstrate a significant zero-order association with conduct problems (see Table 12.1). But with all variables in the final model, this direct association came through.

Also interesting, fathers' child management was positively associated with attachment to school but not with any of the other child outcome variables. Although there were several significant zero-order associations between father management and child outcomes (see Table 12.1), some of these were not statistically significant in the SEM. As shown in Figure 12.2, mother and father parenting behaviors are highly interrelated ($r = 0.69$). Perhaps fathers and mothers encourage similar and effective management skills by one another, but it is the mother's behavior that has the most direct impact on child adaptation. This result may be true because of cultural values that give mothers greater responsibility for child rearing and fathers greater responsibility for providing a family income (see Parke & Buriel, 2007). Whatever the reason for the finding, it is clear that mothers and fathers appear to promote one another's positive managerial skills.

Finally, the SEM showed *direct* associations between neighborhood risk and two of the child outcome variables that were not predicted by the theoretical model. Children living in more dangerous neighborhoods were more likely to demonstrate conduct problems in school and were less likely to become attached to school. We suspect that these results may be the product of peer effects. That is, neighborhoods with higher rates of criminal activity likely have higher rates of delinquent behavior by adolescents as well (see Vega & Gil, 1999). These peer associations would make it more likely that an emerging adolescent in such a neighborhood would be exposed to delinquent peers and even encouraged by such peers to engage in risky behaviors both inside and outside of school. Cutting school and suspensions related to school misbehavior could be the final product of these types of social influences. With these results in mind, we turn to some final observations.

CONCLUDING COMMENTS

We began this report by noting the fact that minority youth are rapidly becoming a larger and larger proportion of the U.S. population. We also reviewed findings indicating that many minority youth are at above average risk for experiencing significant difficulties in their development, including school drop-out and emotional and behavioral problems. These signs of maladjustment often begin during childhood, carry over into the adolescent years, and can have long-term negative consequences during the transition to adulthood (Martin et al., 2010). For these reasons there is great interest in processes or mechanisms in place as children emerge into adolescence that either increase the risk of or promote resilience to developmental problems during the adolescent years. If we can find pathways toward resilience in the early development of minority youth, despite their frequent exposure to environmental risks, then these findings can be used to develop prevention programs to facilitate the development of competencies during adolescence and to increase the likelihood of a successful transition to adulthood.

Consistent with these ideas, we evaluated data from a study of over 500 emerging adolescents of Mexican origin who are participants in the CFP. Based on a culturally informed extension of the family stress model, we predicted that parents who maintain good child management practices, despite exposure to environmental adversities, will have children who demonstrate greater resilience and more positive adaptation during this challenging developmental period. The findings generally were consistent with theoretical predictions. As reported in earlier studies (e.g., Conger et al., 2002), economic pressure experienced by parents predicted greater emotional distress for both fathers and mothers. Emotional distress, in turn, was associated with greater conflicts between parents, which, in turn, were related to less effective parenting behaviors. As predicted, when good child management skills were maintained even in the face of these family stress processes, children were more likely to do well in terms of school performance, attachments to school, and expectations regarding future educational pursuits. They were also less likely to demonstrate conduct problems at school. Interestingly, maternal behaviors had the greatest direct relationship to child developmental outcomes, suggesting that their greater role in the lives of children might account for the differential influence of mothers and fathers.

Particularly important, these findings not only provided support for the family stress model, but they also pointed to important extensions of the model that appear to be especially salient for minority children and their families. For example, parents' experiences of ethnic discrimination were even more powerful predictors of emotional distress than economic pressure (Figure 12.2). Moreover, the stress of living in a dangerous and unsupportive neighborhood, a situation too often experienced by Latinos (Vega & Gil, 1999), had a direct relationship with child functioning rather than the indirect pathway through parent emotions and behaviors proposed by the family stress model. This latter result suggests that the family stress model is incomplete in terms of being an adequate depiction of the influence of exposure to stress for ethnic minority families. We suspect that exposure to deviant peers in risky neighborhoods provides an alternative avenue through which economic hardship affects the lives of minority children. That is, families live in more risky neighborhoods when they are financially disadvantaged and these economic problems appear to affect emerging adolescents not only through disruptions in family functioning, as proposed by the family stress model, but also through the quality of the neighborhood environment, a process not captured by the model. These issues are worthy of future research.

Despite the interesting findings reported here, this research has significant limitations. Most important is the fact that it represents a cross-section in time, and we cannot be certain that the temporal ordering of the variables is consistent with predictions from the theoretical model. We can conclude that the results do not reject significant portions of the model, but we cannot make causal inferences regarding proposed pathways of influence in the model. Nevertheless, the results provide important hypotheses for the next steps in research on the resilience and vulnerabilities of minority adolescents and their passage to the adult years.

With regard to this ongoing study of children of Mexican origin and their families, we plan to follow the focal youth from emerging adolescence to their transition into adulthood. An evaluation of their development during this period of time will allow us to test in a rigorous fashion the degree to which the family stress processes investigated here will have a deleterious influence on various dimensions of competence and maladjustment into the adult years. Of special interest is the expectation that effective parenting practices will help to blunt the negative effects of the multiple adversities these youths often face and thus provide an important mechanism for promoting resilience in the face of significant environmental challenges (see Conger et al., 2010; Masten, 2001).

In addition to the social influences of parents and others who help to promote resilience, Masten (2001) notes that a small set of individual characteristics has repeatedly been related to demonstrations of resilience. These psychological qualities include "cognitive and self-regulation skills, positive views of self, and motivation to be effective in the environment" (p. 234). In the next stages of this research we will study the influences of these individual dispositions and attributes on the ability to overcome environmental difficulties. Perhaps most important, the next stages of the research will also examine individual differences in neurobiological changes, such as development of the prefrontal cortex, that increasingly have been implicated in the tendency of adolescents either to demonstrate sound judgment or to engage in excessively risky behaviors (Albert & Steinberg, 2011; Casey, Jones, & Somerville, 2011). We expect that individual differences in neurobiology will interact with social influences to affect the markers of adolescent competency and maladjustment considered in the current report.

In general, this program of work draws heavily on a transactional or interactionist view of life course development (Burt et al., 2008; Conger et al., 2010; Martin et al., 2010; Schofield et al., 2011). That is, we expect that environmental adversities will tend to exacerbate adolescent maladjustment and impair the development of social and academic competencies. At the same time, however, positive parenting and specific attributes of these youth should help to promote traits and abilities that will foster the successful completion of adolescence and entry into adulthood. These expectations are consistent with findings reported by Schofield and his colleagues (2011). These investigators reported findings for a cohort of over 500 early adolescents who were followed for almost 20 years. The results of their study showed that parent support promoted personality traits that helped to overcome early adolescent adversities and assisted with the successful entry into adult roles of worker, spouse, and parent. In the coming years we will evaluate the degree to which these same dimensions of resilience will be apparent for the focal youth in the California Families Project.

To summarize, the findings from this investigation to date suggest that Mexican-American parents suffer both emotionally and behaviorally when exposed both to economic hardships and to discrimination within the larger society. Even under these conditions, however, their children will likely be more successful if they can maintain effective parenting practices. Prevention programs designed to promote the resilience of Mexican-origin adolescents would do well to focus attention on a number of points in this process, from the economic fortunes of the family to the child-rearing skills of parents. If these findings are replicated in future research, however, successful prevention will need to deal with issues outside the family as well, including giving adolescents better tools and resources for dealing with risky neighborhood environments. Future research needs to test the theoretical ideas evaluated here both through experimental preventive interventions and through community epidemiological studies conducted across time.

ACKNOWLEDGMENTS

Support for this work was provided by funding from the National Institute of Child Health and Human Development, the National Institute on Drug Abuse, the National Institute of Alcohol Abuse and Alcoholism and the National Institute of Mental Health (DAO17902, HD047573, HD051746, and MH051361).

References

Albert, D., & Steinberg, L. (2011). Judgment and decision making in adolescence. *Journal of Research on Adolescence, 21,* 211–244.

Amaro, H., Russo, N. F., & Johnson, J. (1987). Family and work predictors of psychological well-being among Hispanic women professionals. *Psychology of Women Quarterly, 11,* 505–521.

Anashensel, C. S., & Sucoff, C. A. (1996). The neighborhood context of adolescent mental health. *Journal of Health and Social Behavior, 37,* 293–310.

Armsden, G. C., & Greenberg, M. T. (1987). The inventory of parent and peer attachment: individual differences and their relationship to psychological well-being in adolescence. *Journal of Youth and Adolescence, 16,* 427–454.

Baca Zinn, M., & Wells, B. (2000). Diversity within Latino families: New lessons for family social science. In D. H. Demo & K. R. Allen (Eds.), *Handbook of family diversity* (pp. 252–273). London: Oxford University Press.

Bentler, P. M. (1990). Comparative fit indexes in structural models. *Psychological Bulletin, 107,* 238–246.

Bowen, G. L., & Chapman, M. V. (1996). Poverty, neighborhood danger, social support, and the individual adaptation among at-risk youth in urban areas. *Journal of Family Issues, 17,* 641–666.

Brody, G. H., McBride Murry, V., Kim, S., & Brown, A. C. (2002). Longitudinal pathways to competence and psychological adjustment among African American children living in rural single-parent households. *Child Development, 73,* 1505–1516.

Browne, M. W., & Cudeck, R. (1993). Alternative ways of assessing model fit. In K. A. Bollen & J. S. Long (Eds.), *Testing structural equation models* (pp. 136–162). Newbury Park, CA: Sage.

Burt, K. B., Obradovic, J., Long, J. D., & Masten, A. S. (2008). The interplay of social competence and psychopathology over 20 years: Testing transactional and cascade models. *Child Development, 79,* 359–374.

Burton, L. M., & Jarrett, R. L. (2000). In the mix, yet on the margins: The place of families in urban neighborhood and child development research. *Journal of Marriage & the Family, 62,* 1114–1135.

Casey, B. J., Jones, R. M., & Somerville, L. H. (2011). Braking and accelerating the adolescent brain. *Journal of Research on Adolescence, 21,* 21–33.

Casillas, A., & Clark, L. A. (2001). *The mini-mood and anxiety symptom questionnaire (Mini-MASQ).* Poster presented at the 72nd Annual Meeting of the Midwestern Psychological Association, Chicago, IL.

Cauce, A. M., Cruz, R., Corona, M., & Conger, R. D. (2011). The face of the future: Risk and resilience in minority youth. In G. Carlo, L. Crockett, & M. Carranza

(Eds.), *Ethnicity and youth health disparities* (pp. 13–32). Nebraska Symposium on Motivation, Vol. 58. Lincoln, NE: University of Nebraska Press.

Cicchetti, D. (1999). A developmental psychopathology perspective on drug abuse. In M. D. Glantz and C. R. Hartel (Eds.), *Drug abuse: Origins and intervention* (pp. 97–118). Washington, DC: American Psychological Association.

Clark, L. A., & Watson, D. (1995). *The Mini Mood and Anxiety Symptom Questionnaire (Mini-MASQ)*. Unpublished manuscript, University of Iowa, Iowa City.

Cole, J. C., Rabin, A. S., Smith, T. L., & Kaufman, A. S. (2004). Development and validation of a Rasch-derived CES-D short form. *Psychological Assessment, 16,* 360–372.

Conger, R. D. (1997). The social context of substance abuse: A developmental perspective. In E. B. Robertson, Z. Sloboda, G. M. Boyd, L. Beatty, & N. J. Kozel (Eds.), *Rural substance abuse: State of knowledge and issues* (Research Monograph No. 168, NIH Publication No. 97-4177, pp. 6–36). Washington, DC: National Institute on Drug Abuse.

Conger, R. D., & Conger, K. J. (2002). Resilience in Midwestern families: Selected findings from the first decade of a prospective, longitudinal study. *Journal of Marriage and Family, 64,* 361–373.

Conger, R. D., Conger, K. J., & Martin, M. J. (2010). Socioeconomic status, family processes, and individual development. *Journal of Marriage and Family, 72,* 685–704.

Conger, R. D., & Donnellan, M. B. (2007). An interactionist perspective on the socioeconomic context of human development. *Annual Review of Psychology, 58,* 175–199.

Conger, R. D., Ebert-Wallace, L., Sun, Y., Simons, R. L., McLoyd, V. C., & Brody, G. H. (2002). Economic pressure in African American families: A replication and extension of the Family Stress Model. *Developmental Psychology, 38,* 179–193.

Conger, R. D., & Elder, G. H. Jr. (1994). *Families in troubled times: Adapting to change in rural America*. Hawthorne, NY: Aldine de Gruyter.

Conger, R. D., Patterson, G. R., & Ge, X. (1995). It takes two to replicate: A mediational model for the impact of parents' stress on adolescent adjustment. *Child Development, 66,* 80–97.

Cummings, E. M., Goeke-Morey, M. C., & Dukewich, T. L. (2001). The study of relations between marital conflict and child adjustment: Challenges and new directions for methodology. In J. H. Grych & F. D. Fincham (Eds.), *Interparental conflict and child development: Theory, research, and applications* (pp. 39–63). New York: Cambridge University Press.

Enders, C. K. (2001). A primer on maximum likelihood algorithms available for use with missing data. *Structural Equation Modeling, 8,* 128–141.

Feldman, B. J., Conger, R. D., & Burzette, R. G. (2004). Traumatic events, psychiatric disorders, and pathways of risk and resilience during the transition to adulthood. *Research in Human Development, 1,* 259–290.

Finch, B. K., Kolody, B., & Vega, W. A. (2000). Perceived discrimination and depression among Mexican-origin adults in California. *Journal of Health and Social Behavior, 41,* 295–313.

Fincham, F. D. (1998). Child development and marital relations. *Child Development, 69,* 543–574.

Ge, X., Lorenz, F. O., Conger, R. D., & Elder, G. H. (1994). Trajectories of stressful life events and depressive symptoms during adolescence. *Developmental Psychology, 30,* 467–483.

Glantz, M. D., & Leshner, A. I. (2000). Drug abuse and developmental psychopathology. *Development & Psychopathology, 12,* 795–814.

Gonzales, N. A., Pitts, S. C., Hill, N. E., & Roosa, M. W. (2000). A mediational model of the impact of interparental conflict on child adjustment in a mutiethnic, low-income sample. *Journal of Family Psychology, 14,* 365–379.

Harold, G. T., & Conger, R. D. (1997). Marital conflict and adolescent distress: The role of adolescent awareness. *Child Development, 68,* 333–350.

Hauser, S. T. (1999). Understanding resilient outcomes: Adolescent lives across time and generations. *Journal of Research on Adolescence, 9,* 1–24.

Johnston, K. E., & Delgado, M.Y. (2004). Mexican American adolescents' experiences with ethnic discrimination. Poster presented at the Biennial Conference of the Society for Research on Adolescence, Baltimore, MD.

Kishton, J. M., & Widaman, K. F. (1994). Unidimensional versus domain representative parceling of questionnaire items: An empirical example. *Educational and Psychological Measurement, 54,* 757–765.

Lansing, J. B., & Marans, R. W. (1969). Evaluation of neighborhood quality. *Journal of the American Planning Association, 35,* 195.

Laub, J. H., & Sampson, R. J. (2003). *Shared beginnings, divergent lives: Delinquent boys to age 70.* Cambridge, MA: Harvard University Press.

Little, T. D., Cunningham, W. A., Shahar, G., & Widaman, K. F. (2002). To parcel or not to parcel: Exploring the question, weighing the merits. *Structural Equation Modeling, 9,* 151–173.

Luthar, S. S. (Ed.) (2003). *Resilience and vulnerability: Adaptation in the context of childhood adversities.* New York: Cambridge University Press.

Martin, M. J., Conger, R. D., Schofield, T. J., Dogan, S. J., Widaman, K. F., Donnellan, M. B., & Neppl, T. K. (2010). Evaluation of the interactionist model of socioeconomic status and problem behavior: A developmental cascade across generations. *Development and Psychopathology, 22,* 697–715.

Masten, A. S. (2001). Ordinary magic: Resilience processes in development. *American Psychologist, 56,* 227–238.

Masten, A. S., Roisman, G. I., Long, J. D., Burt, K. B., Obradović, J., Riley, J. R., Boelcke-Stennes, K., & Tellegen, A. (2005). Developmental cascades: Linking academic achievement and externalizing and internalizing symptoms over 20 years. *Developmental Psychology, 41,* 733–746.

Matthews, L. S., Wickrama, K. A. S., & Conger, R. D. (1996). Predicting marital instability from spouse and observer reports of marital interaction. *Journal of Marriage and the Family, 58,* 641–655.

McLoyd, V. C., Cauce, A. M., Takeuchi, D., & Wilson, L. (2000). Marital processes and parental socialization in families of color: A decade review of research. *Journal of Marriage & the Family, 62,* 1070–1093.

Muthén, L. K., & Muthén, B. O. (2007). *Mplus user's guide* (5th ed.). Los Angeles: Muthén & Muthén.

Parke, R. D., & Buriel, R. (2007). Socialization in the family: Ethnic and ecological perspectives. In W. Damon & R. M. Lerner (Eds.), *Handbook of child psychology* (6th ed.). New York: Wiley.

Parke, R. D., Coltrane, S., Duffy, S., Buriel, R., Dennis, J., Powers, J., et al. (2004). Economic stress, parenting, and child adjustment in Mexican American and European American families. *Child Development, 75,* 1632–1656.

Portes, A., & Rumbaut, R. G. (2001). *Legacies: The story of the immigrant second genera-tion.* Berkeley, CA: University of California Press.

Radloff, L. S. (1977). The CES-D Scale: A self-report depression scale for research in the general population. *Applied Psychological Measurement, 1,* 385–401.

Roeser, R. W., Lord S. E., & Eccles, J. (1994). A portrait of academic alienation in ado-lescence: Motivation, mental health, and family experience. Paper presented at the Biennial Meeting of the Society for Research on Adolescence, San Diego, CA.

Salgado de Snyder, V. N. (1987). Factors associated with acculturative stress and depres-sive symptomatology among married Mexican immigrant women. *Psychology of Women Quarterly, 11,* 475–488.

Scaramella, L. V., Conger, R. D., & Simons, R. L. (1999). Parental protective influences and gender-specific increases in adolescent internalizing and externalizing problems. *Journal of Research on Adolescence, 9,* 111–141.

Schofield, T. J., Martin, M. J., Conger, R. D., Neppl, T. M., Donnellan, M. B., & Conger, K. J. (2011). Intergenerational transmission of adaptive functioning: A test of the inter-actionist model of SES and human development. *Child Development, 82,* 33–47.

Sloboda, Z. (1999). The prevention of drug abuse: Interrupting the paths. In M. D. Glantz & C. R. Hartel (Eds.), *Drug abuse: Origins & Interventions* (pp. 223–242). Washington, DC: American Psychological Association.

Small, S. A., & Kerns, D. (1993). Unwanted sexual activity among peers during early and middle adolescence: Incidence and risk factors. *Journal of Marriage and the Family, 55,* 941–952.

Small, S. A., & Luster, T. (1994). Adolescent sexual activity: An ecological, risk-factor approach. *Journal of Marriage and the Family, 56,* 181–192.

Statistics Netherlands. (2009). Blaise for windows (Version 4.81) [Computer Software]. Heerlen, Netherlands: Blaise Department. (2002). *Journal of Abnormal Psychology, 30,* 373–386.

Tucker, L. R., & Lewis, C. (1973). A reliability coefficient for maximum likelihood factor analysis. *Psychometrika, 38,* 1–10.

U.S. Census Bureau. (2000). Census of Population and Housing, Profiles of General Demographic Characteristics. No. 36. Cities with 250,000 or More Inhabitants in 2000-Hispanic and Non-Hispanic Groups. Washington, DC.

U.S. Census Bureau. (2010). Current population survey, 2010 annual social and eco-nomic supplement. Washington, DC.

Vega, W. A., & Gil, A. G. (1999). A model for explaining drug use behavior among Hispanic adolescents. *Drugs & Society, 14,* 57–74.

Vega, W. A., Kolodny, B., Aguilar-Gaxiola, S., Alderete, E., Catalano, R., & Caraveo-Anduaga, J. (1998). Lifetime prevalence of DSM-III-R psychiatric disorders among urban and rural Mexican Americans in California. *Archives of General Psychiatry, 55,* 771–778.

13

Psychiatric Hospitalization

The Utility of Using Archival Records to Understand the Lives of Adolescent Patients

KARIN M. BEST AND STUART T. HAUSER

INTRODUCTION

This chapter illustrates the value of thinking anew about existing and easily accessible archival data. Mining archival hospital records and two decades of prospectively collected data provided the opportunity to demonstrate the utility of methods to condense and quantify essential information in archival records as well as address important questions. We highlight the methodological challenges and potential benefits of examining archival psychiatric records to collect valuable information about the individual and family context of hospitalization and to illuminate the processes that shape short- and long-term adaptation following psychiatric hospitalization. We present the system we used to evaluate the feasibility of employing archival psychiatric records to capture important differences among patients, describe the "life chart" technique used to distill the voluminous information, and demonstrate that a measure created for use with contemporaneous data can be reliably and validly used with archival materials to address important and substantive questions about the precursors and sequelae of adolescent psychiatric hospitalization.

THE ADOLESCENT AND FAMILY DEVELOPMENT PROJECT

The Adolescent and Family Development Project (AFDP; Hauser, 1991), an ongoing 30-year longitudinal study of individual development, included a unique sample that provided the opportunity to explore relations among psychiatric hospitalization, parent–adolescent interaction, and lifespan development. The study has been continuously approved by applicable institutional review boards. AFDP was originally designed to explore family influences on ego development, a construct involving cognitive complexity, interpersonal style, current concerns, and impulse control (Hauser, 1976, 1993; Loevinger & Wessler, 1970; Loevinger, Wessler, & Redmore, 1970). To maximize variance in ego development across the sample, approximately half of the AFDP participants ($N = 70$) were recruited after admission to a psychiatric treatment facility and the remainder ($N = 76$) were recruited as freshmen at a public high school. As expected, the ego development scores of adolescents recruited at the hospital, on average, were lower than those recruited at the high school. The hospitalized participants did not differ from their high school counterparts in gender, age, or family composition. Because the recruitment site was unrelated to the original research questions of the AFDP, little information related to the context or course of hospitalization, such as symptoms, diagnosis, psychiatric history, or treatment course, was originally collected. Statistical analyses were completed either with the recruitment site as a control variable or within each recruitment group, in each case equating hospitalized adolescents with one another.

As the project matured, first as the Young Adult Development Project (YADP) when the participants reached age 25, then as the Across Generations Project (AGP) as they moved through their 30s (participants continue to be followed in the twenty-first century, as part of an expanded sample, with a focus on mid-life health behaviors), some differences between the participant groups emerged. Although in general participants have remained loyal to the study—97% of those living participated in AGP—all deaths ($N = 4$) and those who did not participate through the twentieth century were from the psychiatric facility. On average, participants recruited at the treatment facility completed less school, married younger, and had children earlier and more often than the high school sample. These differences, coupled with our long-standing interest in individual development and successful adaptation (Best, Hauser, & Allen, 1997; Masten, Best, & Garmezy, 1990), provided the impetus for a more detailed study of the lives of the psychiatric group participants. The study's aim was to identify the factors and processes that contributed to differences in their adaptation over time.

In developing the theoretical framework for our research, we had to confront the fact that little is understood about the complex longitudinal relations among parent–adolescent interactions, individual strengths and weaknesses, family stressors, adolescent psychiatric hospitalization, and adult adaptation. Research on parent–adolescent interactions most often has focused on linkages to concurrent, contiguous, or short-term longitudinal adolescent personality development, symptomatology, or behavior (e.g., Hauser, 1991; Ge, Best, Conger, & Simons, 1996). Studies of adolescent psychiatric disorder commonly focus on symptomatology and lack consideration of the rich family and individual context of youths' difficulties (e.g., Hankin, Abramson, Moffit, Silva, McGee, & Angell, 1998; Lewinsohn, Gotlib, Lewinsohn, Seeley, & Allen, 1998). Furthermore, studies of adolescent psychiatric hospitalization commonly focus on treatment outcome, are retrospective rather than prospective, study relatively short time frames, have high attrition, and lack observations of parent–adolescent interaction (e.g., Crespi & Ivey, 1987; Pfeiffer & Strzelecki, 1990; Wrate, Rothery, McCabe, Aspin, & Bryce, 1994). Recently, research on adolescent inpatient treatment has included a focus on the health benefits and cost of such treatment (Green et al., 2007). Finally, longitudinal studies of adolescent adaptation and competence have most often focused on risks arising from economic challenges or parent marital status rather than on the adolescent's psychiatric history (Conger, Conger, Elder, Lorenz, Simons, & Whitbeck, 1993; Masten, Coatsworth, Neeman, Gest, & Hubbard, 1995). A promising strategy for unraveling differences in the adaptation of the former psychiatric patients in this sample is linking information collected at the time of hospitalization, just before the adolescents joined the study, with the subsequent prospectively gathered parent–adolescent interaction and individual development data.

To this end, the present study focuses on four questions: (1) Can archival clinical chart data be reliably and validly distilled into a form ("life chart") amenable to research purposes? (2) Can a standardized rating scale developed for use with contemporaneous clinical data be reliably applied to archival hospital records? (3) Does information gleaned from the archival chart records help differentiate among hospitalized adolescents and help us to understand adolescent and adolescent-to-adult development? (4) Can the information contained in archival hospital charts enrich our understanding of adolescent development?

THE PRESENT STUDY

Participants

The psychiatric subgroup of the original AFDP study consisted of consecutive adolescent admissions to traditional treatment units at a university-affiliated psychiatric teaching hospital. Exclusionary criteria included psychosis, mental retardation, and psychiatric difficulties that were secondary to physical illness. At least one parent or guardian had to agree to participate in order for the adolescent to enroll. Thirty-nine male and 31 female adolescents joined the study between 1978 and 1980. When initially hospitalized, they ranged in age from 11 years, 9 months, to 16 years (Mean = 14 years, SD = 1 year). Length of hospital stay ranged from 37 to 921 days (Mean = 192, SD = 198). Participants were assessed annually for 3 years in their teens (AFDP), again at approximately age 25 (YADP), and continued to be assessed at multiple time points as they moved through their 30s (AGP) and into their 40s (PATHS Over Time and Across Generations). Ninety-eight percent of living AFDP participants cooperated with the YADP data collection and 97% of living AFDP participants participated in the AGP.

Methods of Data Collection: Innovative Strategies for Chart Review

Before work could begin, it was essential to establish the feasibility of using charts to extract the data of interest. Although project staff previously had reviewed charts for very limited purposes (e.g., to assign retrospective psychiatric diagnoses and for case studies), no one had explored the breadth or depth of the chart contents. Thus, the first phase of the project was a systematic chart audit to assess the comparability and consistency of the content across charts. Because of the sensitive nature of hospital records, the initial review was conducted by the first author, a clinical psychologist, in the hospital archives.

The review was labor-intensive. Because the original records were created for clinical documentation rather than research, the review was considerably more complex than the typical process of assessing archival research data (see Elder, Pavalko, & Clipp, 1993, for a helpful guide). When reviewing the research archives of others, we assess the usefulness of data available and how they might be recast to answer new questions (Brooks-Gunn, Phelps, & Elder, 1991). In typical archival research, to a greater or lesser extent, a standard set of data exists for each subject, missing data are clear, and the research method and framing hypotheses for the original study are documented. In contrast, the hospital charts used in the present research and typically available from clinical settings varied tremendously in length (roughly corresponding to the different durations of participants' hospital stays). Although hospital and accreditation requirements dictated the completion of certain reports, the content and quality of these reports varied widely by clinician and supervisor. In addition, chart contents evolved over the 2-year recruitment period to include relatively more descriptions of specific behaviors. This change occurred with transition from the theoretically derived *Diagnostic and Statistical Manual (DSM)-II* to the more empirically based *DSM-III* and likely reflect the fundamental shift in diagnostic process associated with the change in diagnostic criteria. Finally, the theoretical framework of reports varied; although mostly psychodynamic (not surprising as this was the predominant approach employed in most psychiatric facilities in the 1970s), the lens through which a given case was conceptualized was sometimes a family systems or biological one.

Several strengths counterbalanced such inconsistencies in the archival material. Notes and reports were quite detailed, as is typical of the documentation at a teaching hospital associated with a major university medical school. Charts included some standardized forms, including assessment of suicidal risk and drug use. The information was collected at the time of hospitalization with no knowledge that the patient was being recruited into a research study or would be followed for over 30 years. In addition, multiple reporters provided information: standard data included adolescent, parent, and clinician self-report as well as adolescent and parent report filtered through the professional training and experience of case coordinators, nurses, psychologists, psychiatrists, and social workers.

Because of the difficulty in sorting through hundreds of pages of data, the senior author placed special emphasis on identifying a promising "core" of structured and semistructured data that were present in almost all records. The review proceeded sequentially. First, four cases were read in their entirety. Next, additional samples of randomly selected sets of four to six charts were read closely. Finally, after approximately half the charts had been reviewed closely, a preliminary *core set* of documents was designated and the contents organized into conceptually relevant subgroups (e.g., admission information and hospital course, testing, and neurological and pharmacological evaluations); the final core set was based on review of all charts. Reports and forms selected from the chart archive provided succinct, pertinent, and detailed information. The final document set included (but was not limited to) admission and discharge summaries, testing reports, physical examination reports, family social work histories, and adolescent reports to clinicians of drug and alcohol use. In addition, when idiosyncratic materials, such as nursing notes, provided highly salient information that was not included in the core data, they were included. Each hospital chart was reviewed a second time to complete the assembly of the contents and confirm the absence of missing data. To maintain confidentiality, the first author duplicated pertinent documents and removed identifying information from the documents before the research archive was transported from the treatment facility to locked storage in the research laboratory. Documents were redacted to remove surnames and distinctive first names. Each document was reviewed three times to ascertain that the names had been obliterated and that all copies were identified only by research number.

Measures

LIFE CHART CODING OF HOSPITALIZATION CONTEXT

A life chart format similar to that refined by Masten and colleagues (Gest, Reed, & Masten, 1999; Reed, 1997) was used to track the occurrence and timing of stressful and unusual events and symptoms in the lives of participants. Events were recorded by hand in spreadsheet format by two raters who independently recorded the presence and duration of 10 categories of events from birth up to hospital admission. Events were recorded in 6-month blocks of time. The categories included both discrete and chronic events: Parental Figure Changes (e.g., separation, divorce, remarriage), Parental Figure Events (e.g., discord, unemployment, illness), Sibling Events (e.g., birth, illness), Loss Events (e.g., deaths of significant figures and pets), Extraordinary Events (e.g., fire, accident, abuse), Precipitous Events (e.g., physical illness, arrests), Symptoms (e.g., drug use, truancy, diagnoses), Treatment History, School Changes and Family Moves (e.g., grade retention, special classes), and Other (adopted, etc.). All events reported in the documents obtained in the chart review in the hospital were entered on the chart; some were reported by multiple informants and others by only one. Sources included adolescent self-report, parent self-report, and professional report. After raters independently compiled a chart, they compared entries and dates of occurrence, returning to the archival record to clarify events and timing when discrepancies arose. The resulting consensus life chart was the source for information used in analyses. The life chart pilot project was completed on 45 of the 70 participants. Pilot cases did not differ from the overall psychiatric sample in gender distribution or age of hospital admission.

Symptom onset. The Symptom, Precipitous Event, and School Changes columns of the life chart were reviewed to identify when symptoms first occurred (or a low-level symptom was significantly exacerbated). Onset was encoded as years prior to hospitalization.

Psychosocial events. After the timing of initial symptom onset was identified, chart categories were reviewed for the 2-year period preceding and concurrent to symptom onset (recall that events were tracked in 6-month blocks of time). When psychosocial events were found in any other column during that 2-year time period, the onset was classified as associated with psychosocial events. When symptoms were reported from infancy or a very early age, or the life chart contained no psychosocial events during the time period, symptoms were classified as not associated with psychosocial events. Examples of psychosocial events experienced by participants included parental divorce and the death or serious illness of a parent or sibling.

Parental relationship difficulties. Parental discord, separation, or divorce was classified as evidence of parental relationship difficulties. The number of years prior to the adolescent's hospitalization that the first or any one of these parental events occurred was noted.

ADOLESCENT FUNCTIONING

The Child and Adolescent Functional Assessment Scale (CAFAS; Hodges, 1995) was employed to quantify the adolescent's functioning during the year prior to hospitalization based on documents obtained in the chart review. The CAFAS quantifies functional impairments in school, at home, and in the community in addition to symptomatology (mood, self-harm, impaired thinking) and parental functioning (meeting the material needs and developmental needs of adolescent). Ratings of functional impairment range from no or minimal (0) through mild (10) and moderate (20) to severe (30). The instrument is designed for use with contemporaneous information such as that available in an in- or out-patient setting and has been reliability used by trained lay-people. Among the CAFAS' strengths are that it includes numerous behavioral anchors for each level of impairment and a set of training and test reliability vignettes. Documents selected as the rating corpus provided a broad overview and specific examples of presenting difficulties and were selected to minimize redundancy with other records (e.g., admission materials, social worker report of developmental and family history, and discharge information). Two advanced undergraduates were trained to use the CAFAS impairment scale, first with the training cases developed for use with the CAFAS; raters demonstrated good reliability with the CAFAS training set on all scales ($r = 0.83$ to 1.00) and, as will be presented in the results section, on ratings of the archival chart data.

YOUNG ADULT FUNCTIONING

Level of education. Level of education completed by the participants in their mid 30s was used as an index of successful adaptation. Measures of achievement, such as grade point average, were purposely avoided because our goal was to obtain an index of competency, as reflected in the ability to complete a phase of education. Thus, high school graduates and those who earned a general education equivalency certificate (GED) were considered equivalent. Level was quantified as 1 = less than a high school graduate, 2 = high school graduate or equivalent (GED), 3 = vocational training beyond high school or some college, 4 = college graduate, and 5 = graduate degree (master's or professional degree).

Hostility. Hostility scores, as an index of less positive individual functioning, were derived from the California Q-sort (Block, 1961; Kobak & Sceery, 1988). First, the Q-sort was modified to be suitable for use by people with no training in psychology and then each participant nominated two friends to describe him or her using the measure. Raters reviewed 100 descriptive statements (e.g., "Is a talkative person"; "Gives in easily; is submissive") and sorted them into three groups: one described their friend "the best" ($N = 33$), another described their friend "sometimes or not at all" ($N = 34$), and the third described their friend "the least" ($N = 33$). Next, each of the groups was resorted following the same instructions, creating nine piles describing the participant from best to least. The two raters' sorts were composited to create a single score. Following Kobak and Sceery (1988), the hostility score was the sum of the position scores of eight individual items: Is critical, skeptical, not easily impressed; Tends to blame others for own mistakes, failures, and shortcomings; Is condescending toward others; acts superior to others; Tries to harm, undermine, or sabotage others; is subtly negativistic; Is deceitful, manipulative, opportunistic, guileful; takes advantage of others; Is hostile toward others; Likes others to be dependent on him or her; Likes to be needed by others; Expresses hostility, angry feelings directly.

Antisocial and criminal behavior. Self-reported antisocial behavior was used as an index of maladaptation (Allen, Leadbetter, & Aber, 1990; Elliot, Huizinga & Menard, 1989). Participants reported whether they had engaged in 30 behaviors (e.g., stolen or tried to steal a motor vehicle, been involved in a gang fight, failed to return change that a cashier gave you by mistake in the prior year). Behavioral categories did not overlap and did not include drug use. To normalize the distribution of reported behaviors, scores were logarithmically transformed.

Results

COMPARING DATA FROM HOSPITAL RECORDS AND THE LIFE CHART METHOD

During the audit phase of the chart review, it became clear that hospitalized adolescents varied tremendously in their background, presenting problems, and hospital experiences, and that chart data held the potential, by differentiating among them, to enrich understanding of adolescent-to-young adult adaptation. The severity and nature of the reasons for admission ranged from an evaluation requested by a school district for truancy to a near-lethal suicide attempt. Some adolescents had been described as difficult from infancy; the difficulties of others seemed to have emerged suddenly. Family histories provided vivid accounts of the stresses and strains experienced by some participants and their families, testing reports documented learning disabilities, and clinician reports detailed symptoms that ranged in number and severity. Although the research corpus was more manageable than the complete charts, information was dense. Further refinement and quantification proved necessary.

The application of the Life Chart method provided an excellent method to filter and consolidate the data. Visually, the life charts provided vivid testimony to differences in the life experiences of participants. Some charts were nearly empty; others were packed with entries, either in limited categories or across the range of stressors. In fact, the psychiatric patients differed in almost every imaginable way. The life chart method also provided information to document symptom development. Symptom onset was distributed bimodally (see Figure 13.1), with approximately half the participants having relatively short-term difficulties (of approximately 2 years duration) and half with long-standing problems (emerging approximately 8 years previous to admission, including one participant with a childhood psychiatric hospitalization).

In half the cases ($N = 22$), the onset of symptoms appeared to be temporally related to psychosocial stressors (see Figure 13.2). In one-fifth of cases ($N = 9$), psychosocial stressors appeared to exacerbate existing low-level symptoms. In 14 cases, symptoms emerged without any noted accompanying stressors, and in six of those the family described the child's problems as life-long or nearly so (first reported before school entry). When the sample was divided into groups of those who had and had not experienced psychosocial stressors in the 2 years prior to symptom emergence, further differences in the pattern of onset were noted. Participants who experienced psychosocial stressors ($N = 31$), on average, had a

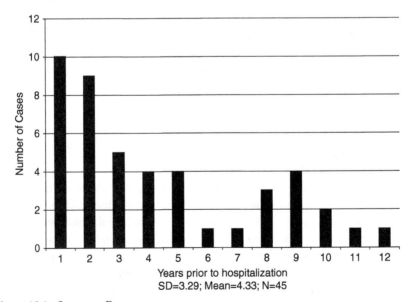

Figure 13.1. Symptom Emergence.

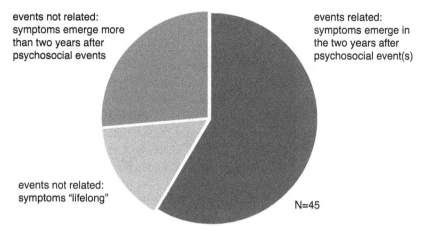

events not related:
symptoms emerge more
than two years after
psychosocial events

events related:
symptoms emerge in
the two years after
psychosocial event(s)

events not related:
symptoms "lifelong"

N=45

Figure 13.2. Relations between Psychosocial Events and Symptoms.

more recent onset of symptoms (see Figure 13.3). Those without stressors had a longer-term course. Post hoc investigation revealed that the one exception, a case with no identifiable stressors and a recent onset, suffered a severe depression described by doctors as biologically based that appeared related to the onset of puberty. Among the participants whose parents experienced discord, separation, or divorce ($N = 27$), symptom onset and the timing of parental relationship difficulties, both scored in number of years prior to hospitalization, were correlated moderately ($r = 0.39, p < 0.05$).

Application of the CAFAS to Archival Records

The CAFAS emerged as a reliable, valid, and useful instrument for quantifying adolescent functioning in this archival data set. The reliability of CAFAS ratings of

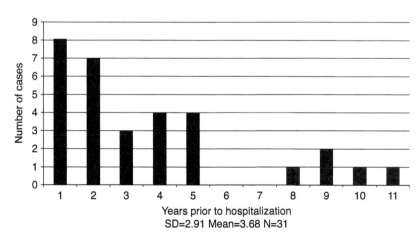

Figure 13.3. Cases with Events: Distribution of Symptom Onset.

the two raters was statistically significant for each domain in the initial pilot of life charts ($N = 26$, $r = 0.44$, $p < 0.05$ to $r = 1.00$, $p < 0.001$) (see Table 13.1). In the pilot set, raters attained reliability $r > 0.75$ on six of the 10 scales. Reliability was highest on scales that assessed easily recognizable behaviors, for example, truancy and school failure (School Scale, $r = 0.92$, $p < 0.001$; exact agreement 96%) and arrests and antisocial behavior (Community Scale, $r = 0.94$, $p < 0.001$; exact agreement 89%). Reliability was lowest on scales that required detailed report of more subtle symptoms and for which raters would benefit from a detailed knowledge of psychopathology (e.g., Mood scale, $r = 0.44$, $p < 0.05$; exact agreement 50%). Reliability was also low on one scale with limited variance (Parents provide family and social support, $r = 0.57$, $p < 0.01$; exact agreement 77%).

Means and standard deviations for the sample are reported separately by participants' gender in Table 13.2. The results show that males were significantly more impaired in community functioning than females, $F(1, 68) = 5.29$, $p < 0.05$, and females were rated as having significantly more self-harm behaviors, $F(1, 68) = 5.02$, $p < 0.05$, and greater drug use, $F(1, 68) = 10.36$, $p < 0.01$.

The CAFAS scale elevations provide evidence for the concurrent validity of the archival CAFAS ratings derived for the present study. Ninety-nine percent of participants were rated as severely impaired on at least one scale (functional impairment or symptom) and 85% were severely impaired on two or more scales, suggesting the appropriateness of psychiatric hospitalization. The one participant

Table 13.1 CAFAS ARCHIVAL RATINGS INTERRATER RELIABILITY
AND EXACT AGREEMENT

CAFAS Scale	r	Rater Agreement
School Impairment	0.92***	96%
Home Impairment	0.87***	69%
Community Impairment	0.94***	89%
Behavioral Impairment	0.76***	58%
Mood	0.44*	50%
Self-harm	0.97***	89%
Substance Use	0.96***	89%
Thinking	0.74***	92%
Parent(s) provide(s) for adolescents' material needs	1.0***	100%
Parent(s) provide(s) family and/or social support	.57**	77%

NOTE: $N = 26$.

*$p < 0.05$; **$p < 0.01$; ***$p < 0.001$.

Table 13.2 MEAN CAFAS ARCHIVAL RATING SCALE SCORES

CAFAS Scale	Males		Females	
	Mean	*SD*	*Mean*	*SD*
School Impairment	25.1	9.1	23.9	10.2
Home Impairment	18.0	13.2	22.3	12.0
Community Impairment*	12.8	14.0	6.1	9.2
Behavioral Impairment	20.3	10.4	18.4	8.2
Mood	21.0	8.5	20.7	7.3
Self-harm*	7.4	11.4	13.9	12.6
Substance Use**	5.6	9.7	14.5	13.4
Thinking	1.5	4.3	2.9	6.4

NOTE: $N = 70$. The higher the score, the greater the functional impairment: 0 = no or minimal impairment; 10 = mild impairment, 20 = moderate impairment, 30 = severe impairment.

*$p < 0.05$; **$p < 0.01$.

who was not rated as severely impaired in any area was rated as moderately impaired in five areas. Some adolescents were rated as severely impaired in four categories, providing evidence that the pervasiveness of participants' difficulties varied considerably. In addition, the sample mean on the Thinking subscale (a measure of odd or impaired reality testing) was at the none or minimal impairment level (Mean = 2.1, $SD = 5.6$), which is consistent with AFDP's recruitment guidelines in which adolescents experiencing psychosis were excluded from the study.

Finally, longitudinal data analyses provide support for the predictive value of CAFAS ratings. Impairment in adolescent functioning was associated with functioning at age 25 in theoretically meaningful ways, and the specificity of connections adds support for the validity of these measures. The more impaired an adolescent's school functioning was in the year prior to hospitalization, the less education he or she had completed by age 25 ($N = 66$; $r = -0.36$, $p < 0.01$). In contrast, impaired school functioning was not associated with peer-perceived hostility or self-reported criminal behavior at age 25. By the same token, adolescent behavioral impairment was associated with both age 25 peer-reported hostility ($N = 59$, $r = 0.31$, $p < 0.05$) and self-reported criminal behavior ($N = 66$, $r = 0.25$, $p < 0.05$), but not with educational level.

RECONSIDER, REUSE, REDUCE, AND RECYCLE

Our long-standing interest in individual competence and positive adaptation provided the impetus to explore ways to understand better the longitudinal adaptation of adolescent psychiatric patients, which led us to examine records of their inpatient stay. Results provide evidence that it is possible to gather valuable data from decades-old hospital charts via the life chart methodology and support robustly the application of CAFAS by trained undergraduates and its use on archival chart materials. That chart data can be successfully "sifted" to create an information-dense archive, and the fact that the archive can be reliability and validly quantified provides promise to researchers interested in better understanding the later adaptation of those once psychiatrically hospitalized.

The question framing this study was simple: do 20-year-old charts contain information that can enrich understanding of adolescent psychiatric patients' lives and subsequent development. Initial review suggested the answer, a complicated "yes." Reports, especially admission information and family histories, provide detailed developmental and symptom histories. Psychological testing reports provide the data to identify learning disabilities. A surprising number of structured forms were present that supplied information about suicidal risk, drug use, weight, menarche, and pubertal development. In short, chart data provided information about the premorbid competency and experiences of the adolescents through multiple methods and from multiple reporters. However, the charts provided no panacea for the researcher. Documentation of treatment methods and response was inconsistent. Therapy notes were only intermittent and hospitalizations were so brief, in some cases, that they provided time only only to stabilize, evaluate, and arrange placement for the adolescent. Finally, symptoms were described in less detail than is the current standard and did not provide the information that would be necessary to assign confidently *Diagnostic and Statistical Manual-IV* (American Psychiatric Association, 2000) diagnoses. [*DSM-II* (American Psychiatric Association, 1968) was the standard during time participants were recruited.]

Given the potential strengths and salient weakness of chart data, a more specific question emerged: Can chart data be distilled reliably and validly into easily usable form? This work suggests the answer is yes. This application of the life chart method, a technique to map multiple concurrent events in the lives of participants and to begin to understand how individual events or the confluence of multiple events relate to adolescent hospitalization, suggests it holds great promise. The spreadsheet format encapsulates, visually and substantively, the challenges faced by each participant; it also provides ready access to a wealth of information. Information culled from the life chart data bank, revealed that (1) the symptom history of these hospitalized adolescents was bimodal with length of problems either relatively short or chronic, (2) psychosocial stressors cooccurred with problem behavior onset in a substantial number of cases, (3) psychosocial events and onset cooccurrence were particularly prominent among adolescents with more recent problems, and (4) the onset of parental relationship difficulties and the onset of adolescent symptoms are moderately correlated. The life chart spreadsheet format makes it possible to identify such relations efficiently. Of course, the quality of the data entered in the life charts depends on the accuracy and truthfulness of the informants. Adults' reports about youth may, at some level, have been skewed by the need to reconstruct events to explain the adolescent's hospitalization. However, many linkages emerged in the life charts that were not stressed or even mentioned directly in the hospital reports. Some families of participants with life-long problems experienced significant psychosocial stressors; however, because the symptoms of those participants emerged at such early ages, it was not possible to disentangle symptom emergence and/or exacerbation from stress exposure and, thus, to associate them with specific events. Finally, the linkages described are only associations that do not take into account the possibility of more complex bidirectional or transactional effects; adolescent difficulties may precipitate or exacerbate parental relationship difficulties, just as relationship difficulties may cause or worsen adolescent difficulties.

The results of this study also provide evidence that the CAFAS, a well-validated measure devised to quantify contemporaneous adolescent functioning, can also be applied reliably to archival chart data. The value of an efficient and easily applied measure cannot be underestimated, especially as a balance against the labor-intensive nature of archival data development and preparation. The pattern of CAFAS ratings, particularly the fact that almost all participants were severely impaired in at least one area of functioning, and many in several areas, was consistent with the need for hospitalization and provided evidence of concurrent validity of this unique application of the CAFAS. Because of the distinctive format and details of chart records, raters were not blind to the fact they were reading hospital records. However, the variation in CAFAS profiles of participants, with some participants rated as severely impaired in multiple areas and others in none or one area, argues against a halo effect. Moreover, the longitudinal relations between CAFAS scale ratings and age-25 peer-reported hostility and self-reported educational level and antisocial behaviors support the predictive validity of the archival CAFAS ratings. These CAFAS ratings also provided an index of adolescent functioning that allowed us to demonstrate the potentially important role of adolescent functioning in later development, at least among those hospitalized. Finally, the specificity and psychometric qualities of the CAFAS are a great improvement over measures of adaptation used in previous follow-up studies (e.g., Crespi & Ivey, 1987).

Thus, by all indications, the information gleaned from these archival records helps differentiate among hospitalized adolescents and contributes to our understanding of adolescent and adolescent-to-adult development. Although all participants experienced the stressor of hospitalization and the separation from family and friends that this entailed, their premorbid competencies, hospital courses, and discharge plans varied tremendously. Chart review documented the greater or lesser severity of participants' symptoms, the chronic versus recent onset of difficulties, the varying number of previous hospitalizations and evaluations, the emergency or relatively routine nature of the admission, and the vast variation in family circumstance.

Will these differences relate to later adaptation as participants emerge into adulthood? Subsequent analyses (and, of course, time) will tell. It is impressive, given intervening events and experiences, that functioning in the year prior to hospitalization was correlated significantly, albeit modestly, with educational attainment, peer-rated hostility, and self-reported criminal behavior 11 years later. More important than the stability in behavior suggested by these simple analyses, however, will be the contribution of this dataset to helping us understand the processes underlying continuity and discontinuity in such behaviors. The answers to the questions inspired by this work have laid the foundation for the investigations of our primary interest: What factors associated with institutionalization predict later adaptation? The fact of hospitalization? The extent or degree of functional impairment that leads to hospitalization? Symptom presentation? Treatment availability? Parents' flexibility to meet the adolescents' changing needs?

Previous work has suggested that parenting behaviors, as mediated through adolescent ego development, contribute to the prediction of educational attainment and ego resiliency (Best, Hauser, & Allen, 1997). With chart data available we can proceed to understand better what contributes to adaptation within the high-risk hospitalized group. For example, will enhanced knowledge of adolescent functioning, intelligence, and family circumstance further improve the ability to predict later adaptation? And might relations between premorbid competencies and later outcome vary by domain of functioning? The decades of prospectively gathered data from this unique sample provide an unprecedented opportunity to explore these and other questions.

The present sample provided a unique opportunity to explore the sequelae of adolescent hospitalization. Although some of the sample's characteristics may limit the interpretation and generalizability of findings regarding the psychiatric sequelae of hospitalization, the sample's characteristics do not impeach the usefulness of methods used. Participants were patients at a university-affiliated teaching hospital in New England and do not represent the population in general or constitute a representative sample of adolescent psychiatric patients. Participants also were recruited from traditional treatment units rather than the intensive family intervention ward at that hospital and thus may not be wholly representative of even that specific hospital's population. Indeed, the adolescents were not randomly designated to receive psychiatric services, nor, if services were needed, were they randomly assigned to type of service or treatment facility. Although information about AFDP participants recruited at a high school provides a comparison group that also has been followed for over 30 years, the high school and hospital groups cannot be compared in great detail because we lack the information about the early development and family relationships for the normative group that psychiatric histories would provide. In addition, both the high school and hospital recruits came from middle-class to upper middle-class white families and the results of this research therefore cannot be generalized across social class or ethnicity. The availability of detailed information about the lifetimes of 70 participants and the on-going nature of this study provide an unusual opportunity to begin to understand the process of adaptation over time. Taken together, the results we have reported provide the foundation for a detailed study of such processes.

The process and methods applied to this sample provide strong support for the feasibility of using archival hospital records to generate reliable and valid information about individuals. Archival records are an underutilized resource, in large part because they contain so many pieces of information. This work demonstrates that archival records can be reliably and validly quantified for use in research and, thus, have the potential to enhance greatly our understanding of the lives of those who experience psychiatric illness. Archival information may provide a valuable adjunct to retrospective self-report in prospective studies and in follow-back designs. As an adjunct to more conventional methods, they have been neglected and deserve another look.

ACKNOWLEDGMENTS

Deep thanks are extended to Soundhari Balaguru, Lisa Fucito, Andrew Gerber, Nozomi Murakami, Elizabeth K. Schnitzer, and Grace K. Song for their many contributions to data preparation, rating, and data management. Many thanks to Ronald L. Rogowski, Marc S. Schulz, and Robert J. Waldinger for their intellectual stimulation and encouragement, to E. L. B. Rogowski for technical consultation, and to C. B. B. Rogowski for tracking completion of this work.

Karin M. Best gratefully acknowledges the support of Stuart T. Hauser, Joseph P. Allen, and Judith Crowell who provided access to data from the Adolescent and Family Project and the Young Adult Development Project. These projects, the first two phases of a 30-year longitudinal study, have been supported through grants from the National Institute of Mental Health, National Institute of Child Health and Development, MacArthur Foundation, and Spencer Foundation. Karin M. Best began this study while supported by a post doctoral training award from the National Institute of Mental Health through the Family Risk and Resilience Consortium (MH19734).

References

Allen J. P., Leadbetter, B. J., & Aber, J. L. (1990). The relationship of adolescents expectations and values to delinquency, hard drug use, and unprotected sexual intercourse. *Development and Psychopathology 2,* 85–98.

American Psychiatric Association. (1968). *Diagnostic and statistical manual of mental disorders* (2nd ed.). Washington, DC: Author.

American Psychiatric Association. (2000). *Diagnostic and statistical manual of mental disorders* (4th ed.). Washington, DC: Author

Best, K. M., Hauser, S. T., & Allen, J. P. (1997). Predicting young adult competence: Adolescent era family and individual influences. *Journal of Adolescent Research, 12,* 90–112.

Block, J. (1961). *The Q-sort method in personality assessment and psychiatric research.* Springfield, IL: Thomas.

Brooks-Gunn, J., Phelps, E., & Elder, G. H. Jr. (1991). Studying lives through time: Secondary data analyses in developmental psychology. *Developmental Psychology, 27,* 899–910.

Conger, R. D., Conger, K. J., Elder, G. H., Jr., Lorenz, F. O., Simons, R. L., & Whitbeck, L. B. (1993). Family economic stress and adjustment of early adolescent girls. *Developmental Psychology, 29*, 206–219.

Crespi, T. D., & Ivey, A. E. (1987). Adolescent psychiatric hospitalization: A historical review of the efficacy of inpatient treatment. *International Journal of Family Psychiatry, 8*, 47–61.

Elder, G. H., Pavalko, E. K., & Clipp, E. C. (1993). *Working with archival data*. Newbury Park, CA: Sage.

Elliot, D. S., Huizinga, D., & Menard, S. (1989). *Multiple problem youth: Delinquency, substance use, and mental health problems*. New York: Springer-Verlag.

Ge, X., Best, K. M., Conger, R. D., & Simons, R. (1996). Parenting behaviors and occurrence and co-occurrence of adolescent depressive symptoms and conduct problems. *Developmental Psychology, 32*, 717–731.

Gest, S. D., Reed, M-G. J., & Masten, A. S. (1999). Measuring developmental changes in exposure to adversity: A Life Chart and rating scale approach. *Development and Psychopathology, 11*, 171–192.

Green, J., Jacobs, B., Beecham, J., Dunn, G., Graham, D., Kroll, L., Tobias, C., & Briskman, J., (2007). Inpatient treatment in child and adolescent psychiatry—A prospective study of health gain and costs. *Journal of Child Psychology and Psychiatry, 48*, 1259–1267.

Hankin, B. L., Abrahamson, L. Y., Moffitt, T. A., Silva, P. A., McGee, R., & Angell, K. E. (1998). Development of depression from preadolescence to young adulthood: Emerging gender differences in a 10-year longitudinal study. *Journal of Abnormal Psychology, 107*, 128–140.

Hauser, S. T. (1976). Loevinger's model and measure of ego development: A critical review. *Psychological Bulletin, 83*, 928–955.

Hauser, S. T. (1991). *Adolescents and their families*. New York: Free Press.

Hauser, S. T. (1993). Loevinger's model and measure of ego development: A critical review II. *Psychological Inquiry, 4*, 23–29.

Hodges, K. (1995). *Child and Adolescent Functional Assessment Scale*. Ann Arbor, MI: Hodges.

Hodges, K., & Summerfelt, W. T. Reliability and validity of a multidimensional measure to assess impairment: The Child and Adolescent Functional Assessment Scale (CAFAS). Personal correspondence.

Kobak, R. R., & Sceery, A. (1988). Attachment in late adolescence: Working models, affect regulation and representations of self and others. *Child Development, 59*, 135–146.

Lewinsohn, P. M., Gotlib, I. H., Lewinsohn, M., Seeley, J. R., & Allen, N. B. (1998). Gender differences in anxiety disorders and anxiety symptoms in adolescents. *Journal of Abnormal Psychology, 107*, 109–117.

Loevinger, J., & Wessler, R. (1970). *Measuring ego development: Vol. I*. San Francisco: Jossey-Bass.

Loevinger, J., Wessler, R., & Redmore, L. (1970). *Measuring ego development: Vol. II*. San Francisco: Jossey-Bass

Masten, A. S., Best, K. M., & Garmezy, N. (1990). Resilience and development: lessons from children who overcome adversity. *Development & Psychopathology, 2*, 425–444.

Masten, A. S., Coatsworth, J. D., Neeman, J., Gest, S. D., & Hubbard, J. S. (1995). The structure and coherence of competence from childhood through adolescence. *Child Development, 66*, 1635–1659.

Pfieffer, S. I., & Strzelecki, S. C. (1990). Inpatient psychiatric treatment of children and adolescents: A review of outcome studies. *Journal American Academy of Child and Adolescent Psychiatry, 29,* 847–853.

Reed, M. (1997). *Technical Report on Adversity Ratings: Measurement of Lifetime Stress Exposure.* Institute of Child Development, University of Minnesota.

Wrate, R. M., Rothery, D. J., McCabe, R. J. R, Aspin, J., & Bryce, G. (1994). A prospective multi-centre study of admissions to adolescent inpatient units. *Journal of Adolescence, 17,* 221–237.

Looking Beyond Adolescence

Translating Basic Research into Clinical Practice

MARC S. SCHULZ AND PATRICIA K. KERIG

The chapters in this volume present cutting-edge research and theory about development from early adolescence through the transition into young adulthood. In so doing, the authors of these chapters have much to contribute to clinical efforts designed to prevent difficulties or remediate psychological problems across this time of life. Evidence-based approaches to intervention, which increasingly are being adopted in psychology and other health fields (e.g., Kazdin, 2008; Sackett, Rosenberg, Gray, Haynes, & Richardson, 1996; Spring, 2007), view basic research findings as a critical pillar of knowledge for informed clinical work. A similar view emerges from the perspectives of developmental psychopathology (Hinshaw, 2008) and prevention science (Coie et al., 1993) in which a core goal is to identify the causes of disordered functioning in order to eliminate or mitigate the impact of the causes. Thomas Insel (2009), the Director of the National Institute of Mental Health (NIMH), recently highlighted the critical role of basic scientific research in shaping interventions:

> The challenge for those who seek to prevent and cure mental illness is awesome. In the past, we advanced via serendipitous discoveries, stumbling on treatments that helped people to get better but not well. In the future, to find effective preventions and cures, we will need a more disciplined scientific approach, based on identifying individual risk and the pathophysiology of each disorder. (p. 132)

In this light, the chapters in this volume provide a resource guide for clinicians working with adolescents and young adults. By enhancing our understanding of stage-salient tasks, the contributors to this volume highlight areas of vulnerability, challenge, and change that are linked to difficulties in adaptation and the development of psychopathology (Holmbeck, O'Mahar, Abad, Colder, & Updegrove, 2006). The chapters also help identify opportunities and potential impediments that are likely to influence the process and effectiveness of therapeutic interventions. In this concluding chapter, we highlight some of the implications of the contributions to this book for clinical intervention efforts.

In Table C-1, we identify salient risk and resilience processes that are discussed by the investigators who contributed to this volume. For clinicians, sources of risk, such as self-regulatory difficulties (Boeninger and Conger, Chapter 2, this volume), point to areas of difficulty that may underlie presenting problems or may need to be a target of intervention. In a preventive context, the sources of risk act as early warning signs that can be targeted to reduce the likelihood of development of a disorder or problematic outcome in the future (Coie et al., 1993). In turn, the sources of resilience presented in Table C-1 can guide clinicians in identifying strategies or processes that may help adolescents weather challenging circumstances. These sources of resilience could also be the focus of health promotion or prevention programs that are intended to build or preserve well-being in the future.

Information about risk and resilience is most effectively applied when clinicians also have an informed awareness of normative development. For example, clinicians who are familiar with normative developmental trajectories in peer relationships (Way & Silverman, Chapter 4, this volume) and romantic relationships (Kerig, Ward, & Swanson, Chapter 6, this volume; Shulman, Scharf, & Shachar-Shapira, Chapter 5, this volume) during adolescence are better able to assess the degree to which variations in these normative trends warrant therapeutic attention or may just be minor deviations from normality (Kerig & Wenar, 2006). Moreover, this basic developmental knowledge facilitates alliance-building with adolescents by preparing clinicians to understand the core experiences that organize, preoccupy, and challenge the lives of teenagers.

THERAPEUTIC IMPLICATIONS OF STRIVINGS FOR AUTONOMY AND IDENTITY FORMATION

From a clinical perspective, a central challenge to establishing an effective working alliance with adolescents is their eagerness to avoid feeling or appearing dependent on adults (Spiegel, 1989). In the throes of seeking greater autonomy (McElhaney & Allen, Chapter 7, this volume), the prospect of needing to rely on an adult authority figure for assistance can be threatening to many adolescents. Recognizing the threat and presenting therapy as a way to assist teens in living their own lives rather than being told how to live is one strategy that has been suggested for clinical work with adolescents (Spiegel, 1989). By working with adolescents to identify alternative approaches to the difficulties they face, therapists can present themselves as agents of autonomy promotion rather than as fosterers of dependency. The narratives presented by Hauser and colleagues (Chapter 10, this volume) of adolescents hospitalized for psychiatric difficulties present a dramatic illustration of the adaptive significance of adolescents' struggle to maintain a sense of autonomy (and control) in the therapeutic context.

Table C.1 Sources of Risk and Resilience during the Transition from Adolescence to Adulthood Illustrated in the Present Volume

	Sources of Risk	Sources of Resilience
Individual Context	Emotion dysregulation (Schulz & Lazarus, Chapter 1) Suicidal thoughts (Boeninger & Conger, Chapter 2) Conflict between stage-salient adolescent tasks and those of teenage parenting (Pittman et al., Chapter 8); psychological unpreparedness for parenthood (Florsheim & Moore, Chapter 9) Poor self-regulatory capacities (Boeninger & Conger, Chapter 2)	Maturation of developmental capacities (Way & Silverman, Chapter 4) Identity attainment (Kroger, Chapter 3) Individuation (emotional maturity, self-assertion, capacity to manage conflict; Pittman et al., Chapter 8) Ego development (self-reflection, agency, self-complexity, mastery, self-esteem, coherence; Hauser, Allen, & Schulz, Chapter 10) Perceived successful resolution of stage-salient tasks (Boeninger & Conger, Chapter 2) Coherent and meaningful narrative formulation (Shulman et al., Chapter 5; Hauser et al., Chapter 10)
Family Context	Intrusive monitoring (Way & Silverman, Chapter 4) Parents' unresolved past issues and dispositional representations (Shulman et al., Chapter 5) Parents' current stage-salient issues and life course challenges (Shulman et al., Chapter 5) Difficulty balancing parental protectiveness with allowance for age-appropriate exploration (Shulman et al., Chapter 5) Psychologically controlling parenting (Kerig et al., Chapter 6) Interparental conflict, poor child behavior management (Conger et al., Chapter 12)	Perceived family support (Diamond et al., Chapter 11) Youths ability to elicit parental support and affirmation (Diamond et al., Chapter 11) Maternal support (Way & Silverman, Chapter 4) Positive parental attitudes about and structuring of friendships (Way & Silverman, Chapter 4) Youth acceptance of and empathy toward parents (Hauser et al., Chapter 10) Paternal empathy (Hauser et al., Chapter 10)

	Harsh and uninvolved parenting (Boeninger & Conger, Chapter 2) Parent–youth conflict (McElhaney & Allen, Chapter 7)	Intimate and supportive friendships (Way & Silverman, Chapter 4) Valuing of relationships; reflectiveness about others' motives, feelings, thoughts (Hauser et al., Chapter 10)
Peer/ Interpersonal Context	Masculine stereotyping (Way & Silverman, Chapter 4) Lack of/poor quality friendships (Way & Silverman, Chapter 4) Emotional stress and increased mental health problems associated with unintegrated/negative sexual experiences (Shulman et al., Chapter 5)	
Environmental/ Societal Context	Poverty (Conger et al., Chapter 12) Risky neighborhoods (Way & Silverman, Chapter 4; Conger et al., Chapter 12) Racial hostility in the school climate (Way & Silverman, Chapter 4); racial discrimination (Conger et al., Chapter 12) Homophobia (Way & Silverman, Chapter 4); stigma related to sexual-minority status (Diamond et al., Chapter 11) Economic stress (Conger et al., Chapter 12) Psychiatric hospitalization (Best & Hauser, Chapter 13; Hauser et al., Chapter 10)	Positive school climate (Way & Silverman, Chapter 4) Positive quality of coparental relationship among teen parents (Florsheim & Moore, Chapter 9) Parental restriction of autonomy in high-risk environments (McElhaney & Allen, Chapter 7) Culturally defined beliefs, meanings, and functions of parent and youth behaviors (McElhaney & Allen, Chapter 7)

Similarly, clinical work with families would benefit from recognition of the challenges that parents face in facilitating healthy autonomy in their adolescent children while still maintaining a strong caregiving relationship. Bromfield (1997) speaks of the tightropes that children string for their parents in describing the difficult balance facing parents of adolescents. Both Shulman, Scharf, and Schachar-Shapira (Chapter 5, this volume) and Kerig, Ward, and Swanson (Chapter 6, this volume) develop these ideas further by considering how parents' responses to their child's budding sexuality complicate this balancing act. Kerig and colleagues (Chapter 6) highlight the relevance of parents to adolescents' ability to establish intimate peer relationships that involve a healthy balance between autonomy and connection, with adolescents' perceptions of their parents as being controlling linked to problematic adolescent outcomes. The chapters in this volume by Pittman and colleagues (Chapter 8), McElhaney and Allen (Chapter 7), Florsheim and Moore (Chapter 9), and Hauser and colleagues (Chapter 10) extend our understanding by examining the process of autonomy development in contexts that go well beyond typical white, middle-class family life cycles and environments. For example, Hauser and colleagues (Chapter 10) show that even in the context of being hospitalized and dealing with substantial anger and resentment toward their parents, resilient adolescents show signs of reaching out to parents in family interactions. In sum, the elucidation of the complex nature of the linkages between adolescent autonomy processes and parenting across multiple family contexts provides clinicians with important knowledge for assisting parents in walking the tightropes that adolescents string and for helping adolescents develop autonomy in healthy and adaptive ways.

Identity formation is often a focus of therapeutic work with adolescents (Holmbeck et al., 2006). Kroger's meta-analytic studies (Chapter 3, this volume) present critical information about normative patterns of identity development and the implications of progress in identity development for well-being. This research points out that it is not just the content of adolescents' identity that may have adaptive implications, it is also the way in which adolescents explore and define their identity. By focusing on identity development as a process, clinicians can facilitate healthy exploration and consolidation of identity throughout the adolescent period.

For clinicians working with sexual-minority youth, Pachankis and Goldfried (2004) have emphasized the importance of being aware of adolescent identity processes and parental responses to youth during the coming-out process. Consistent with this, Diamond, Butterworth, and Allen (Chapter 11, this volume) review research on the role of family members in fostering or hindering the development of sexual-minority adolescents and young adults. They remind us of the dangers of oversimplifying by emphasizing, consistent with the developmental psychopathology constructs of equifinality and multifinality, that there is no single pathway to optimal adjustment or a single developmental progression for sexual-minority youth. Rather, Diamond and colleagues present a differential developmental trajectories approach that emphasizes the importance of understanding a range of factors that can shape the individual trajectories of sexual-minority youth. In their review, they also highlight common stressors facing these youth, such as social marginalization, harassment and internalized shame, and possible strategies for coping with these challenges. In this way, this chapter is an invaluable resource for all mental health professionals who are likely to work with sexual-minority youth and their families.

TRANSDIAGNOSTIC APPROACHES TO PSYCHOPATHOLOGY

A recent approach to understanding and treating psychopathology highlights common psychological mechanisms that might underlie multiple diagnostic entities (e.g., Harvey, Watkins, Mansell, & Shafran, 2004). The rationale underlying this transdiagnostic approach is that the same fundamental psychological process can be responsible for multiple manifestations of pathology. Self-regulatory processes, especially emotion regulatory processes, are a central focus of this approach (e.g., Kring, 2010; Sloan & Kring, 2010). Brown and Barlow (2009), for example, describe underlying emotion regulatory vulnerabilities that are common to a number of anxiety and mood disorders.

Schulz and Lazarus (Chapter 1, this volume) highlight the multiple components of emotion that are part of emotion regulatory efforts and remind us that emotion regulatory efforts are in the service of goals that adolescents prioritize in particular moments. Much clinical work is directed to helping clients develop more effective strategies for managing their emotions and striving toward their goals in the face of adversity or vulnerability. Building on these ideas, clinical work with adolescents can help adolescents identify and explore their priorities and long-term objectives so that their efforts to regulate emotion can be in the service of meaningful and healthy goals. Self-regulatory difficulties are also a key risk factor for adolescent suicide, which is a major public health concern (Boeninger and Conger, Chapter 2, this volume). Boninger and Conger identify important self-regulatory processes across behavioral, cognitive-affective, and motivational domains that may put adolescents at risk for suicidality or other maladaptive responses when challenged by difficult life circumstances.

IMPLICATIONS OF EARLY PARENTHOOD FOR EFFORTS TO PROMOTE HEALTHY FAMILY DEVELOPMENT

Spurred by accumulating research that identifies strong linkages between the interparental relationship and children's development, there have been a number of initiatives to develop interventions designed to enhance couple relationships early in the family life cycle (Lawrence, Rothman, Cobb, & Bradbury, 2010). With few exceptions, these and other preventive interventions designed to enhance couple relationships have tended to involve mainly couples who may not be at the greatest risk for relationship difficulties (Sullivan & Bradbury, 1997).

More diverse and more vulnerable populations are often the least likely to be able to access prevention services. One notable exception is the Supporting Father Involvement (SFI) Project in California that is designed to deliver a couples-based intervention to poor, unmarried couples (Cowan & Cowan, 2010; Cowan, Cowan, Pruett, Pruett, & Wong, 2009). Continued efforts to reduce obstacles to participation in efforts that promote healthy family development are critical. One of the challenges to developing these programs has been the relative lack of research focused on less privileged populations. The research programs of Florsheim and Moore (Chapter 9, this volume) and Pittman and colleagues (Chapter 8, this volume) provide critical information about how we might extend interventions that are intended to promote positive family development to young parents growing up in less privileged circumstances. By identifying common challenges and developmental tensions, these research programs also highlight opportunities for intervention that might address these challenges.

THE ROLE OF NARRATIVES IN THERAPEUTIC WORK

Several of the chapters in this volume (Shulman and colleagues, Chapter 5; Pittman and colleagues, Chapter 8; Florsheim and Moore, Chapter 9; and Hauser and colleagues, Chapter 10) highlight the role of narratives about the self and one's experience as markers of adaptation in challenging circumstances. Narrative construction is increasingly being emphasized as an important aspect of personality with significant consequences for well-being (Lilgendahl & McAdams, 2011; Pals, 2006). The stories that individuals weave about themselves offer critical information about how they respond to challenges and difficulties. Over the past two decades, narrative approaches to therapy, in which these stories are a central focus, have become an important approach to treating individuals and families (Madigan, 2011). Basch (1980), in describing his work with George, an 18-year-old young man, uses painting as a metaphor to illustrate the place of narratives and their reworking in therapy:

> George was painting a picture of himself for me, and I was going to let him finish it. Then he and I could step back and together look at and comment on this or that detail, add finishing touches, or perhaps erase large parts of the canvas and start afresh (p. 141).

The focus of narrative approaches in therapy includes attempts to help individuals add depth to their understanding of difficult events or circumstances, provide greater overall coherence to their personal narrative, and shift the focus of narratives from one of personal *or* external blame to a more balanced perspective between one's own role in shaping adaptation and the contextual factors that are at play (Freeman, Epston, & Lobovits, 1997; Madigan, 2011; Weingarten, 1998). The chapters in this volume provide illustrations of how these elements of narrative development are linked to adaptation during particular family challenges

(Shulman and colleagues, Chapter 5; Pittman and colleagues, Chapter 8; Florsheim and Moore, Chapter 9; and Hauser and colleagues, Chapter 10) and during acute psychiatric illness and recovery (Hauser and colleagues, Chapter 10). Florsheim and Moore (Chapter 9), for example, use case studies of young men experiencing an early transition to fatherhood to demonstrate the adaptive advantages of constructing an authentic, coherent, and meaningful storyline about one's life and self. Hauser and colleagues emphasize similar themes during a very different developmental challenge—adapting to and recovering from psychiatric hospitalization early in adolescence.

CONCLUSIONS

The risk and resilience processes that are identified in this chapter reflect the overarching framework of developmental psychopathology that informs this volume (Achenbach, 1990). A central tenet of both the developmental psychopathology (Hinshaw, 2008) and prevention science perspectives (Coie et al., 1993) is that there is a reciprocal relationship between clinical intervention and research. Intervention efforts should be informed by basic research about processes of risk and resilience, and interventions, in turn, inform our understanding about basic mechanisms of adaptation and pathology by providing tests of theoretical tenets that arise out of basic research. The contributors to this volume have done much to expand our knowledge base about the developmental tasks of adolescence and key risk and resilience processes across the adolescent transition. In this way, they have provided a critical knowledge base to arm clinicians and for clinical research programs to test and refine in future investigations.

References

Achenbach, T. M. (1990). Conceptualization of developmental psychopathology. In M. Lewis & S. M. Miller (Eds.), *Handbook of developmental psychopathology* (pp. 3–14). New York: Plenum.

Basch, M. F. (1980). *Doing psychotherapy.* New York: Basic Books.

Bromfield, R. (1997). *Playing for real.* New York: Penguin Books.

Brown, T. A., & Barlow, D. H. (2009). A proposal for a dimensional classification system based on the shared features of the DSM-IV anxiety and mood disorders: Implications for assessment and treatment. *Psychological Assessment, 21,* 256–271.

Coie, J. D., et al. (1993). The science of prevention: A conceptual framework and some directions for a national research program. *American Psychologist, 48,* 1013–1022.

Cowan, P. A., & Cowan, C. P. (2010). How working with couples fosters children's development: From prevention science to public policy. In M. S. Schulz, M. K. Pruett, P. K. Kerig, & R. D. Parke (Eds.), *Strengthening couple relationships for optimal child development: Lessons from research and intervention* (pp. 211–228). Washington, DC: American Psychological Association.

Cowan, P. A., Cowan, C. P., Pruett, M. K., Pruett, K., & Wong, J. J. (2009). Promoting fathers' engagement with children: Preventive interventions for low-income families. *Journal of Marriage and the Family, 71,* 663–679.

Freeman, J., Epston, D., & Lobovits, D. (1997). *Playful approaches to serious problems: Narrative therapy with children and their families.* New York: Norton.

Harvey, A., Watkins, E., Mansell W., & Shafran, R. (2004). *Cognitive behavioural processes across psychological disorders. A transdiagnostic approach to research and treatment.* New York: Oxford University Press.

Hinshaw, S. P. (2008). Developmental psychopathology as a scientific discipline: Relevance to behavioral and emotional disorders of childhood and adolescence. In T. P. Beauchaine & S. P. Hinshaw (Eds.), *Child and adolescent psychopathology* (pp. 3–26). Hoboken, NJ: John Wiley & Sons.

Holmbeck, G. N., O'Mahar, K., Abad, M., Colder, C., & Updegrove, A. (2006). Cognitive-behavior therapy with adolescents: Guides from developmental psychology. In P. C. Kendall (Ed.), *Child and adolescent therapy: Cognitive-behavioral procedures* (pp. 419–464). New York: Guilford.

Insel, T. R. (2009). Translating scientific opportunity into public health impact: A strategic plan for research on mental illness. *Archives of General Psychiatry, 66,* 128–133.

Kazdin, A. E. (2008). Evidence-based treatment and practice: New opportunities to bridge clinical research and practice, enhance the knowledge base, and improve patient care. *American Psychologist, 63,* 146–159.

Kerig, P. K, & Wenar, C. (2006). *Developmental psychopathology: From infancy through adolescence* (5th ed.). New York: McGraw-Hill.

Kring, A. M. (2010). The future of emotion research in the study of psychopathology. *Emotion Review, 2*(3), 225–228.

Lawrence, E., Rothman, A. D., Cobb, R. J., & Bradbury, T. N. (2010). Marital satisfaction across the transition to parenthood: Three eras of research. In M. S. Schulz, M. K. Pruett, P. K. Kerig, & R. D. Parke (Eds.), *Strengthening couple relationships for optimal child development: Lessons from research and intervention* (pp. 97–114). Washington, DC: American Psychological Association.

Lilgendahl, J. P., & McAdams, D. P. (2011). Constructing stories of self-growth: How individual differences in patterns of autobiographical reasoning relate to well-being in midlife. *Journal of Personality, 79,* 391–428.

Madigan, S. (2011). *Narrative therapy.* Washington, DC: American Psychological Association.

Pachankis, J. E., & Goldfried, M. R. (2004). Clinical issues in working with lesbian, gay, and bisexual clients. *Psychotherapy: Theory, Research, Practice, and Training, 41,* 227–246.

Pals, J. L. (2006). Narrative identity processing of difficult life experiences: Pathways of personality development and positive self-transformation in adulthood. *Journal of Personality, 74,* 1079–1110.

Sackett, D. L., Rosenberg, W. M. C., Gray, J. A. M., Haynes, R. B., & Richardson, W. S. (1996). Evidence based medicine: What it is and what it isn't. *British Medical Journal, 312,* 71–72.

Sloan, D. M., & Kring, A. M. (2010). Introduction and overview. In A. M. Kring & D. M. Sloan (Eds.), *Emotion regulation and psychopathology: A transdiagnostic approach to etiology and treatment* (pp. 1–9). New York: Guilford.

Spiegel, S. (1989). *An interpersonal approach to child therapy.* New York: Columbia University Press.

Spring, B. (2007). Evidence-based practice in clinical psychology: What it is, why it matters; what you need to know. *Journal of Clinical Psychology, 63,* 611–631.

Sullivan, K. T., & Bradbury, T. N. (1997). Are premarital prevention programs reaching couples at risk for marital dysfunction? *Journal of Consulting and Clinical Psychology, 65,* 24–30.

Weingarten, K. (1998). The small and the ordinary: The daily practice of a postmodern narrative therapy. *Family Process, 37,* 3–15.

Abwender, D. A., 103
accommodative challenge, 79
Achenbach, T. M., 5
Across Generations Project (AGP), 288, 289
action tendency, 24
ADHD. *See* attention deficit hyperactivity disorder
adolescence
    boundaries of, 5, 8
    as construct, 8–9
    ego development in, 288
    extended, 9
    late, 6*t*, 7*t*, 8, 9
    normative development in, 305
    parenthood in, 9, 177–78
    stages of, 6*t*, 7*t*, 8
    working alliance during, 305
Adolescence Experiences Interview, 120
Adolescent and Family Development Project (AFDP), 287, 291–94, 298, 301
    CAFAS in, 295, 296, 296*t*, 297, 297*t*, 299
    recruitment in, 288, 290, 297, 300
Adult Attachment Interview, 120
AFDP. *See* Adolescent and Family Development Project
African Americans. *See also* Baltimore Multigenerational Family Study
    friendships of, 98, 99
    parenting by, 164–65, 166, 168
    in school, 105–6
    as sexual minorities, 259

agency, 239–40
    after psychiatric hospitalization, 241–42
    communion and, 135
    of fathers, 219–20
    for resilience, 241–42
    strong, 241
AGP. *See* Across Generations Project
Aiken, L. S., 145
Alden, L. E., 136
Aldwin, C. M., 45
Allen, J. P., 36–37
Anashensel, C. S., 274
Anders, A. F., 135
anger, 22–23, 24
Anthis, K. S., 78
Anthony, E. J., 243
antisocial behavior, 293
anxiety, 69
anxiety, separation, 67
appraisal, 20, 37
    primary, 21, 22
    reappraisal and, 27, 31–32
    secondary, 21, 22–23
    self-, 241
Archer, S. L., 72
archival records, 287, 289, 290, 300–301
    CAFAS for, 295, 296, 296*t*, 299
Arnett, J. J., 8
Årseth, A. K., 70–71
Asian Americans, 104, 105
Asian cultures, 163

attachment
  caregiving system and, 116
  coping and, 47
  development of, 138
  emotional regulation and, 36
  friendships and, 101–2
  in identity status model, 70–71, 80
  intergenerational transmission of, 116
attention deficit hyperactivity disorder
    (ADHD), 48
authoritarianism, 67, 69–70, 165, 166
authoritativeness, 165, 168–69
autonomy, 134
  of boys, 148
  context of, 156, 162–63
  culture and, 167–68
  development towards, 155–56
  goal of, 161
  individuation and, 192–93
  mutual, 135, 136, 138–39, 145, 145f, 146
  negotiation of, 168
  with neighborhood risk, 156
  outcomes of, 162
  overreliance on, 136
  in parent-child relationship, 161–62,
    165, 308
  in romantic relationships, 148–49
  self-focused, 135–36, 140, 148–49
  support for, 180
  therapist's role in, 305
  timetables for, 164–65
  values and, 162–63
awareness, self-, 239, 241

Bakan, D., 135
Baldelomar, O., 80
Baltimore Multigenerational Family
    Study, 184–94
Bandura, A., 241
Barber, B. K., 137, 139–40, 147
Barlow, D. H., 309
Barrett, K., 19, 21
BARS. See Behavioral Affect Rating
    Scale
Basch, M. F., 310
BEE. See Beliefs about Emotional
    Expression
Beeler, J., 254

Beery, S. H., 103
Behavioral Affect Rating Scale
    (BARS), 274
beliefs
  about emotions, 35
  of families, 104
  about friendships, 104
  as identity, 32–33
Beliefs about Emotional Expression
    (BEE), 35
Ben-Ari, A., 253
Benjamin, L. S., 205
Berzonsky, M. B., 72
Berzonsky, M. D., 73, 76
Beyers, W., 72
binding, 118, 128, 243
Biringen, Z., 116
bisexual. See sexual minorities
blame, 22, 249–50
Blos, P., 115
Bosma, H. A., 77, 78
boundaries
  of adolescence, 5, 8
  of parent-child relationship, 88–89,
    137–46
  of relationships, 136
Bowen, G. L., 274
Bowlby, J., 146
boys
  friendships for, 87, 91, 92, 93, 98,
    100–101, 106, 107
  intimacy for, 93, 101
  masculinity for, 93–94
  self-focused autonomy of, 148
Branje, S., 73, 74, 77, 80
Bretherton, I., 116
Bromfield, R., 308
Bronfenbrenner, U., 86
Brown, T. A., 309
Browne, M. W., 142
Burzette, R. G., 269

CAFAS. See Child and Adolescent
    Functional Assessment Scale
California, 269
California Families Project (CFP),
    269–82
California Q-sort, 293

Campos, J. J., 19, 21, 26
Campos, R. G., 19, 21, 26
caregiving system, 116, 128
Carlson, E., 182
Cauce, A. M., 181
CECS. *See* Constraining and Enabling
    Coding System
Census Bureau, U.S., 270
Center for Epidemiologic Studies
    Depression Scale (CES-D), 274
CES-D. *See* Center for Epidemiologic
    Studies Depression Scale
CFP. *See* California Families Project
Chapman, M. V., 274
Child and Adolescent Functional
    Assessment Scale (CAFAS),
    292–93, 297*t*
  predictive value of, 297
  reliability of, 295, 296, 296*t*, 299
child management, 275, 277, 278*t*,
    279–80, 281
children
  enabling by, 244
  suicide of, 43
Children's Report of Parental Behavior
    Inventory (CRPBI), 141
Child's Report of Parental Behavior
    Inventory, 141
Chinese-Americans, 94, 99, 165
Chinese culture, 164, 165, 166
Claussen, A. H., 116
Cobbs, G., 137
cognition, 179, 184
cognitive map, 138
Cohler, B. J., 49, 56–57, 246
Cole, J. C., 274
Cole, P. M., 19
collectivism, 163
coming out
  age at, 255
  denial with, 256–57
  ethnicity and, 258
  in families, 227, 253–63
  to family subsets, 256
  predictors of, 257–58
  rates of, 255
commitment
  identity, 73–74

  in identity status model, 68–69,
      72–73
communication
  parental facilitation of, 243
  in parenting, 188–93
  for resilience, 243
communion, 135
community functioning, 296
conflict
  between goals, 30
  identity status model and, 78, 79
  interparental, 274–75, 277, 278*t*
  in parent–child relationship, 165,
      167–68, 180
  in romantic relationships, 271,
      277, 278*t*
Conger, R. D., 269
Connections Studies, 95
conscientiousness, 48
Consolidators, 76, 77
Constraining and Enabling Coding
    System (CECS), 144
Contemplation of Change scale, 78
Cook, T. D., 181
Cooper, C. R., 134
coping
  age-related, 45
  attachment behavior and, 47
  cognitive strategies for, 45–46
  definition of, 26, 44
  developmental history and,
      46–47, 56
  dyadic, 45, 46–47
  emotion-focused, 26–28
  in families, 261
  problem-focused, 26, 28
  research on, 34
  self-destructiveness as, 44–46
  with stress, 26
  substance abuse as, 45–46
  suicidality as, 44–45
coping potential, 22, 23
core relational theme, 21–22, 32
Costin, S. E., 98–99
credit, 22
criminal behavior, 233, 293
Criss, M. M., 147
Crittendon, P. M., 88, 116, 137

Crouter, A., 103
CRPBI. *See* Children's Report of Parental Behavior Inventory
culture. *See also* specific cultures
  autonomy and, 167–68
  identity and, 80
  values by, 163
Cummings, E. M., 33

Darby-Mulliins, P., 253
daughters
  fathers and, 130, 148
  mothers and, 88, 119–25, 126–30, 147, 148, 237–38
  as proxy, 128
  romantic relationships of, 120, 122–26
Davies, P. T., 33
death, 236
delegating, 118, 124–25
Dennis, T. A., 19
depression, 237
  from discrimination, 271
  friendships and, 91–92
  with puberty, 295
  from romantic relationships, 114
developmental psychopathology, 5
Diagnostic and Statistical Manual (DSM)-II, 290
Diagnostic and Statistical Manual (DSM)-III, 290
Diagnostic and Statistical Manual (DSM)-IV, 298
Dialectical Behavior Therapy, 58
Diffuse, 66, 69, 72, 73
discipline, 48
discrimination
  depression from, 271
  parenting effect of, 273, 278*t*
display rules, 29, 34
Dispositional Representations (DR), 88, 116–17, 119, 126–27
divorce, 233
Dodge, K. A., 147
Doernberger, C. H., 225
Doty, N. D., 262
DR. *See* Dispositional Representations

DSM. See Diagnostic and Statistical Manual-II; *Diagnostic and Statistical Manual-III*; *Diagnostic and Statistical Manual-IV*
Duality of Human Existence (Bakan), 135
DuBois, D., 99
dysfunctional behavior, 233

Eccles, J., 181
economic hardship measures, 273
economic pressure, 273
effortful control, 47
ego development, 31, 70, 288
ego identity. *See* identity
ego-involvement, 22
Ekman, P., 29
Elder, G. E., 181
Elizur and Ziv, 256
emerging adulthood, 6*t*, 7*t*, 15
  self-narrative in, 49–50
  suicide in, 43, 50
emotional distress, 274, 277, 278*t*, 279. *See also* stress
emotional security, 33
emotional valence, 139–40, 145, 146–47, 148–49
emotions
  beliefs about, 35
  cognitive development and, 31
  cognitive-mediational theory of, 14, 19–37
  core relational themes of, 21–22
  definition of, 21
  as dynamic, 36–37
  expression of, 35
  response tendencies with, 23–24, 24*f*
  showing, 239
  signals of, 27
  social context of, 32
emotions, regulation of, 236
  attachment behavior and, 36
  in cognitive-mediational theory, 25–26
  developmental factors with, 30–33
  display rules, 29, 34
  feeling rules, 29, 34
  goals of, 28–29

governing of, 25–26
mechanisms of, 26–27
as mediator, 37
meta-emotion, 34–35
multichannel assessment of, 36, 38
multiple, 29–30
through parenting, 31
research in, 19–20, 33–37
timing of, 25
enabling
by children, 244
of individuation, 180, 243
Epstein, J. L., 104–5
Erikson, E. H., 16, 31, 33, 64, 71, 74,
    79, 217
Estrada, A. U., 102
ethnicity
coming out and, 258
of families, 102
friendships and, 94, 98–99, 100, 104
in FTP, 50
in school, 105–6
and sexual minorities, 258–59
etiqueta, 258–59
European-Americans, 99, 165, 168
European culture, 164
Ewell, K. K., 103
exceptional functioning, 233
expelling, 118

false self, 137
families. *See also* parent-child
    relationship; parenting
adaptability of, 262
beliefs of, 104
cohesion of, 262
coming out in, 227, 253–63
coping in, 261
denial in, 256–57, 261
ethnicity of, 102
friendships and, 93, 101–3
hostile exchanges in, 36–37
leave-taking from, 9
morality in, 243–44
non-traditional, 9
positive focusing behaviors on, 243
with psychiatric hospitalization, 292

resilience in, 261
revealed differences procedure,
    243–44
for sexual minorities, 249–63
social skills in, 93
solidarity of, 163–64
subsets within, 256
support from, 252–53, 257–58
trigger events in, 261
vulnerability in, 260
families of choice, 155–56
family stress model, 270, 270*f*, 271, 276,
    279*f*, 281. *See also* stress
family systems theory, 243
Family Transitions Project (FTP)
ethnicity in, 50
recruitment for, 50–51
self development in, 54, 54*f*, 55, 55*f*
self-regulation in, 54–55, 55*f*, 56, 56*f*,
    57, 58
social roles in, 52, 54
suicidality in, 53, 54–55, 54*f*, 55*f*, 56,
    56*f*, 57–58, 59
fathers
agency of, 219–20
child management by, 278*t*, 279
daughters and, 130, 148
emotional distress of, 277, 278*t*, 279
identity as, 218–19, 220
individuation of, 217, 218
parenting involvement of, 193–94,
    200, 202, 203, 206, 207*t*, 208,
    209–16, 218
psychoeducation for, 220
self-narrative of, 220–21
support from, 102
therapy for, 220
violence of, 239
feeling rules, 29, 34
Feldman, B. J., 269
FIML. *See* full information maximum
    likelihood
Finch, B. K., 271
Fleeson, J., 138
Florsheim, P., 205
Foreclosed, 66, 69–70, 71, 72
Freud, Anna, 115

friendships
   of African Americans, 98, 99
   attachment behavior and, 101–2
   beliefs with, 104
   for boys, 87, 91, 92, 93, 98, 100–101,
      106, 107
   changes in, 92–93, 99–101
   context of, 93
   depression and, 91–92
   developmental importance of, 91
   effects of, 106–7
   ethnicity and, 94, 98–99, 100, 104
   families and, 93, 101–3
   gender and, 87, 91, 94, 98, 99, 100, 106
   of girls, 91, 98
   for immigrants, 94, 99
   influences on, 93
   intimacy in, 94, 98, 106, 107
   macrocontext of, 92, 107
   parenting and, 85, 87, 103–4
   school adjustment and, 93
   school context for, 104–6
   skills for, 103
   social provisions in, 97
   types of, 94–95
   valuing of, 87
friends with benefits, 140
FTP. *See* Family Transitions Project
full information maximum likelihood
      (FIML), 53, 276
Furman, W., 140
Furstenberg, F. F., 181
future expectations, 22

gay. *See* sexual minorities
gay-related stress, 251–52
gender. *See also* boys; daughters; fathers;
      girls; mothers
   friendships and, 87, 91, 94, 98, 99,
      100, 106
   in identity status model, 71, 75
   in parent-child relationship, 143*t*, 144*t*
   psychological control and, 143*t*, 144*t*,
      146, 147–48
   roles, 258–59
George, C., 116, 117, 128
Giordano, P. C., 140
Girl Interrupted (Kaysen), 231–32

girls
   friendships of, 91, 98
   other-focused connection of, 147–48
global psychiatric symptomatology, 233
goal congruence, 22
goal-corrected partnership, 185
goal relevance, 22
goals
   of autonomy, 161
   common, 33
   conflict between, 30
   of emotional regulation, 28–29
   parenting, 161
   socialization, 163
Goldfried, M. R., 308
Gonzales, N., 181
Goosens, L., 72, 73, 76
grade point average (GPA), 275, 278*t*, 279
grandmothers, 182–83, 185–86, 187
Graves, D., 181
Gross, J. J., 19
Grotevant, H. D., 134
Grove, K., 181
Guardians, 76, 77

Hand, L. S., 140
Harmon, E. L., 137
Harter, S., 135–36, 137
Hauser, S. T., 31, 36–37, 269
Hauser, Stuart, 4
Heatherington, L., 262
Herdt, G., 254
Hierarchical Regression Analysis and
      Growth Curve, 97
Hiraga, Y., 181
Hirsch, B., 99
Hochschild, A. R., 29
homophobia, 87, 107
hookups, 140
Horowitz, L. M., 136
hostile recognition, 257
hostility, 293

identity, 13. *See also* projective
      identification
   beliefs as, 32–33
   commitment, 73–74
   crisis, 74–75

culture and, 80
definitions of, 16, 65, 134–35
development of, 65, 74–76
ego, 64–65
Erikson's concept of, 64–65, 218
of fathers, 218–19, 220
formation of, 308
intimacy and, 218
Minuchin on, 134
as sexual minority, 258
Identity Achieved, 66, 68, 69, 70, 71, 72
identity dimensions, 72–73
identity status model, 74
    accommodative challenge in, 79
    adjustment types in, 76–77
    anxiety, 69
    attachment behavior in, 70–71, 80
    authoritarianism, 67, 69–70
    commitment making, 72–73
    commitments, 68–69
    conflict and, 78, 79
    Consolidators, 76, 77
    developmental continuum of, 77
    Diffuse, 66, 69, 72, 73
    ego development, 70
    equilibrium in, 79
    exploration in breadth, 72, 73
    exploration in depth, 72, 73
    Foreclosed, 66, 69–70, 71, 72
    gender in, 71, 75
    Guardians, 76, 77
    identification with commitment,
        72, 73
    Identity Achieved, 66, 68, 69, 70,
        71, 72
    identity exploration, 78–79
    identity stability in, 75–76, 77
    intimacy, 71
    locus of control, 69
    meta-analysis of, 67–71
    moral reasoning, 70
    Moratorium, 66, 69, 70, 74, 75
    Pathmakers, 76, 77
    progressive movement in, 77, 80
    ruminative exploration, 73
    Searchers, 76–77
    self-esteem in, 68–69
    social context of, 78
    subgroupings within, 72
    trajectories in, 76
    variables in, 67
Identity vs. Role Confusion, 65, 71
IIP. See Inventory of Interpersonal
    Problems
immigrants, 94, 99
impulsive-aggressive behavior, 49
independence, 241
individualism vs. collectivism, 163
individuation, 155
    autonomy and, 192–93
    competencies for, 179–80
    constraining, 180
    definition of, 179
    disruption in, 181
    as dyadic, 185
    enabling, 180, 243
    of fathers, 217, 218
    importance of, 180–81
    of mothers, 181–82, 183, 186–93
    in parenting, 143t, 178, 180, 181–82,
        183, 183t, 184, 186–87, 188–93, 217
    promotion of, 180, 181
    relationships and, 180
Insel, Thomas, 304
institutional self, 218
internal working models, 116
interpersonal orientation, 89
interpersonal skills, 220
interpersonal spillover, 216–17
interventions
    evidence-based approaches to, 304
    for parenting, 58, 193
    research for, 304, 311
    for resilience, 58–59
    for romantic relationships, 309–10
    for self-destructiveness, 58
    with sexuality, 130
intimacy
    for boys, 93, 101
    capacity for, 217
    in friendships, 94, 98, 106, 107
    identity and, 218
    in identity status model, 71
    interpretation of, 92
    need for, 86
    resistance to, 219

Intimacy *vs.* Isolation, 71
intolerance, 251
Inventory of Interpersonal Problems
  (IIP), 141–42
Iowa, 50
Iowa Single-Parent Project (ISPP), 50, 51
Iowa Youth and Families Project
  (IYFP), 50–51, 275
ISPP. *See* Iowa Single-Parent Project
Israel, 256
IYFP. *See* Iowa Youth and Families
  Project

Jack, D. C., 136, 137
Jenuwine, M. J., 49, 56–57
Jesperson, K., 70
Jones, D. C., 98–99
Jones, J. E., 243
Joyner, K., 99

Kao, G., 99
Kaplan, N., 128
Karweit, N., 104–5
Katz, M., 226
Kaufman, A. S., 274
Kaysen, S., 231–32
Kegan, Robert, 217, 218
Keijsers, L., 73, 74, 77, 80
Kerig, Patricia, 3, 4, 5, 8, 9, 11, 13, 85, 86,
  88, 89, 134, 137, 139, 141, 142, 146,
  147, 148, 149, 155, 225, 304
Kermoian, R., 26
Al-Khayyal, M., 243
Kobak, R. R., 293
Kohlberg, L., 70, 243
Kohlberg moral dilemmas, 233, 243
Kolody, B., 271
Kroger, J., 68, 69, 70–71, 72, 75, 80
Kunnen, E. S., 77, 78
Kupanoff, K., 103

Laird, R. D., 147
Lang, C., 116
Larson, R., 31
Latino cultures, 163, 164, 165, 258–59
Latinos, 94, 102. *See also*
  Mexican-Americans
  discrimination against, 271

Mexican-Americans as percentage
  of, 269
  in school, 105–6
Lavner, J. A., 262
Lazarus, R. S., 19, 21, 26
Leonard, S. A., 102
lesbian. *See* sexual minorities
Lieber, D., 243
Life Chart method, 229, 288–90
  archival records for, 293–94, 295, 296,
    296*t*, 297*t*, 298
  CAFAS for, 292–93, 295, 296, 296*t*,
    297, 297*t*, 299
  coding in, 291–92
  symptoms in, 292, 294
life history theory, 128
Lillevoll, K. R., 69
Listening Guide, 97
Loevinger, J., 70
Longmore, M. A., 140
love, 91
loving denial, 256–57, 261
Luthar, S. S., 225
Luyckx, K., 72, 73, 76

MacCallum, R. C., 142
machismo, 258–59
Madden-Derdich, D. A., 102
Magruder, B., 258
Main, M., 128
Malik, N. M., 262
Manning, W. D., 140
Marcia, J. E., 70–71, 75, 80
Marcia, James, 66, 79
Marcoulides, G., 145
Marold, D. B., 137
marriage
  age at, 58
  divorce, 233
  before parenting, 200–201
Martin, S. E., 19
Martinussen, M., 68, 69, 70–71, 75, 80
masculinity, 93–94, 101, 258–59
Maslin, C., 116
MASQ. *See* Mini Mood and Anxiety
  Symptom Questionnaire
Masten, A. S., 282
McAdams, Dan, 219, 220

McHale, S., 103
Meeus, W., 73, 74, 77, 80
men, 71
meta-emotion, 34–35
Mexican-Americans, 99
  in California, 269
  in California Families Project, 269–82
  family stress model with, 270, 270*f*,
    271, 276, 279*f*, 281
  neighborhood risk for, 274, 277, 278*t*,
    280, 281
  poverty of, 270
  stress for, 227–28
Micucci, J. A., 8, 9
Mini Mood and Anxiety Symptom
    Questionnaire (MASQ), 274
minorities, 94. *See also* sexual minorities
  as majority, 270
  stress for, 271
minority stress, 251
Minuchin, Salvatore, 134, 137
moral dilemmas, Kohlberg's, 233, 243
morality, 243–44
moral reasoning, 70
Moratorium, 66, 69, 70, 74, 75
mother-daughter dyad, 127
mother-grandmother relationship,
    182–83, 185–86, 187
mothers
  adolescent, 177–78
  child management by, 278*t*, 279–80
  daughters and, 88, 119–25, 126–30,
    147, 148, 237–38
  development of, 177–78
  emotional distress of, 277, 278*t*, 279
  good enough, 121
  individuation of, 181–82, 183, 186–93
  individuation-promotion of, 180, 181
  influence of, 117–18
  protective behavior of, 128
  resilience effect of, 228
  romantic relationships of, 120–21,
    122, 123, 125, 127
  script of, 127–28
  self-preoccupation of, 128, 129
  support for, 182–83, 221
  support of, 87, 102
  unmarried, 201

motivation, 48–49
Mounts, N. S., 103
Muller, A., 256–57
Mumme, D. L., 26
Murdock, T. B., 253
mutual autonomy, 135, 136, 138–39, 145,
    145*f*, 146
mutuality, 135

Narrative Guide, 234
narrative review, 67
National Institute of Mental Health
    (NIMH), 304
Neff, K. D., 135–36
neighborhood, risk in
  autonomy and, 156
  for Mexican-Americans, 274, 277,
    278*t*, 280, 281
  values with, 164
Network of Relationships Inventory
    (NRI), 96
neuroticism, 49
NIMH. *See* National Institute of Mental
    Health
NIMH Family Research Consortium,
    3–4
NRI. *See* Network of Relationships
    Inventory

Olsen, J. A., 139–40, 147
Olson, Bradley, 219, 220
Osofsky, J. D., 193
other-focused connection, 136, 140,
    147–49

Pachankis, J. E., 308
parental facilitation, 243
Parent-Child Boundaries Scale
    (PBS-III), 141
parent-child relationship
  autonomy in, 161–62, 165, 308
  boundaries of, 88–89, 137–46
  conflict in, 165, 167–68, 180
  emotional valence of, 139–40, 145,
    146–47, 148–49
  gender in, 143*t*, 144*t*
  goal-corrected partnership in, 185
  longitudinal research on, 288–89

parent–child relationship (*Continued*)
  projective identification in, 88,
    118, 128
  reciprocation in, 244
  religion through, 48
  role reversal in, 147
parenthood, 9, 129, 177–78
parenting
  abusive, 47–48
  adaptive, 117, 121–22
  by African Americans, 164–65,
    166, 168
  authoritarianism, 165, 166
  authoritative, 165, 168–69
  binding in, 118, 128, 243
  child management, 275, 277, 278*t*,
    279–80, 281
  communication in, 188–93
  comparisons in, 113, 115
  constructive, 271–72
  context of, 117, 162
  delegating in, 118, 124–25
  discrimination effect on, 273, 278*t*
  DRs in, 116–17, 119, 126–27
  economics of, 273
  emotional regulation through, 31
  expelling in, 118
  father's involvement with, 193–94,
    200, 202, 203, 206, 207*t*, 208,
    209–16, 218
  friendships and, 85, 87, 103–4
  goals of, 161
  harsh, 44, 54, 54*f*, 137
  individuation in, 143*t*, 178, 180,
    181–82, 183, 183*t*, 184, 186–87,
    188–93, 217
  interpersonal orientation from, 89
  interventions for, 58, 193
  life-stage issues in, 118
  marriage before, 200–201
  monitoring, 103, 128
  motivation from, 48
  psychological control in, 137–38,
    139–40, 143, 143*t*, 144*t*, 145, 145*f*,
    146–48
  reflective function in, 119
  resilience and, 243
  restrictiveness in, 169, 172

romantic relationships and, 85–86,
    115–16, 200–201, 206, 207, 207*t*,
    208, 208*t*, 209–17, 295
  school effect of, 277
  self-development and, 54*f*
  self-regulation and, 15, 47–48, 54–55
  by SES, 164–65, 166–67, 207*t*
  sexuality and, 87, 118
  stress effect on, 270, 270*f*, 271
  styles of, 164–66, 168–69
  suicidality and, 44, 58
  symptom onset and, 298
  timetables for, 164–65
  uninvolved, 44
  values in, 163–64
Partridge, M. F., 116
Pathmakers, 76, 77
PBS-III. *See* Parent-Child Boundaries
    Scale
peer acceptance, 29
Perceived Social Support Scale for
    Friends (PSS-FR), 96
personality development, 219
perspective taking, 184
Pettit, G. S., 147
Phinney, J., 80
Pincus, A. L., 136
positive focusing behaviors, 243
posttraumatic stress disorder, 64
poverty, 270
Powers, S. I., 35
preadolescence, relationship in, 91
prevention science, 304
projective identification, 88, 118, 128
protection, from a distance, 128
PSS-FR. *See* Perceived Social Support
    Scale for Friends
psychiatric hospitalization, 34
  admission to, 293
  agency after, 241–42
  appropriateness of, 296
  control in, 237, 238
  effect of, 231, 235, 299–300
  ego development and, 288
  families with, 292
  psychosocial events with, 292
  school and, 297
  as secret, 236

self-report of, 298–99
for substance abuse, 238–39
for suicidality, 236
symptoms for, 292
psychoeducation, 220
psychological control
  gender and, 143t, 144t, 146, 147–48
  in parenting, 137–38, 139–40, 143,
    143t, 144t, 145, 145f, 146–48
  romantic relationships and, 148–49
  self-report of, 148
psychopathology, 233
psychosocial events, 292, 295f, 298
psychosocial stage theory, 16
psychosocial stressors, 294–95, 295f,
  298, 299
puberty, 5, 8, 9
Puzzle Task, 186–87

Quality of Relationship Inventory
  (QRI), 204, 207–8

Rabin, A. S., 274
R.A.P. See Relationships Among Peers
reappraisal, 27, 31–32
relational aggression, 139
relationships. See also specific
    relationships
  boundaries of, 136
  individuation and, 180
  intergenerational transmission of, 88
  model of, 138
  mutual autonomy in, 135, 136
  other-focused connection in, 136
  platonic, 140
  in preadolescence, 91
  quality of, 46–47, 86, 87
  self-focused autonomy in, 135–36
  self-narrative about, 88
  sexual, 140
  with therapists, 238
relationships, romantic, 47, 49
  age gap in, 122, 123
  autonomy in, 148–49
  conflict in, 271, 277, 278t
  of daughters, 120, 122–26
  depression from, 114
  duration of, 114

idealization of, 123
importance of, 140, 145–46
interpersonal skills for, 220
interventions for, 309–10
of mothers, 120–21, 122, 123, 125, 127
other-focused connection in, 148–49
parenting and, 85–86, 115–16,
  200–201, 206, 207, 207t, 208, 208t,
  209–17, 295
psychological control and, 148–49
self-focused autonomy in, 148–49
stress from, 114, 115
suicidality and, 55, 55f, 56, 56f, 58
Relationships Among Peers (R.A.P.), 95
religion, 48
research. See also specific research
    studies
  on coping, 34
  on emotional regulation, 19–20,
    33–37
  for interventions, 304, 311
  microanalytic coding techniques in, 36
  on parent-child relationship, 288–89
  person-centered, 9
  self-report data, 35, 148, 298–99
  variable-centered, 9
  video-recall, 35
resentful denial, 257
resilience
  agency for, 241–42
  child management for, 281
  communication for, 243
  definition of, 226
  family domains of, 261
  interventions for, 58–59
  mother's effect on, 228
  as multidimensional, 232
  parenting and, 243
  psychological qualities for, 282
  sources of, 306t, 307t
resistance, 219
resources
  personal, 54–55
  suicidality and, 54–55
response tendencies, 23–24, 24f
restrictiveness, 169, 172
revealed differences procedure,
  243–44

Ricard, R. J., 98–99
Richards, M. H., 31
Ridgeway, D., 116
risk, 179
  in neighborhood, 156, 164, 274, 277,
    278t, 280, 281
  sources of, 306t, 307t
risk-taking, 45
Rohner, R. P., 139, 146–47
Rutter, M., 226
Ryan-Finn, K., 181
Ryeng, M. S., 68

Sales, L. J., 102
same-sex attraction. See sexual
  minorities
SASB. See Structural Analysis of Social
  Behavior
Sayfer, A. W., 31
Scale of Intergenerational Relationship
  Quality (SIRQ), 186
Scaramella, L. V., 269
Sceery, A., 293
Schludermann, E. H., 141
Schludermann, S. M., 141
school, 48
  adjustment to, 93
  African Americans in, 105–6
  conduct at, 275, 277, 278t, 279, 280
  effects of, 237
  ethnicity in, 105–6
  friendships and, 93, 104–6
  as marker, 292–93
  parenting effect on, 277
  psychiatric hospitalization and, 297
  suicidality and, 55, 55f, 56f
School Performance Scale, 275
Schulz, M. S., 35, 36–37
Schumacker, R., 145
Schwartz, S. J., 73, 74, 77, 80
Searchers, 76–77
second toddlerhood, 5
secret
  for boys, 92, 100
  in friendships, 87, 92, 98, 100
  psychiatric hospitalization as, 236
  for sexual minorities, 256
Seifer, R., 135

self
  false, 137
  institutional, 218
  socially implanted, 137
self-appraisal, 241
self-awareness, 239, 241
self-destructiveness, 231, 296
  as coping, 44–46
  interventions for, 58
self development
  in FTP, 54, 54f, 55, 55f
  parenting and, 54f
  suicidality and, 55, 55f, 56f, 59
self-efficacy, 241
self-esteem, 48, 68–69
self-focused autonomy, 135–36, 140,
  148–49
self-harm, 296
self-in-relation theory, 134–35
self-involvement, 22
self-mutilation, 231
self-narrative
  coherence of, 240–41
  in emerging adulthood, 49–50
  of fathers, 220–21
  importance of, 310
  as marker, 245
  Narrative Guide for, 234
  about relationships, 88
  significance, 246
  suicidality and, 49, 57
self reflection, 45, 119, 241
self-regulation, 13–14, 43. See also
  emotions, regulation of
  assessment of, 51–52
  parenting and, 15, 47–48,
    54–55
  social roles and, 48–49
  suicidality and, 15, 44, 54–55, 55f, 56,
    56f, 57, 58
self-report data, 35, 148, 298–99
self-representation, 234, 235
self-silencing, 136
Separating Parents and Adolescents
  (Stierlin), 118
separation anxiety, 67
SES. See socioeconomic status
sex-role stereotyping, 87, 93–94, 101

sexuality. *See also* sexual minorities
  interventions with, 130
  parenting and, 87, 118
  questioning of, 260
  stress from, 114–15
sexual minorities
  African Americans as, 259
  coming out of, 227, 253–63
  definition of, 250–51
  ethnicity and, 258–59
  families for, 249–63
  family systems perspective on, 261
  gay-related stress for, 251–52
  identifying as, 258
  intolerance of, 251
  language for, 258
  secret for, 256
  violence against, 251
SFI. *See* Supporting Father Involvement
    Project
Sherman, M., 116
Simons, R. L., 269
SIRQ. *See* Scale of Intergenerational
    Relationship Quality
Skinner, E. A., 49
Smith, T. L., 274
Smits, I., 73, 76
social context
  of emotions, 32
  of identity status model, 78
social deviance, 233
socialization goals, 163
socially implanted self, 137
social partners, 45, 46–47
social roles, 48–49, 52, 54
social skills, 93
socioeconomic status (SES), 164–65,
    166–67, 207*t*
Soenens, B., 72, 73, 76
Solomon, J., 116, 117, 128
South Asian culture, 258
Sroufe, L. A., 134, 138
stage-salience, 5, 6*t*, 7*t*, 8
status, 49
Stein, J. A., 35
Stern, D. N., 117, 135
Stierlin, H., 118
Stolz, H. E., 139–40, 147

stress. *See also* gay-related stress;
    posttraumatic stress disorder
  coping with, 26
  for Mexican-Americans, 227–28
  for minorities, 251, 271
  parenting effect of, 270, 270*f*, 271
  from romantic relationships, 114, 115
  from sexuality, 114–15
  suicidality from, 44
stressors, psychosocial, 294–95, 295*f*,
    298, 299
Structural Analysis of Social Behavior
    (SASB), 204
substance abuse
  as coping, 45–46
  as dysfunctional behavior, 233
  psychiatric hospitalization for,
    238–39
Sucoff, C. A., 274
Sugawara, H. M., 142
suicidality
  assessment of, 53
  as coping, 44–45
  FTP and, 53, 54–55, 54*f*, 55*f*, 56, 56*f*,
    57–58, 59
  parenting and, 44, 58
  psychiatric hospitalization for, 236
  resources and, 54–55
  romantic relationships and, 55, 55*f*,
    56, 56*f*, 58
  school and, 55, 55*f*, 56*f*
  self development and, 55, 55*f*, 56*f*, 59
  self-narrative and, 49, 57
  self-regulation and, 15, 44, 54–55, 55*f*,
    56, 56*f*, 57, 58
  from stress, 44
suicide
  of children, 43
  in emerging adulthood, 43, 50
Sullivan, H. S., 86, 91, 93
support
  for autonomy, 180
  from families, 252–53, 257–58
  from fathers, 102
  for mothers, 182–83, 221
  of mothers, 87, 102
Supporting Father Involvement (SFI)
    Project, 310

symptoms, onset of, 294*f*
    notes of, 298
    parenting and, 298
    for psychiatric hospitalization, 292
    psychosocial events with, 295*f*, 298
    psychosocial stressors with, 294–95,
        295*f*, 298, 299

therapist, 238, 305
therapy
    engagement in, 238
    for fathers, 220
    notes from, 298
    working alliance in, 305
Thompson, M., 193
Thompson, R. A., 19
transdiagnostic approach, 309
trigger events, 261
Tromsø Meta-Analytic Studies of Ego
        Identity Status, 75–76
trust, 236

University of Rhode Island Change
        Assessment measure (URICA), 78
University of Virginia, 106–7
Updegraff, K., 102, 103
URICA. *See* University of Rhode Island
        Change Assessment measure

values
    autonomy and, 162–63
    cultural, 163
    family solidarity, 163–64
    with neighborhood risk, 164
van de Schoot, R., 73, 74, 77, 80
Vansteenkiste, M., 72, 73, 76

Vega, W. A., 271
Vernberg, E. M., 103
veterans, 64–65
video-recall, 35
violence
    of fathers, 239
    against sexual minorities, 251
volatility, 13–14
vote counting, 67
vulnerability, 260

Waldinger, R. J., 35, 36–37
Waldner, L. K., 258
Walsh, F., 261
Ward, M., 182
Waterman, A. S., 72, 75, 77, 80
Weiss, R. S., 97
Welsh, D. P., 35
West, S. G., 145
Whitbourne, S. K., 79
Whitesell, N. R., 137
Wiggens, J. S., 136
Willoughby, B. L. B., 262
women, 71
working alliance, 305
World War II, 64–65
Wright, V., 35
Wynne, L. C., 243

Young Adult Development Project
        (YADP), 288, 289
Young Parenthood Study (YPS), 201–21

Zeanah, C. H., 135
Zigler, E., 225
Zimmer-Gembeck, M. J., 49